Converted on LSD Trip

David Clarke

Luke 5. 9 *For he was astonished, and all that were with him, at the draft of fishes which they had taken.*

Ordering Information:

Prime Seven Media
518 Landmann St.
Tomah City, WI 54660

Printed in the United States of America

3

AUTHORS NOTE

Please excuse the typo's, errors in grammar and spelling. As hesays he was virtually illiterate until the age of 21 after which he learned to read usinge the bible and classical Christian literature to educate myself.

Please take time to understand what he has written as he trying to communicate with you as to get proof readers to work for love is very difficult.

Davis says he is sure all the New Testament writers, some of which were unlearned men, had the same difficulties.

A Foreword by Malcolm Kirkham

I first met David Clarke around 1965 in Aylesbury, a town just north of London. David went to the local secondary modern Grange school and I went to the Grammar School. Our worlds collided though when through mutual acquaintance I found the R & B band he played for "Fowler Mean". I joined as the singer. We became firm friends, the other band members were very straight and po faced but Dave and I connected I was aware of his older brother mike he was notorious in Aylesbury and no one messed with him. He was also an entrepreneur and extremely intelligent. On a different path Mike could have succeeded in any field.

Dave and I had many adventures during our times together. He was naturally inclined to steal however and his brazen nature astounded me. If he saw something he wanted he just took it. This is something he shared with his brother. Dave and I drifted apart when he was incarcerated along with is brother in one place and I in another for separate crimes. After 50 odd years we are in touch again. This book get details the life and times of a criminal, his redemption and his present day mission. It is also a snap shot of a period time and a place. End Of.

Malcolm Kirkham 06 May 2017

B Foreword Dr Philip Fleming
By Dr Philip Fleming MA. BA, Bch. FRCPsych. DPM

"Converted on LSD Trip"

This book, the personal testament of David Clarke, was first publshed as **Converted on LSD Trip** but now, **'Let Chrisitan Men Be Men'** in an autobiographical style. It charts his life, which became one of criminality and drug taking though an experience in 1970 of finding God whilst under the influence of LSD. Cynics may say that this was just an effect of drugs, but it is clear that the experience changed his life. Later when in court facing charges he admitted to many other crimes and was fortunate in receiving three years conditional discharge and not a prison sentence.

Since then David has combined his work as a lecturer in electronics with his mission of spreading the word of God. This is a scrupulously honest book recording both the difficulties he has faced as well as the successes in his life since 1970. A continuing worry is the fat of his brother, currently serving a long prison sentence in a Philippine jail who himself has recently found God.

"This is an inspiring story of a life that has been turned from crime to a positive account and may be of help to others who find them selves directionless and involved in crime and drug misuse".

Dr. Philip M. Fleming. MA. BA, Bch. FRCPsych. DPM.

Consultant Psychiatrist with special responsibility for drug and alcohol misuse.

C Foreword Gregg Haslam

Rev. Gregg Haslam Senior Minister Westminster Chapel, London

Gregg Haslam

"David Clarke tells the story of his troubled violent past and his extraordinary life, in such a way that it re-tells the story of Jesus' love that's available for us all. Christ has the power to renew and reclaim anyone's wasted years, no matter we've done, or how deep our shame. He can re-launch our lives on a brand new future that we could never have planned for ourselves."

Westminster Chapel

London SW1E 6BS

D Foreword Samuel Ntoyimondo

Chaplain HMPS Nottingham

" This moving story demonstrates the goodness and mercy of God and it is a clear proof that no one is beyond God's grace, mercy and love. Whatever wrongdoings we do, God continues to call us back to Him and if we accept, He fulfils His plan for us to give us hope for the future. "

E Fifty Years On; A Celebration

Fifty years ago David Clarke made a confession to the police of 24 crimes and appeared in Aylesbury Magistrate Court[1], on 9th February 1971.

In court Clarke related the reasons for his confession. In summing up and sentencing the Chairman of the magistrates said, "We have considered what we aught to do and have come to the conclusion that your evident desire to become a martyr is one thing we are not going to gratify". He gave Clarke a conditional discharge for 3 years pointing out that the sincerity of your conversion could be shown by his behaviour during that period.

It was 30 years later, in September 1999, that David got news of his older brother Michael Clarke's own conversion to Christianity. Michael had served 5 years, of a 16 year prison sentence[2], in the Philippines, that he decided to go on a mission of help to the Philippines[3]. This was to bring help and relief to his brother. This part of the story[4] was reported as news by Portsmouth News. Their story was also reported in The Oldham Chronicle[5], the town where the brothers were born.

David visited Michael in New Bilibid Prison, for the first time in 2001. This is the National and Maximum Security Prison. He visited Michael several times over the next four years and the brothers worked together within the prison with Religious Volunteers, and many prison inmates, seeking to help former criminals in their own rehabilitation.

The brothers vision was to equip former converted criminals to return to their own villages, towns or Cities and preach the gospel to their own friends and relatives.

The first inmate to be released with this commission was William O Poloc[6] who was released, in August 2002, after serving 14 years for homicide. Several other prison inmates testified, in their own hand written accounts, their own stories of reformation, which David writes about in their book, Trojan Warriors , that contains 66 testimonies of converted criminals.

---

1   Why He Confessed To 24 Crimes
2   I Pray I might save my criminal brother
3   Mission of Help 13th September 2001
4   The News August 19th 2000
5   Oldham Chronicle 11 January 2001
6   Introducing William O. Poloc

But Sadly Michael died[7]of Tuberculosis in New Bilibid Prison before their vision of bringing help to many had been realized. Michael's story[8] was reported in the Eastbound Herald, on 27th September, 2012,

Since August 2002, William Poloc[9] has worked in Baguio City Jail and Benguet District Jails, working with inmates and former criminals, and founded several church groups, called Christ-Centered Churches and a Theological Institute.

God's work here in the Northern Philippines bloomed most especially here in the city of Baguio. The Baguio Christ-Centred Church is the mother church of all the Christ Centred Churches in the Philippines namely; The Pilot- Christ-Centred Church, The Kamog Christ-Centred Church, The Christ-Centered-Church Theological School(TULIP), The Christ-Centred Radio Ministry, The Christ-Centred Jail Ministries etc..). We'll, we are truly blessed by these works He has entrusted to us. To God be the glory!

Website http://www.bccc.com (Facebook)

Email: williampolocsr@yahoo.com

Christ-Centered Ministries Philippines

In celebration of this work David has republished and sent 12 theological books[10] dedicated for the use of students, teachers and pastors and for Christs Centered Church groups. It is intended that these theological text books will be the basis of study for a theological degree, for qualifying students of Christ Centered Churches.

The publication date, of these books are by chance, 16th January 2020, which is virtually 50 years to the day of David's original conversion from Crime to Christ, which took place, on 16th January 1970. This Jubilee is the year of release , a practice of bringing release to those in captivity and, bondage and a release from old dcbts.

This mission of help was called Trojan Horse International.

David is now 71 years old and has been invited to visit and preach this year to the10 affiliated churches, Baguio, but the Covet 19 lock down prevented it.

This new publication of Converted On LSD Trip tells the whole story

---

7   Man Dies In Prison In The Philippines

8   Brother's Book looks at a former criminals life 27th September 2011

9   William Poloc's Testimony

10   A Body Of Doctrinal and Practical Divinity, Books I,II,III,IV,V,V,VI and VII.

About The Author

David Clarke, was born in Oldham Lancashire, in 1949.

During the 60's he and his older brother Michael began to enjoy lives of crime, promiscuity and infamy during their teenage years, whilst living in Aylesbury, Buckinghamshire, They lived with their parents and younger sister in Aylesbury and became criminals. They were both sent to prison in 1967 for malicious wounding and carrying a firearm without a license. David served his time in a young persons Borstal Training Institute at Dover, and Michael served his time in Maidstone Prison.

On leaving Dover Borstal in 1968, David was determined to have a good time living a life of crime, with no fear, or belief in God, respect for society, parents, or the wider family. He proceeded on a three-year career of undetected crime until he met a Christian woman who informed him that his life style was wrong.

It became David's opinion that Christianity was for people who could not enjoy life, or stand on their own two feet.

On the 16th of January 1970 David was arrested whilst he experienced a bad trip on LSD, but not by the Police. It was by Jesus Christ who spoke to him after he had cried out to God for help. Jesus said to David that the horrors that he had experienced was nothing compared to what hell was like.

David turned away that Friday night, from a sinful life of crime and immorality to follow Christ as best he could.

David began to read the bible immediately, and other Christian books, and attended a wide range of churches. He finally confessed to the police to 24 crimes that he had committed during his release from Borstal in 1968 and his conversion in January 1970.

David eventually joined the Bierton Strict and Particular Baptist Church in 1974. And then trained as a Lecturer commencing teaching electronics at Luton College of Higher Education, and taught for 22 years in colleges of Higher and Further education, until 2001.

The Bierton Church, which was founded in 1831, became a Gospel Standard listed cause in 1981, and in 1982 David was called by the Lord and sent by the church to preach the gospel where ever the Lord opened up the door for him to speak.

David then sought to reach his old friends from the past, and organized a preaching meeting at the Bierton chapel in 1983, inviting all his old friends to come and hear of all what the Lord had done for him. Providentially that preaching meeting was televised on video and is available on YouTube under the title:

"David Preaching at Bierton Strict and Particular Baptist", 5th June 1983" (Click to view).

David recalls that it became apparent after this meeting his real troubles began, and as a result he seceded from the Bierton Church in 1984. An account of this secession was written by David's own hand entitled, "The Bierton Crisis".

This story is a complete account of David's early life, experience of conversion from crime to Christ and life in the Bierton Strict and Particular Baptist Church. He concludes that men may begin well in their faith towards God, trusting in the person and finished works of Jesus Christ alone for their salvation, but then **fall from grace falling** into the error of seeking to please God by works according to their own inventions or distortions of the Law of Moses. They fall into the trap of making themselves **"perfect in the flesh"** and then judge others who do not act like them.

The story continues to the time of Michael's arrest in the Philippines, in 1995, and his 16-year prison sentence.

The story goes on through to Michael, David's brother's own conversion from crime to Christ, in New Bilibid Prison some 30 years after David own conversion to Christianity. This occurring after he was convinced that Jesus was the Christ, the son of the living God, through reading CS Lewis's book, "Mere Christianity". It tells of his baptism as a Christian in an old oil drum in that prison in September 2000.

This story demonstrates the manifold grace of God, in saving two brothers from a life of sin, crime and immorality, through the person of the Lord Jesus Christ.

This book is really David's confession and testimony written for the **defence and confirmation of the gospel**. David also believes the things that have happened to him have fallen out rather unto the furtherance of the gospel. Phil 1. verse and 7 and verse 12.

David's solution to help and assist in the promotion of the gospel of the lord Jesus Christ is the creation of the Bierton Particular Baptist Open College (an Internet Cloud and also in the formation of Bierton Particular Baptist College in Pakistan. This is outlined in the last chapter of this book. Those wishing to be trained and educated In the doctrines of grace can enrol and obtain all the assistance they need.

1 CONFESSION TO 24 CRIMES

(The court case)

It was real, absolutely real, but none of my friends really believed me. All I could do was tell them what had happened to me, and that was what I did. I told them all, the long, the short and the tall. As many of them as I could.

They thought I had gone mad after taking LSD.

Jesus Christ had spoken to me and rescued me from a bad LSD trip on Friday evening, 16th January 1970. He had said that what I had been going through was nothing compared to what hell was like. I now knew the way and was determined to tell the others. I had become a Christian and no longer needed to live the life style that I had adopted, which had involved crime, drugs, promiscuity, flash cars and fame. I had been born again.

I was now responsible for sorting out all my stolen gear. What could be done with a builder's shed and stolen cars? I still had in my possession many stolen goods, which included the 48-foot by 24-foot. Builder's shed, which we had stolen one night from a building site at Berkhampstead, and a lovely "G" reg. Mini, stolen from Hemel Hempstead, which was in the process of being "rung". Ringing meant replacing and old mini with legitimate registration documents and number plates with a new one. My new mini was being used to replace it. This was to be my new car. I also had a Morris Minor Traveller, which had been "rung" and was being used as a hire car. I had stolen garage equipment, which included an air compressor, electric welding equipment, spray guns and a trolley jack. I also had several pieces of electrical test equipment, which included oscilloscopes, AVO meters and Colour TV's. I had all the garage equipment I needed to repair and spray cars.

I had a lovely Citroen DS car in the builder's shed, which was being repaired. I obtained this car through swapping it for a colour TV set. The only problem was that I had stolen the TV set from an old people's home called Redfields , in Winslow, Buckinghamshire.

I also had two nice speedboat engines, getting ready for the summer of 1970. All in all I had had a real good time full of excitement and fun.

In fact I had been stopped in the midst of my career, which involved stealing all kinds of goods to have a good time. I had intended to have a caravan, a speedboat, water skis, aqualung diving gear, flash cars, motorbikes, clothes and so on, all through stealing. I was in fact stopped whilst in the midst of my career but not by the police. It was Jesus Christ who had called me by name and I followed him.

What To Do With Stolen Goods After One Becomes A Christian

I thank God he intervened again a year later and His hand was clearly seen once more. I had no one else to help. As I write this I take encouragement in the faithfulness of God to me in never leaving me or forsaking me. I realize now I was kept through the power and grace of our Lord Jesus Christ to bare witness today, to many people of the goodness and mercy of God.

The Problem Was Solved By A Visit From The C.I.D.

I was sitting at the table in our kitchen at 37 Finmere Crescent one evening in late 1971, when a knock came on the door. I had two visitors, a detective constable Robson and a younger man. I was greeted quite politely but with sure and certain words " You are charged with stealing a colour television set " and "would you accompany us down to the police station to make a statement".

I knew instantly what I must do and say. I saw the hand of God and believed this was all his doing but I did not know the outcome. Leaving the outcome to God I asked the two men to sit down in the kitchen and I admitted the charge. At this DC Robson seemed most relieved, for he said to me later, he had thought I would be very difficult and awkward and deny the charge.

I explained I would certainly come with them to the police station and make a statement but I wanted to speak to them about other things first. I said I had many crimes I wished to tell them about but wanted to tell them first of all why I was informing them.

I wanted it to be known that they would not have been able to find out about my crimes unless I confessed to them. I wanted to testify to the saving work of Jesus Christ that he had saved me from my former criminal way of life a year previously and that I did not wish to get off lightly with this confession but rather bear testimony for Christ. For in no way could my crimes be discovered unless I tell them and owned up to them. I had a lot of property, which could be returned.

I went with them to the police station and spent the rest of the evening making written statements giving details of my crimes. I was detained that evening in the police cells at Walton Street police station in Aylesbury, not that I was a stranger to prison cells. My shoelaces were removed but I was allowed my New Testament (Authorized Version, working man's pocket addition).

I had to appear in Aylesbury Magistrates Court on the 9th February 1971 and answered two charges of burglary and one of theft. I also asked for 21 other crimes of theft to be taken into consideration, all of which had been committed since I left Borstal, between September 1967 and 16th January 1970. I had decided I did not need legal representation, as I would speak for my self.

With my past record of probation and Borstal training it was quite expected that I would be sent to prison. I was quite OK with this because I deserved it and I believed God was in this and had a definite purpose in this event. I prepared for this by setting my affairs in order at home and gave directions that my Mini Traveller, which I had rebuilt, was to be given to

Barry Crown, if I got sent down. I believed that whatever happened to me the outcome was of God and there would be good reason for it. I thought I might be being sent to prison so as to preach the gospel to inmates. A friend of mine Mr Peter Murray was concerned about my court appearance and suggested I get some written testimonials from some of my Christian friends and he felt he ought to appear in person and speak on my behalf. The friends who wrote were Barry Crown, Cyril Bryan, Tom Thompson and Eric Connet. I am including these letters, which were sent to the court. These people all testify to the saving grace of God in changing my life. These are some of the written testimonies:

Testimony of Barry Crown

R.B Crown 45, Mitcham Walk, Aylesbury. Buckinghamshire

To the Clerk to the Magistrates

Dear Sir,

6th February 1971

I am a graduate of Salford University, and hold a B.Sc. in Civil Engineering. I am at present an employee of Aylesbury Borough Council, working under Mr. Hanney, the Borough Engineer and Surveyor. I have held this post since September 1970.

Shortly after taking up residence in Aylesbury I befriended Mr. David Clarke whom I met at the Full Gospel Church, Rick fords Hill. I found David to be a true and sincere Christian seeking to spread the Gospel of Jesus Christ and to give personal testimony of the salvation through Jesus Christ, which he himself had experienced.

David told me how he had been miraculously converted on January 16th 1970. And have the subsequent change in his whole manner and outlook to life. Before his conversion he confessed to a life of drugs and theft, but now he no longer had any desire or pleasure in such things, since Christ destroyed the power of such in his life.

For the six months I have known David I have been a witness to the truth of his testimony and I know him as a person who is a completely honest and trustworthy follower of the Christian faith.

Yours Sincerely,

R. B. Crown.

Testimony of Cyril Bryan

176 Cambridge Street Aylesbury

To the Clerk to the Magistrates   2/2/71

Dear Sir,

I am privileged to write a testimony to you concerning David Clarke, and I count it a privilege because it is to the glory of God.

I have known this young man through conversations and meeting with him, through the church I attend in Aylesbury. The Full Gospel Testimony Church at Richford's Hill.

What I wish to bring to your notice is the wonderful change that has taken place in him as a result of him believing the gospel and receiving the Lord Jesus Christ as his personal saviour, according to the scriptural instruction and ordinances.

The change of character and speech is miraculous, as are all the works of God, and as a believer in the Lord Jesus Christ for 30 years; I know that David Clarke is a transformed person, by the grace of God. As are we all who know the reality of the new birth as taught by Johns Gospel.

You will know his past life, I testify to his new life in Christ Jesus. Yours Sincerely,

C Bryan.

Testimony of Mr E Connet
E.H. Connet
125 Park Street,
Aylesbury,

2nd February 1971

TO WHOM IT MAY CONCERN

This is to certify that I have known Mr. Clarke for a period of approximately 9 months since his conversion to Christianity. I am fully persuaded that he has turned his back on his past life and changed for the better.

He is now earnestly endeavouring to make amends for his past mistakes and even influence others to turn their lives over to God, as he has done.

My object in writing this testimonial is that it may help to throw some light on David's character from one who knows him as a Christian.

Yours Faithfully,
E Connet.

I Speak In Court

I appeared in court on the 9th February 1971, dressed in my dark blue (Mod) suit. I pleaded guilty and then a report from the police was read and I was given leave to speak for myself. I spoke extempore (without notes- trusting in the Lord for all the help I needed) describing my pre-convention days up to my conversion. I also spoke about life since being a Christian explaining my difficulties with respect to the stolen goods that I had in my possession.

I was able to speak of what Jesus had done for me in a way that only God could have worked.

After this Peter Murray spoke on my behalf confirming my testimony.

This happened on Tuesday 9th February 1971, a date that proved significant to me 3 years later.

I was amazed, so were all my Christian friends. The magistrates thought I was trying to be a martyr. I do not know how or why. They obviously thought I should be sent to prison but part of my punishment would be I was not going to get what I wanted. God smiled. We smiled with him. It was good to be a child of God.

The Bucks Herald Weekly Paper

The whole court appearance was reported in the local newspapers and in the national Evening Standard

The news headlines of the Bucks Herald read, " Why he confessed to 24 crimes" and " Converted on LSD trip". Whilst the Bucks Advertiser read " Man speaks of horrors on LSD".

The following are copies of those headlines all of which were fairly accurate.

Bucks Herald Script

The Bucks Herald 11th February 1971.

David Clarke, who had a three-year career of undetected crime, experienced a "Christian conversion" whilst suffering from the effects of LSD, he told Aylesbury magistrates, on Tuesday. After wrestling with his conscience for a year, he confessed to 24 crimes, and gave information leading to the recovery of over £1000 worth of stolen property. In court he pleaded guilty to charges of steeling a £300 colour television set from an old peoples home, a £20 spray gun, and a hydraulic jack. He asked for 21 other charges to be taken into consideration, including stealing a builders shed, two cars, and an electric arc welder, two other TV sets, two compressors, and a road trailer. Clarke (21) of Finmere Crescent said that his reputation in the town had been that of a man who was enjoying himself. "I used to sell drugs to young people, and indulge in permissive sex" he declared.

Seeking Truth

"Religion to me was rubbish, and for sissy people who could not stand on their own feet", he said. "Within my heart I was searching for truth, and a meaning to life". He had good prospects of getting on in life he went on but "was not satisfied with what I had, I was greedy, selfish and boastful." Clarke had been using pep pills, and marijuana since he was 16 he told the court, but it was after taking LSD that he experienced, what he described as, "a major thing in my life". He described the "torment" he suffered, as a result of taking the drug, and went on "I warn any young person who hears my testimony, "The effects of LSD are so bad, and I warn you to stay clear". While in this condition he said he, "Called on the name of Jesus" and his torment went from him.

Voice Of Christ

"Jesus Christ spoke to me as clearly as I speak here today saying, "David, I am with you".

Mr Murray, of Manor Crescent Wendover said he was habitually sceptical of sudden conversions, and preferred to put them to the test of time. The time, which had elapsed, since Clarke's profession of faith had convinced him that this young man would now be salt and light to society". "He is in truth, a new man, and had experienced what Christ called a second birth". Murray said Clarke now put himself out to be of assistance, read the bible intensely, always carried a New Testament, attended a wide circle of churches and would spend hours in discussion on spiritual things.

Difficulty

Clarke's difficulty during the months spent deciding how to make amends for his past had been the problem of accusing himself, without informing on others.

Passing sentence the chairman of the magistrates, Colonel I. Tetley, told Clarke, "You have pleaded guilty to three offenses and asked us to take into consideration 21 others, and except a record over a short period of time, which is quite the worst we have ever seen, we have considered what we aught to do and have come to the conclusion that your evident desire to become a martyr is one we are not going to gratify".

He gave Clarke a conditional discharge for three years pointing out that the sincerity of his conversion could be shown by his behaviour during that period.

The outcome of the court case was a complete surprise to us all, and we were overjoyed. A Christian friend, Mrs. Chapski of Broughton Avenue Aylesbury, invited us all back to her home for coffee.

DC Robson informed me that they had discovered I was the person who had stolen the television from Mike West. An enemy of Mike West had tipped them off about the stolen Television. Mike West appeared in Court on the same day as myself and was fined £25. He nearly lost his job with the insurance company that he worked for. His encounter at court, to his embarrassment, also appeared on the front page of the newspaper alongside the article about my conversion.

After this I gave Mike West his Citroen car back that I had swapped for the colour TV. I had re sprayed it a bright Banana yellow, and replaced the engine. At lease he was able to sell it and get some money back. I now know, and take encouragement that God works well and sorts things out when we cannot do so.

As far as the other stolen goods were concerned the police managed to take away most of them but the firm who owned the builders shed sent a trailer. The ironic thing is that I could get no help to load the shed on the trailer. In the end Mrs. Knight was the only one to help. This was very hard work but between us we managed to load it on the trailer late one night. To give you some idea of the value of the stolen items. The shed was said to be worth £400. The mini was brand new and worth £672. The price of a terraced house at that time was £2000.

I Tell My Story

I wish to tell my story starting when I was born (natural birth) and lead the reader until my conversion when the Lord Jesus spoke to me (second birth).

I then wish to speak about being a Christian and seeking to follow the Lord and meeting with the many and varied Christian groups and people. I wish to share with the reader how I learned the distinctive truths of the distinguishing doctrines of grace and sovereignty of God, which led me to joining the Bierton Strict and Particular Baptist Church.

In this account I relate my call to preach and I list the many churches I share the gospel with until the very sad occasion of my secession from the Bierton Church due to a departure for the truth. The church fell into the error of allowing general redemption being taught and a falling away into the error of the Law of Moses becoming their rule of life and conduct, rather than the Gospel. My secession being fully recorded on my publication, **"The Bierton Crisis"**, which I now believe could serve as a real help to many churches as in this account I name the many errors that I found to be prevalent, in those days amongst believers, and I point out the truth and scriptural view, which opposed those who held differing views.

It is my desire that this will serve to help and edify fellow Christians, and those seeking the truth as it is in Jesus Christ.

2 MY EARLY LIFE

I was born on the 16th February 1949 at 9.50 AM, in Boundary Park General hospital, Oldham, Lancashire. My mother's name was Elsie Dyson Clarke who was married to my father Thomas George Clarke some time after the war. She informed me that this hospital was next to Oldham Athletic football ground.

We lived with my mother's father in his house at 26 Fleet Street, Clarksfield, Oldham. My granddad's name was Watts Ormrod and he was a retired craftsman and senior member of a Trades Union.

Boundary Park Hospital

This Is Where I Was Born

His hair was white, which I am told happened due to an accident at work when a large rivet was pushed through his hand. I had a brother, who was two and a half years older than me, Michael John (spelt Michael instead of Michael due to my mother's stubbornness when he was named at the registrar's office. The official informed her that the way she had spelt Michael was in fact wrong, and my mum reacted at being corrected and insisted it would be spelt just as she had written it.

The Clarke Family

Michael David Granddad Ormrod Dad Mum

My Parents

Thomas George Clarke   Elsie Dyson Clarke

My mum and dad were both in the armed forces and were very proud to be British. Dad was in the Army and mum was in the Royal Air Force.

I was christened at Christ's Church, Glodwick and my Godfather was David Maltby of 382 Barton Road; Stratford and was a sides man at the Church on Barton Road. He gave me at that time a bible with a text of scripture written on the inside cover. Prov. 3. 6 "In all thy ways acknowledge him and he shall direct thy paths ".

I have found a baptism certificate dated 3rd April 1949, where it states I became a member of Christ the child of God, and an inheritor of the "Kingdom of Heaven". This however is wrong, as I did not become a member of Christ until I was born again on The 16th January 1970, which I speak about later.

I remember attending the church and Sunday school at Christchurch, which was just along the road from our house in Fleet Street. On one occasion I was so cosy, sitting on the pew, I fell asleep and woke up with a jolt wondering where I was, just as the vicar had finished his sermon. I had been lulled into sleep by the stimulating sermon. I haven't changed even to day. I must have been about 3 or 4 years old. It was my mother's idea to take my brother and I to Sunday school.

My Baptismal Certificate

Holy Baptism

A member of Christ, the child of God, and an inheritor
of the Kingdom of Heaven

Name .... David Clarke

Place .... Christ Church

Goodrich, Oldbury

Signed .... y. Moran

Date 3rd April 1949

David's Baptismal Certificate 3rd April 1949

St Barnabas School

At Sunday school I remember we painted pictures of houses and still remember wondering why did the teacher draw the house with the door in the middle of the building and windows either side of the door. This was because I knew we lived in a house in a terrace and our door was to one side, just like the other houses in the street. I had no spiritual impressions of the Lord Jesus Christ from these times.

Barnabas Sunday School

St. Barnabas Sunday School Building

Just across the street from our house there was a great Roman Catholic Church building, and living accommodation, surrounded by a high wall. It was built of red engineering bricks and several stories high with stained glass windows alone the long church building. I remember looking up at the crooked lightening conductor and I still get the feeling of austerity and awkwardness when wondering what was behind that wall. It produced the same feeling in me when I had the story of Toby Twirl red to me. In that story he meets a giant who lived behind a great high walled castle. I was afraid to go near, or to even think of climbing the wall, or trespass in the grounds. I did not know it was a Roman Catholic Church building until about 25 years later when my mother informed me.

At that time I knew of no other religion than that of the Church of England, I assumed my mother was right in all such matters and so the Catholics were wrong.

I remember the street lamps because a man use to come around each night to light them as they were gas and he had a small ladder, which he carried with him, pointed at one end. He climbed the ladder and lit the lamps each night. I assume they were gas lamps.

Roman Catholic Building

The Roman Catholic Building

The Back Of Our House

Back Yard of 26 Fleet Street (Where I lived)

I remember my favourite sweets were what was called Kylie, it is called sherbet now. We could also buy a very small loaf of bread called a penny loaf.

At that time when I was about 4 years old I wanted to go to another Sunday school (I did not know at the time it was at a church building), which was at Lee's Road. My mother must have taken me there before. On this occasion it was Saturday morning and I did not believe there was no Sunday school that day. After being dressed I think my mother must have humoured me and did not take me seriously. I said I was going to Sunday school. I left home, I do not think my Mum realized and I walked at least two miles along Balfor Street and along the busy Lee's Road and found the building, to my disappointment it was all locked up. On my return I wandered off and got lost and ended up asking for help from a Laundry Shop. They put me in the window as a lost boy and called the police. I was soon returned home. I think my Mum was horrified how far I had been.

Back Alley

Back Alley at 26 Fleet Street

I commenced my school days at "Clark's Field" Infants' School. My brother Michael John was already attending and was in the third year when I started.

Clark's Field Infants School

Clark's Field Infants School (David bottom right)

I remember my first day at school in the classroom with other children.

The ceilings were high and there were things like sand pits and black board easels and old fashion classroom desks and tables.

The girl next door, Vivian Butler, began school with me and I can remember her crying for her Mum. I remember not feeling the need to cry and I tried to comfort her and assure her all would be well.

My Auntie Edith was very good to us boys and we would visit her every Saturday. She lived with my Granddad's sister. She was called Auntie Alice. Auntie Edith would take us out to a great park in Oldham and on the way home we would call in at the chip shop. In those days chips were real chips, cooked in real fat. One of our favourite meals she would cook was potato pie, with red cabbage. In the house there was a cellar, which I always liked to visit. I think at one time washing was done in the cellar.

At that time my brother was probably the only close friend I had, although we were not too close. He was just there. We use to go swimming on a Saturday morning to the "Waterhead Baths". This type of swimming baths was typical of the old-fashioned baths of the time. They were small, the water green, and walls tiled cream. At the side of the pool there were slipper baths where you could sit up to your chin in hot water and carbolic soap was supplied to wash with. It was very cosy. In fact the whole atmosphere was warm and cosy, not like the cold clinical swimming baths of modern times. Next-door was the washhouse where mum used to go at the same time to do washing.

One Saturday morning I nearly drowned and was saved by the attendant called Norman. I had tiptoed backwards and as the pool got slowly deeper and deeper I found I could not touch the bottom. It was through the providence of God that the attendant turned to see me reaching upwards out of the water. I couldn't speak. He dived in to rescued me and I can still feel the fear today of nearly drowning.

Across the road from the swimming baths was a slaughterhouse, next door to inhabited houses. We were very curious and would look through the slatted windows and see the men kill the pigs, sheep and cattle. This was awesome and ghoulish and a fearful thing, but we were very curious and wanted to see how the men slew the animals. There was blood, animal intestines, animal heads bones and blood. The smell was awful and not pleasant at all, and it seemed as though the pigs knew they were going to be slaughtered, and their end was come. I have wondered about my brother since then, as he was two and a half years older than me and how this may have affected him. Later on in life he demonstrated a callous way, which was characteristic of killing without mercy just like these slaughter men.

About this time I remember coming home from school and in the dusk of that day the house seemed unusually quiet. I noticed some blood on my brother's book and my mum told me there had been an accident. My brother had fallen down a basement stairway shaft at school and landed on his back. He was concussed and I remember then feeling how precious life was. My brother could have died through the fall. It was awesome. I still had no recollection of God during this time.

Oldham

Oldham is a town in the north of England, not far from the city of Manchester, and during the 19th century was an industrial community famous for its cotton mills. In fact, my grandfather was a great supporter of the Trades Union.

As a child I remember the old mills, red brick built with huge chimneys towering high above the buildings. Also the water reservoirs, which we were always warned to stay away from. My mother had spoken about children being drowned in them and this was sufficient for me to obey her.

An Oldham Mill

Typical Old Mill Oldham

3 GARSTON INFANT SCHOOL

We moved from Oldham to Garston, Watford when I was 5 years old and my mum took me to my first day at school, which was at Garston Infant School. I was in the second year of the infants. My mum had arranged for me to walk home with a girl called Vivian who apparently lived in Coats Way where we lived. Not that I knew my address because I didn't. All I knew was we had move to a place called Garston, so I assumed we lived in Garston Road.

When it came to walking home I had to follow Vivian, but she took me by a way I had never been before. A completely different way, and across a park to what was the other end of Coats Way. She left me there and I had no Idea where I was, as I did not recognize anywhere at all. Feeling uneasy about all this I realized I was lost. So I made my way back towards the school and began to ask people where Garston Road was. There was no such place but I insisted I lived in Garston Road. A man with a red Bedford dormobile offered to take me back to school to find out where I live so off we went. The schoolteacher said I lived in Coats Way where Vivian had took me but I said I didn't live there, as I could not recognize the place. The man took me back to Coats Way but I could not recognize where I lived. He drove from one end to the other. It was quite a long Way with a Council estate on one end and private houses at the other end. This was where I lived 149 Coats Way. I saw my Mum in the front garden - so I arrived home after being lost on my first day at school.

German Teacher

My classroom teacher was a German woman called Miss Kitchener. She spoke with a German accent and I spoke with a broad Lancashire accent. We did not hit it off and I was hopeless at reading the flash cards. It seemed as though I was singled out and proved to be a dunce, as I could not really read. Being small I think I messed about to divert attention from my inability to do class work.

One day when I arrived at school I found a pair of pumps (they called them plimsolls now), which I later found out belonged to Vivian on my desk and I did not like them being there. Feeling rather indignant I place them in the dustbin. I think I might have asked the teacher, "please Miss, whose are these pumps?", But was ignored, as she did not understand me, so in the bin they went.

The next day Vivian's mother came to school wanting to find out where her plimsolls had gone. The caretaker said he had found them and placed them on my desk. When I was questioned I was in trouble and Miss Kitchener said my mum would have to buy a new pair as I had thrown them away. I felt this unfair and felt really picked on. I know my mum came to the school and had an argument about the pumps and the fact that a German teacher was trying to teach English. This was only few years after the war with Germany had ended.

David And The Hamster

At that time my mum had to work late and it was arranged for me to wait in the classroom after school until my mum came to pick me up. This was shortly after the event with the plimsolls. The class had a pet hamster and this little creature got all the attention from every one. I was the one that got no attention but rather got into trouble. One evening whilst I was waiting in the classroom for my mum to collect me, the teacher left the classroom for a short while.

I went towards the hamster cage and thought to my self why do you get all the attention. I know what I am going to do with you. I took the hamster out to the cage and closed the door. I looked at the hamster in the in the eyes and went over to Vivian's desk and put it inside, shutting the lid quickly thinking that will pay her back for getting me in trouble over her plimsolls. I sat back in my chair before the teacher returned and went home with my mum as though nothing had happened.

The next day I went into class as quiet as I could and keeping out of the way. I waited patiently for the eruptions. Then suddenly, Oh Miss, screamed Vivian, the hamster is in my desk. It had weeded and messed everywhere through out the night. Every one gathered around the desk to see at the same time. I felt very guilty. One boy tried to suggest the hamster had escaped and climbed up the table leg and got through the whole drilled for the spilled ink to drain. A good idea I thought so keep thinking that thought. Then some one asked how did it get out of the cage as the door was closed. I was feeling very, very guilty now and wondered if Miss Kitchener was thinking had I done the deed the night before. I kept quiet and to this day they do not know how that hamster got there. During this time my brother was attending the Lea Farm Junior School, the school I was to attend the next year or so.

Congregational Sunday School

My mum use to take me to Sunday school from time to time and I didn't mind going. One day (about 1958) on the way home from normal school I would walk past the Congregational church building, rather a modern building, and the vicar lived in a Gypsy stile caravan in the church grounds.

Garston Congregational Church Building

Congregational Church Building

The church building was always left open and we often went in the church building on the way home. I saw, on one occasion, some boys took the money out of the collection box, which too was left unlocked. I could not understand this. Why where things left unlocked for boys to steel from. One day after school I met the vicar when I was looking around the church building and I asked him why is the building left open and why it the collection box not locked. His reply puzzled me. He said the church should be always open for people because God was like that if people fell they need to steel the collection then they must need it badly. He did not feel the box should be locked. I was puzzled and said but why? The vicar was sure it was the right thing to do. That stayed with me to this day and people get angry some times with me for not locking up my house.

At this same church I can remember the Easter services. I had no Idea what the gospel was nor did I understand the Easter story.

I remember sitting in the pew during the Easter service listening to how they crucified Jesus wondering why Jesus did not come down from the cross. I felt he could have done so and confounded all them Pharisees, but why didn't he do so. I knew the story about his death and resurrection but did not know what it all meant. I never did find out until 14 years later when I was 21 years old when I learned to read the bible for my self. It was then I learned that Jesus had to die to take away my sins. That he died in my place to set me free from sin, self and death.

It was about this time (1959) that my mum encouraged me to play the piano. My mum's favourite artist was Perry Como and "Side Saddle" was a piece of mum's favourite music, which I learned to play. I had music lesson with a Miss Mary Lee, a music teacher in Garston and eventually I graduated with a merit Grade 1 (Primary) RSA in Pianoforte. This was July 1960.

The sort of music, which was popular in those days, was. "Yellow Polka Dot Bikini, My Old Man's a dustman, by Lonnie Donnigan, Living Doll by Cliff Richards. Also the Hula-Hoop was a craze at that time.

Cecil The Sissy And Air Pistol

Living not too far away from us in Coates Way, was a boy who my brother nicknamed Cecil, as this sounded like a suitable name for a sissy. He was a cripple in the sense that his feet were curved inwards and he walked awkwardly. He must have been about 10 years old. My brother poked fun at him and I too soon followed suit. We would sing about him a song called Cecil, Cecil a Cecil feet. He would try and avoid us.

One day Cecil came on his bike down to the woods that we called the dell. We were playing up the trees and had made a catapult out off one of the great branches of the trees. One person would sit in the branch and two or three other kids would pull on the rope till the branch was fully bent. The rope would be released and the person would be catapulted up in the air. They would have to hold on tightly other wise they would end up in the trees.

On this day my brother had it in for Cecil. We took his bike and put it into the catapult making sure it was catapulted up into the trees. We thought this was great fun but Cecil did not.

His mother came to our house and complained to my mum about our bullying Cecil but my mum seemed to have no mercy. She said Cecil had got to learn to look after himself and he was a sissy. I felt mum was wrong as I knew how bad we were and my mum seemed to have no mercy. I felt bad however.

Shortly after this incident my brother encouraged me to take our newly acquired air pistol to school, and Cecil was the one who my brother bullied and threaten to shoot in the playground. On reflection my brother seemed to have no mercy at all. My brother must have been in the final year and I in the first year of Lea Farm Junior School.

David at Lea Farm Junior School

David At Lea Farm Junior School

It wasn't long however before my air pistol was found and confiscated. After assembly one of the boys had taken it out of my desk and was running around the classroom with it when the teacher walked in. I was in trouble again with the Headmaster and this would have been another time I got the cane for bringing a dangerous weapon to school.

Wrexham Holiday

Michael and I must have been about 7 and 10 years old and Mum and dad had renovated an old Ford convertible car whose number plate was BBU.

Mum had bought the car whilst we were living in Oldham and dad was working in Watford. Dad had moved to Watford to get a job, and was living with his mum (our grandma at Ash Tree Road Garston, Watford). Mum and dad were able to by a house at 149 Coats Way Garston and it was mum who decided to buy the car to get Michael and I down from Oldham to Watford.

It was this car that I often fell out of when the breaks were hit. It caused me to move forward and push open the door lock and the door opened the opposite way round. I would end up on the road outside the car. Dad eventually was able to put a safety chain on the handle to stop this happening.

Dad had rebuilt the engine and painted it black and green, Mum made a new convertible top using her sewing skills. It was a bit like Noddy's car it was really good.

In this car we went to Brixton for a holiday and it was there mum and dad bought Michael and I a fishing rod each. I had a wooden cane one and he had a metal rod. I remember I was always jealous of what he had as I always thought his things were better than mine.

Keen to try the rods out near the sea harbour Michael rushed to the waterside just around the corner and soon came back crying. He said a man had taken his rod and thrown it into the sea. Dad rushed around but no one could be seen. We looked for the man on his bike but no one was to be seen. It is only now that I look back that I believe Michael had quickly put the rod together pretended to fish by casting an imaginary line and the rod top had gone straight into the see. He probably felt he would have been told off by our dad and be in trouble. So he invented a story about a man on a bike.

When I look back it is incidences like this that I learned about the way Michael thought and worked and in later life it made one wonders at the tales he told.

The Fair Ground, Stolen Bike
Every year the fair would come to Garston and I really looked forward to ride the dodgem cars. All the kids would go to the fair and spend lots of time watching. I can remember two brothers who worked on the fair and these were like heroes, and we would wonder who was the strongest and speculate which one could lift a dodgem car above his head. We would also listen to the latest pop music, which played through large loudspeakers. This was before any one had personal radios or cassette players. There was no Top of the Pops on TV. So the fair was the place to hear pop music.

I was probably about 11 or 12 years old, and this year I remember stealing £3 from my mum's purse. I felt very guilty and bad at the time and I still feel the shame as I write about it now, but this was spent on the fair. I am thankful for the truth that the blood of Jesus cleanses us from all sin. This became my only way of me dealing with my sin when I became a Christian and still is.

My brother at that time had a paper round and use to get up early each morning and so he began to earn his own money. I remember him obtaining all sorts of new things like writing cases, pens, pencils, ink cartridges, etc.. all the little things one would like but could not afford. I soon realized that my brother was not buying them but stealing them from the shop where he worked.

On the odd occasion I would go and help him deliver the papers. I enjoyed this as it took me to places I had never been before.

On one occasion we had to deliver papers to a hospital or residential home, and around the back of the building we could see the kitchens and we helped our selves to the cakes, which had been freshly cooked. I learn from my brother how easy it was to get things I wanted.

I always looked up to my brother and often envied the things he did and had. I remember him going to Switzerland, with the school and him coming home with all kinds of goods. Like a walking stick, flick knives, and badges etc.. Flick knives were illegal and to have a flick knife was a good thing.

My brother soon got in to bows and arrows, and air rifles and pistols swords and sheath knives, which seemed good to me. In fact we use to hide all these weapons under the floorboards in our shed, which was at the bottom of our garden.

At this time I remember my mum and dad buying me a new bike. It was a red Californian, with curved crossbars etc.. I thought it was great and was ever so pleased with it. One day the bike went missing, and I knew some one had taken it, so I was very upset.

When I went out looking for it I noticed up the road an accident had taken place, as there were cars stopped and people milling around. To my horror I saw my nice new bike crumpled and just lying at the side of the road. The boy who had taken it had been knocked off the bike and was lying in the road awaiting an ambulance and every one was trying to take care of him.

I thought to my self never mind about him, as he had stolen my bike, but look at my new bike, all bent. I was very upset. No one however took any notice of me, neither were they concerned about my bike being damaged. The boy's name was Michael Abbes and we had been friends until recently and I seem to remember that he had broken his legs in the accident.

A Stolen Crystal Set

My interest in radio, which we now call electronics, started the day I heard a crystal set operate. I must have been 10 or 11 years old.

My mum and dad belonged to the Camping Club of Great Britain and every weekend we would go camping to Chertsey, where we had a tent pitched.

One weekend my brother stole a crystal set from a camper's tent. It consisted of a small tuning capacitor in a blue plastic case and a crystal diode, together with a set of headphones. I was amazed as it worked and became interested in radio from that day forward.

Camping at Chertsey

Dad at Chertsey Camp-site   Dad By Our Canoe

I sent away for a set of parts to build a two transistor reflex receiver, and put the thing together as best I could. I wired the circuit as I thought the diagram showed, and crushed it all together to fit inside its plastic case. It didn't work and I was most disappointed. I didn't realize that all the wires were shorted together when I crushed it into the plastic case. Another friend of mine's dad helped me out. He was a radio technician in the Royal Air force and he rebuilt the receiver and showed me how to wire circuits up. From that time I began to learn about how things worked and taught my self-many things with the help of others.

Another friend of mine had a dad who had a radio workshop and I was very envious of all the equipment that he had in his garage. I remember the boy being confident enough to take apart out of an old radio for me, without any sense of fear. I was quite impressed. I taught my self quite a lot and began to learn about transistors.

One day on the way home from school we climbed over the fence of someone's back garden and discovered a shed full of radio parts, and equipment. There were valves, tuning condensers, transformers etc.., we took what we wanted and thought no more of it.

This hobby was to last me a long time and helped me to get a job in radio and television servicing and to Technical College at a later date. During this time I had no sense or knowledge of God and I had stopped going to Sunday school.

Stealing Radio Equipment

One day on the way home from school we climbed over the fence of someone's back garden and discovered a shed full of radio parts, and equipment. There were valves, tuning condensers, transformers etc.., We took what we wanted and thought no more of it.

This hobby was to last me a long time and helped me to get a job in Radio and Television Servicing and to Technical College at a later date. During this time I had no sense or knowledge of God and I had stopped going to Sunday school.

A Visit From The Police

About this time I manage to break into a work man's hut which was at the gravel pit situated on not to far from our home. Me along with other kid would play there during the evening and climb on top of the work man's working shed. There were also two large tanks of hot water and we would after dangle our feet in the water and wash our selves after getting dirty. On this occasion we managed to break in the shed and I managed to steal a wireless receiver. It was a valve receiver in a wooden box. I took it to pieces and saved the chassis and had it in my bedroom at Coats Way. Some how the police were tipped off and they came and searched our house for the stolen goods. I was thankful I had got rid of the wooden cabinet as they found no evidence of the break in.

4 SENIOR SECONDARY SCHOOLS

My first senior school was in Garston, as I had failed the 11 plus. It was at this school I first heard a boy play a tune called , "Apache" by the Shadows, on an acoustic guitar and I was very impressed. Michael had already started at this school and did well at cricket, boxing and basketball. I was not good at any of these things but rather was interested in my radio hobby.

Michael and Boxing

I soon learned the my brother had a reputation at school as a boxer and I recall attending the school competition for sports and Michael won the boxing at that event. He would have been in the fourth year and about to leave school. On that occasion my uncle John and Dad were there and Uncle John after Michael's win went and congratulated the looser, in order to keep him encouraged. Parents were like that in those days.

Michael at Butlin's

Michael In The Horizontal Striped Jumper

The Senior Clarke Brothers

Uncle John and my Dad Tom Clarke

My Visit to Soho

It was towards the end of my first year, at Francis Coombe Secondary modern school, that I ventured out to London on the train, with a friend of mine, Paul Dorrington. This was to visit the second hand electrical shops, to buy radio parts. I loved visiting Tottenham Court Road for this purpose and it was on one of these visits that we stumbled across Soho and noticed the strip clubs.

These aroused our curiosity. Paul and I plucked up courage and paid to go in and sit at a table. We could see a nude lady sitting on a chair and were given a sketchpad and pencil and encouraged to draw her picture. I felt I was growing up. Afterwards we paid one or two more visits and became wiser.

When we moved to Wilstone, a village near Tring in Hertfordshire, my radio and television hobby helped me pass the time and kept me out of too much trouble.

5 Our Move To Wilstone

In 1961 we finally moved to Wilstone a village near Tring and Michael and I went to Tring Secondary modern school called Mortimer Hill. I can remember my brother wearing winkle picker shoes and some of the girls from the next village couldn't help but say oh look at those shoes. They were just different and I suppose they felt threatened.

Michael at Tring School

Michael With His Friend Notice the Winkle Picker Shoes

It was during this time that I taught myself more about Radio and amplifiers.

I became absorbed in this hobby. I met a man in the village called Cluck Turney, who was the man to know about televisions and radios and he gave me a lot of help. He taught me about valve amplifiers and allowed me to build a power amplifier, from all the spare parts that he had. It was a push pull amplifier using two PX4 valves and a triode driver. I had to rewind the driver and output transformers in order to get it working. I learned a lot from Cluck Turney.

Home Made Public Address Amplifier

Amplifier Using PX4 Valves

On one occasion I was able to connect a microphone up to my amplifier and I directed the speaker out of my bedroom window and spoke to people out side our shop. On this occasion I saw a woman in her rear garden called Ethel. I called out with the amplifier as loud as possible saying Ethel, Ethel I am watching you. I heard many years later that she thought it sounded a bit like God speaking from the sky.

Keeping Myself Busy

To occupy myself I made things of interest. I made a kart with a large wind sale.

Keeping Busy

My Land Yacht

A pair of stilts and all the kids in the village wanted a pair. On one occasion I made an electric shock machine from an ignition coil a battery and a mechanical vibrating mechanism used in an electric bell. I tested it out on the kids in the village by getting them to hold hands, in a circle and one kid at each end of the circle held the electrode.

When I switched the machine on they all got a sharp electric shock. It was a success.

Keeping Busy

Electric Shock Machine

I later had a visit from the local policeman as I had stolen a 12-bore shotgun from an old barn and brought it home. When I showed it to my next-door neighbour he recognised the gun and realised who it belonged too and so he informed the local policeman to get it returned to its owner.

Stolen Shot Gun

Stolen Shot Gun From the Farm

Whilst at Tring School a friend of mine Duncan Miller found a baby fox cub in a wood, and I wanted to keep it so I took it home. Unfortunately my Grandma, who had come to stay, freaked out when she saw it as she was frightened and to my dismay my brother killed it and to this day I felt he was callous.

I Ride A 350 cc Triumph

My brother mixed with all the lads who had bad reputations and no one would dare up set them and he was in the final year at Tring Secondary Modern school. He was friends with all the lads who were in trouble.

One friend was Bod Shearer, who lived on a farm in Tring and I recall Michael having an old 350 cc, Triumph motor bike, with girder front forks. I took courage and rod this bike in the field and was quite pleased with myself for having the courage to riding such a big bike. I had, until that time, only ridden a moped.

The Motorbike

Michael's 350 CC Triumph Motor bike

It was during this time at Wilstone my brother got sent to his first spell in Detention Centre. He had made a knuckle-duster at school, in the metal work classes, and tried it out by hitting some boy in the village. What happened was some lads had found our moped in the field and had a go at riding it without our permission. Not that they would know whom to ask, but my brother felt he would sort them out for riding it. I think it was an excuse to use the knuckle-duster he had made.

When the police were called in he made out the knuckle duster was made as a part for the moped and my mum was certain this was true and she defended my brother to the hilt. I knew it wasn't true and my brother did a spell in Detention centre for 3 months, for grievous bodily harm. I did not go along with my brothers' violence and could not understand it. His reputation spread and at school the teachers began to identify me with my brother and I think they began to be wary of me too.

My brother mixed with all the lads who had bad reputations and no one would dare up set them.

Village life proved too much for my mum and she became depressed, due to they way things were, and the trouble Michael had gotten into so it was decided to sell up and move to a new house in Aylesbury.

The Moped

Our Moped in Wilstone Field

The Big Freeze 1962

Once we had sold the village shop mum and I moved to Oldham whilst Michael and my dad moved into lodgings in Aston Clinton. This was while the house they had bought off plan was being built. Mum and moved to live with my aunt Edith at 26 Fleet Street, in the town where I was born and had to go to school. This was Clark's Field Senior School and I became a bit of a celebrity simply because I was from "London". This status increased when I told the "lads" about my trips to Soho. It was here that I first heard of the Beatles as they were playing in Oldham at that time. The song I remember that was popular, "Love me do", by the Beatles, which came out in October 1962.

During my time in Oldham we were there for about three months, I built a balsa wood, controlled line, aeroplane, a radio transmitter for a remote control aircraft and learned to ice skate. We had a very cold winter, the coldest on record and the snow fell and the streets froze over. My mum bought me a pair of second hand ice skates and I learned to skate on the frozen streets in Oldham.

Short Stay Back To Watford

After staying for while in Oldham we moved back to Watford and lived with my Dad's mum. On this occasion I had to go back to Francis Coombe Secondary School and I renewed acquaintances with my former friends. It was during this time I made my own transistor radio set. This was before printed circuit boards were available. It was a two transistor reflex receiver and I was very proud of it, as it was the size of a matchbox. I also missed riding the moped and so I got up very early one morning and walked into Watford where I knew a motorbike was parked and stole it. I drove several miles to a secret place and parked it up and went home. I later used it for joy riding with my friends. I walked miles that morning and my mum never knew about it.

Michael also would visit us at Watford and see his old friends who played in a pop group and on one occasion he gave me a pair of bell-bottom trousers and a shirt, with a long pointed collar. Michael and his friend wanted to take me to the dance that was held at Leavesdon, on a Friday or Saturday night. I really enjoyed myself there and wanted to go again. I met some of my friends from school there and one boy noticed my clothes and said that I was a Mod.

Unfortunately for me after this I began to get bullied at school by a group of boys who were what you might call "Jack the Lads". I learned afterward the reason and it was to do with Michael. One of the boys was from Australia and was the ringleader of this gang and he had a girl friend at the school called Pat Petty. She was every boy's dream of a girl. Well Michael had met her at the Leavesdon dance and chatted her up. This Australian boy was jealous and a soon as they realised that I was Michael's brother they had it in for me.

My First Matchbox Radio

It was during this time (13 years) I obtained a circuit diagram for a Two transistor Reflex Receiver and with the components.

My Two Transistor Wireless Receiver

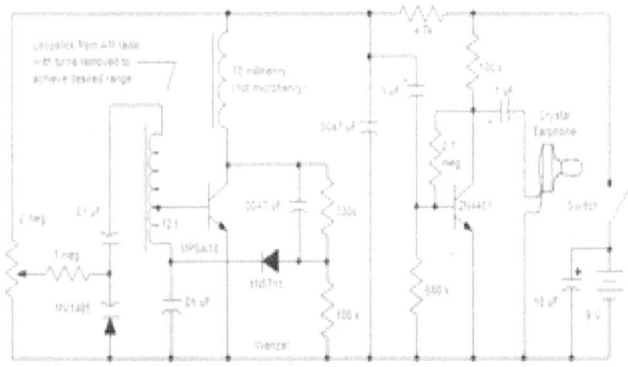

Here Is The Circuit Diagram

I obtained from Tottenham Court Road, London, I built this on a small paxolin board. This was before printed circuit boards were readily available. I was very pleased with this as it had good sensitivity and selectivity and was about the size of a matchbox.

6 AYLESBURY: OUR NEW HOME

Our new house was situated on the Bedgrove Estate, in Aylesbury and was ready for us to move in, in April of 1963. However before we left Wilstone I had enjoyed riding a moped in an old orchard, in the village. It belonged to a friend of Michael and I was allowed to ride this moped. It was a 50 cc NSU Quickly and was kept in his orchard.

Once we had moved into out new house in Aylesbury I was able to return to Wilstone and take the engine from the moped frame and put the engine in a home made go kart. I made this go- kart from builder's wood that I took from the building site. I use the moped engine, a set of wheels from a child's three wheeler tricycle, and various parts from a cement mixer. I then began to ride this machine around the new roads on the housing estate. However I was eventually stopped by the local police and warned that it was illegal to ride this Go Kart on the roads and soon after that the local newspaper came and gave me a write up in the Bucks Herald.

David's Do It Your Self-kart

David's Do It Your Self Kart 1963

An Aylesbury boy was able to return to school after the Easter holidays and proudly tell his friends, " I've made a Go Cart in the holidays." He is 14 years old,

On Sunday of last week a friend gave David (pictured above) and old moped. As he was unable to ride it he as he is too young he dismantled it. He then made a Kart frame from some pieces of wood, four old wheels and a set of handlebars and the moped engine.

My NSU Quickly Moped

My Moped

Within three days it was in working condition and David estimates it will do 20 miles and hour.

Incidentally David, who has lived in the town for only a month has very little real interest in engines. His main hobby is in radio construction work and one of his proudest possessions is a transistor radio, which he built that is slightly larger than a matchbox.

I Steel Push Bikes

It was during this space of time, before starting my new school; I met another lad called Ian Motrem. We encouraged each other to steel push bikes. In fact the first day that I went to school I stole a bike to come home from school.

I eventually got a Francis Barnet 150 CC motorbike, which my brother had stolen from Aylesbury College, with some other lads. I kept this in a field on the Bedgrove Estate near our home. It was great fun to have a motorbike and I would ride across the fields to school and return home during my lunch hour. However one day some one stole my motorbike and Ian Motrem informed me that he thought he knew the person that had taken it. I went to this person's house early one morning, during my paper round, and found a motorbike in his garage. This wasn't my bike but I took it anyway. This ended up in me being charge with garage breaking and being put on probation for two years.

Stolen Francis Barnett 150 CC Motor Bike

My Francis Barnett Motor Bike

7 I MEET MRS GRACE KNIGHT

My teenage years leaving School

My first recollection of any religious person having any effect on my life was when I was about to leave school, at the age of 15 years old.

My mother had spoken to a Mr K H Knight who was the proprietor of Central Bucks T.V. and had arranged for me to have a part time job working after school and on a Saturday. This was until I left school and took up full time work as an apprentice to Mr Knight.

I am told years later that my letter of job application was so badly written and the spelling so awful it was laughable. However I was taken on despite my inability to write, spell or use correct grammar, or read properly. This was during my last year at school.

I first met Mrs Grace Knight, one Saturday morning, whilst working for her husband Ken. She was in hot pursuit of her husband and shouting at him for doing some thing she disapproved of.

I was in the workshop, with Norman Garret the other apprentice, and I thought- wow what an awful dragon of a woman and pitied Mr Knight from that moment on.

Through Mr Knight (Ken) I was introduced to the Radio and Television servicing trade and often went with him into customer's houses to repair TV's and install television aerials.

I spent many hours with Ken going to peoples homes and soon learned that he was not faithful to his wife. Not that it bothered me, as I knew what Grace was like from our first meeting. The idea of sexual promiscuity was very attractive to me. When we went out enjoying our selves Mrs Knight would be left at home or in the workshop minding their two children Allison and Mark. They also had a big dog called Rufus.

By this time I had left school and was interested in our band, as we wanted to make music. Ian Myers was the bass guitarist and he built his own guitar amplifier from a circuit design and published in Practical Wireless. He built the amplifier I helped him with the speaker cabinet and it was used in all our future gigs.

I soon began to realize the things I enjoyed were not the things Mrs Knight approved of, or found interesting. I thought she was a right "kill joy" and was boring. She was a Christian what ever that meant and I soon realize her values were not the same as mine. What I considered good and enjoyable she would call it sin and sinful. She would also complain to her husband that I was always with him and he gave her no time. It seemed she was often driven to despair by him never being in on time and being very unreliable. He would often leave her for hours whilst we were at work out on jobs.

Conversation On The Intercom

On one occasion Norman Garret's mum complained to Mrs Knight the Norman her son, was not getting the training he needed because Ken was always taking me out with him. I heard this conversation over the shops intercom. Mrs Knight said yes I was a nuisance and she did not like me one bit and it was not good that I should be out with her husband all the time. Upon hearing this I felt angry and went down the stairs to where they were and confronted them both saying that I had heard what they had said about me. They were embarrassed and I am sure this did not help our relationship. I really thought Mrs Knight was an ogre.

I began to attend Luton College of Technology, to learn about Radio and Television Servicing, and travelled by bus, one day a week, from Aylesbury to Luton; it was about an hour's and a half's run. I think it must have been due to Mrs Knight and her religion that I began to notice the texts of scripture put up out side churches as I past by on the bus, they were called "Way side pulpits". I began to memorize the verses such as:

" Righteousness exalteth a nation but sin is a reproach to any people"

And also another:

" Jesus said if you find life difficult learn of me and the burden I shall give you will not be too difficult to carry".

At that time I had no idea of the meaning of these texts of scripture but found it amusing to quote them to Mrs Knight at any in appropriate moment thinking it would embarrass her.

On one occasion I remember being dressed in an old blanket made into an undercoat from my brothers Mod anorak. I was standing on the corner of the street near to the workshop one Saturday morning with Mr and Mrs Knight. I quoted at the top of my voice these two scriptures in order to embarrass Mrs Knight. I am not sure how they felt about it but little did I know that one day I would learn the truth of these texts and become a preacher of the Gospel myself.

Mrs Grace Knight became a great help to me and lived until 2001. Here is a link to a video of her funeral.

(Click to view)

Obituary Grace Maude Knight

A Confident 15 year old

I enjoyed working for Mr Knight because he seemed to appreciate my help and abilities and would trust me to drive the van at 15 years old. On one occasion he was short of a driver and had to deliver a television. So he dressed me up in a sheepskin coat and gave me dark glasses to wear with instructions to deliver a TV to a house in Quarendon. I was very pleased to do this even more when it turned out that I was delivering the TV set to one of my school friends called Gillespie.

On another occasion I was given the job of replacing a complete I.F. board on a new Ferguson 850 T.V. receiver in a customers home. A qualified engineer in a workshop setting normally would have done this but this unconventional approach was normal to me. Mr Knight had complete confidence in me at the age of 15 years old. I am sure the customer was not at all happy at this 15 year old repairing their lovely brand new Television receiver.

During this time I was still making music in the group and when I was 16 Mr Knight's business failed and went into liquidation so I found myself another job. I got an apprenticeship with Sale and Mellor at Radio a TV shop in Aylesbury. I worked there until I got in trouble with the police when I was sacked at the age of 17 years.

Stolen BSA Bantam

BSA Bantam 125 CC Motor Bike

It was shortly after this time that I got into trouble with the police for breaking into a garage and stealing a motorbike. I had a Francis Barnett 150 CC, which had been stolen from the field where I kept it and a friend of mine told me that it was in this garage, along the Tring Road. At first I was just interested in getting my bike back but when I opened the garage door I was disappointed not to find it - just a 125 BSA Bantam.

I thought well its better than nothing so I decided to take it any way and wheeled it out of the garage and back to our field, to use it later. The police later caught me and for this first crime I was charged with garage breaking and put on probation for two years.

A Holiday in Newquay

At this time Mum and Dad took me and my sister Margaret , who was about 3 years old, to Newquay for a holiday. I didn't know what kind of place it was but when we got there it was great. The sand the sea and the surfing and views were a treat to see. It was here that I conducted my first blag (a scheme or scam) as I wanted to explore the Headland Hotel, which was an impressive hotel.

The Headlands Hotel

Anyway on this occasion I took Margaret by the hand and we walked down the drive right into the hotel. As we approached a steward of some kind came up to me and asked if he could help. I confidentially replied no thank we are staying here. He stood upright, in embarrassment and said, oh yes I remember the little girl. So we blagged it and I wondered around the hotel with my 3 year old sister, admiring the hotel.

The Hotel Where The Witches Was Filmed

The Headlands Hotel Newquay

My brother and I were to returned to Newquay for a holiday in 1967 just before we were both sent to prison.

8 OUR ROCK GROUP

It was after this that decided I wanted to play the electric guitar and I remember a lad called Alan Lawrence, from Tring Secondary Modern School, having an electric guitar and bringing it to school. He plugged it into the schools record player and it sounded great. I wanted to learn to play like him. The first guitar I owned was an electric Hofner Futurama Two and a friend called Steve showed me how to play Twist and Shout and it was this that got me really interested to play properly.

Steal An Amplifier Catholic Church

I put together my own guitar amplifier using the P.A. amplifier that I had stolen from the Catholic Church on the North Orbital Road in Watford. It didn't bother me even when my conscience spoke to me about it being wrong to steal as I believed the Catholics were wrong anyway according to my mum.

My First Guitar Stolen Amplifier

Liner Concord 30 Amplifier

Top View using EL34 Output valves in push pull

Underneath the Chassis

Hand Wired Main Chassis

(I had inherited a prejudice against the Catholic Church, from my mum, and so when I took the amplifier I ignored my conscience by saying to myself they were wrong any way).

I then began to get more interested in making music and during my last year at school we formed a band and we played at the end of term school dance. Our Gym teacher, Mr Pottinger, organized this event.

The Fowler Mean our Rock Group

Ian Myers was the base guitarist and later Robby Woods became our lead guitarist. On that occasion though, at the school do, Willie Barrett was lead guitarist. He was the only one of us to make musical fame. He became known as Wild Willy Barrett and played music with John Otway.

Wild Willy Barrett

Wild Willy Barrett

A Secret

Willy Barrett's dad was a brilliant man, a musician and a craftsman, he made an excellent bass guitar for either Willy or his friend. He wanted an amplifier for Willie's electric guitar and the bass player friend said he had a 30 Watt Linear Concord amplifier for sale, for a small amount of money and I jumped in quickly before they made their mind up and bought it from this man. This is the one in my picture.

How ever I then agreed to sell my 15 Watt linear Concord amplifier that I had stolen from the Catholic Church, in North Watford to his dad for a little bit less money and they bought it of me. I was very pleased but felt a bit guilty because they got a rough deal and really they should have had the 30 Watt amplifier which was much better than mine. Little did they know I had stolen the amplifier.

Aylsebury Musicians

Wild Willy Barrett and John Otway

My Vox A.C. 30 Amplifier

My Vox AC 30 (Cost Second hand £60)

I had a new amplifier that was a Vox AC 3.0. and replaced the amplifier that I had stolen from the Catholic Church. One of our regular spots, on a Saturday night, was Courts Dance School, just off Kingsbury Square. Here is our music play set:

The Fowler Mean (Play Set) Click to view and listen

After leaving school we reformed the group and began to play music at various dance halls and I named the group "The Fowler Mean".

We often played at Courts School of dancing in George Street in Aylesbury and other venues in Aylesbury. In Tring and the Bulls Head and the Anthony Hall in Aston Clinton. One of the other bands we played with was The Must Be Blue with the organist Pat Archer.

We would play all cover music by groups such as, The Rolling Stones, The Who, The Small Faces, The Kinks, Ottis Reading and John Lee Hooker. We played, "My Generation", but I knew it was not quite right and I never did find out how to play the right cords to this day. The opening chords we played were four down strokes on G followed by four downward strokes on F but that is not right. I always thought if ever I met Pete I would ask him to show me how to play those opening chords. I really enjoyed playing with the band but was eventually sacked and it was then that Malcolm Kirkham and I began to knock around with each other.

The Fowler Mean

Dave Clarke (left) with Robby Woods (top) Ian Myers

Our Favourite Band The Who

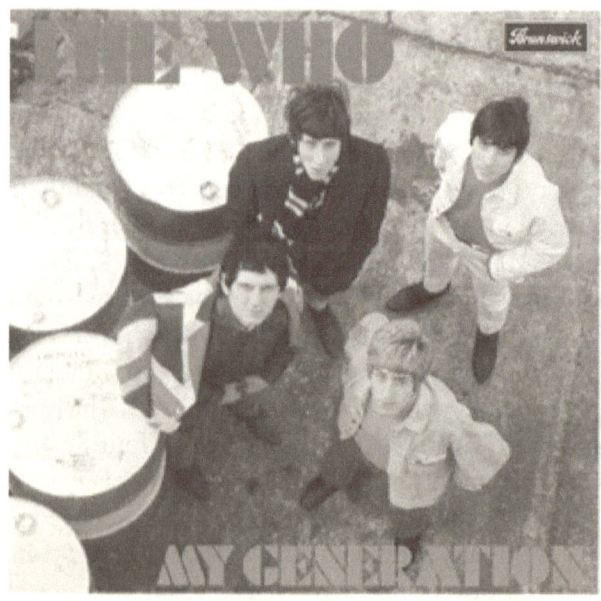

John Entwhistle, Pete Townsend, Keith Moon, Roger Daultary

My favourite band was The Who. This group introduced something to music that was new. It was volume. My Generation was the real hit that made the Who. I can remember hearing them, at the Grosvenor Dance Hall, in Aylesbury. Pete Townsend was the lead guitar, John Entwhistle on bass, Keith Moon on drums and Roger Daultary lead singer. There was not a band to touch them they were brilliant. We saw them on a number of occasions including places like Borehamwood and the Bedford Corn Exchange.

I remember their amplifier line up (being interest in amplifiers) Pet Townsend had:

Pete Townshend Amplifier line Up

Two A.C. 100 Amplifiers in Parallel

John Entwhistle Amplifier line up

4 X A.C. 60 watt Vox Bass

Amplifiers and their PA system was Vox columns and Shure microphones.

The volume added another dimension to the experience. I call it Rock and Real Music, It added depth to the sound and none of us had experienced anything like it before

These were all classic Who numbers and none forgettable pieces of music

Malcolm Kirkham use to be one of our singers which made 5 in the band and we use to go out together on our scooters. I had inherited my brother's Lambretta TV 175 CC and Malcolm had a 150 CC new Lambretta and we began to mix with the Mods in Aylesbury and district.

He had been sacked from the group because he messed about. Malcolm would always arrive late and never be in time to set up the equipment. He was always combing his hair or having to press his trousers, and he general fooled around. He was nicknames Cocoa the clown.

After mixing with the other lads in Aylesbury I soon found out my brother was well known and when it was made known I was Mike Clarke's brother it was like having a license to or say any thing, I was accepted. I was one of the boys. I recalled the times my brother had told me of the parties they use to have and I began to want to get involved in all the fun. Pep pills, scooters, Mod fashions, dances, girls and permissive sex. All of which I found positive and attractive as we were looking for a good time in the world.

The image I had of my brother was that he was quite a character and had a way with girls. I remember that was how I wanted to be and follow him in fame. I remember one impressive occasion I must have been just 16 and met one of Michael's friends who was a Mod. One Saturday night out side the Grosvenor he came dressed in brightly coloured trousers and a black plastic mac wearing girls make up around the eyes. This was the in thing to do and I thought this is good and liked it.

The normal mode of transport was either a Lambretta or Vespa scooter with crash bars, back rests, spare wheel carriers and mirrors. The scooters would be custom sprayed and generally a world war green Parker or black plastic cape was the uniform. All of this became the world I wanted to be in.

Oxford Bags

I remember my brother coming to see us at Rockley Sands, in Bournemouth when I was away with my parents on holiday. I must have been 15 years old. He came dressed in a brown suit with 22 inch, Oxford Bag trousers, with small turn-ups. His top was a white crew necked and red stripped tea shirt. Also brown brogue leather shoes. This was some fashion that I had not seen before. It was the Mod fashion.

He told me he had to return to Aylesbury to do some repairs and tidy up mum and dads house as they had a party and the place had been wrecked. Apparently all the Aylesbury Mods and from the district had been to his party held at Mum and Dads house. They had rolled up the carpets and put them in the garage but the bathroom sink had been pulled off the wall as some girl had got drunk and sat in it. He told me of the promiscuity and it all seemed good fun. This was the year 1963 or 4 when the Beatles and Rolling Stone came to fame. Also Gerry and the Pacemakers had a hit records at the time called, "I Like it".

My First Girl Friend

I met Susan, at a Friday night dance being organized at the Aylesbury College; she was 15 years old and looked great. She had blond hair in a Bob style. I was 16, wearing my navy blue Mod suit. I had arrived on my Lambretta.

I asked her to dance and later asked if I could take her home. I was feeling great when she agreed and so I covered up my learner plate, which was just under the rear, number plate and took her home. This was the beginning of my first love. The relationship only lasted a few months. When she told me she wanted to finish the relationship I was heart broken and she sought to encourage me by saying I would find some one else. I never did and had no interest in finding any one else. My only interest in girls after that was for sex alone- not friendship or anything else.

Another Who song that expressed my emotions at that time and I first heard this at Borehamwood.

The Mod Image

Lambretta Scooter Blond Girl Friend Sue

During this time Malcolm and I mixed with the Mods in Aylesbury we were both 16 years old and we began to meet with these older lads and were curious to try pep pills (purple hearts, black bombers and Dexedrine) and smoke hashish, or grass, so we began to make some inquiries where to get some. In the mean time we would experiment smoking crushed codeine tablets and dried banana skins. This was purely to satisfy a curiosity and to experience new things. The was a pub in Aylesbury called the, "Flee Pit" situated in Kingsbury Square and it was there we understood we could buy hash. However at 16 years old I went in this pub and became very embarrassed as on the wall behind the bar were displayed ladies knickers in various styles and colours. I felt embarrassed because the sight aroused me as at that time there was very little pornography and the sight of a woman in a short skirt and legs was very provocative for a 16 year old, On reflection I had a very high libido. Which led to a very promiscuous life style.

Carknapping (Steeling Cars)

Shortly after this I remember my brother coming home about 9.30 pm in a hurry. He had not long been released from Detention Centre. Our parents were away and I had a girl friend there. In came my brother and told me of his narrow escape from the police. About six of his friends had been out in a stolen car, not taxed or insured, when the police had stopped them along the Tring Road. They had all jumped out and made a run for it. It was soon after this that my brother got sent to Borstal Training for some crime or other. Never the less it all seemed a good life style and I wanted more of it.

I had discovered I could buy chloroform from a chemist and this was much better than sniffing carbon Tetrachloride or the glue substances people began to experiment with. Shortly after this Malcolm Kirkham, after trying something like, this took it in his head that he could fly on his scooter. He broke his arm and smashed his scooter in the process but fortunately not his head as he was wearing a dear stalker crash helmet he had stolen a few days before.

The names of some of the lads we knew and come to mind were: Stuart Knight, Keith Guntrip, Ian Wilton, Dill Dorwrick, and Terry Tatem (Now dead), Phil Davis, Brian Collier, Mickey Coil, Roy Miles, John James, Dave King, Jimmy Findlay, Phil Davis, and the like all of which had one thing in common. They wanted fun and were the lads of Aylesbury. (Time of writing this is the year 2000).

My Lambretta Scooter

Lambretta TV 175 CC

At that time after being sacked from the group we began going to a nightclub called the Banbury Gaff. Here we would stay up all night taking pep pills (we use to say getting blocked) dancing and talking and in the morning end up in a cafe eating toast before driving back to Aylesbury. Soon after this Malcolm began to mix with the lads from Oxford and he was later sentence to some time in prison, for some crime or other. During this time my brother was in Borstal and at the Gaff I met Alan Dodd. He was my brother's partner in crime and had escaped from Borstal and was living on a barge in Oxford. He told me at the time he had a gun and all this type of living impressed me as it seemed rather exciting. We would spend time at the Gaff talking with other lads about the crimes we had done and planned various schemes and bragged and boasted about things we had done.

From this experience of mine I can say that there is no prevention or cure from this kind of criminal mind set. Once on that route you are on the road to serious crime, as all that I knew at that time will confirm. I can also say that a girl friend could really help some one like that avoid getting into too much crime.

The Great Train Robbery

It wasn't long after the Great Train Robbery that we were finding our feet as criminals.

Bridgo Bridge

The Scene of the Robbery 1963

The great train robbery had taken place on August 8, 1963 at the Bridgo Bridge in Linslaid, just up the road from us in Aylesbury. The thieves laid an ambush for the mail train running from Glasgow to Euston and stole more than £2 million. For 125 years, the train had run uninterrupted until that night, when it was stopped by a red light in Buckinghamshire. Bruce

Reynolds who crafted the robbery, was caught in 1969 and sentenced to 10 years in jail.

We were very impressed at this crime.

The Kray Twins

In the 1960's, the Ronnie and Reggie Kray were seen as prosperous and charming celebrity nightclub owners and were part of the Swinging London scene. A large part of their fame was due to their non-criminal activities as popular figures on the celebrity circuit, being photographed by David Bailey on more than one occasion; and socializing with lords, MP's, socialites and show business characters such as the actors George Raft, Judy Garland, Diana Dors, Barbara Windsor and singer Frank Sinatra.

"They were the best years of our lives. They called them the swinging sixties. The Beatles and the Rolling Stones were rulers of pop music, Carnaby Street ruled the fashion world... and me and my brother ruled London. We were fucking untouchable..." – Ronnie Kray, in his autobiographical book, My Story.

The Twins

Ronnie and Reggie Kray

Kray's Imprisonment

On 8 May 1968, the Kray's and 15 other members of their firm were arrested. Many witnesses came forward now that the Kray's' reign of intimidation was over, and it was relatively easy to gain a conviction.

The Kray's and 14 others were convicted, with one member of the firm being acquitted. One of the firm members that provided a lot of the information to the police was arrested yet only for a short period.

Out of the 17 official firm members, 16 were arrested and convicted.

The twins' defence, under their counsel John Platts-mills, QC, consisted of flat denials of all charges and the discrediting of witnesses by pointing out their criminal past. The judge, Mr Justice Melford Stevenson said: "In my view, society has earned a rest from your activities." Both were sentenced to life imprisonment, with a non-parole period of 30 years for the murders of Cornell and Mcvitie, the longest sentences ever passed at the Old Bailey, (Central Criminal Court, London) for murder. Their brother Charlie was jailed for 10 years for his part in the murders.

Mods Scooters, Bikes Bubble Car

Shortly after my brother came out of Borstal a form of transport was required for two. A solution to this came through my brother who persuaded me to swap my scooter for a two-seater, Issetta 350 cc bubble car. I had inherited the scooter from my Michael when he was sent to Borstal but by now it had been renovated. I had rebuilt it in the spare bedroom at home and re sprayed it British racing Green. It was a Lambretta T.V. 175 cc. The fuel tank and tool compartment was stove enamelled gold. It had a dual seat with a passenger back rest with very little extras. There had been crazes whereby crash bars, wing mirrors, wheel racks and anything made of chrome were generally attached to such machines, but not mine. I was proud of this Lambretta. It had to go to make way for the sky blue Bubble Car.

Pete Townsend Gives Us A lift

Before this time we had to thumb lifts, to get to where we wanted too if the scooter was out of action. On one occasion we were keen to get to Bedford, as The Who were playing at the Corn Exchange. We were dressed in our Mod mohair suits and carried a small suitcase with our night things in. We got as far as Ampthill and were stuck at the corner of the Ampthill to Bedford road and were about 20 miles from Bedford. We were stuck and Michael went into a pub to get a drink whilst I stayed on the corner trying to thumb a lift. As my brother needed a lift as well. To my relief and just after Michael had gone to the pub, a two seater red coupé Jaguar pulled up to offer me a lift. I rushed up to the window of the car, carrying our small suit case, feeling very relieved that I had a lift, but at the same time anxious as my brother was still in the pub. I said to the driver cheekily would he mind waiting a minute, The driver was fine and said OK. However to my surprise and amazement I realized whom the driver was it was Pete Townsend, the lead guitarist of The Who. Of course that made our day. By this time Michael had arrived and we both squeeze into the front seat of Pete's Jaguar. We told him who we were and that we were off to Bedford to their gig at the Corn Exchange.

As we drove into Bedford we stopped and Pete asked me to ask some girls the directions to where The Who were playing. Sure enough they knew and pointed us in the direction of the Corn Exchange. It was a great evening.

Pete Townsend's Jaguar

Pete Townsend MK1 Jaguar

9 THE BUBBLE CAR

The bubble car belonged to David Ness of Chiltern avenue in Aylesbury, who had been given it by his brother. There was only one thing wrong with it. We had to bump start it as the starter motor did not work. (Push it and the put it in gear and jump in once the engine had started).

Our New Form Or Transport

Front Loader 300 BMW Issetta Bubble Car

In this vehicle we had many adventures because we were liberated from the two- wheeled scooter and could cram four people in this vehicle, if we wanted. Neither of us had passed our driving test to drive a normal car but I had past my test to drive a motorbike and my license allowed me to drive the three-wheeler bubble car. We were able to carry blankets spare clothing etc..

all in the dry. We carried all that we needed for a night out in that case. It was ideal for catching girls. The front opened up and it could be driven with the front door open. All we did was drive up to the bird we wanted to catch and stop in front of her. Open up the door and drive forward. She had no option but to fall in and we would drive off with her in the car. It was questioned was any girl safe with us around.

Dr Clarke's Case

Whilst Michael was in Borstal, he had made for me a wooden case, like a brief case, that he had written on the side, Dr Clarke. This was for a bit of fun. However I carried, in that case, a bottle of Chloroform, whiskey and a fake gun (it was a starter pistol that fired blanks and looked real). We used the case to frighten people , as they soon learned what was inside the case.

The Doctors Case

Dr Clarke Case

On one occasion we went into the Crombie shop, just off Kingsbury Square intending to frighten the manager of the shop.

What had happened was that I had a blue mohair navy suit made to measure by him . How ever the jacket did not fit right and even after many alterations it did not fit properly. This was whilst Michael was in Borstal. So on Michael's release, and him hearing about the suit, we decided to go an get our own back and frighten the manager to pieces. He was about 21 years old and we were younger. So we went into the shop and put Dr Clarke's case on the counter and proceeded to get the chloroform out of the case intending to put the manager to sleep. We had no other intentions but simply to frighten him. When he realised what was about to take place, he was terrified and I had to stop Michael from knocking him out with the Chloroform. On one occasion we set off to Margate, on one Bank holiday. This was a custom amongst our generation of Mods. We all seemed to migrate to Yarmouth, Margate or Brighton. This was Whitsun bank holiday.

Off To Margate

1966 and Mod and Rocker riots were common. On this trip to the coast my brother was true to form he had borrowed a 22 Webley air pistol from Pat Jones and was determined to have a good time. He had fired the occasional pop shot at one or two girl's bottoms, which cause many amusements to us all. This was not what I would have normally done because I remember how shocked I was at 11 years old a boy I recalled boys having air gun fights in the woods on the way home from school. I thought then how dangerous and stupid it was. However her was my brother older than I acting fearlessly. I just went along with it suppressing my natural cautiousness.

As we past through the various towns in London the air pistol was used to cause alarm. (As I write I shrivel up at the thought of what was done) We found it amusing to shoot at ladies bottoms as their reactions of shock was funny. As we passed through Lewisham several people must have reported the mystery air gun shooter and at least one lady was wounded.

Caught By The Police

Traffic police on route to Margate stopped us. These men briefly searched our car but found nothing suspicious and let us go. My brother had hidden the pistol just in time and we did not allow this close shave stop our adventure. Persons (girls) bathing at night were targets for our folly and we found it amusing to see and her scream from a female. It was not intended to wound or harm but that really was inevitable.

Our BMW Bubble Car

300 CC Bubble Car

During this weekend we moved on to Ramsgate and again moved with a spirit of naughtiness decided to steel a tray of peaches from a fruit and vegetable shop. The bubble car was to be used as the get away car. The shop was half way down a hill with houses on either side of the road, it was decided I should take the peaches and my brother to drive the get away car. I lifted the tray of peaches and jumped in the car as it rolled down the hill making a chug, chug, noise-attracting attention. Naturally we were spotted and reports were made to the police but we did not know this.

Our foolishness was brought to an end when the same traffic police that had stopped us in London, on the way home, picked us up. I could tell from their faces that they had it in for us.

A quick search of our vehicle revealed a stolen handbag. If only we had got rid of it, I thought. Then the air gun pellets and finally the air gun itself. That was it we were arrested, the policemen having a snarl on his face and almost laughing as us. We were charge with malicious wounding and two cases of stealing. A woman in Lewisham had been travelling in a side car and been hit in the neck by the air pistol by my brother.

I was granted bail but my brother detained in custody. We had decided that I would say I had done the shooting and my brother was a sleep. This was to get my brother off a prison sentence as he had already done two spells in Detention Centres and two years in Borstal. I had only had a probation order and had an apprenticeship. I thought I would only get a fine but I was wrong.

Our Mum managed to obtain bail for my brother and we appeared in Kent Quarter sessions several months later.

On recollection I can remember a prison officer, at the Rochester Borstal, where I had visited my brother a year previously, had said to me that I would be sent to Borstal if I didn't watch out. I said. "You must be joking". I was sent to Borstal just as he said I would be for confessing to this crime. We were charged with malicious wounding.

On reflection I think my brother was not being a good brother to me. He should not have let me do it.

Bubble Car Blows Up

During the time we were awaiting our court appearance we went one night to Bedford in the bubble car. On the way home the bobble car caught light and blew up as the petrol tank was above the engine. We managed to walk to Woburn Green and decided we would have to sleep the night there. After routing through some ones garage we found an old mattress and blankets and there was a newly piled mound of grass on the village green. This was where we made our bed and it was very comfortable. We put up our umbrella that we had rescued from the bubble car and slept soundly until the morning. The police, who wanted to know what we were doing - as if they could not see, waked us up. When we explained the bubble car had blown up they said oh yes they had seen it up the road. So they let us go without any further questions. I arrived at work that morning but was soon to be dismissed because I was due to appear in court and they were not prepared to trust me any more. This was the last of the bubble car as my parents managed to sell it when we were in prison.

I Get The Sack

Once my boss Mr Sale found out I had been caught by the police he gave me the sack and so I had no job and was about to appear in court on charges of malicious wounding and carrying a fire arm without a license. So in revenge I had a plan. I knew where the money and the takings of the shop were stored over night.

Plan A Break In

So shortly after this I instructed my apprentice, Pat Jones, to break into the shop where I used to work and had been given the sack, and he was to take the money.

The Shop

Shop Front High Street

The Break In

His task was to climb on top of the garage roof, lift the tiles off the roof of the shop and break through into the loft, and then the ceiling. Go into the rear toilet and take the money. A great plan so we thought Then only trouble was that the money bag had not been placed in the spot that I instructed Pat to go to. So he did the job, did not get caught but we got no money.

The Plot

Sale And Mellor Shop Rear

The Fire Arm

The Offending Weapon

10 CANTERBURY PRISON

When my brother appeared in the Kent Quarter Sessions court I pleaded guilty to the charges of malicious wounding and carrying a fire arm without a license and my brother pleaded not guilty on all accounts.

I was sentenced to Borstal Training, which meant I could do any time between 6 months to two years. That would depend on me to some degree on how I behaved.

Canterbury Prison together

My brother was detained in custody until he appeared in court a month later during, which time we were both detained in. Our time in Canterbury Prison was in one sense a time of continuous fun and just another of our good times together, even though I had just received an awful sentence. Upon arrival at Canterbury Prison we were taken into the reception hall. Here we were with other newly sentenced young persons and being with my brother made it that much easier for me, and it gave me confidence because he had been to Rochester Borstal, and Detention Centre on two occasions, before and he knew the ropes. Canterbury Prison

Canterbury Prison in Kent

This housed young persons who must have been typical of the criminal population of England at the time. In this prison we shared our experiences with others who had been sentenced to three, four and six months, and many had already been to approved schools, detention centres and Borstal before. Some were on their second or even third visit to prison. There was an element of excitement and curiosity about what made people like they were?

In the reception hall we were issued with prison clothing. Our fingerprints were taken and photographed and we were each given a number. After this the medical officer (all prison officers were called screws) had inspected us and we were taken to our cell (called a Peter). At that time we were three's up. My brother and I and a lad from Liverpool. In this cell we were to remain for a few days until we were issued work. The cell was approximately 12 foot by 9 foot and housed a bunk bed and a single bed. A table, chair, water jug and urinal pot.

Canterbury Prison

Canterbury Prison Gates

At half past six each morning our sleep was broken with a bang on the door and words saying "Slop out". This meant we had to get up make up our beds and empty the urinal pot. We then could get hot water for a wash in a jug for a shave and return to our cell. A razor blade was issued and collected after and then we were banged up until breakfast.

At breakfast time we were unlocked and had to line up in single file to collect our food. This was served up on a specially shaped metal tray, which was recessed in three places to retain the food.

A typical breakfast would be a scoop of porridge, four slices of bread, a knob of margarine, a sausage or piece of bacon with beans and a large mug of tea.

The bread dipped in porridge became one of my favourite meals but on one occasion this practice of dipping bread in my porridge offended one inmate (when I was in Dover Borstal) he expressed he thought what I was doing was a disgusting habit. I just ignored him with contempt.

One of the ways we past time, when locked up in the cell, was to play "Blind Man Buff". One of us would be blindfolded whilst the other two crept about and hid from the other, while the blind man tried to catch the others. There were all sorts of places to hide in such a small cell. We enjoyed this game we would jump from bed to bed which made the game that much more fun.

During this time I found time killing boring so I tried to read one ore two books. The books I found I could read were James Bond as these were about my level and the Beano and Dandy comics. Any other reading would be too difficult to me.

On the days we were not working, each morning and afternoon was exercise. This was where all the inmates walked as a body around the prison yard. No doubt each prisoner looked at the high walls and every building looking for a possible way to escape. During this time we could talk with whom we pleased, those that attempted an escape were made to wear yellow patches so they could be spotted easily. These times became a time of communication and formed the prison grape vine

Hair Style Change

On one occasion I decided to change my hairstyle. So during the wash period my brother removed the safety edge from the Government Issue razor and was able to shave my head. It was much easier to wash in the mornings with no hair and much fresher. However I had gone against the prison rules and was put on a Governors report and put in solitary confinement for a period of time.

At the meal time it cause an amusing stir and I was to get laughed at when one of the cooks slapped a handful of strawberry jam on my bald head. After this when my hair grew a little I was able to razor a parting in my hair which was really the beginning of the hair fashions for the skin head.

What Sentence Have You Got?

I could not help but notice the various characters and the first points of conversation were "What sentence had you got and what was your crime, or crimes". After this an inquiry would be made as to your previous convictions and prison sentencing.

Our time at Canterbury came to and end when my brother was found guilty and was sentence to two years prison at the Kent Crown Court.

I was a witness at his trial and was detained in the cells below the courtroom. When my brother was brought below, handcuffed to a prison officer, I was shocked and disappointed that he had been found guilty. In fact all our plans had come to nothing and I was to do a stretch in Borstal. He was found guilty of malicious wounding as well and was sentenced to 2-year prison.

On that occasion my mother was not allowed to see either of us and we were taken from the cells in Kent back to Canterbury prison that dark wet night. As we approached the prison gate I saw my mum with tears in her eyes out side the prison gate. We both waved and motioned to the prison officer to say she had come to see us and his reaction was, "So what, she can't see you because you are now prisoners". She had not got a visiting permit. She had travelled from Kent to Canterbury late that night to try and see us but she was rejected.

From that time we hated that prison officer called Titmouse. He was about 6 foot 7 inches tall. My brother, weeks later, after we were separated laid into this screw because of the hate. He head-butted him (nutted) and of course was on a governor's report and put in solitary confinement. This I heard through the grape vine when I was at Wormwood scrubs awaiting my allocation to Dover Borstal.

Wormwood Scrubs

I was moved from Canterbury Prison to Wormwood Scrubs in London, which was a Borstal allocation centre. After a period of four weeks it was decided I was to go to Dover Borstal. A closed Borstal called the Citadel. For the first time I was on my own and was moved from one cell to another having to share some times with others. I did not really enjoy things here, as it was lonely being on my own.

The Scrubs

Wormwood Scrubs

Dover Borstal (The Citadel)

We were allowed to go to church on a Sunday, which I did to break the monotony. How ever I remember being horrified by the fact that I saw some inmate tearing pages out of the bible to role cigarettes. This was probably the first sense of me acknowledging the existence or fear of God.

When at Dover Borstal I was placed in an open dormitory with five other lads. Here I had to learn to survive. There was a 6 foot 6 inch Lad nicked named Te Oh who was bullied mercilessly by a 5 foot 6 spectacled bottle job, called Vince Bowker. I saw this bullying the moment I arrived and Te oh was made to do this, do that, and he would say yes Vince, no Vince and so one hoping to get off lightly. In the end Te oh turned and lashed out on

Vice Bowker and that put stopped to that. I was determined I was not going to let that happen to me. I stood my own ground whenever I sensed any one trying to bully me. I was in fact nick named Flash Clarke because I had all kinds of goodies like, cocoa, coffee, milk and sugar and even Ovaltine and had one of the senior green ties make me Ovaltine in the morning.

Borstal Boy

One bully, 6 footer, was moved into our dormitory because he had mercilessly bullied another inmate. We got on well until I tied his shoelaces together one morning for a joke but he didn't see it that way. When he realized who it was that did it he threw these tied shoes at me in anger and this gave me a black eye. As he came at me to hit me I was quick enough to hit him on the jaw bringing him down to the ground. After that he kept out of my way and the screw that could see my black eye ignored it. I think they must have known how to deal with bullies.

Electrical Installation Course

Whilst at Dover I went on a six months training course doing Electrical Installations and I worked really hard obtaining top marks every week and I use to be rewarded half an ounce of tobacco for coming top of the class. I traded this with an inmate for his ration of milk each morning and cornflakes and an egg each Sunday morning.

We had to attend church on a Sunday and were would be marched to church in whatever the weather. We would have to be dressed in our best gear after Sunday morning inspection. I remember I had no sense of respect for God or anything like that. In fact when the vicar Rev. Whally took us for talks before we were to leave Borstal I can remember ridiculing him in front of all the inmates. I thought it was a huge joke.

Paternity Suite

Whilst serving my time in Borstal I was served with a summoned to appear in court to answer a paternity suit. A former girl friend was pregnant and I presume the Social Services had made her declare whom the father of the child was in order to get the finances but I am not sure as I never spoke to her about it. In fact I do not remember knowing any thing about it until I had to appear in court. The first time in court I admitted I was the father because I could have been even though I knew she had been with other men. At the time. I was ordered to pay maintenance out of my three shillings and six pence a week, at the rate if one shilling and three pence per week. I had no idea of the serious nature of being a father or bringing up children or any idea of taking responsibility for my actions.

Dover Borstal

Dover Borstal (The Citadel)

My mother how ever was very anxious and after listening to the evidence given by the girl, she maintained it was not possible for me to be the father, as the timing of the events did not fit. She encouraged me to appeal and she really fought the case for me. This I did and with the aid of a Solicitor the girl had to prove I was the father of the child. When I look back it must have been humiliating for the girl because she had to explain when and where these events took place. My defence solicitor asked where the event or events took place. With incredulity he questioned her how could things take place in a bubble car, in the daylight. This I think on reflection was humiliating for her.

The suit was not proven and I was release from the charge. My probation officer Mr Moorland Hughes asked me many years latter, when I became a Christian and had to appear in court over my confessions to many crimes, "Was I the father of the child", I replied I might have been.

The child was called David and my mother say's he had ginger hair. She had seen him out with his mother in Aylesbury whilst I was still in Borstal. He must be around 33 years old now.

I met all kinds of lads here in Borstal, car thieves, burglars, forgers, and gamblers. None of us had any idea for the reason of our existence but were probably looking for the best in life never finding it.

When I was released I was determined to have a good time. I wanted the best clothes, a good car, a speedboat, and a caravan. You name it I wanted all these things and intended to obtain them by one means or another. I had learned many criminal ways and had no intention going straight. I just had no intention of getting caught at any crime I may choose to be involved in.

11 MY RELEASE FROM BORSTAL

I was released from Borstal a year later and it was during this time I began to get into all kinds of things and criminal activities in Aylesbury.

My Gold Mini

My First Car 850 CC Mini

I bought my first real car for £100 when I came out of Borstal. It was a gold mini 850 cc.

I decided to visit my brother who was now in Maidstone Prison and I visited him when I could. Whilst he was there he met an inmate senior man from Cyprus who told him some fantastic story, which we both believed. We had ideas of being involved in gold smuggling.

It led to my brother absconding from prison and being on the run from the law for a year. He was offering us the opportunity to make money by smuggling gold. The idea was we had to pretend to be just married, we would have a suitable partner and we would carry the gold strapped under our clothes making out we were newly weds. This would reduce the chances of being stopped by customs and so get the gold through. We were prepared to take the risk. It sounded exciting and that was what I wanted.

The plan was that when my brother came out on home leave we he would go to Greece. We had to a contact in London all set up by the Greek man and take it from there. We were all hyped up but the was no such person or arrangements and we felt really let down.

However my brother decided he could not face going back to prison so he just did not return. He changed his name to Kenny? And managed to stay away from the police for a whole year before being picked up whilst working on a building site in Aylesbury.

At this time I was doing a Government training course in Enfield Middlesex and Michael got some work with a shop filling company and worked in London. He decided he would live above the shop, which was near Kings Cross, where they were working and so I was able visit him during the week.

For a bit of fun one morning we decided to go to the cafe down the road dressing in our pyjamas and dressing gowns bringing with us our own cornflakes. We went into the shop and asked for breakfast bowls and milk and sugar. This seemed a funny thing to do and it all went down well.

Michael soon got fed up being there on his own so he decided he was leaving.

So one night we took all the companies tools and equipment and returned to Aylesbury where our parents lived.

During this time I renewed friendship with Pat Jones and we did many things together. My brother had got a girlfriend now and I was seeking to have a good time.

On one occasion I showed Pat Jones the powerful effect of chloroform and knocked him out so he was unconscious. Moved by my strange sense of humour I cut several chunks of hair from his head and when he came too he had no idea what I had done. I found it great fun when I took him home and saw his mother's face. Of course he had no idea what she was upset about. I just left and got out of the way laughing to my self.

It was after this that Pat Jones got the first skinhead hair cut in Aylesbury. No one would normally cut all their hair off it just was not yet fashionable. He did it and I was proud of him. I am sure he set the trend of the Skinhead fashion.

Mods, Skinheads, Greasers at Yarmouth

On one bank holiday weekend in 1969, when I was working for Radio Rentals in Hemel Hempstead, Pat Jones and I decided to go to Yarmouth and meet with the Aylesbury Mods, later called skinheads.

I took my firms Ford van in which we would sleep the night. On this particular weekend I was sleeping in the back of the Ford van that Sunday afternoon and Pat Jones was out with some of the lads. They had a run in with a crowd of Greasers.

Greasers were motor bikers who would fight with knives and motorbike chains. It was a very similar to the Mods and rockers you see in The Who film Quadraphenia. They were the sworn enemies of skinheads.

Mods On a Bank Holiday Weekend

Mods at Margate and News Reports

This company of Greasers had come across Pat Jones and his crowd when out on the sea front in Yarmouth and they were combing the area for skinheads, to pick a fight with. There were too many of them and Pat Jones and the crowd was on the run and I was happily asleep in the back of the van quite safe. Or I would have been had not Pat Jones came running up to the van shouting and screaming to get out and run or do some thing. He ran off just having just called attention to these Greasers. As I looked up and came too and looked out of the van window I could see a crowd of Greasers grinning and running towards the van. They knew they now had a victim in a van. I was concerned it was the firms van so had to get away. There wasn't much I could do so I locked the doors quickly and jumped into the driver's seat hoping to drive. Unfortunately I was awkwardly parked. As I tried to start the engine a great whack came from the roof of the van. The van was hit a number of times with motorbike chains and I heard shouts of glee. Then they began to rock the van seeking to turn it over. They lifted it and rocked it as I tried to drive forward then backwards. I must have hit one or two as I managed to gut get away in time for a beating. That was all thanks to Pat Jones!

This how ever was all part of our fun getting into scrapes of one kind or another. On the way home that week end we decided to tow a four wheeled sea side bike back to Aylesbury so I got Pat Jones to ride the bike whilst we towed this bike all the way from Yarmouth to the outskirts of Norwich before deciding to lead it outside a pub as I began to realize we would be captured by the police going through London. It was all good fun and it made us laugh.

Newquay Here We Come

It was the summer of 1968, shortly after my brother had been released from prison and I had served time in Borstal. We had decided to go on a holiday, seeking the sun.

Our Holiday to Newquay

Newquay The Place Of The Sun

He had become friendly with a girl called Karen Mead but that did not stop our plans. We were going to go off with no plans to return. Michael had a nice long wheeled base Bedford van. This was fitted out with our equipment to live and we fitted a double mattress on the roof with a tarpaulin like tent. This was to be our sleeping arrangements.

It was decided we would make our way to Newquay in Cornwall as I remembered going there with my parents when I was 16 years old. That year the sun was hot, the surfing was good and a really nice summer. We were off to seek the sun.

Our Bedford Van

This Is Where We Slept For 6 Weeks

Our first mischief that we planned but fail to do was the stealing of a speedboat, moored in the water at Barnstable. That evening we had planned to swim out to the boat and cut its moorings and float it down river to load on a trailer. That after noon we borrowed tools from a workshop and got some welding done to make a tow bar for the van. We needed a tow hitch to drive away with the stolen speedboat and trailer that night.

All went to plan until that night when we got the trailer ready but when we looked at the cold dark water, it being pitch black, we both lost our bottle and decided to call it off. We left Barnstable disappointed

The Beatles Magical Mystery Tour

I had been to Newquay before and I told Michael all about it. It was the place to go for surfing and to seek the sun. The Beatles had been there before us and stayed at the Atlantic Hotel and were filming their notable film Magical Mystery Tour. The Beatles stayed at the Atlantic Hotel in Newquay. They booked into The Atlantic Hotel in Newquay on Tuesday 12 September 1967 and left on Friday 15th. Newquay was a famous place to go on holiday and we knew why.

Our Holiday A Place of the Sun

Our first mischief that we planned but fail to do was the stealing of a speedboat, moored in the water at Barnstable. That evening we had planned to swim out to the boat and cut its moorings and float it down river to load on a trailer. That after noon we borrowed tools from a workshop and got some welding done to make a tow bar for the van. We needed a tow hitch to drive away with the stolen speedboat and trailer that night.

The Atlantic Hotel Newquay

The Atlantic Hotel Where The Beatles Stayed

All went to plan until that night when we got the trailer ready but when we looked at the cold dark water, it being pitch black, we both lost our bottle and decided to call it off. We left Barnstable disappointed..

I Am A Waiter At The Gull Rock Hotel

Our first bit of work, which we did, was to work in "The Gull Rock Hotel" in Newquay. I was a waiter and my brother was a kitchen porter. I had never been a waiter before but soon picked it up.

We were given sleeping quarters but we soon realized this kind of work and life was not what we wanted. The hours were unsociable hours. So the next morning we decided not to go to work, just stay in bed. We made a huge joke of it and expected to get the sack.

Sure enough we were knocked up when it was realized we were late but still we did not surface. When we decided to get up we went to the chef believing we had got the sack and so to collect or pay. To my surprise they hadn't sacked us but had just thought we had too much to drink the night before and were prepared to over look the sleep in. I said no we would leave and we each got the £1 each we had earned for the day's work.

In or mischief we went back to the sleeping quarters the next day where the girls were sleeping and jumped into bed with two of the girls. They didn't want this really and made a bit of a protest but before we left the manager's wife had been informed and came to see what was happening. As she came into the bedroom we were seen in bed with Angela the chambermaid. The manageress screamed, "Oh! Angela how could you". The girl got the sack and I felt really bad about that afterwards.

Shortly after this we decided to rob a petrol station to get some money. My brother tried to disguise him self by wearing a long girls wig but this made him stand out even more because he was flat chested and had no hips like a woman and this attracted attention rather than do the opposite. That idea was discarded so I decided I would take the money. When the attendant was looking after a motorist I crept up to the till and took the notes and ran away behind some building. Then quickly dressed in an old overall coat and then walked slowly away without being noticed.

We Return Home To Aylesbury

In the end I noticed my brother writing to his girl friend and somehow we decided to return home to Aylesbury.

After this I began to spend time with Pat Jones as my brother got more involved with his girl friend. Pat Jones and I got into all kinds of things, which I will mention later on. I was 20 years old and he was just 16 years so he began to learn many things off me, all which was probably bad for him.

It was after this I managed to get a job with Radio Rentals in Hemel Hempstead

This was a good job and at 20 years old I was the only Colour TV Engineer in the Hemel Hempstead branch and with a company car.

Our Trip To Shoreham

About this time we went on a sailing trip to Shoreham near Brighton. This weekend we were invited to go sailing with Ken and Grace Knight. I took Mary Bilton a girl friend of mine, Bernie Gilbert and Alison Knight. Whilst we were there Mrs. (Grace) Knight went off to stay with a Christian friend in Brighton. Not that I knew that at the time I just thought she did not like sailing and it was a Sunday and she wanted to go to church.

The History Of The Jews And 1967

We were all invited back to this Christian man's home. He was called Tom and was a manager of an insurance company in Brighton. That afternoon he sat and talked to us all about the bible. I was almost convinced by his talk and began to believe there was more to the bible message than I had ever really liked to admit before. He told us about the history of the Jews and all future events. It was all foretold in the scripture. The history of Israel was recorded and the return of the Jews to the land of Israel in 1967 was clearly a sign of the last days.

I was very impressed at what he said. So much so that I began to tell my friends at college the very next week all about it. This made me read parts in Deuteronomy about the curses that would come upon the Jews if they forsook Moses Law and reject the Lord Jesus Christ.

Pat Jones And The Bully

At this time Pat Jones was in his final year at school and he informed me of a bully who would relentlessly give him grief at school. The school was the Grange Secondary Modern School in Aylesbury. The school I had attended until June 1966.

One day at the evening youth club held at the school I decided we would sort this bully out so I instructed Pat ' Bones" to do as I said. I was dressed in my long Crombie over coat, which my mum had altered for me, and inside I kept a large long rubber torch, which was ideal for use as a cosh. Not too hard to break the skull and not too soft to do no harm. Just about right to knock some one on the head and possibly knock them out.

This was the plan. We were to go to the youth club and search out this bully. The Grange youth club was held behind the school buildings in some prefabricated buildings. It was early evening and not too dark and a few people were around. Here we looked out for the bully.

I gave Pat Jones the large heavy rubber torch and said to him when he sees the bully he must call out to him, " Come here" and walk towards him. When he came right up close he was to shout at him the words, " I have had enough of your nonsense and if you don't watch out I am going to set Dave Clarke on to you". He was then to point in the direction away from him so at to make him turn around and say' " look he is over there". When he turned around he was to hit him on the head, as hard as he could with the torch. Then say, " Now I am going to do it again and roar at him.

The plan went perfectly. We saw the bully dressed in a Denhim Jean jacket he had slight ginger hair. I am sure his nickname was Ginger) .I had never met him before. Pat Jones shouted out to him and sure enough the bully came walking like a gorilla with his arms swinging by his side. Almost running to get at Pat Jones eager to get him. I was happy because this was where he was going to get the treatment. Pat did exactly as instructed. He said look over there and as he turned around Pat walloped this bully hard on the head. Every eye was on the two in conflict. The bully was stunned and his hands went up to his head to hold it as it hurt. Then Pat shouted at him to say he was going to give it to him again and sure enough the bully ran away as predicted. I encouraged Pat to chase after him to make sure he now knew his place. Every one looking on looked in amazement.

From that day forward Pat Jones had no more trouble from that bully. I felt quite satisfied in dealing this way with the bully.

How would Jesus have us deal with bullies today? This is a real problem to parents in a world of violence like to day. I was not a Christian but this remedy actually worked in Pat Jones's case.

12 CONVERSION FROM CRIME TO CHRIST

Having worked through and experience many things I often thought about life and its meaning. I could recall the absolute emptiness of my soul after going out for the evening and coming home. All was empty and what was the point to it all. I was seeking an answer to life, the universe and every thing.

A Bad LSD Trip

The following is an account, taken from memory and notes made of my experience of conversion to Jesus Christ on Friday, 16th January 1970.

Towards the end of 1969 I was continuing my studies at Luton College learning Radio and Television Servicing. We would often engage in discussions and it was quite easy to divert our lecturer onto subjects like spiritualism and the like. We would discuss what we would do if another world war came. We would talk about the future as portrayed by Nostradamus, drugs and our experiences. At that time I was informed of a new film called Easy Rider and wanted to see it. On one occasion I obtained some hashish mixed with opium and smoked this during our break time. This was so effectual I made use of the sick room at college to sleep and enjoy the illusionary effects of the drug, which amused my student friends.

On another occasion in January 1970 I had obtained 4 tablets of LSD from Peter Coppenhall, a student friend from Bedford, he was one of my fellow students at Luton College, and I decided to take them the following Friday night 16th January 1970

On this Friday night the 16th of January my brother I decided to each took half a tablet and Pat Jones had a quarter. He had been a close friend of mine (he was only just 16 years old) for some time and I use to think of him as my apprentice. I taught him all my bad ways. There was little we did not do together. I had known him whilst he was at school and encouraged him in crime, sniffing chloroform, smoking (marijuana, hashish, weed etc..) drunkenness, violence and permissive sex. He was known amongst our friends as "Bones", Patrick Bones.

My brother was going out that night with his girl friend Karen Mead so Pat Jones and I decided to walk up town and not risk driving for we did not know the effect this drug would have on us. I was dressed in my old clothes deliberately for I did not know what might happen too us. We tried to thumb a lift but eventually caught a bus and got off at the bottom of the High Street. As we walked past the "pictures" I noticed the film "Easy Rider" was being shown so we decided to go and see it.

We wanted to take some one else with us, some one who was in their right state of mind, so we went up the billiard hall and found Bernie Gilbert and Mike Ellis but they said they would only come and watch the film with us if they too had some acid.

I decided this was OK, and so we got a taxi back to my house to get the rest of the Acid. Bernie had half a tablet and Mike Ellis the other quarter. So all four of us were about to trip on acid whilst watching the film Easy Rider. We arrived back at the "pictures" about 8.45 PM and I fumbled a bit with my ticket as the acid had begun to take effect. Bernie and Mike suggested we go and sit up in the balcony but I thought to my self, what if we decide to jump off? I was tripping now and just followed them up the stairs. We sat two in front and two behind, but Mike and Bernie's trip had not yet begun as they acted and spoke normally.

The Film Easy Rider

Peter Fonda and Dennis Hopper

They seemed to know how to give the correct lighting and sound effects. How ever Bernie and Mike seemed to be jumping about all over the place and it was irritating. I still was sitting in my seat when all the people had gone, before I decided there was nothing more to do. So we decided to up and go but Mike and Bernie were annoying me because they were mucking about.

All my thoughts and feelings began to reverberate four times over and thought patterns were being reflected and at the same time building and snowballing.

We walked outside the cinema and I said to the boys, "Man you are all on the wrong scene you can't be turned on". Then I heard Mike and Bernie say he's turned into a wizard (Hippie) and there was a club room for wizards like me (The Dark Lantern Pub in Aylesbury). I then began a downward trip, which ended in the horrors. I began to feel paranoid thinking they were now sorry for me and were being polite in hiding their feelings from me.

As we went further up the road Mike Ellis asked if I wanted a scrap with some blokes across the street. It was as if he was testing me out to see if I was the same person he knew. I said no I didn't. I thought they had thought I had gone mad and they wanted to test me out. We went further up the high street and Bernie began to mess about and pull faces at me and make noises. I hid in a shop door way and told him to stop it and Pat Jones pulled Bernie away saying don't do it as he didn't understand. My horror began when I could not face the thought that they thought I had cracked up and gone mad. This feeling was too much for me to bare. More was to come.

We decided to go to the Crown pub and Brian Sale came up to me and spoke but I was out of my mind by now with this feeling of paranoia and could not speak sensibly and came out with a load of nonsense, so I had to say quickly I was drunk because I didn't think he would understand other wise.

I then saw my Michael sitting with his girl friend and I went up to him and told him what was happening. He laughed and motioned to wined me up like a clockwork toy and then my mind began to distort so much so I had to run out of the pub to get away. Pat Jones followed me and I kept thinking the others were following us. I kept looking back as I didn't want them following me as they annoyed me. We left the Green Man and walked towards Mount Street, via Richford's Hill and along Friarage Road. On the way down it seemed like a scene from a picture book and was like Alice in Wonderland with all the street lamps lit up.

The torment of my mind had grown so much that I could not bare the pain but I could not get rid of the torment. Ken and Grace Knight lived at Mount Street. We went down there with no real aim and as I arrived just outside their house Jock Macallion, another friend of mine, was about to leave and drive off. I jumped in besides him and told him my situation. After telling him I was tripped out of my mind I was thinking he would take me home and as I was about to ask him he said, "Dave you are a worried man". I knew this and I now though so did every one else and being told that did not help me at all. My mind was about to blow so I had to run again. I jumped out of the car and into 24 Mount Street where Ken and Grace were. I wanted to escape and so I told them my plight but I could not explain to them what was happening to me. Grace Knight recalled she thought I was in serious trouble and began to question me. This didn't help so I had to say forcefully I must have peace so they took me out to the summerhouse to lie down in peace.

No one seemed to understand the torment of mind I was in and no one could help me at all. I told Mrs Knight to leave me alone to work it out on my own and let me lie down. Then the torment got worse. I knew it was only the LSD doing it but I could do nothing about it I would have to wait till it had taken its course. I thought it could be 12 hours or so but to me each moment seemed like an eternity of torment and I could not endure this any more.

I lay down and tried to settle my mind by thinking good thoughts and different things but my mind would not be controlled. The thought came, " I may be driven to kill myself to get rid of the pain", but I was horrified at the thought and the more I tried to stop thinking like it the more I thought about it. I looked around to see if there was a mirror or glass in the room and wanted to get rid of it just in case I cut my throat or wrists. I just did not know what to do I was at the end of my self.

In this condition it was evident I could not help myself. My friends could not help; my brother had not helped. Mr and Mrs Knight couldn't help and I could not help myself.

In this desperation it came to me to call out to God for help. So I cried out calling on the Lords name saying, "Jesus please help me". At that moment my mind went blank and his name appeared in the imagination of my mind but the torments soon came back again. I called out again and his name appeared twice and the happening repeated. I called four times in all and his name appeared four times and formed a square in complete emptiness.

I then began to feel emotional and wept but I didn't know why and at that moment Mrs knight came to the chalet door to see if she could help. It was then, at that, a flood of guilt overcame me. I was convicted of the sin of Adultery and did not know what to do. I beckoned Mrs Knight to come in and said to her did she realize how bad I was and what I had done. I asked her to tell me the way what could I do.

Mrs Knight had spoken to me about Christian things and some how I knew she knew the way. Mrs Knight sat down and quoted the scripture saying, " For God so loved the world that he gave his only begotten son that who so ever believed on him should not perish but have everlasting life." (John 3 verse 16).

Dave I Am With You

After this Jesus spoke to me, I heard his voice as clearly I am writing this he said, "Dave I am with you. You have been searching for a long time, this is what our Father says. What you have been going through is nothing compared to what hell is like. I replied with thanks giving saying thank you, Jesus thank you.

Mrs knight I think thought that I was speaking to her she but she did not know what was going on.

It seemed that the words that Mrs Knight had spoken, were in fact the way out and pathway to my escape. It appeared as though I was at the bottom of a pyramid and the words were the way to the top and if I were to follow the words I would escape. I replied thank you Jesus thank you.

I then thought of hell and my thoughts were about the Pat Jones, Bernie Gilbert and Mike Ellis and I said what about the others. Jesus spoke again and said, " all I could do was tell them".

I replied feeling it an impossible thing to do to convince them "but what more could I do" I was feeling the agony of the LSD horrors and knew I wanted to warn my friends of the hell to come. I reasoned within my self they will think I have gone mad on LSD how could I convince them, I wanted to do more than tell them. I asked what more could I do.

All I could Do Was Tell Them

In order to answer my question the Lord took me back in time to show me all I could do was tell them. A number of weeks earlier I had reason to read about the curses that were to come on the children of Israel if they forsook their God. Deut. 28 v 53. And though shall eat the fruit of thine own body. (I knew nothing about the back ground to these things) I thought it was saying people would be so hungry and having no food to eat a woman would be driven to eat her own after birth. Which of course was shocking. With this in mind these weeks earlier I was trying to shock this girl at work. I was working for Radio Rentals as a Colour TV engineer and I said to this receptionist how would she like to be so hungry to have to eat her own after birth? She responded with expected repulsion " How could you say such a thing". I simply said I hadn't said it but God has. This thing repulsed her and she did not want to know anything about what I was saying (Not suppressing). However to this incident Jesus took me and asked me, " what did the girl do when I spoke to her"? My answer was she shut her ears, as she did not want to know. It was repulsive to her. His reply was to me that, " if I tell people about Hell and what I had learned and they screw their faces up and do not want to know I could do no more." The condition of the person listening is not my responsibility but theirs. All I could do was tell them. So tell them I would.

To these questions Mrs. Knight thought I was asking her, because I was speaking aloud, but before she could answer I had been answered directly from the Lord.

When Jesus stopped speaking I felt as though I was falling back into my torment and I prayed again, "Please don't leave me". My reply was, " I will never leave you".

Why Boast

Jesus then questioned me and asked me, "Why boast". This is because I was naturally prone to boasting amongst my friends just to make a good impression. I reason within myself now and now knew I had no need to boast of anything. So from that day I have always avoided boasting.

My torment ceased from that time and the rest of the night passed with various thoughts going through my mind. I do not think Mrs Knight was fully aware of what had taken place.

The next day was Saturday and I was due in to work but I decided to take the day off. I phone in briefly saying I was not up to work.

13 WHAT AFTER SALVATION

Pat Jones had spent the night in the caravan parked at the side of the Knight's home, together with Paddy who had no where else to live. We spent that day together and I told them both of my experience. I assumed and expected them to fully understand and see what had happened.

Instinctively things were different with me. An internal change had come about and by it I had new desires. I no longer wished to live as I had lived and wished to be rid of my bad ways. No one told me I had to give up any particular way of life, I found within me an internal desire to choose the good and refuse the evil.

Evidence of the New Birth

Upon reflection I say this was the evidence of the new birth and I later found this experience spoken of by the Lord Jesus Christ in Johns gospel. John 3. Jesus answered and said unto him, Verily, verily I say unto thee, except a man be born again, he cannot see the kingdom of God. The Apostle Paul also writes the same in Cor. 5 17. Therefore if any man were in Christ Jesus, he is a new creature: old things are past away; behold all things are become new.

I knew also there was a part of me which was just the same and when I would do good evil was also present with me. The Apostle Paul in Romans also expressed this. Rom. 7 verse 21. I find then a law that when I would do good evil is present with me.

Whilst this was my experience I found it impossible to convey this to my friends even thou I tried ever so hard.

What To Do With Stolen Goods

I had in my possession much stolen property. In fact hundreds of pounds worth of stolen goods. I was no longer prepared to live off the benefits of stolen goods. What should I do? I had involved others in my crime of stealing and these could not help me now. In fact Mike West came to see me the next day and when he heard me explaining Jesus had spoken to me he began to fear I might go to the police and confess my crimes. I did not actually say to him I wanted him to return the Colour TV set, which I had stolen and swapped for his Citroen car but he was concerned, as he did not know what to think.

Poor Mike he must have panicked thinking I was about to go to the police, as he was concerned some of the stolen goods that I had left in his garage were a stolen including the mini engine sub chassis. I don't remember what happen to these parts but I asked Mike to dispose of them. I was later informed they had been dumped in the reservoir.

That Saturday evening both Pat and I decided to go to the Social Club at Park Street.

This was the usual thing for us to do on a Saturday night. I had determined to go and see my mates to explain what had happened to me. We walked down there but did not go in. After seeing one or two people I broke my news to them. I cannot remember what I said. I had no desire to stay so went back to the Knight's home. My inclination to live it up as normal was no longer with me. I now seemed at a loose end not knowing what next to do. From that time forward Pat Jones began to realize things had really changed for me.

The next day, being Sunday, Mrs Knight took both Pat Jones and I to the local Baptist Church in Southcourt, in the evening. I distinctly remember the passage of scripture the preacher spoke from. It was in Exodus where the whole nation of Israel was about to enter the Promised Land. However they listened to the evil reports of the 10 spies and did not take heed to the voice of the two good spies. Who gave encouragement to go in and possess the land? I remember also I saw, whether he preached this or not, that this was a picture of the body of Christ - the church of that day.

Seek To Tell Others

After the meeting Mrs Knight introduced me to a Martin White who gave me a copy of the New Testament called the Good News for modern man. I began to read this straight away. This I received gratefully and began to read it every day

The following days were spent in the after glow and certainty of this new life that had opened up to me. I thirsted for knowledge, the knowledge of God in Jesus Christ. I told the folk at work about my experience and could not remain silent about the things I was learning.

Southcourt Baptists

South Court Baptist Church

My evenings were spent at Mrs Knight's home discussing the scripture with some of her Christian friends. Both Pat Jones and Paddy all seemed interested to hear.

My own ignorance never read the Bible

I am now amazed at my own ignorance then for until then I had never read the bible for myself. I did not know what the Acts of the Apostles meant. Within two weeks I had read the New Testament and thought I understood it all. I soon learned from the scripture that in the economy of Salvation it was the blood of Jesus Christ shed on the cross at Calvary that was the means of me obtaining a free pardon for all my sins. And also that I was given freely a righteousness to justify me before God.

In this respect the Lord Jesus was a true substitute and he died for me without cost at all to me. These were the things, which I learned and as it were drank in like water from the well of salvation. I learned them by reading the scripture and did not know them from the night Jesus spoke to me.

Difference at College

I attended college that week but there was a difference. I had decided I would not dress in my usual clothes to show off. Which would have been Levi jeans, white boots with red toe caps (or whatever colour I chose to spray them), a Ben Sherman shirt and loose leather jerkin. I felt I must not only be more sober but dress more soberly too i.e. not show off as I use to do.

So I dressed in my best trousers, which were from my Prince of Wales cheque suit, shirt and normal pull over and normal shoes. O course I had to tell all my friends about my experience. I protested to them look I even dress differently. They could not believe me. I told one of the lecturers, Mr. Jones, in front of them all but I was just given a smile of wonder.

I Tell Rupert

That same week I felt constrained to go and tell my friend Rupert, a West Indian from Jamaica. He lived in a room, at 14 Bicester Road Aylesbury so Pat Jones and I went to see him. As soon as I met him I told him what had happened in front of his new girl friend but Rupert's reply was, " I told you Dave not to take LSD ". Again they were none plus, they could not believe even though I tried my best to convince them.

Turning From The world

Being in the world but not of it. It was now wrong for me to continue in the way of life that I had lived in the past. My back was now turned from the world that I once laid hold on, and had built for myself. I was self-seeking (ones own glory), asserting self without considering others, stealing, and thoughts of adultery, fornication, drug taking, drug selling, boasting, drunkenness, violence and worldly ambition. I say worldly ambition because I believe we all have worldly ambitions but when we are converted and come to Christ we are called to forsake it; that is forsake the world and its ambitions.

We all have our own worlds to forsake when we become a Christian. Some have a religious world to turn from; as a person may have been born in a religious family or have a circle of religious friends but in their world they have their own natural fallen nature to contend with. Fallen human nature seeks to gratify its desires and as such sin the whole day long. A religious person still has all the workings of a natural man as those who have no religion. Any thought or act, which is born out of selfishness, greed, pride, avarice, thinking evil of others, back biting, slander and prejudice may all be practiced by those in a religious or none religious world. So to forsake the world means to forsake all those thoughts and actions, which are natural to us, and are contrary to the way of Christ.

Religious And None Religious Persons

Need to turn from their world

Some persons have no religion or religious friends, yet they too have natural desires and a fallen human nature, which they seek to please. Ambitions of fame for its own sake, the love of money, selfishness, the practice of gossip, evil speaking of others, are all to be turned from. It doesn't matter whether you be in a religious or none religious person we are to world are to be forsaken the world from which we come from when we seek to follow Christ. We are called to be in the world but not of it. This is really what John Bunyan sought to express when he told his story of the man who turn his back on the city of destruction. One of the problems how ever was that his story only described the picture of those who were none religious and the pattern of their life styles. In reality a religious person, one who is not born again, has a pattern and life style, which is equally wrong and such need to be turned from. It is very easy for such a person to think because they do not do certain things that they see people in a none-religious world do, to look down and judge them thinking they are better than them. Not so, we all have a world to turn from. When a person is born again they have an ordinary life natural to them and are part of the natural world but we all must turn from our world in order to follow Christ

Kept By The Power And Grace Of God

I now had an inward and real desire not to continue in those ways, which I have just mentioned, for they just perpetuated my former sinful self, of which I had, had enough. A change of heart had taken place. This was the fight. That is not to say I could not be tempted to find pleasure in such sins there was a part of me still the same but I had a desire to put to death sinful thoughts and actions. Should I allow wrong affections to move me I was self-condemned with an accompanying self-abhorrence and I knew was not pleasing to God. By the grace of God I was able to resist and fight against sin.

14 WHAT TO DO WITH STOLEN GOODS

I was now moved by a new set of principles but here in lay a problem. I had erected a 48-foot by 12-foot wooden builder's shed on waste ground belonging to the Water Board next door to the Knight's home at 24 Mount Street. This became my garage and workshop. I had stolen the builders shed from a building sight in Berkhampstead. I had persuaded Mr. Knight to drive his lorry whilst me, Pat Jones and Paddy lifted the shed panels from the building sight late one night.

In this shed was my newly acquired Citroen DS car, which had formally belonged to Mike West of Wendover. I had swapped it for a colour TV that we had stolen from old peoples home called Redlands, in Winslow. I had some lovely garage equipment which included a trailer, ark welder, trolley jack, air compressor, spray gun, tools, speed boat engines even a stolen car and various other items all of which by one means or another I had stolen or burgled.

My Citroen DS Car

What could or should I do now. I was responsible for at this stuff. Conscience would not permit me to continue to make us of all this stolen gear. What should I do? Should I just dispose of it all and brush the past behind me? How should I dispose of it if I decide to do so? I could not sell the goods for what would I do with the money. Conscience would not allow me to use it. I had in fact so much stolen property go through my hands, which had been disposed of by one means or another, none of it could be recovered anyway.

My Citroen DS what I acquired

Citroen Ds Except Mine Was Banana Yellow

I had only just stolen a nice new Mini car, which was about to be used to make me a lovely new car.

Stolen Mini from Hemel Hempstead

The body had been cut up and disposed of in my parents' garage in Finmere Crescent Aylesbury. (Whilst cutting up the body with the arc welder the hydrolastic suspension fluid caught light a nearly burnt the car and garage to pieces).

I had also another stolen Morris Minor Traveller, which I had swapped the number plates and disposed of the old body. This was and used it as a hire car. I think on reflection with hindsight and the faith I now have in God I would have been able to act differently than I did.

The Stolen Mini

My Stolen Mini

I was able during this time to return one or items of stolen goods. Late one wet night in February 1972 Pat Jones and I loaded the trolley jack into my firms van. I am not quite sure what Pat Jones thought about all this but I drove up to the garage from where I had originally stolen the trolley jack and parked on the forecourt.

Returning The Trolley Jack

The garage had been closed for the night (next to the Broad Leys pub on the Wendover Road, Aylesbury) and whilst no one was about I opened the van door and swiftly and quietly lifted the jack and placed it down on the forecourt. We then drove off as fast as we could. I often wondered what did the owner think when it was returned several months later.

I had no real advisers or any one who really knew the depths of my crimes and the amount of acquired stolen goods I had. I was faced with this problem what ever happens to me was no real concern but I did not feel I could involve others and get them into trouble. Mike West was very fearful in case I confessed all to the police and he must have been puzzled by what was going on. I had hoped he would have offered me the colour TV back and I would have given him the Citroen back but he wished to keep the Colour TV so I gave him the Citroen any way, as I felt I could not use it.

The Broad Leys

The Broad Lees Wendover Road

Dealing With Sin and Temptation

I did not need anyone to tell me what was right and wrong. I knew the difference and in particular the sin of fornication. This is sexual activity out side of marriage. Sexual temptation was really fierce and strong to me, but by the grace of our Lord Jesus Christ I fought the fight against them. So much so that I had to avoid meeting girls because of a natural inclination, which had I given into would not have been good for them or me. The words of Jesus are clear that the very thought of sex with another man's wife was to commit the sin of adultery and I agreed. This area of my life was really difficult to me and would be to any new believer.

Hippies In The Shed

Pat Jones began to acquire new friends and some were what we called hippies. They smoked pot, took drugs and generally did nothing but think about life etc.. We invited them down to Mount Street as I felt it would be right to speak to them about Jesus Christ. About five or six came and they ended up sleeping in the shed.

The Shed at Mount Street

Whilst trying to speak the gospel to them I saw no real effect so I was disappointed. Perhaps one day I will see some fruit. I felt it OK to use the shed to house the hippies. About six lived in the shed for a number of weeks until they moved on. I thought I was putting it to good use.

My problems were solved by an intervention of God and his hand was clearly seen by all one year later.

The Hippy Shed

The Stolen Builders Shed on Water Board Ground

This solution came by the knock on the door. It was the C.I.D when I was arrested for stealing the colour TV set from "Redfields" old peoples home in Winslow. See part 1.

15 GOING TO CHURCH

During the first few weeks of conversion unto Christ, in February 1970 there were a series of meetings held at Limes Avenue Baptist Church. The person speaking was Mr. Lance Pibworth and a girl called Geraldine Dunbar was being baptised.

Limes Avenue Baptist Church

Limes Avenue Baptist Church Aylesbury

I saw my first baptism here. After the meeting a man informed the congregation that if any one wanted to talk about any thing or ask questions they could stay behind. On this occasion I had brought Pat Jones and Paddy along to the meeting. I was dressed in my overalls and leather jacket, which I always wore when working on cars- I wasn't dressed up at all. I knew God did not look on the outward appearance but man may do so it did not bother me that we were not dressed for the occasion. I asked to see the minister Mr Sibthorpe and we three were invited into his study. I explained to Mr Sibthorpe about my conversion and wanted him to confirm that what I was saying to Pat Jones and Paddy was in fact true. On that occasion I half expected him to baptise me, there and then. I was under the impression, from reading the scripture, a minister of Christian were under direct command to baptise new believers as soon as they believed. I was very disappointed that he did not command me to be baptised that night. I knew nothing of church membership, modes of baptism, doctrinal distinctions and the like only that I should be baptised.

Shortly after this I met a man called Charley Tweedy, of the Church of Christ meeting (it is now a Seventh Day Adventist Church) at Stoke Mandeville Road, Aylesbury. He maintained that unless you are baptised you couldn't be saved.

He held some kind of responsible position in this Church so I explained to him about my conversion after which he gave me his telephone number to ring him if I needed too. I knew he was wrong about baptism but felt constrained to speak to him as I reasoned according to him, " I shall be damned if I die today if I am not baptised". I felt the need to reassure him that was not the case and he need not worry. When I rang him he seemed non plus nor moved with concern that I was not yet baptised. Again I was disappointed.

I Attend Various Churches

I had not been accustomed to go to any particular church but did go to a Sunday night meeting with Mrs. Knight. This was the Assemblies of God; Pentecostal church meeting at Rickford's Hill and Pastor Baker was the minister. Here I was received without any question and made to feel welcome. This was also the church Cyril Bryan went to and where I met Barry Crown.

Giving A Testimony

On one occasion I was asked to give an up to date testimony as to the Lords dealing with me that week. So dressed as I was, in my working clothes (overalls) not knowing a difference between working days or Sabbath days, I went to the front of the congregation and gave a clear and detailed account as to how I had combated the devils suggestion to steel a car battery that week.

I had some trouble with my car battery and I needed a new one. The temptation was this. Here was I, passing Adam's Garage, on the Tring Road in need of a car battery. Just over the fence belonging to the garage were several car batteries. All I had to do was nip over the fence and help my self. This was the way I had thought in the past and would have done just that all one time. Not now. This kind of thinking was the old man of whom I had to continually combat and I knew Satan had a hand in the matter. To avoid this temptation I rebuked the devil and told him to clear off in Jesus name. On that occasion I told them the exact language I had used to the devil. I said to the devil, "Bugger off Satan". I was quite unaware of the bad language I had used, and a number of years later Barry Crown remembered that Cyril Bryan gently reproved me for my speech. I did not know that I had said any thing amiss so was unaware that I had even been reproved for using bad language. I don't think I knew what the words meant any way.

Church of God near Stoke Mandeville

The Church of God, Mandeville Road Aylesbury

I Am Baptised

I knew from the scripture and believed I should be baptised and I expected Pastor Baker of the Assemblies of God Church to command me to be baptised. I knew this was the command of Jesus and it signified the new birth, which I had already experienced. It also symbolized my union with the Lord Jesus Christ in his death and resurrection. That through his death I was to reckon myself dead to sin and my former sinful ways and that by his resurrection I was to reckon myself risen with him to the newness of life, which is in him. No one spoke to me about being baptised.

Rickford's Hill Assemblies of God

Assemblies of God Church Building

At that time shortly after the Limes Avenue meetings I was taken to another group of Christians meeting at Fleet Street in a large shed. These were West Indians and the Pastor was Mr Bruce from Luton. This group also was having a series of meetings leading up to a baptism. I heard they had permission to use the baptistery at Limes Avenue Baptist Church so I asked Pastor Bruce to baptise me. He said he would and asked me to attend baptism classes that week with other people being baptised.

Fleet Street Pentecostal. Pastor Bruce from Luton was the overseer did not know what this was all about but presumed it was to make sure the person being baptised knew what it was all about. I was not told that after the baptism I was expected to join the church meeting at Fleet Street.

Fleet Street Pentecostal

Fleet Street Pentecostal Meeting Hall

I was baptised (dipped or immersed) upon the confession of my faith in the Lord Jesus Christ early one Sunday morning at 7.00 a.m. at Lime Avenue Baptist Church. My friends turned up, Pat Jones, Paddy, Paul Brooks, Mrs. Knight and Mrs. Chapski. Pastor Bruce baptised me in the name of the Father, Son and Holy Ghost, according to the command of our Lord Jesus Christ. Matth. 28 19.

Where Pastor Bruce, of the Assemblies of God Church, meeting at Fleet Street, Aylesbury, baptised me. I say this because I had met some that were teaching baptism was only valid if it was administered in the name of Jesus only. The reason being that they say the name of the Father is Jesus and the name of the Son is Jesus and the name of the Holy Spirit is Jesus. Gordon Smith, of Albert Street, informed me that some considered it was necessary to be re baptised in the name of Jesus only and that all other baptisms were invalid. I was not impressed by their reasoning and stress upon the singular name of Jesus to the exclusion of the Father and Spirit for Jesus had commanded baptism to be performed in the name of all three persons.

Mormons and Baptism

It was about this time that two Mormons spoke to me, whilst I was on the drive of our home in Finmere Crescent, and they were insisting that my baptism was invalid, as it was not conducted by a person having the right authority. As I had read the scripture and understood what baptism was all about, I realized that these men were wrong. In later years I came across similar views by some Primitive Baptists in the Philippines, but there too were wrong. I had been baptised, according to the terms of the lord Jesus, and that by immersion. My baptism was as valid as if John the Baptist had baptised me himself.

I knew that as far as I could discern from scripture, a man could be dipped, ducked, dragged, drenched, soaked, sprinkled or dribbled with 10 thousand gallons of water it would make not a scrap of difference to his spiritual state. Baptism could not affect the new birth, remove sin or make a natural man a spiritual man for that was the sole prerogative of Him that proceeded from the Father and was sent by the Son. John 15 26. The new birth being the effect not of the will of the flesh, nor of the will of man, but of God alone. John 1 13. Therefore Baptism could not save a sinner.

Baptism In The Spirit

I soon realized there were few churches in Aylesbury that believed the Baptism in the Holy Spirit was a distinct experience to being born again. I had no reason to doubt this and took it as a truth revealed in the Scripture.

I had no problem with this, as that was how I had read the bible. I actually felt I was baptised in the Spirit when I first believed and Jesus spoke to me. The only thing I seemed to lack was speaking in tongues. This had not happened.

I remember speaking to Mr Sibthorpe, the pastor of the Strict Baptist Church at Limes Avenue, about these things and he gave me an article written by John Stott who denied the Baptism in the Spirit, as I knew it. I was amazed at the way these people twisted and wriggled out of what God had plainly spoken about.

At that time I read as much as I could because this experience was not recognized by any other group of Christians apart from the Elim Pentecostal Churches. The best book that I read, at that time, was by Derek Prince called, "From Jordan to Pentecost". This gave a very clear and biblical position about speaking in tongues and it being the evidence of the baptism in the spirit.

This was what happened during the time of the apostles.

The Christian Life

Being converted unto Christ was by no means an outward imposed principle I was not under a set of rules. I was not under any kind of legal fear to serve God. A rule, which says do this and you will be OK. There was no rest in works that I could do. . It was in fact the rule of faith. It was to walk by faith, without which it is impossible to please God.

I was what the scripture describes a, "new man", with an inward desire to follow the Lord Jesus Christ. The scripture expressed these as God writing His laws upon the fleshly tablets of the heart Heb 8. 10- 13. I began to read the bible straight away and I read the Good New bible within two weeks of receiving it, which was good going for me who could barely read. I was able to understand most of what I read and thought I understood it all at first.

The Divine Nature of Jesus Christ

Before this time I was ignorant of its contents and very soon the principal points of the gospel became very clear to me: The divine nature, or deity of Jesus Christ was essential to understand. Hell was real just as heaven was sure. The actual reality of Adam and Eve and the fall of our first parents. The need for the shed blood of Jesus Christ to remove sin. That salvation and the forgiveness of sins was by faith alone, without works done by us. We were not under the Law of Moses as the Jews were but under Christ Jesus' under his rule by His law the gospel of love and grace.

I remember trying to tell one of my friends about following Jesus saying that I didn't have to give up any thing to become a Christian. I simple found that I did not want to do certain things any more. It was not difficult. This lad came up to me sometime after this and I am sure he misunderstood me and in front of several other lads said, isn't it right you don't have to give up any thing to be a Christian. He was expecting my answer to be no you can carry on just as you are. However I said that's right you don't have to give up any thing except sin. This silence him and I think they all got the point

Preaching Not Musical Entertainment

I learned that Gods way of saving people was through the preaching of Christ and him crucified. That the new birth was a must. What amazed me was the apparent lack of zeal and knowledge of them that had professed faith in Christ. Also how these persons tended to try and entertain people by means of music instead of preaching.

Giving My Testimony

On the 22nd May 1972 I was asked to give my testimony to a meeting of people in Luton to about 400 people. I was not sure what the meeting was all about so I simply spoke as I felt right to do. I spoke the gospel as best I could. I was not fully conversant with the doctrines of grace but I was soon to learn the word more perfectly. Providentially this meeting was recorded and may be viewed on:

(Click here) **Converted on LSD Trip 1972 David Clarke**

Every Day The Sabbath Day

Every day was the Lords day to me, as I awoke I was conscious of the presence of God and when I slept, yea even in my dreams. I knew of no distinctions of days such as holy days or the Sabbath day for I knew these to be abolished or fulfilled in Christ. Jesus Christ being the sum and substance of all the Mosaic Sabbath. He was the body that cast the shadow of Moses Law. Col. 2 16-17.

Authorized Version of the Bible

At the Assemblies of God Church, at Richford's hill, we had a representative from the Trinitarian Bible Society speak. Mr Cyril Bryan confirmed his belief how important it was to use a good translation of the Bible. It was pointed out to me that the modern versions often left out or changed the texts of scripture, which clearly taught the deity of Christ. From that time I began to be cautious of new versions and was happy to stick with the Authorized Version. This was helpful because all the books that I had begun to read quoted from the Authorized Version and not modern translations.

Giving Money

On another occasion I was attending the evangelical meetings at Fleet Street Pentecostal church and there was an appeal for money to support the young musicians. The man making the appeal was so moving I felt I ought to give all I could. I reached to my pocket and put in the collection plate all that I had. I was giving as unto the Lord. I was given to believe it was for the Lords work and it was needed. I was happy to give. Shortly after this the same steward who had collected the money came back to me from the front of the meeting hall speaking and motioning to me with the roll of notes in his hand saying was I aware how much I had given. I said yes it was OK. It was probably about £200 as I was still use to carrying that sort of money around with me (1970).

Shortly after this at another meeting there was a visiting evangelist called C D Gilbert preaching and he too made similar moving appeals for money. I had also spoken to him about the tattoo on my arm. This was because I regretted having it. He had been saying if I believed God then it would go by a miracle. I asked him would he pray to have it removed. At the same meeting he appealed for money with a prophecy saying the Lord had told him that each one had to go to their bank tomorrow and draw 10 per cent of all their money and give it to his fund the next day. It followed by another vision of an accident that was going to take place if it was not done. At the same meeting he said there was some one in the meeting that doubted God and they must get of their seat and come forward that if they did not then another warning was issued. I knew because of our previous talk he had me in mind. I also knew his prophecy and visions were not of God but generated to control and manoeuvre people like witchcraft. I opposed this and would have nothing to do with it.

I even went to Mr Eric Connet and informed him that this type of talk and action was not genuine. Mr Connet was a preacher at the church and had some influence and could have helped to correct error.

I write this for the sake of any that may feel similar pressure from them who say that God sends them. Not all that is spoken in the name of Jesus is of God.

The Lord loves the cheerful giver. The Lord does not need our money. He wants our hearts. All that we have is His when this is the case. We are stewards of all that we own. I learned like the Sabbath there is no Sabbath day for every day is Sabbath, so with money there is no tithe of 10 percent but all our possessions are the Lords, not just 10 percent.

Doing The Work Of An Evangelist

I found it my natural desire to preach and speak about Jesus to who ever I could. I remember working on a car in Mount Street one Sunday morning and a crowd of street kids all who I knew were playing around doing nothing. I was dressed in my overalls and leather jacket and I suggested they come with me to church. I decided to take them to a former Brethren Assembly called Granville Street Evangelical. I knew all these lads and realized we were all untidily dressed and that we may not be readily accepted. I knew however the scripture, which taught when you are invited to a meal, then take the lowest seat or place in the room. I decided we should adopt this principle so when we went into the hall, part way through the meeting. We slipped in and I beckoned them all to sit down on the floor. This we did without any noise. These lads were Paul Mitchell, Clifford Atley (Tatty), Michael Clarke and one or two others.

Granville Street Evangelical Church. Aylesbury (former Brethren) where I took the lads from the street to the meeting one Sunday morning. All the eyes of the congregation seemed to be on me. The meeting was stopped and a man came up and sure enough according to the scripture we were invited to sit on chairs towards the front of the meeting room.

Granville Street former Brethren Church

Granville Street Evangelical

Later on in that meeting they had what was called the "breaking of bread". They were an open communion church and their custom was to allow any believer to partake of the bread and wine. As the bread and the cup passed by they could help them selves. This bread and wine spoke of the death of Jesus till he come again. On this occasion however when the plate and cup came to our row it was passed by. We were judged as ineligible. I felt upset at this, as the stewards had judged us by an outward appearance and not as God. The problem then I suppose," I did not dress as a Christian".

I meet Peter Howe minister of the gospel

It was at this time I met Mr Peter Howe, a former pastor at Hearne Bay Evangelical Church, who also befriended my friends Paul and Sue Aston. Paul was a bible student studying at Watford and valued any help he could get. It was soon after this that Mr Peter Howe became the Pastor of the Ivanhoe Particular Baptist Church and Paul and his wife became members.

I was a Hyper-Calvinist

Mr Howe made it clear to me he was against what he called Hyper Calvinism which he stated was the position of the Gospel Standard Baptists. It was not possible to make head way with him, as he seemed insistent he was right. He was what is now called a Fullerite. He mocked the term "Dead Elect" a term that I understood to refer to the elect who were still dead in their trespasses and sins. I had no problem with this term and I had heard Mr Hill from Luton, use this from time to time.

Doctrinal Summery

By this time I had come to a fairly comprehensive knowledge if gospel truth. I had come to believe in the Sovereignty of God. The divinity of the Lord Jesus Christ and his eternal Sonship. The value and authority of the Authorized Version of the bible. The everlasting purposed of the trinity of persons in the Godhead Predestination. Election, Justification by imputed righteousness and the new birth, and a call to glorify God in declaring these things to others. And having knowledge of these things more than others abled me to discern the many errors of many who too professed faith in Christ. I was shocked at the ignorance of so many.

I Hear Dr Martin Lloyd Jones Preach

I was encouraged by my friend to go to various Christian churches and on one occasion the church meeting at Long Crendon who had a visiting preached at their yearly anniversary service, he was Dr Martin Lloyd Jones.

Long Crendon Evangelical Church

Long Crendon Evangelical Church

This is where I heard Dr Martin Lloyd Jones preach This man had a real gift to preach and I could tell he understood doctrine, but he was never outspoken as to his belief in absolute predestination, although you could tell he would know these things and many more. I heard him also on another occasion as he preached also at the Ivanhoe Particular Baptist Church where Peter How had become the minister, and where Mr And Mrs Dix senior were members, along with Paul Aston and wife.

16 GETTING A JOB

This was a problem to me but I believed in God and I believed that I knew that through the grace of our Lord Jesus Christ I would be provided for.

I had been dismissed from Radio Rentals due to my confession of stealing one of their colour Televisions from the old peoples home in Winslow. All I knew was how to fix televisions and I was qualified to City and Guilds 111. I decided to take the first Job offered me through the labour exchange; this was with a firm called Electroloid in Aylesbury. I was being employed as a wireman and on the interview the foreman called Dennis asked why I had left my former job. I was determined to be honest so I explained I had been dismissed for theft. At this he asked no more questions and I was given the job. I was also able to negotiate for one day off a week, without pay so I could finish off my college course.

I soon acquired a good knowledge of the equipment, which I wired up and began to read the circuit diagrams. My knowledge was such that I was able to fault find and develop test equipment.

Electroloid were a company involved in making equipment for electro plating and the particular equipment I was involved in making was the controllers for the automatic dipping of parts that required plating. A microprocessor now would replace the whole control unit.

I was soon asked to go out on sight and trace faults on installed equipment. After six months I had been given the task of commissioning a controller in Southend. This involved doing what ever was necessary to get the new equipment operative. I spent a week away from home and successfully completed my task. I drew diagrams for the owner explaining how to fix things if things went wrong. The owner of the firm was so pleased he invited me to apply for a job as the maintenance engineer. However I declined the invitation, as I was not ready to leave Aylesbury as I had just found Christian friends. On reflection I perhaps should have gone after the job as I now realize Christians are all around not just in Aylesbury.

Acting Foolishly

I began to get bored and impatient when I wasn't trouble shooting, which lead me to act foolishly. I began to experiment with charging lead acid car batteries and notice how the gasses were emitted from the battery when charged at a high rate of charge.

During my tea break I decided I wanted to collect these Hydrogen Gasses in a very large plastic bag. The size of which, would cover and over coat. I then charged the battery at the rate of 50 A/H and soon the bag was filled with gas. I thought what would happen if this ignited so decided on a way to do it. I took two match heads and wrapped thin wire around them and then connected this to two long pieces of insulated wire. I hid behind a large metal cabinet and connected the wires to the car battery. This acted as the detonator. The "Bang" was so loud, the building shock and the whole factor stopped. The foreman came looking to see what had happened. I was so embarrassed I came out from behind the cabinet like a scolded dog with my tail between my legs. The manager whose name was Tom, asked what was happening. Before he spoke my conscience slew me. I felt a fool and had dishonour Jesus. I simple said the hydrogen from the car battery had ignites but all was well. I told my work college all about it when they returned from break. I laughed about it but inwardly felt ashamed and had let Jesus down because I had acted foolishly. Boredom, pride and self-seeking became a snare to me and I soon began to joke and mess about at work and I felt unclean.

Working For Self

I had worked for Electroloid for some time and I began to be dissatisfied with the repetitive work although the opportunities, which were opening up to me, were not identified by me. Or rather I did not welcome the fact this may involve me travelling away from home to work and missing my Christian friends.

At that time my brother was out of work and Jock Macallion who was replacing windows on a council estate in Richmondsworth had offered us work. So hastily I handed my notice in and my brother began to work together again. This work soon how ever came to an end but we soon found work in a building site as carpenters. We were paid £10 a day, which was good money and this lasted a few weeks. One day on the site the men laughed at me when I told them about the Lord Jesus Christ. It didn't bother me but my brother for the first time ever stuck up for me and told them what I was saying was true.

Delivered from fire Morgan Sports Car

After this we decided we would have to earn money at welding and spraying cars. I had the equipment and know how so we hired a barn in Little Horward and set up in business. It was cold at that time of the year in January and so we heated the workshop with an oil-burning stove called a "Salamander". We were supposed to use heating oil or paraffin but we used old engine oil.

This heater we called, "Sally the oil burning goose", because of the shape of the chimney. This was a dangerous heater as I shall now relate and I believed God delivered me from a catastrophe.

Sally The Oil Burning Goose

One day I had in the workshop a Morgan sports car, which was in for re spray. It was worth £1000 (1972). I was working alone preparing this car with old Sally burning away merrily but she began to bubble and spit. This meant water was in the oil. Normally when this happened we would shut her down and re-lite her but on this occasion she would not have it, She was so hot she erupted and oozed out gallons of hot engine oil, which flooded the floor. This went up in flames. The flames leapt up to the ceiling burning the polythene ceiling stretched across the rafters. The fumes and smoke and heat were so terrific I cannot describe the event and terror that I found my self in. What should I do? What could I do? All Alone in the middle of a field, in a wooden barn with a pool of leaping flames just about to burn down the Barn, and the Morgan car in side. My heart immediately motioned my soul to seek direct help from God. I had done all I could now I prayed aloud unto God for his intervention. I then left the barn with my back to it and my eye fell on an old damp tarpaulin big enough to unfold and use as a fire blanket. In I went using the opened damp tarpaulin as a blanket and threw it over the burning pool. The flames were put out and smoke filled the place. The flames reappeared a few time but I soon put them out. God had answered my prayer and the flames were put out. The barn was saved and our equipment. Here God gave me the wisdom and courage and initiative to apply a natural remedy to my dilemma. God had saved me yet again. Praise God.

About 15 minutes later Mike West and his wife arrived and the knights for a visit. They said I looked as white as a sheet. No wonder, so I explained all that had happened. From that time Mr. Knight inquired about getting insurance against such accidents but the insurance company refused it on the grounds it was too risky. Shortly after this I decided I would have to look for another kind of work.

I Find Work In Lowestoft

I found a job advertised in a national paper working as a faultfinder at the Pye TV factory at Fleet, Lowestoft. This was in the spring of 1972. I decided to take the job. I moved into a Y.M.C.A hostel leaving my home in Aylesbury and parents house. At the same time KK took a job at the same factory and both he and his wife moved to Lowestoft for a short while. They eventually decided not to stay.

The Elim Pentecostal Church

I felt very lonely but soon got involved in the Elim Pentecostal Church in the town. I visited the local Christian bookshop and ordered a book called, "The Sovereignty of God", by Arthur Pink. It was soon made known amongst the young people that I was a Calvinist because the mother of one of the girls served me in the shop. I found this out one evening when I was attending the young peoples meeting and on that occasion the girl (about 20) said she thought I was a Calvinist as I had bought this book from the bookshop. She then asked me directly saying was I a Calvinist.

I am a Calvinist I Speak To The Elders

I said yes I believed in the sovereignty of God. She was the daughter of one of the senior members of the Elim Church. Her response was YUK! And she turned around and walked away. I certainly felt hostility then. I decided I would speak to the elders of the church about some of the things that I had learned but the idea of God choosing some and leaving others was not received very well at that church. They also rejected the doctrine of Particular Redemption.

Whilst at the Y.M.C.A. I became very lonely and woke with a bad taste in my mouth. My mouth in fact tasted like the inside of a zoo keepers boot. This was a saying of Mike West. I decided to treat my self and ended up very ill. I began to take Andrews lived salts and at first this was very refreshing. It was so good I began to take it all the time, until one day at lunch I had stomach pains and when I tried to eat a salad then pain increased intensely. This set off a reaction, which lasted months and ended up me being treated for duodenal ulcers.

I Speak At The Factory

I remember speaking to one of the workers at the Lowestoft factory about Jesus Christ. I had told him all have sinned and come short of Gods standard. He did not accept he was a sinner as he had lived a good life and loved football. He asked me how going to a football match could possibly be wrong in the eyes of God and I gave a quick retort saying the scriptures say, "Go not with a crowd to do evil." I was thinking of the football hooligans but at that he said I was ridiculous.

In the summer holiday of that year I returned to Aylesbury and decide to apply for a Job as a television service engineer, in Tring. This was at Mr. C. J. Ward & Son. I got the job and so I left the Pye Lowestoft Factory.

17 PENTECOSTAL HOLINESS BIERTON

When I returned to Aylesbury, the summer of 1972, I attended the opening services of the newly opened Pentecostal Holiness Church, in Bierton, Buchinghamshire. A Rev. Gordon Hills, from High Wycombe, was the preacher and was the pastor at an Elim Pentecostal Church.

Pentecostal Holiness Church Bierton

Pentecostal Holiness Church Bierton

Five points of Calvinism

There was a series of meetings for one-week and I soon realized that he too was a Calvinist as each night his theme in preaching was one of the five points of Calvinism: Total depravity, Unconditional election, Limited atonement, Irresistible grace, and Perseverance of the saints. I certainly felt encouraged and assumed Mr Harrison the minister of the Bierton Pentecostal Holiness Church were in agreement with these truths. At last I felt here was a place where truth and the baptism in the spirit went hand in hand. I was so encouraged.

I began to attend as a regular and got involved in the young people's work and very soon we had far to many kids from of the street to deal with. I was hopeless at discipline and how to control them. There was a wonderful opportunity but I found I was out of my depth and did not cope. Not only that but no one else knew how to cope either so the youth work was closed.

Working for Mr C J Ward and Son

It was during the summer holidays when the Lowestoft Pye factory closed down that I looked for work nearer my home and I applied for an interview with C.J. Ward and Son, of Tring. When I arrived for the interview it was said by Mr Ward, the owner, the reason why I had got the job was because I was on time exactly. I had not planned it that way I just arrived at that time. I started work on the 14th August 1972. With a salary of £2000 per year. I was very thankful to God for His mercy to me.

City and Guilds London Institute Award

During my time working for C.J Ward and Son I completed my college learning a Luton College of Technology and was awarded a final Certificate In Radio and Television Servicing, including a Colour Television Endorsement. This was course 48 and was the highest qualification in that subject that was later to prove very useful.

This was where I worked. However none of the staff at C.J. Ward had time for Christian things. In fact I felt I was considered as less than nothing. I was ridiculed when I said in the bible God mentioned there was a Synagogue of Satan. I was not the only one treated with contempt however as they also treated the apprentice as a servant, a and often humiliated him, which he did not like.

Dr Gill's Doctrinal Divinity

Whilst working for C. J Ward and Son the practice was to break for lunch between one and two o'clock and whilst all the staff returned to their homes for lunch, I was left alone for an hour each day during my break from work.

C J Ward and Son Where I worked

C. J. Ward and Son. 72 Weston Road, Tring, Herts

It was during this time I studied the scriptures and read various Christian books. You might say, "I esteemed Thy word more than my necessary food." I read "Mercies of a Covent God", By John Kershaw, the life of John Warburton, Martin Luther's "Bondage of the Will," William Huntington's "Kingdom of God taken by prayer".

My Theological Training

I also read Dr John Gill's Body of practical and Doctrinal Divinity. All of these books I had managed to obtain from America. It was my friend Peter Murray who recommended these theological books to me. I found this book very, very helpful and it was here that I learned the extent of the doctrines of grace. It was my school of learning, which was to last a number of years.

In my reading I studied John Calvin's Institutes of Christian Religion and in all I had to learn so many new words that my list covered several pages of full size paper. I had come a long way since reading comic and paperback books like James Bond, by Ian Fleming. All of these theological and spiritual books I now consider recommend reading. One excellent book was on by J.C. Philpot, The Eternal Son ship of Christ" along with an excellent sermon,

"Winter Before Harvest".

Michael Goes To Spain

At this time Michael had decided he wanted to live in Spain and so sold his house in Brackley and bought himself a Bobcat Catamaran. He lived in this boat in Denia and began to enjoy the delights of the Mediterranean sun.

Bobcat Catamaran

Michael's 8 Metre Bobcat Catamaran

Michael difficulties did not stop however as it wasn't long before a hurricane hit the harbour in Denia and his Catamaran was dashed upon the rocks and one of the hulls was damaged. This happened however before the bad whether and he had invited mum and dad and me for a two week holiday. One side of the ship sank and after the hurricane cleared it was lifted out of the water with crane in order to repair the boat.

My Visit To Spain

My parents arrived and Michael found them accommodation on a friend boat and Michael collected me from Alacante Airport. I spent my first holiday from work helping Michael repairing the hull on his catamaran. On that tip I took with me Martin Luther's book, **The Bondage of the Will**, a translation from German into English by Erasus Middleton

I Leave The Pentecostal Holiness Church

At this time I had become unsettled at the Pentecostal Church over a few issues that I did not know how to deal with. When explaining to the minister, a Mr. Harrison, that I wanted to leave because they did not teach the doctrines of grace. He said I ought not to leave because of a little bit of doctrine being different. This I found rather strange and did not agree.

A Denial of Imputed Righteousness

I found the issue with Mr E.C. Connet serious because he did not believe or teach that the righteousness of the Lord Jesus Christ was imputed to us for our Justification. Although he had been a help to me he was one of the teachers in the church.

Mr Harrison said he believed in the total depravity of man (not that he used these words) he said that there must have been a little bit of good, though ever so small in us for God to love us and want to save us.

I knew that God set his love upon us and we had need of mercy and there was no good thing in us to recommend us to God. God did not love us because we are lovable. I realised God set his love upon us (the elect) before the foundation of the world. God did not love every body like this.

Scripture Should Guide Us Not Feelings

I also found the issue of being led by feelings rather that the Word of God very awkward.

I began at that time to question many things and realized how easy it would be to be deceived if we were lead by our feelings and not the Word of God.

An example of this was shown to me when the pastor Mr Harrison informed the church that the Lord had shown him the bungalow, which he wanted him to have. This was in Windermere Close in Aylesbury. He said he knew it was the Lords will because he had offered the people a cut price and it was immediately accepted. This was the means, which Mr Harrison knew it was the Lords will.

The next thing the church was informed was that there were 17 clauses in the deed of purchase, which were unacceptable, and therefore the Lord did not want Mr Harrison the buy the property. This was an example of what I mean, the Lord no more told Robert Harrison to buy the bungalow than he did to refrain from buying. I did not feel or believe that was being lead of the Holy Ghost.

Arminian Righteousness

Mr E.C. Connet was another man whom I respected and he attended the Pentecostal Church at Bierton. One day in conversation with him, about the things of God and what I was reading and learning, he turned on me and said it was doctrinally wrong to say the righteousness of Christ was imputed to us for our Justification. This was because each one of us had to have a righteousness of our own. Jesus had his own righteousness for himself and we to needed our own righteousness.

I was shocked and on every occasion I could I sought to reason with him, from scripture, that what I spoke about was true. I argued that as in Adam all Die so in Christ should all be made alive. So the imputation of sin (in Adam) also pointed to the imputation of righteousness (in Christ).

That as the sin and guilt of Adam (note: not the sin of Eve) brought about the imputation of sin to the whole of humanity so the righteousness of Jesus - his life and death brought about a righteousness that was imputed to all that believe. I stated that on this account only do we have right standing with God.

One Sunday morning he turned on me in anger and said all I did was talk about doctrine and never about the Lord.

I felt so wounded I just did not know what to do; I had always looked to this man for support and help. I groaned in spirit feeling so alone in this situation. I wondered how should I handle this.

These were the reasons for me leaving the Pentecostal Holiness Church at Bierton.

I Am Made Redundant

In 1973 during the economic crisis and the Governments imposition of a three-day week C. J Ward and Son fell upon hard times. And I received a letter dated 8th of Feb. 1974 informing me of my redundancy. This date became significant to me.

I was at home at the time of receiving this letter and when I realized I was unemployed I looked at the date of the letter. From this date I took courage, which helped me fight the haunting fears of not being able to get a job due to my past criminal record. The Judge Col. Tetley at the Aylesbury Magistrates Court had given me a conditional discharge from punishment from the crimes I had committed that lasted for three years. This was on 9th February 1971. In other words my three years (to the day) was up. I could now seek work knowing I was free from condemnation under the law and had no need to inform a future employer of my past criminal record (Unless they asked).

It was as though my God and Father were saying to me don't worry I will take care of you. I could now look for work knowing and feeling I was free with a clean sheet to start from.

Letter informing me of my redundancy

From: C.J. Ward & Son 8th February 1974

To: Mr. D Clarke

37 Finmere Crescents Aylesbury.

Dear David,

It is with deep distress the due to the present day economic position I greatly regret that we have to terminate your employment as from today week.

Rest assured this has no adverse reflection on your work or you present unfortunate illness, and will be more than pleased to give you any reference, which may be of help to you.

Should the economic position improve I would be pleased to consider any application you may wish to make at any time, and always pleased to see or help in any way possible.

Yours Sincerely,

C. J. Ward. Enclosed P.45 and N.I. Card.

Please note we have sent off your National Health certificate and have not deducted any money from this on next week's remuneration.

The following reference was enclosed

To whom it may concern.

Mr. David Clarke has been in our employ since August 1972 and has always proved himself to be industrious, courteous, efficient and reliable worked whom we have been pleased to have on our Staff. Since being with us he has taken advantage of Day College to obtain his City and Guilds endorsement to add to his previous knowledge and certificates. We can thoroughly recommend him for any similar position and wish him well in such. We regret that the present government and country unrest and economic position leaves us with great regret to dispense with his services.

C. J Ward.

18 WORKING FOR GRANADA TV RENTALS

It was within two weeks of my redundancy that I had obtained a new job, working for Granada TV Rentals, as a service technician.

I started work for Granada TV Ltd. on 25/2/1974 being paid £37.27 per week. This car had a company logo printed on the side of the vehicle so one knew for whom I worked. I say this because this became a point of issue at a later date. I also was granted £3.72 per week as a vehicle allowance.

I Am Promoted To Service Manager

Within 6 months of working at Granada I was promoted to workshop manager and I found the work very challenging and rewarding. I found working for Granada a fresh breath of air and got on real well. The only problem was I worked too hard and was inefficient which led to a real case of depression, which I will relate later.

Granada TV Rentals Aylesbury

Michael Nicholson left, David. Phil Reason Middle, Tony Burnham and Mrs Royce-Taylor

My visit to Northern Ireland

I was encouraged to have a break from work and in July 1974 I was invited by Owen McCrystal to visit his home in Northern Ireland, He lived in a town called Omagh in County Tyrone. Owen had a television business called, "Crystal T.V.". He started his business by bringing a van load of second hand T.V. sets from England to the town of Omagh and began to rent them out and repair washing machines and TV's. I was invited out to teach one of his employee's, called Ivan. I taught him how Colour T.V.'s work. Owen maintained he was a genius as he could fix TV sets without knowing how they worked. He maintained any one could repair a T.V. set if they knew how they worked so he must be a genius as he could repair them not knowing how they worked. Owen's wife was a Catholic and I think they viewed my religious beliefs with scepticism.

I was unaware of all the conflicts in Ireland and completely ignorant. I had heard people speak evil of Ian Paisley and all I knew was that the Rev. Ian Paisley had preached this sermon called, "Second Mile Religion" and I knew from that sermon he was a man of God and preached the truth about the Lord Jesus Christ. I decided on my way through Belfast I would stop the night and visit the Martyrs Memorial Church where Ian Paisley was the pastor the next day.

Martyrs Memorial in Belfast

Martyrs Memorial Church building, Ravens hill Road Belfast

I Seek Ian Paisley

When I arrived in Belfast I was amazed to see all the soldiers with guns checking every body and watching out for trouble. It was the 12th of July 1974. When I arrived on the streets in Belfast I noticed all the shops and doorways were barred up and the streets very clear with soldiers on every corner. I was unaware of what the 12th of July was all about. It was the end of the day and a lot of parades and marches had gone on that day. It was a day of celebration to some people. I ended knocking on a guest house door to find two ladies running this guest house. I had arrived unannounced with a large suspicious suite case in my hand from England. I said would like to stay the night and asked if they knew where Martyrs Memorial Church building was. They looked at me "gone out" and asked me what was an English man was doing visiting Belfast during all these troubles. I said I wanted to hear Ian Paisley preach. I said I had heard him preach on a record and he preached the gospel. They said they were Catholics and they would be too afraid to go and hear him preach even though they would like to. They made me welcome and I had a pleasant stay learning a bit about the troubles in Northern Ireland

Suspicious Looking Suit Case

In the morning as I carried my suspicious looking suit case through the streets of Belfast I had occasion to ask a milkman the way to Martyrs Memorial Church and he replied I was in the wrong part of Belfast to be asking directions to that place and directed me along a certain road. I realized this must have been a Catholic area but I was really so naive I did not know what was going on at all.

The Wrong Part of Belfast

I ended up in a Newspaper shop asking directions and my eye caught the picture of a man called "Carson", on a post card. To make conversation I asked the shopkeeper who was this person Carson and she spoke scathingly to me say I ought not to ask such questions like that. I then realized I must have been in the wrong area.

I arrive at the Martyrs Memorial Church and Dr Paisley was preaching. It was a very large building with figureheads of the martyrs all around the building. Dr Paisley preached faithfully the truth about Jesus Christ and could not understand why people should oppose him like I had heard. In that meeting I heard no mention of Politics I only heard about Jesus Christ and what he had done for sinners. I concluded it must be his tone of voice or way of speaking I felt people must not be listening to his message but rather the tone of voice. I could imagine him speaking against the enemies of the truth using his tongue like a "Bastard file". After the meeting I asked Dr Paisley to direct me to some one who could help me get to Omagh, as I was a visitor. I finally got transport that day to Omar and ended up joining a group of Christians, from the Free Presbyterian Church in Omar. I was given an orange sash and joined their march along the streets and lanes of Omar. We then went to a meeting and the Preacher was Rev. William Macray.

I had a good time in Omar staying at my friend's home. Owen did not believe the gospel, he was a nominal Roman Catholic and we had long talks about the things of God. He employed a man called Ivan who confided in me that he was a Christian but he did not like to say too much to Owen as it might not go down too well for him and Owen could give him a hard time.

The pace of life seems so much slower than that in Aylesbury and every one I spoke to seemed to have a knowledge as to what it means to be, "born again" or to "be saved". Even Owen and his wife, who were Catholics, knew these terms and used them. It was not like this in England. I had a good time in Ireland and would like to go again.

We Go To The Reformation Conference

Isaac And Esther Crying Their Eyes Out

Dr Ian Paisley says they were tears of repentance

This meet we televised a may be viewed online at the following links. (Click below)

Dr Ian Paisley Preaches At Hounslow (click to view)

A few years later my wife and I went to hear Dr Ian Paisley preach in London with our two children Isaac and Esther to a Reformation Conference, on 14th May 1983 in order to hear Dr Ian Paisley preach. At this meeting Isaac and Ether sat on Dr Ian Paisley knee and cried their eyes out as we took a photograph.

We Employ Michael Nicholson

When I returned from my holiday we had a vacancy for a technician so in my capacity of workshop manage I contacted Michael Nicholson, of C J Ward, asking him if he wanted a job with Granada. He was the apprentice of C J Ward, and whilst working for them he told me he wanted to leave as soon as he could. He was fed up with being treated second rate. He hated having to stub out John Wards cigarette ends.

He came to Granada and past all the tests and was accepted. He joined Granada as a Technician in October 1974.

I am Poached by C. J Ward and Son

It was in October 1974 that I received a call from Mr. C J Ward asking me if I wanted a job.

I went for the interview and asked all kinds of questions as this company had recently made me redundant. I explained my problem about being a Christian and having the three-year conditional discharge over Mr Ward and he seemed sympathetic saying he had not realized this at all. I told him about the Lord Jesus Christ and what he had done for me. He said had I told him these things before he may have been able to help.

I was offered £50 per week (I was only getting £ 40 a week at Granada) plus a company car - with a day off - I was really tempted. When he offered me £60 per week and would I start straight away and not work my week's notice I said yes, thinking this was the right thing to do. I had never had things so good. He wanted me to make a decision there and then, on the spot, without hesitation.

I thanked God for the promotion and this offer and Mr Ward seemed pleased as though he had won a prize. Here I was being offered £1000 per year more than I was getting at Granada.

After the interview I felt and asked the question was it the right thing to do and thought about my boss Tony Burnham - how would he cope? He had been good to me and got me the promotion at Granada. I then had second thoughts.

After thought and prayer I felt I should not take up the job so I rang Mr Ward saying I had decided against working for him.

The following is his letter, which shows I had obviously upset him. His letter certainly caused me concern so he got my reply.

Letter from Mr. Ward

Dear David,

I have to thank you for your letter dated 8th October, I have personally not written before as I have been trying to reconcile your actions with your religious beliefs, to this "God which spoke to you".

You spent all one Friday afternoon asking about four pages of questions, I began to think it was myself asking for a job, which apparently were answered to your satisfaction and you agreed to take the position at a wage well above your actual capabilities but I was willing to accept, capabilities which in part we paid for you to acquire, you shock hands with me to seal the bargain and when I asked if you required a contract you paid me the compliment of saying " No your word is good enough Mr Ward". What a pity that I cannot now pay the same compliment to you, as within 24 hours you had broken our agreement. One does not expect this from religious people of conviction; your religion is obviously different to mine. Just how it this compatible with seducing our apprentice away from us before he had completed his contract for which he so willingly, and at his own request signed for.

Yours Sincerely,

C J Ward.

My reply to Mr Ward

This reply from Mr Ward irritated me and I felt he was acting in spite so I wrote my reply 31/11/74

Dear Mr Ward,

I am sorry to hear you seem so bitter about my break of contract with you. I wrote firstly to apologize for inconveniencing you and wasting your time and money. My conscience had troubled me over saying I would start work for you and then turning your offer down.

What more can I say I know me saying sorry will not undo what has happened all I can do is apologize. Please accept my apology.

Surely you realized the reason why I asked you so many questions was because it was such a major decision I had to make. You wanted an immediate answer straight away so I had to weigh all the facts so to act in my own interest. Just as you acted in your own interest when you dismissed me before.

I am most grateful for your efforts in supplementing my training, which I realize, cost you money also. But Mr. Ward you did sack me I never intended to leave. And therefore I am under no obligation what so ever to you in that respect.

I did explain to you about Michael the last time we met. I hid nothing from you.

Whilst I worked with Michael he told me as soon as his apprenticeship was finished he was leaving you. It was under this impression I contacted him regarding working for Granada. I thought his contract finished this summer gone.

I never intended that he should break any contract. I explained to him that you had always treated me fairly and that he must make his own decisions. It was well within your own ability to freely agree to disannul the contract without aggravation to you or Michael. I am sure Michael would not have left unless you had agreed to dismiss him.

As to enticing and seducing him away and your religion being different from mine on this point it seems that is what you attempted to do with me when asked me to leave Granada without giving a weeks notice.

Your last point I admit my religion is different to yours.

The Lord God whom you speak against is my Lord and God. He is your creator and both you and me are accountable to him alone for our actions, words and thoughts. If He chooses to start a work of change in such a sinful person as my self and you speak against his work it is He you defy and not I. The Lord Jesus Christ came into the world to save his people from their sins. Not for the sake of the righteous. Only sick people need a doctor. I am the sinner and am in need of his forgiveness and mercy.

However I don't like upsetting people I hope you receive my answer to your letter and consider what I say. I don't wish to be on bad terms with you as I like you and admire your business ability.

Yours Sincerely,

David   Clarke.

Shortly after this Mr Ward was in serious difficulties, which those that know him will know all about.

Victor Prince The Crombie Over Coat

"In all thy ways acknowledge him and he shall direct thy paths"

The following extract is taken from my loose-leaf diary and relates to a remarkable experience, which demonstrates the wonder and way of the Spirit of God leading and teaching a believer.

On Friday, 30/8/74, it was my day off from work and during the day I was rebuilding our garage roof at 37 Finmere Crescent, Aylesbury. During the day I was thinking about the way God had dealt with me and led me thus far. I realized that each one that was child of God was special and God dealt with them personally. Each person had his own peculiar special work of God in his or her own life. This work was a personal work done in no other it was special to them. All were saved, being involved in a common salvation, but the work of God was peculiar and special to that individual. In this frame of mind I began to wonder about a particular trouble I had caused a certain Mr Victor Prince, many years earlier.

Mr Prince was a tailor and some years previously (about 5 years) I had employed him to make a Crombie over coat when I had just been released from Borstal. It was to cost £45 and I gave him £5 deposit to start the work. At that time I was living in London doing Government training course learning about Television servicing. My brother was due to be released from prison on home leave. He had a coat made by some one a year previously and on his home leave he came to see the coat before it was finished. After hearing how long it had been in the making he said it was taking far too long and he persuaded me to tell Mr Prince it was not good enough. He then picked holes in the coat in front of Mr Price and told him top stick the coat. Later on the telephone we were both nasty to Mr Prince. He thought I was saying I could not afford it and offered to keep it until I could. It was made especially for me and really would nod do any one else. I left it with Mr Price and thought no more of it until then when I was on the garage roof.

I felt bad about the way I had treated him and would have apologized to him if I could.

Contemplation On Divine Predestination

My mind was thinking upon the subject of predestination and reasoned that God had planned every thing in creation to bring about a display of his glory and Grace in Jesus Christ. I was a person created by God being responsible and accountable to God having a definite purpose for my existence. I was alive and active but God was working in and through me. I had been predestined to obtain salvation by Jesus Christ. This work of salvation being the means of displaying God's love, mercy and grace towards me. It was not my free will that saved me but Gods free grace that made me willing in the day of His power. Therefore glory was due to God the Father, Son and Holy Spirit.

Feeling wretched over the way I treated Mr Prince I had resolved in my mind to pay the money I owed Mr Prince and apologized to him if ever I was to meet him again.

It was one week later on a Sunday the 8 /9/74 that I saw the amazing hand of God at work. Mrs Knight of Mount Street spoke to me on the way home from the Pentecostal Church at Bierton. She said her and Ken had met someone they had not seen for a long time. I stopped her speaking and told her it was Mr. Prince. She was amazed and wondered how I knew. They had met Mr. Prince in Aylesbury and he had though of asking Ken to repair his TV as it had gone wrong. They said perhaps they would ask me to do it and if he remembered me. He certainly did. Mrs Knight was able to inform him of me becoming a Christian and he left it to them to make arrangements to get his TV fixed.

I had not mentioned a thing to Mrs Knight and there was no way of this happening by chance. God had done it.

The first Sunday after this we all went to visit Mr Prince but he was out at a harvest thanks-giving service at a Methodist church. So we made arrangements to go on 18th of September. At first I did not know what to say as I was extremely embarrassed so I said very little. I soon repaired the TV and then spoke to Mr. prince about what had happened. I apologized and offer to pay the money I owed him quite forgetting about the coat.

It turned out he still had the coat even after several moves and the money owing was £38. All I was asked to pay was £34 so I paid this by cheque (Cheque number 183901). I now had my coat; it is dark blue Crombie over coat and still have it today.

19 Bierton Strict and Particular Baptists

I felt lead and right to leave the Pentecostal Church and attend the Bierton Strict and Particular Baptist Church. I felt I could no longer in conscience stay or continue at the church even though I had affection for all the people there when there was a company of people across the road at the Bierton Strict and Particular Baptist Church. They held to and professed the very gospel I had received. From that time I commenced to attend as a member of the congregation at this cause of truth.

Distinguishing Doctrines of Grace

A friend, who lived in Wendover, Mr Alan Benning, informed me that the Strict and Particular Baptist Church at Bierton, believed the doctrines of grace and that a Mr J Hill, a Gospel Standard minister (of Luton Ebenezer Church) was engaged to preach on an anniversary service in the near future. I was keen to hear him preach. So I began to attend their week night prayer meeting.

My hopes had been raised that I would hear the truth about Gods free sovereign grace for it was reported that Mr. Hill was a Gospel Standard minister. I was given to believe I would hear those truths preached by William Huntington, William Gadsby and John Kershaw. I had read their autobiographies and found their writings very helpful during my time at C. J. Ward and Son, and was encouraging by them as they gave all the praise and glory to Jesus Christ the Lord and not to man.

I started to go the Bierton church just before Mr Hill preached that anniversary year on the Wednesday night prayer meeting, and sat at the back of the chapel. At that time I had no idea of the manor of service or church government nor of any other ministers engaged to preach on a Lords Day or weeknight services.

Denham's Hymns

The folk at Bierton used Denham's collection of hymns called "The Saint's Melody" and the substances of these hymns were very pleasing to me. Even the singing pace was different to all the other churches I had attended being that much slower.

Miss Bertha Ellis would play the foot-peddled organ and the hymn-book used was Denham's Collection 19th century. The hymn singing was about half the speed of the hymns sung at other churches and the words of the hymns were wonderful and glorifying to God. The stile of meeting was generally Hymn, reading from the scripture (Authorized version King James), Hymn, Prayer, hymn, Sermon, finally hymn and then a closing prayer. A short while after I began to attend on a regular basis I was asked by Mr. King if I would engage in prayer when asked too. It was the custom for men to pray the women would keep silent.

I did engage in prayer and after the meeting Mr King asked me kindly to pray in future in reverent language and address God in terms of thee and thou rather then you and your because it could offend people. That was there custom.

I went away feeling offended thinking all kinds of thoughts. I was upset thinking what difference does the language make etc.. but I bowed to their request and adopted their form of speech in order not to offend. I now find it difficult, to day, to break from that habit of using thee and thou. I.e. Reverent language when addressing God.

Bierton Baptist Chapel

Bierton Strict and Particular Baptist Chapel. The Church was founded in 1831

The Doctrines of the Gospel

I was convinced the Word of God was infallible and the only rule of conduct and religious practice. I believed the scripture taught us of a sovereign true and living God. That though God be one God, the only self existent being, one in essence and nature, there subsists in the divine essence three divine persons; The Father, Son and Holy Ghost. I believed that person were truly and properly God by nature and that from all eternity. I believed that the divine nature was not divided but one in essence and each divine person possessing the whole of the divine essence.

I believed the scripture taught the Lord Jesus Christ is that only begotten son of the Father full of grace and truth, the only saviour of (Gods elect) lost sinners. He being one person yet having two natures. Being God from all eternity the divine Son of the Father and by nature truly God. Yet at the incarnation he took to himself that which he was not; our human nature and so was truly man. Hence the glorious complex person of Jesus Christ is the Christ that should come into the world to save sinners. I believed that His glory was veiled during his time of humiliation.

This Jesus Had Called Me

I believed this same Jesus had called me by his grace directly and made him self-known to me, outside of the circles of any Christian church. It was he whom I sought and believed in when I went and heard Mr. Hill preach at the Bierton Anniversary Service he preached the distinguishing doctrines of grace very clearly. At that time I did not know many preachers who preached these things except, I had heard I heard Dr. Ian Paisley, on a record and that sermon was called "Second mile religion".

I had also heard Dr. Martin Lloyd Jones preach but he seamed not to emphasize the distinguishing doctrines of Grace, although it was evident that he believed in the sovereignty of God.

The churches I had attended, until this time, around Aylesbury and district appeared to only know of Arminian doctrine and held to a the false doctrine of universal love towards all mankind and a general atonement as distinct to particular redemption.

Not All Preaching Was Good

Not all the preaching at Bierton was good as we had a range of visiting ministers. Some times I would groan and suffer 45 minute of difficult things to listen too. Very few were Gospel Standard ministers and some were opposed to the Gospel Standard position, they often liked to refer to the 1689 confession, a confession that I soon realized was in error. The Scottish Free Presbyterian's Churches boasted of their 1646 confession as the best. Again I soon learned that this too was in error. Some of these preachers used notes whilst others did not. Not that, that helped, as some I felt would have benefited from notes to preach. Some preachers would not use notes and speak as they felt lead too. But I realized that too was no guarantee they could be listened too.

Miss Ruth Ellis

She was one of our members and she was a gem of a person and always ready to share a word or hymn. On several occasion mid week we would visit her and she would read from her books stories about choice Christian experience.

Unfortunately Ruth died and she ended her days at Bethesda Home in Harpendon.

Mr and Mrs Gurney were members and their son John attended our church as a member of the congregation. I noticed a plaque over the fireplace of their home and it read, "A Sabbath well spent brings a week of content but a Sabbath profaned, what err may be gained is a sure for runner of sorrow. I noticed this, as when I looked at the churches original trust deed there was no mention of Sabbath day keeping. It was only brought up in the spurious set of article presented to me when seeking membership of the Church.

Miss Bertha Ellis

She was a mother in Israel and looked after most of the visiting ministers and played the organ at our meetings, giving way to visiting people who were also able to ply such as John Snuggs and Mr Dix from Ivanhoe.

Miss Bertha Ellis informed me that the church was formed in 1831 and opened by the son of John Warburton. She had the minutes of that meeting which were signed in his own hand and the deed of trust upon which the church was formed. These articles of religion were very good and acceptable.

After my warm reception I was looking forward to hear Mr Hill of Luton preach at the anniversary service.

It was good to hear Mr Hill preached and he invited me and Alan Benning to his home in Luton and I spent time with him at his home.

Church Anniversary Services

During this time I was able to take time out of my work and attend the various Gospel Standard Baptist church anniversary services, which were held by other causes of truth. And it was because I was working for Granada TV rentals that I was a blessing because I was able to take time out of work to attend the various church anniversary services in our area. Had I been working for C.J. Ward and Son this would have proved impossible? I really looked forward to these meetings and seeing the various friends of our church and I often took with me some of the members of ours. These churches that we visited were, Linslaid, Prestwood, Barton Le clay, Waddesdon Hill, and Keeche's Chapel, in Winslow.

We also had our own anniversary services and visitors from the different churches in our area and from a far who came to our meetings.

It was at our anniversary meetings that I learned not every one was in favour of the Gospel Standard Articles of Religion. In particular Mr Dix senior expressed it and his wife (parents of Kenneth Dix the Pastor of Dunstable Baptist Church) that they opposed the articles and some, of the ways these Strict Baptists. I felt uneasy about hearing such things but kept them to my self.

Linslaid Strict and Particular Baptist Church

Linslaid Strict and Particular Baptist Chapel

This is where Mr Collier was the pastor. During this time Mr Alan Benning informed me of the Linslaid Strict and Particular Baptist, which was a listed Gospel Standard church, and from that time were we able to visit from time to time.

On one anniversary service we went to hear a Mr Andrew Randall's who apparently had been involved with the Brethren and I could tell from our conversations that he was aware of doctrinal issues of the day, and he had a very serious disposition.

Waddesdon Hill Strict Baptist Chapel

Another favourite anniversary was at Waddesdon Hill, where Mr James Hill was the preacher. This was a Gospel Standard cause and was founded as a Particular Baptist church in 1752.

Waddesdon Hill Strict and Particular Baptist Chapel where we heard Mr Hill, Pastor of Luton Ebenezer church, preached. and Mr Collier. I use to take Bertha and Ruth Ellis, Alan Benning and Grace knight to these meetings. I remember these meetings with fondness

Waddesdon Hill Gospel Standard Chapel

Waddesdon Hill Gospel Standard Cause

Benjamin Keeche's Chapel

At Winslow

At this time, on one occasion each year, an anniversary meeting was held at Ketch's Chapel, the oldest place of non-conformist place of worship in England and Dr Ian Paisley was the preacher. I attended this meeting for a number of years afterward and was greatly blessed and heard Mr Collier from Linslaid and Mr Ramsbottom from Luton preached at those meetings.

Benjamin Keeche's Chapel at Winslow

Keeche's Chapel

Benjamin Keeche's Chapel Winslow where I heard Dr Ian Paisley, Mr Collier and Mr Ramsbottom preached.

Prestwood Strict and Particular Baptist Church

Prestwood Gospel Standard

Another one of the local churches that we attended on their anniversary services (that is Alan Benning, Bertha and Ruth Ellis and Mrs Grace Knight) was the Prestwood Strict and Particular Baptist Church. This church was a Gospel Standard listed Church.

Prestwood Strict and Particular Baptist Chapel. I was here that I first heard Mr Sparling-Tyler preach.

Barton Le Clay Hope Chapel

It was at this chapel that I took both Bertha and Ruth Eliss to hear Stanley Delves and on another occasion to hear Jessie Delves preach.

Meeting Other Christians and Friends

During this time I met John Snuggs from Eaton Bray who had come to work in Aylesbury. He came to our wee knight prayer meetings at Bierton and he introduced me to some of his friends who attended the young peoples meeting that were held once a month at Bethel Strict Baptist Church in Luton. Mr Ramsbottom would give a talk or lecture and afterward we were invited to the Bethesda Rest Home at Harpendon where we were given refreshments and able to meet and talk to other people from the various churches in the district. I found these meetings very helpful to meet other Christians.

Excessive Work And Depression

At this time I was working for Granada TV Rentals and within a few months had been promoted to Workshop manager. I thoroughly enjoyed the job but I found I spent more and more time thinking about work than any thing else. I was taken up with work.

The things of God paled. I went to the meetings but I could not shut off from work.

I soon realized I was not a good manager and found myself doing all the work. I worked long hours and my days off. Although I got the job done and we were the best branch in the district it was all at my expense.

After several months of this intense work I began to find I could not cope with the stress the job demanded and went though horrifying bouts of agony and fear of not being able to cope. I began to think I was experiencing flash backs from the bad trip on LSD. This time how ever it was in the cold light of day with no LSD etc.. I was so ill I wanted the ground to open up and swallow me thinking this would remove me from all the pain I was going through.

Heavens as Brass.

My manager Tony Burnham, who was not a Christian had noticed a change in me as at one time, when I first began to work there, I continued my habit of reading during my lunch time break and he noticed me reading John Calvin's book on Daniel.

Due to my excessive workload I forsook my devotions and worked all the hours I could.

One afternoon on the garage roof at Mount Street I cracked up and realized I could not cope any more. I couldn't make decisions I could not think straight every problem was too much to face.

I ended up resigning from the manager's job and becoming a normal technician. This ended in me feeling a failure and depression set in that lasted about 3 years. It was during this time I learned that the Christian life could be very painful, which caused me to seek deliverance and rely totally on the God of all grace. I found my self-feeling very lonely and wondered if I would ever find a wife and marry.

I found the hymns and preaching at the Bierton Strict Baptist Church very helpful. In particular one hymn by John Newton I recall was most helpful.

John Newton's Hymn

I asked the Lord that I might grow
In faith, and love, and every grace;
Might more of His salvation know,
And seek more earnestly His face

'Twas He who taught me thus to pray,
And He, I trust, has answered prayer;
But it has been in such a way,
As almost drove me to despair.

I hoped that in some favoured hour,
At once He'd answer my request;
And, by His love's constraining power,
Subdue my sins, and give me rest.

Instead of this, He made me feel
The hidden evils of my heart,
And let the angry powers of hell,
Assault my soul in every part.

Yea, more, with His own hand
He seemed Intent to aggravate my woe;
Crossed all the fair designs I schemed,
Blasted my gourds, and laid me low.
"Lord, why is this?" I trembled cried; "
Wilt Thou pursue Thy worm to death?"

"Tis in this way," the Lord replied,
"I answer prayer for grace and faith."
"These inward trials I employ,
From self and pride to set thee free;
And break thy schemes of earthly joy,
That thou mayst seek thy all in me."

---

20 I JOIN THE BIERTON CHURCH

After a short while I wrote to the church expressing my wish to join the church at Bierton, as I believed that I had that responsibility having experience the new birth and being baptised. I reasoned that I ought to support the cause of Christ at Bierton.

I was received into church membership at the Bierton Strict and Particular Baptist Church on 8th January 1976.

A problem arose because in the articles of Religion that were given to me were not those listed in the trust deed of 1831 and I could not subscribe to them. There were two articles that I could not subscribe too.

Mr Hill of Luton Ebenezer helps

I discussed my concerns and misgivings with Mr Hill, the Pastor of Luton Ebenezer church, who fully understood my concerns and after looking at the original articles of Religion , for the Bierton Church, it was realized that there was no record as to how these articles had come into existence. So the church was bound to be subject to their original articles of religion. These were listed in their trust deed of 1831 and these did not contain these items I could not in conscience subscribe too.

The church was please to allow me to join them upon my confession faith and my acceptance of the original Articles of Religion, and not the spurious ones. There was in fact no record of how these other articles of faith came to be in use.

Articles of Religion: The problem

Article 12. We believe that Christ has set apart a day of rest, to be kept holy, and for his honour and glory, which is the first day of the week, commonly called Sunday, Mark 2 27. Acts 16 13. Hebrew 4, 9.

I did not believe that was true or that these scripture taught that.

Article 16. We believe all infants who die in their infancy go to heaven by virtue of the death of Christ. Matth 19 13, 14&15.

Again I could not say I believed this. I grant if they do go to heaven then is must be by virtue of the death of Jesus. These scriptures quoted do not teach this view.

A Church Member Dies

Sadly, soon after I joined the church at Bierton, the husband of Mrs Evered died, who was a church member, and I was invited to the family funeral. I was later invited to the family home in Aylesbury and on that occasion I was asked to share my testimony, at the family meeting, after the funeral to which, I felt privileged to do. It was here that I met the Groom family, who were members of the Prestwood Strict Baptist church and had moved to Brighton.

I Am Introduced To Mr Sperling-Tyler

I had previously met Pastor Mr Sperling Tyler, at a meeting at the Prestwood Strict Baptist Chapel, in 1975, when Mrs Evered introduced me to Mr Sparling-Tyler, soon during my early days attending the Bierton Church. On that occasion Mr Tyler was very gracious and asked me had I found the lord Jesus Christ as my personal saviour to which I replied, " No but rather He had found me".

I Am Introduced To Pastor Frank L. Gosden

Mr Frank L Gosden Gilead Chapel Brighton

Mr Frank L. Gosden was the Pastor of the Church at Gilead where Mr and Mrs Groom were in attendance and they wanted me to meet their pastor. Frank L. Gosden also pastored churches at Heathfield (1939-1957) and Gilead, Brighton (1959-1980). Mr. Gosden once said that he believed a twofold test could be applied to every preacher: Will the things he speaks be things that will matter when we come to die? And will the things he speaks be a help to a poor, broken-hearted sinners?

Gilead Chapel Brighton

Gilead Chapel Brighton

Mr and Mrs Groom and Mrs Evered arranged for me to visit Mr Gosden, in order for me to share with him my experience of conversion and I was very honoured to do this. We spent the afternoon together, at his very modest home, and he gave me a gift when I was leaving. It was his very own personal copies of Dr. John Gill's commentaries of the whole bible, in 6 volumes, for which I felt very privileged to receive. And this became my

143

source of instruction ever since. At that time I have obtained a very old copy of William Huntington's book entitled the Everlasting Love of God towards His Elect. On reading this it became very clear that the Arminians were in the dark and I felt if only I could talk to them then the opposition that I had experienced from those that I had met at Lowestoft would surely disappear and the news be received with gladness. Mr Groom commented on my reading the book expressing he felt it very deep reading. I can recommend this to any one to read.

Before Mr Frank L. Gosden was the pastor of Gilead church in Brighton Mr J K Popham (1847 to 1947) was their pastor who was the former editor of the Gospel Standard.

For 55 years pastor of Gilead Chapel Brighton. Editor of the Gospel Standard from 1905 -1937. Besides being a minister of the gospel he was a gifted writer and theologian. He was called upon to deal with many controversial issues of the times. His booklet Spiritual Counsel to the Young is still in print as are many of his sermons. A book on the life of letters of J.K. Popham was written by J.H. Gosden

Under the title 'Valiant For Truth'

James Kidwell Popham 1847-1937

A Visitor James from Scotland

On one of these occasions we had a visitor from the group meeting at the Bethlehem Meeting hall, at Penn, where John Metcalf, was their Pastor. I learned one or two things from our visitor, who was called James. He was a former Scots Presbyterian and I think from the Free Presbyterian Church of Scotland whom I learned were renowned Calvinists. These I learned and opposed the Gospel Standard views of the none-offer of the Gospel and also the view that the Law of Moses was not the rule of life for the believer. They held to a view of a free offer of Christ to all men, a view I could not go along with, as Christ died for the elect only. Christ was to be preached to the entire world but He was not on offer.

The Law of Moses

Not The Rule Of Life For The Believer

Also I knew that the Law could not be the rule of life for the believer because of their union to him in His death and resurrection whereby they are delivered form the Law of sin and death and had rule of life which was the whole gospel of Christ the perfect law of liberty.

James informed me that the Presbyterian's were against John Metcalf and his teaching because he too like William Huntington taught, like the Gospel Standard article convey that the Law was not the rule of life for the believer but rather the gospel was. This I agreed was the truth.

James came to our weeknight prayer meeting; his name was James and he later informed me that he wanted to hear Mr Sparling-Tyler preach, who was the Pastor of the church meeting at the Dicker. So I agreed to take him one Lord's Day. He had a problem though, because I worked for Granada TV Rentals and I had a company vehicle which, had the name of my company written on the side of the car. This was an embarrassment to him as he was acutely aware of the disapproval of many, who were opposed to any church member who had a television set. He wanted me to park the vehicle away from the chapel car park, so as not to show we were connected with the chapel. I felt slightly irritated with this mode of thinking but was sensitive enough to know how much he felt embarrassed, so we parked my company car out of the way. We then heard Mr Tyler speak in the Morning, afternoon and evening. Meetings of the church. It was here that I met the son of Mr Tyler and his wife who both attended the Linslaid Strict Baptist church.

Television A Concern For Many

In respect to the television I began to realize this had become an issue, not only amongst the Strict Baptists but also the Brethren. I had reason to consider the whole matter at a later date,

Zoar Strict Baptist Chapel

Zoar Strict Baptist Chapel, Lower Dicker

This was built in 1837 and enlarged in 1874. There is an extensive graveyard on three sides

Not All Preaching at Bierton Good

Our visiting preaches came from various local and far away places and only a few were from Gospel Standard causes, let alone gospel standard listed ministers. As I recall the names of some of those who visited us and preached, we shall see who were from Gospel Standard causes and who were listed ministers.

Our Ministers were:

Mr Hill, Luton, Pastor of Ebenezer Luton and one of our Trustee's GS
Mr Collier, Pastor Linslaid Bethel Strict and Particular Baptist GS
Mr Goode, Pastor, Dunstable Baptist
Mr Martin Hunt, Colnebrook Gospel Standard
Mr King, minister, Bierton Strict and Particular Baptist (Bierton Trustee)
Mr Martin White Colnebrook
Mr C. A Wood, Pastor Croydon, Strict and Particular Baptist GS
Mr Hope, Pastor Reading, Strict and Particular Baptist
Mr Howard Sayers, minister, Watford Strict and Particular Baptist GS
Mr Crane, minister, Lakenheath Strict and Particular
Mr Tim Martin, minister, Blunham Strict and Particular Baptist
Mr Levy, minister and Deacon, of Dunstable Baptist
Mr John Gosden, minister, Southbourgh
Mr Lawrence, Evangelical from Harold
Mr Ramsbottom, Pastor Luton Bethel, and Gospel Standard editor GS
Mr Scott Pearson, Pastor, Baptist
Mr Baumber, minister Bedford Providence, Strict and Baptist (Trustee)

Mr Tim Martin, Blunham Strict Baptist (Trustee)

Mr Sayers, Pastor, Watford Strict and Particular Baptist

Mr Dawson Strict and Particular Baptist Kent

Mr Tanton, Tenterdon Strict Baptist

Mr Gould, minister, Limes Avenue Baptist

Mr Dix, pastor Dunstable Baptist and Trinitarian Bible Society representative

Mr Terence Brown, minister and Secretary of the Trinitarian Bible Society

Mr Redhead, minister of Pottern End?

Mr Gerald Buss, minister Strict and Particular Baptist

Mr Buss (senior) Strict and Particular Baptist

Mr Howe Pastor of Ivanhoe Particular Baptist

Mr Paul Rowland (Presbyterian leanings)

Mr. G. Ashdown of the Protestant Alliance

A Range Of Doctrinal Differences

It became apparent to me, through listening to the various visiting ministers and my conversations with them, that we had a range of ministers with differing degrees of understanding of scripture. Some had and held opposing views to each other. We had those who held to the 1689 confession of faith some the 1966 Strict Baptist confession, some who were convinced of the Presbyterian position. Some holding to "duty faith and repentance" and one who could not accept the Bierton Articles of Religion of 1831.

I Am Appointed Secretary

And Correspondent

There came a time when we needed a correspondent and Secretary and I agree to take on this role and had the responsibility of engaging minister for the coming year. It was all-new to me and found it very difficult and a real sense of responsibility.

I had to deal with a request expressing in a letter from Colnebrook Strict and Particular Baptist Church who had informed the church (via me the secretary) that one of their members, Mr Martin Hunt was under censorship. Martin Hunt was one of our visiting ministers, who I found to be a very nice and polite man and had a good understanding of scripture. How ever Mr King and I were asked by the church to speak to Martin about this issue being raised and it was difficult to understand the problem. It was to do with particular redemption so in the end I asked Martin if he could subscribe to our Bierton Articles of Religion of 1831. His reply was no he could not. This resolved the matter and the Church decided not to invite

Martin to preach again. This helped us not to judge this issue he had with his church but rather enabled us to respond to the concerns of the Colnebrook Church in the correct way.

Church Minutes A Cause Of Concern

It was my responsibility as secretary to keep church minute and the church book and during this time I was able read the issues that had been spoken about and the decisions that were made before I became a member. I was shocked to find the Mr and Mrs Evered had put forward motions to prevent certain visiting ministers from preaching due to un-substantiated beliefs about their conduct. I knew that this would be contrary to the gospel and so I raised the matter with the church and stated the need to put the matter right. Unfortunately to one member who was implicated in this form of slander was so upset it was felt best to leave the matter as it was. I realized from that moment I had crossed Mrs Evered.

I continued being the secretary and correspondent until I married and moved briefly away to Leicester.

21 Caterham Strict Baptist Holiday

I meet my wife

It was during this time in 1976 I felt loneliness and fell into depression and friend's of Alan Benning, Paul and Susan Aston invited me to go with them on holiday with a Christian group, to Switzerland. Paul was a student at a Watford Evangelical Bible College and so I went. It was on that holiday that I was made more aware of a holiday being arranged by Caterham Strict Baptist being, held at the Elim Pentecostal Bible College,at Capel. It was here that I met my wife to be that year who is Irene Protheroe, from Shepshed in Leicestershire where Paul Cook was the Pastor of the Evangelical Church.

I Meet Other Evangelicals

In Coventry doctrinal differences

My wife Irene had lived in Coventry and introduced me to her Christian friends including the Minister and Pastor of Holbrook's Evangelical Church. Here I meet good friends who had a desire to follow the Lord however in discussion they realized my views on predestination, particular redemption, the relationship of the Christian to the Law of Moses and the none offer of the gospel proved a divide between us. How ever we were able to discuss matters and agree to differ. These conversations enlightened me further to the differences between the Evangelicals and Strict and Particular Baptists and exclusive position of the views expressed in the Gospel Standard Articles of Religion. I was being cast into the mold of the Gospel Standard Baptists. I also learned that the minister of the London Evangelical Church called Westminster Chapel, where Dr Martin Lloyd Jones was a minister was now

R.T. Kendal who taught a 4 point Calvinist position namely not particular Redemption. This raised the alarm bell in my mind.

Preparation For Marriage

We were engaged to be married in December 1977 and I had obtained a place on the Technical Teacher Training Course as Wolverhampton Teacher Training College. I resigned from my job at Granada TV Rentals and I moved into student lodgings at the college.

Mean while we purchased a house in Wigston at 64B Moat Street, which turned out as a good buy.

Our First Home

64B Moat Street Wigston

This is the first house we purchased and Irene lived here whilst I was living in student lodgings at Wolverhampton and me move in together the on our wedding day, 9th December 1976.

Regarding Marriage Counselling

During the time and lead up to my Marriage I was really concerned about the idea of birth control, as in conscience I was uncertain as its morality. In this connection I asked our only male married church member about the subject. I was very embarrassed but had to settle the matter for conscience sake. To my dismay the only response and reply to the question was, "moderation in all things". This was my answer to a very serious question. As I look back it is laughable and now realize how unhelpful ignorance was.

Marriage

I married my wife Irene Protheroe on the 9th December 1977 and the wedding took Place at Bethel Evangelical Church at Wigston.

Our move to Luton

My first teaching post was at Luton College of Higher Education and I commenced lecturing in Electronics in September 1978. And we were able to rent a council house at Lewsy Farm in Dunstable. The funny thing was that we were obtained permission form the council to keep our two goats in the coal shed in the rear garden building in Wigston were we were married on December 19 th 1977.

Bethel Evangelical Church

Bethel Evangelical Church

Our move to Linslaid

My concern was that I wanted to be in a church with a Pastor particularly now that I had a wife who had been just introduced to the Strict Baptists, so I decided we should attend the Linslaid Strict and Particular Baptist church where Mr Collier was the pastor.

Our Home In Linslaid

Our home in Linslaid

"Fairholme", Queen Street

We continued here for as short, while when we realized it would be more economical to purchase a house in Linslaid and I travel to Luton to work. In that case we would be near the local church. And so we were able to buy our house called "Fairhome'" for £14,000 with a mortgage in Linslaid.

The Isle of Skye

And the Presbyterian Churches

It was my desire to visit Scotland and some of the Presbyterian Churches we rented an old school house in Waternish on the Isle of Skye and we had to cross to the island on a ferry to Porter to get there. It turned out that the Old School house had belonged to Donavan who was a pop star during the 60's. It was a very quite place but very peaceful building at Staffing where I answered the question.. We were not aware at the time that the Presbyterian churches celebrate their communion twice a year and that particular "Sabbath" as they called it was the occasion of their "Mount of Ordinances". It was their communion to be held in the morning of that day. We attended the meeting in the morning and we were made very welcome and were asked where we were from.

Free Presbyterian Church

Free Presbyterian Church

Speak To The Question

During the meeting each male in attendance and whom the elders knew were asked to speak or answer a biblical question. And as their custom was, which I was totally unaware, I was addressed as Mr Clarke from the Strict Baptists would you please speak or answerer the question. This meant that I had to speak about a verse of scripture presented by the elder to the congregation. The verse of scripture was, Philippians 1 [1 v.] "For unto you it is given in the behalf of Christ, not only to believe on him, but also to suffer for his sake;" To which I gave my answer and exposition of the verse.

I believe my exposition was accepted for after the meeting we were invited to renew our covenant vows and partake of the communion.

Not knowing what this meant I declined, as I knew nothing of renewing covenant vows from the scripture.

Called Before The Elders

After the communion meeting I was called by one of the men and told to put my jacket on and come before the Elders as they wish to ask my why I had not partaken of their communion. When I explained my reservation and ignorance of their practices they were pleased to be of further help. We were then invited to lunch at one of the Elders home.

Silence Woman These Are Guests

We had a delightful time and at the head of the table was a senior man in his 80's along with other visitors. One of the other guests enquired of us about the differences between Strict Baptists and Presbyterian's. It came a shock to the lady, who had asked the question, that we do not baptise infants. She exclaimed, "What? You do not baptise infants?' At which point the senior man stepped in by saying, "Silence Woman these are guests". Which I found rather amusing but was not put out by the question and would have freely spoken about it.

Portree Rev Frazer MacDonald

That evening we went to the church in Porter where Rev. Frazer MacDonald was the minister.

Free Presbyterian Church

Portree

Church Building Noticeboard

Portree Free Presbyterian Church

This minister was a very good preacher and lifted up the Lord Jesus Christ and as their custom was they invited all men to come to Christ and he was very urgent in his exhortation.

I Was Questioned The "Free Offer"

We were later invited to another home, that evening, along with other guests and at one time I was challenged as to why I did not hold to the free offer of the gospel, as we had heard that night. It wasn't the time or place to go into detail but I realized then that there were real differences between the Free Presbyterian Churches of Scotland and the Strict Baptist (Gospel Standard) Churches in Great Britain and differences that were not to be ignored.

A Return To The Bierton Church

On our return from Sky we decided we could return to Bierton and give more support to the cause. This of course meant a move and the realization of finances, as property in Bierton was very expensive. This meant selling my property in Aylesbury to raise the money.

Angels Come To Help

(or so I thought)

I had bought a terraced house at Canal Side Aylesbury before I got married and I had renovated it. I had borrowed £3000 from Barclays' bank and was paying this back over a period of 3 years.

My House at Canal Side Terrace in Aylesbury

3 Canal Side Terrace, Aylesbury. My first House

In September 1977 I left Aylesbury and went to Wolverhampton Polytechnic (Formerly Wolverhampton Technical Teacher Training College) to train as a teacher. I rented out three rooms with shared amenities and had kept a room reserved for myself downstairs.

My mother looked after all the bills and collected rent. Whilst I was at Wolverhampton the boy friend of the lady who lived as a tenant asked if he too could rent a room. This seemed OK so I let a room to him. They soon got married and I saw no real problem. They then asked if they could have just the one double room. I explained that I needed to rent all the rooms but they could have the double room for an appropriate rent. I also said they could use my room down stairs when I wasn't there.

I thought things were OK but I had a problem three years later (October 1980) when I wanted to sell the house. I knew nothing about the law and the **Land Lord and Tenant Act.** I soon found a buyer for the house and made an offer to buy a house from Mr Groom at Great lane Bierton who was the son of Mr Groom Senior from Brighton.

The couple that rented rooms from me decided to claim they had right of occupation, which prevented me from selling the house. I went through all kinds of indignant feelings and was angry with them. They knew I had rented the rooms to them on condition if I wanted to return they would have to leave. They called in the **Rent Officer** and the officials coming in reducing the rent I was charging them. In the end I decided I would have to take them to court to get them to leave.

I had to say to Mr. Groom I could not proceed with the purchase and he was very upset as it messed all their plans up and cost him extra money because of the housing chain, which had been broken. He even asked me to meet the extra costs he had incurred. He felt I was morally obliged to pay towards the costs (£1000) due to us not being able to proceed with the purchase. I felt upset by this too.

I felt God was on the side of the righteous a believed it necessary to take my tenants to court to get them to leave. I felt if I were to present my case to the court I would get an order to get these people to leave.

I knew nothing about the law and did could not afford a Solicitor so I did it my self. I believed I could do all things through God who strengthened me.

The Judged asked me what the case was all about. I proceeded to read my script but he soon stopped me. He said you cannot do that and without explaining why asked the defendants solicitor to state the case.

Apparently you have to present things in a certain order and way and it must conform to a certain protocol. I knew nothing about protocol or the law all I knew was I had been wronged and I was looking for Justice.

The judge said I ought to seek legal help. My case was dismissed much to my dismay and my mother stopped up and protested in the courtroom. I got up and left saying no more. Needless to say I was dismayed and dumbfounded. Where was God where was justice. I realized then the law of out land has nothing to do with morality or right and wrong but was pedantic was according to strict rules. This was not justice. I looked to God for help. I had believed God would appear for my help.

What was All That About?

When I returned the next day to Canal Side to sort things out in the house the man, he was a big Irish man, said what was all that about last night? I did not know what he was talking about. I said what do you mean? He said, " Two men had been around with lumps of wood last night and said they wanted them out". I was amazed, as I knew nothing about it. I said I didn't know anything about it and he should go to the police.

I thought that these must be angels sent from God to warn them not to trifle with me. I felt comforted that this was the case. I began to believe it that things were going to be OK.

In the end I had to employ a Barrister to represent me and many months later the couple agreed to buy the house from me at a market rate. It cost me at least £800 in legal fees.

It was a number of years later that my brother confessed to me that he together with another friend of mine Pet Sinfield had been those Angels.

Prevented From Buying A House

As I have already mentioned we had to pull out of buying his bungalow but he was upset by the fact we did not proceed with the purchase. This was his letter to me, which caused me concern.

17th November 1980

Dear David,

As you can see after you had withdrawn from the sale of Great Lane we were put in a very difficult position, because as you remember we had been given until the end of December to complete the purchase of this property. This proved to be quite impossible, and although the builders have been very helpful, they had to increase the price to us by £1500.

We had not bargained for this when we got our mortgage, and together with extra Solicitors fees that were involved, found us at the end of the sale needing to borrow the extra money. This of course must be paid back in the near future and we felt that, as this was not our fault really, that you might feel you could help us with a £1000 of it. We did give you the preference over the cash buyer we had because we wanted to help friends at Bierton Chapel.

If we could have managed in any other way without writing to you, believe me we would have done so.

Trusting that Irene and the children are well. May God bless you all?

Yours   Sincerely,

John G

My Reply was as follows:

Dear Mr. G Re: Your letter dated 17th November 1980

I am pleased for you that at last you have moved to your new home but am sorry that the move proved more expensive than you anticipated.

Your request came as a surprise and has caused my conscience much exercise over the morality of the issue; since it would appear you feel Irene and I are obligated to repay some of your losses. However after careful reasoning we do not share the same view and do not accept the obligation. Not only so Irene and I are unable to do so as we are in financial difficulties our selves.

I would like to add that had we felt obliged then by the grace of God we would have offered payment for your loss. This did occur in my last transaction when trying to sell Canal Side. I presumed to give the intended purchaser vacant possession within a month of the exchange of contract but I was unable to do so since my tenants refused to leave. In this case I felt obliged to him and offered to pay the expenses of my intended purchaser because he had proceeded to purchase on that basis.

When we spoke to you we did not keep you in the dark over our circumstances and did keep you informed, and our arrangements were subject to contract, which at that time had not been drawn up nor signed at the time of our withdrawal.

I do apologize over the matter for it seems God in His providence intervened having His own reasons and although at the present time we cannot see why.

He may be pleased to show us one day.

Yours with Christian regards,

David Clarke.

Dealings like this always leave a bad taste in the mouth but I had to leave it in Gods hands. This shows that Christians are not immune from the normal trials of life and that this chain in buying and selling has a knock on effect. Mr. Groom felt I had let him down so I should compensate him. I too had been let down by the tenants.

Such is life and goes to show we are not immune from the normal difficulties men face in this world in business.

22 BIERTON GOSPEL STANDARD CAUSE 1981

During these times there were several moves, initiated by Mrs Evered for the church to join the Gospel Standard list of Churches, as she had been our secretary and was finding it difficult to obtain supply preachers. Her sister Mrs Groom and her brother in Law were members of Prestwood Strict and Particular Baptists and really wanted Bierton to become a listed church. I knew some members were quite happy with the ministers that were engaged to speak and did not see the need to become a Gospel Standard listed Church.

It was during the time we were trying to move back to Bierton, that on the 16th January 1981, our church decided to join the Gospel Standard list of Churches. Mr Hope, Pastor of Reading, Strict Baptist Church was the Chairman of the meeting and he agreed to do all the necessary documentation regarding this matter and we were duly listed as a Gospel Standard cause. Mr King had made the proposal and seconded by Mrs Evered and a unanimous decision by ballot was taken. It was agreed we became a Gospel Standard listed cause.

This was not how ever without opposition from without the Church. Mr Dix, the Pastor of Dunstable Baptist Church, stated to me personally that we were out of order and it was illegal for us to adopt the Gospel Standard Articles of religion and its Rules of Conduct. This I write about in "The Bierton Crisis 1984.

Ruth Ellis a Church Member Dies

At this time Ruth Ellis who had been a great encouragement to my wife and I before I married and I use to visit her regularly with a friend and have good fellowship in the lord. She eventfully need looking after and ended her days at the Bethesda Home in Harpendon. I believe it was noted that one could always have choice conversations with her on spiritual matters.

Mr Collier, Pastor of Linslaid

In early April 1982 Mr Collier from Linslaid came to our Church midweek to our prayer meeting and he spoke on the subject of the Falkland war, this was because England was at war with Argentina in 1982. He informed the Church of the ancient conflict between the Roman Catholic system and the Reformation in Europe. Argentina being a Catholic country. Mr Collier was a friend of Dr Ian Paisley and through his connection we were able to here Ian Paisley preach in Mr Greens Church in London. It was always good to here him preach, as he was an excellent preacher even though he differed over certain points of doctrine.

In connection with Mr Collier it was remarked by his family that, "If he had been disturbed by events in the first twenty-five years of his pastorate he was even more profoundly disturbed by developments since. Blatantly heretical statements from so-called Church leaders, the fresh impetus given to the ecumenical drift by the charismatic movement, the historic visit of the Pope to this country in 1982 - all these things affected him deeply. His response, however, was not to project himself back into the past in a nostalgia for better days. It was to work for the present and for the future. It was to recognize that God is still working today in raising up a witness to the gospel. He found encouragement in his contact with other ministers both within his own denomination and outside; and it is a simple matter of fact that the extent of such contact increased in his latter days."

I Meet Dr Ian Paisley At Oxford

At this time there was a memorial rally held in Oxford to remember our Martyrs Cranmer, Latimer and Ridley. And I remember Ian Paisley echoing the words, Fear not we shall light a fire in England that will never be put out". Shortly after the accession of Mary in 1553 a summons was sent to Latimer to appear before the council at Westminster. Though he might have escaped by flight, and though he knew, as he quaintly remarked, "Smithfield already groaned for him," he at once joyfully obeyed. The pursuant, he said, was "a welcome messenger." The hardships of his imprisonment, and the long disputations at Oxford, tolled severely on his health, but he endured all with unbroken cheerfulness.

On the 16th of October 1555 Hugh Latimer and Ridley were led to the stake at Oxford. Never was man more free than Latimer from the taint of fanaticism or less dominated by "vainglory," but the motives, which now inspired his courage, not only placed him beyond the influence of fear, but also enabled him to taste in dying an ineffable thrill of victorious achievement. Ridley he greeted with the words, "Be of good comfort, master Ridley, and play the man; we shall this day light such a candle by God's grace in England as (I trust) shall never be put out."

He "received the flame as it were embracing it. After he had stroked his face with his hands, and (as it were) bathed them a little in the fire, he soon died (as it appeared) with very little pain or none."

Archbishop Cranmer, on the day of his execution, he dramatically withdrew his recantations, to die a heretic to Roman Catholics and a martyr to others. His legacy lives on within the Church of England through the Book of Common Prayer and the Thirty-Nine Articles, an Anglican statement of faith derived from his work. He renounced the recantations that he had written or signed with his own hand since his degradation and as such he stated his hand would be punished by being burnt first.

He then said, "And as for the Pope, I refuse him, as Christ's enemy, and Antichrist with all his false doctrine". He was pulled from the pulpit and taken to where Latimer and Ridley had been burnt six months before. As the flames drew around him, he fulfilled his promise by placing his right hand into the heart of the fire and his dying words were, "Lord Jesus, receive my spirit... I see the heavens open and Jesus standing at the right hand of God."[97]

Rescuing Michael's Roles Royce

(About 1982)

Whilst these things were going on my brother got into serious difficulties. His business was failing and he became very depressed so much so he did not know how to sort some of his problems. He came to me one day explaining he had sold his Roles Royce to a person in Milton Keynes for £7000 and he was still owed £3,500. He was too ill to sort it out. The person kept giving one excuse after another as to why he could not pay the money.

I felt indignant and was not prepared to sit down and see some one-take advantage of my Michael because he was ill and could not sort his problems out.

I said to Michael come on I will go with him and get it sorted. I dressed in my Crombie over coat and suit and looked very official and we went to this person's house in Milton Keynes. I told Michael not to worry I would deal with any problems. When the person answered the door, early on morning, I said who I was and what we had come for and that I was a Christian and we intended to sort out the issue with the Roles Royce. The bloke looked at me gone out.

Michael decided he wanted the car back and so it was agreed that he would pay back the £3500 in cash and take the car. I found out that the previous deal had been done between another person as well as this man and the car was in his garage somewhere else. Also a problem with a finance company had arisen. This all seamed straight forward and we left with the intention (or so I thought) to return with the £3500 cash and collect the car that day.

My brother then explained that he understood that these men had raised money through a finance company to buy the car and he only got half the money. I then feared if he gave up the £3500 cash to them he would loose that as well, as the finance company would claim ownership of the car. He had already gone to the police but the police said it was not a problem they could deal with so my brother felt real down about the whole issue. He said he could not remember signing any forms with a finance company but I began to feel the case was not a straight forward, as it first seemed. Michael kept saying he could not remember what had happened.

I got the impression Michael had been party to some deal and was keeping some thing from me and these men had just tucked him up for £3500 and they now had no money to pay. Michael informed me years later that he did not know about this and that these men took him advantage of him, whilst he was ill.

Michael decided to get the car back so he paid a couple of his heavy friend's £250 to go and collect the car. Sure enough the next day the Roles Royce was in bed in my garage at Bierton, out of the way. I felt much better even though my brother didn't. This did not stop my brother worrying because apparently there was more to it than first met the eye there was some problem with the finance company.

I felt let down by Michael for not telling me all this. Had he told me all this in the beginning instead of being devious. (Michael now tells me I was wrong) I could have helped him. In the end the finance company contacted Michael and he by then realized the car belonged to the finance company. Michael, through not being able to cope with the worry, agreed to return the car as he realized the deal they had done was not straightforward.

This was all out of my hands and on reflection I think it would have been better to keep the car and give the finance company the £3500, but at the time I was not able to sort the issue out for Michael because he had kept things from me.

I felt upset for my brother because he had lost his car and all that money. We are always wise after an event.

23 A CALL TO PREACH THE GOSPEL

I believe that God puts the desire to preach and speak His Word into the hearts of them whom he calls. This desire was placed in my heart the day Jesus called me to hear him and believe in him. My desire to help others turn from the way that leads to hell and to Christ himself for salvation, was acknowledge by Jesus the night I got saved. His reply to me, when I asked what about the others, was all I could do was tell them. What better way than to preach the unsearchable riches of Christ to men.

I had spoken on a number of times at Bierton Church during the weeknight prayer meeting from the table not the pulpit. Gradually however I felt more and more uncomfortable when sitting in the pew just listening to sermons. Particularly when things were not very well expressed and some times serious errors were being spoken. It grieved me to listen to the ignorant talk off the religious whose eyes were blinded to the truth of God and who sought to bind burdens on peoples backs. This issue over the hat and lady visitor and a head covering which write about latter was an example. Not that I am against a head covering for a woman but what had happened to this lady visitor was wrong.

I Did Not Believe In Bible Colleges

When I first became a Christian I did not believe in Bible Colleges. Thinking I do not want men to teach me, I wanted God to teach me. From what little I had seen of vicars and so called trained men I felt Bible Colleges were of no use because these people are not even born again.

Wolverhampton Polytechnic

Teacher Training

So I dismissed the idea of Bible college for me, never the less I wanted to learn all about God and speak his word in clarity and truth. This desire turned me to read about the lives of men of God. I went from reading the Beano and Dandy comics and James Bond books to the Bible and then on to the writings of John Bunyan, Dr. John Gill, John Owen and Calvin in a matter of two or three years. It was when I met my wife to be that she encourage train me to be a teacher and that is why I attended the Technical Training College in Wolverhampton, to learn how to teach technical subjects.

An Ulterior Motive

My ulterior motive was to learn how to teach so that I could then teach the gospel. I took one year out from work and studied at Wolverhampton Polytechnic and finally graduated with a teaching Certificate in Education. This was awarded by Birmingham University in 1978.

I believed that I could learn from secular professional teachers how to teach and then would then be able to take the substance of what God was showing me and then present it to men in a way they could understand. This was my desire.

I took my first teaching post at Luton College of Higher Education

commencing teaching in 1978

Wolverhampton Teacher Training Group

David (B center Right) at Wolverhampton Polytechnic

I Inform The Church At Bierton Of My Felt Call To Preach

It was during this time at Luton College and at Bierton Church that I felt it right to make known my desire to the church as I believe I was being called by God to preach the word of Jesus Christ.

The church asked Mr. Hill of Luton and minister of the Gospel and Mr. Hope of Reading, both Gospel Standard ministers invited me to share with them my calling..Questioned about the Law of Moses

Mr Hill questioned my belief regarding the Law of Moses and both he and Mr Hope listened. I expressed my understanding of the believers relationship to the Law of Moses and concluded that the Law of Moses did not make the Lord Jesus righteous as he was always righteous.. He had an essential righteousness independent of the Law. He did not have to fulfill the Law to become righteous. He always was righteous. Had he been judged according to the law he would have been declared righteous and so he was.

That imputed righteousness is the righteousness of God, given to all who believe, that Christ's Righteousness imputed justifies us, without our works according to the Law.

Mr Hill's Conclusion

Mr Hill concluded that my leading was right and Mr Hope agreed. It was then put to the church that I should preach and exercise any gift I had. This was duly done and people came from Albert Street Strict Baptists Church, Oxford and Eaton Bray Strict Baptist Churches, to hear me preach the word of God that weeknight meeting at Bierton.

Sent by the Church to Preach

It was agreed without question that I should preach, as the Lord opened up the way, and from that day in 1982, letters came from different churches asking me to preach at various Strict Baptist Chapels throughout the country. This was my call by the Lord and being sent by the church to preach the gospel, as the Lord open up the door for me to speak. This came with the blessing of the church believing that the gifts and callings of God are without repentance.

I Preach At Various Churches

In fact I was so overwhelmed with being asked to preach at so many places, I could have been preaching three times on a Sunday every week of the year and during the week on week night services. This was on top of my full time work, which involved teaching two nights a week at Luton College as well as continuing my studies with the Open University.

In a very short period of time I was engaged to preach at the following Strict Baptist Chapels throughout the country:

Place	Church
Oakington	Strict and Particular Baptists Gospel Standard
Eaton Bray	Strict and Particular Gospel Standard
Oxford	Hope Strict and Particular Baptists Gospel Standard
Uffington	Strict and Particular Baptists Gospel Standard
Grove	Strict and Particular Baptists Gospel Standard
Evington	Strict and Particular Baptists Gospel Standard
Stamford	Strict and Particular Baptists Gospel Standard

Leicester	Zion Strict and Particular Baptists Gospel Standard
Luton	Ebebezer Strict and Particular Baptists Gospel Standard
Reading	Zoar Strict and Particular Baptists Gospel Standard
Fenstanton	Strict and Particular Baptists Gospel Standard
Attleborough	Strict and Particular Baptists Gospel Standard
Beeches Road	Independent Baptists
Bradford	Strict and Particular Baptists
Nottingham	Strict and Particular Baptists Gospel Standard
Matfield	Strict and Particular Baptists Gospel Standard
Blackheath	Strict and Particular Baptists Gospel Standard

Hats Or Head Coverings For Ladies

Trouble was on its way in the form of religious oppression. On Sunday morning, in 1983 I took to church Dick Holmes' daughter. Dick was well known in Aylesbury and he had 4 daughters and two sons. I worked for him as a trainee aerial rigger. She had been through a divorce and was having a very difficult time. I suggested she came with me to church, as she needed help from God.

She was dressed in tight black slacks and a short top, which showed all her figure. She had long peroxide blond hair and her face was made up. This mode of dress was a striking contrast to the elderly ladies who dressed very modestly with very little make up on and all ware hats to cover their heads in church.

Unfortunately this was too much for Mrs. Evered who came up to me after the service (I call it a meeting because the meetings of the New Testament churches were not called services) and she said to me the next time I bring a female to chapel I should tell her to wear a hat.

Mrs. Evered said that all Gospel Standard Churches insisted women cover their heads and so should we.

I responded that by saying, " what ever others do that was their concern they were wrong if they enforced the covering of the head upon a none church member and women visitor having no profession of the Christian faith."

I said she must raise this issue at our church meeting.

This spirit of legalism naturally took me back. Here was a young woman in sever distress needing the mercy and love of God as revealed in Jesus Christ and all Mrs. Evered seemed to be concerned with was the wearing of a Hat.

I knew the principle of a believing women dressing modestly and being in subjection to her own husband and covering her head in worship. I also knew the principle of the woman not exercising authority over the man or teaching a man but this action of Mrs Evered to use the phrase, "took the biscuit".

I was a man and was being instructed by a woman, Mrs Evered, to order or insist a visiting unbelieving female wear a hat In order to uphold the principle that it was a shame for a woman to worship God without a head covering.

This covering according to the scripture was to show the angels she was in subjection to the man and not usurping authority over him.

Mrs. Evered missed the whole point of the gospel and in her religious zeal to maintaining an outward form of religion transgressed the rule she sought to maintain.

This religious spirit was not of God and I believed the gospel needed to be preached to set men free from such darkness. But who would do this?

A Spanking From the Pulpit

I was very conscious of the instruction that I was responsible to God for the discipline of my children and knew the scriptures, which speak of spoiling children through lack of discipline. And the exhortation that if I spare the rod of correction I would spoil the child (Prov. 13. 24). The other scripture, which spoke to me, was that of how a good father ought to " Rule his house well, his children being obedient and subject to him ". That if I did not know how to rule my own house how should I be able to take care of the church of God (1 Tim 3. 5 - 12. I believed the scripture spoke clearly about corporal punishment and it was a must. (Prov 29. 15 and Prov 23. 13).

The first occasion I felt the need to exercise corporal punishment was on Isaac when he was very small. As I write this now I smile and I am sure he would do too. I think he needs corporal punishment now at the age of 20 years old.

Isaac had done some thing, which warranted correction, and I felt this occasion I would use the rod of correction. I was a small thin garden cane, a green one. I made him stand away from me and I said it hurt me more than it would hurt him, to have to correct him like this. He was about 4 years old. I smacked his bottom with the cane and he jumped and couldn't say a word for a few moments. Then he burst into tears saying, " daddy that stings". From that day forward that cane was called the "stinging stick". That was not the last time the stinging stick was used.

On another occasion I was preaching in Bierton Chapel and Isaac and Esther were sitting with there mum on the back row of the chapel. During the sermon Isaac was playing his mum up and he would not sit still and kept messing about. His behaviour was unacceptable. I was gradually becoming cross with him until I felt I must do some thing about it.

I stopped speaking and said to the congregation " excuse me" and climbed down the pulpit steps and went to the back of the chapel. I picked Isaac up and took him out side the chapel and informed him I was displeased with his behaviour and gave his three smacks on the bottom. With this he burst into tears and when he stopped I took him back in the chapel and placed him besides his mum. I then went back into the pulpit and apologized for the interruption and proceeded with the sermon as though nothing had happened.

I heard afterwards the spanking was heard through out the chapel and a couple of the ladies were horrified at what I had done but they said nothing to me. I felt I had done the right thing using the rod of correction to drive foolishness from the child (prove. 22. 15).

Is Corporal Punishment Correct ?
Hatred stirs up strife's but love covereth all sins. (Prov. 10. 12)
Prov 10 13. A rod is for the back of him that is void of understanding.
Prov 13 24. He that spareth the rod hateth his son: he that loveth him chasteneth him betimes.
Prov 19 18. Chasten thy son whilst there is hope spare not for his crying.
Prov 19 29. Judgments are prepared for scorns and stripes for the back of fools.
Prov 19 30. The blueness of a wound cleanseth away evil: so do stripes the inward parts of the belly.
Prov 22. 15 Foolishness is bound up in the heart of the child but the rod of correction will drive it far from him.
Prov 23. With hold not correction from the child: for If 13 - 14 thou beatest him with the rod he shall not die.
Prov 29 15. The rod and reproof give wisdom: but a child left to himself bringeth his mother to shame.
Answer: Yes.

24 The Papal Visit 1982

This year Pope John Paul 11 was due to visit Britain. This was to be the first time in 400 years.

Very few people saw the significance of this and I felt the need to inform people about such an event.

I wrote to the Bierton Church, which meet on the 16th January 1982 (This was 14 years to the day of my conversion) asking if we could invite a member of **The British Council of Protestant Christian Churches,** using the Bierton Chapel to meet and to teach clear biblical principles as to how we could act responsibly and maintain a Godly witness in the present time. I suggested it would be helpful to many churches in the area.

Mrs. Evered expressed the Bierton Chapel was not the place to hold such a meeting but some other place like the village hall. Mr. King said they had Roman Catholic friends and would not wish to offend them!

From this time I began to wonder about the church at Bierton and believed I would see the hand of God out against her.

I remembered, "They that honour me I will honour".

Our Home In Bierton

187 Aylesbury Road Bierton

I held the meeting in my house and invited several people from different churches and Rev. Gordon Ferguson came and preached for us. We eventually was able to buy our home in Bierton it was a detached bungalow just down the road from the Bierton Chapel. I felt really blessed by God to own it and being so near to our chapel. I had been shocked by the reluctance of the Bierton church to use the chapel to conduct a meeting informing people of the error of the Papal system of Rome, and how we might act righteously in the present day since the Pope was to visit Britain that year.

I had seen the Pope on the TV screen, when at Wembley Stadium, and the whole crowd, thousands of them, were singing praise to the Pope. They were singing, "He's got the whole world in his hands". And the Pope received that praise. I saw it and heard it with my own eyes and ears. This man is an Anti Christ. I felt I must speak out other wise the stones would do.

I write to D.B. An Anglican Vicar

Since the recent visit of the Pope to Britain, on May 28th 1982, I was compelled to examine the claims of the papacy and the Roman Catholic Church.

After that time I was very much alert to the activity of the Church of Rome and the trend for the Anglican Church to move closer to Rome. About one year after this time I read an article in a magazine called "Contact", by Rev D.B. An Anglican Vicar at Walton Street Church of England. I was move to write to him.

Here is the letter:
187 Aylesbury Road Bierton Buckinghamshire

Dear Mr. Brewin,   17th August 1982

Having read your article, which appeared in May's issue of "Contact" (1982), titled Roman Catholicism, I am constrained to write to you as a preliminary step. For you express views concerning Roman Catholicism and Pope John Paul II which are not shared by many Christians. You indicate your views concerning the Pope by stating the John Paul the II are a man of deep spirituality and courage and so worthy of our respect. You say he is a Christian, and a Christian Leader, although you differ on the authority he and his church lays claim too. Never the less there are common grounds between Anglicans and Roman Catholic as fellow Christians and belonging to a Christian Church.

You list four basic areas of common ground for this recognition:

A You are (Anglican and Roman Catholic) are both people of Christ.
B Are both people of the bible
C Have Sacraments of Baptism and Holy Communion
D Are both people of the Holy Spirit.

You then express the real differences, which you believe ought to be remembered.

Now as a minister of the Gospel of the Lord Jesus Christ I write to you believing your article and beliefs do endanger the flock of Christ, over which you are and over seer and I would be failing in my responsibility should I remain silent and not approach you.

May I then go through some of the points you mention?

A You are both people of Christ

The justification for saying this is that both churches call upon the name of Christ and worship Him as saviour and Lord. My question to you is where is the evidence of this? To own him as saviour and Lord is to call upon no other name than his. This being demonstrated by rejecting all others whether lords of lordesses. Is this true of both churches?

My evidence is the present Pope John Paul II calls upon Mary the Queen of Heaven in prayer. (Quotation from "Return to Poland" Collins)

Before the Black Madonna of Jasn Gora (where he had many times in the past whispered "totus tuus" i.e.. completely yours) there he re consecrated Poland to the immaculate heart of Mary as the Queen of the popish kingdom.

He further told the image " I consecrate to you the whole Church- every where and to the ends of the earth. I consecrate to you all humanity; all men and women. All the peoples and nations. I consecrate to you Europe and all the continents, I consecrate to you Rome and Poland (who are) now united through your servant. Mother accept us all! Mother do not abandon us! Mother be our Guide!

This shows a plain contradiction to you first statement that the Church of Rome calls upon Christ's name as Lord. How can is be said of him he is a man of God of deep spirituality worthy of our respect and a Christian. A man stooped in idolatry and spiritual darkness.

B You are both people of the bible

The evidence for this statement is that since the Vatican Council, 20 years ago, the Roman Catholic Church has put great emphasis on bible study for individuals and groups. With a profound effect.

But which bible do they advance to be the word of God is my question. My evidence is that:

a) The tradition of the Roman Catholic Church is of equal authority with the bible and the Apocryphal books must be considered as scripture. (Council of Trent 1545). Hence the bible which the Catholics are lead to read contains the Apocrypha and the reason being they require 11 Maccabees 12 verse 40 - 45 to teach and maintain their heretical doctrines of prayers for the dead. (The Apocrypha must be accepted as scripture under the penalty of a mortal sin).

b) The bible is subject to the churches interpretation of the Douay or Confraternity i.e. those versions, which are tailored to teach Catholic Doctrine, and notes are the version put forward as scripture. Again it is still a mortal sin for a Catholic to read a Protestant version except the R.S.V. (Catholic Edition). Hence the Catholic is not free to read the scripture and interpret it for himself. The Roman Catholic Church under the infallible Pope when reading the bible must rule him. For there can be no other interpretation than what the Church dictates.

C   Both have the Sacraments of Baptism and Holy Communion

This however is without qualification. My evidence is that the Roman Catholic Church have the Mass and Sacrificing priest, both of which are heretical and opposed to the Holy Communion or Lords Supper.

As for baptism the Roman Catholic Church maintains the doctrine of baptismal regeneration by which means all past sins are forgiven. Hence baptism is essential to salvation. (See Trent catechism) quote Infants, unless regenerated unto God by the grace of baptism, whether their parents be Christian of infidels are born to eternal misery and perdition). Hence we see the Church of Rome has no Christian Ordinances but the reverse.

D   Your are both people of the Holy Spirit

Your evidence for this is that the renewal movement has made a good impression upon the Roman Catholic Church with the effect of bringing many Christians together even within the Church of England. Here you place undoubted reliance upon renewal and gathering together imputing this work to the Holy Spirit. Hence concluding the Spirit of God makes no distinction so who are we to put up doctrinal barriers hindering our gathering together with which we please?

Here I would ask the following: If both communions have the same Spirit of truth, light and love for Jesus Christ why are they not lead in the same way. If the Holy Spirit say, " Come out of her my people that ye be not partakers of her sins (Rev. 18 verse 4) what spirit is it that keeps them in the Church of Rome or moves the Anglican Community to seek such unity with her. Rome is an Apostate Church.

If the spirit which is in the Roman Catholic Church which leads them to blaspheme the Son of God in the sacrifice of the mass and bow down to idols and seeks the aid of departed saints then what spirit moved Luther and the reformers to obey the truth and leave Rome, and the Papal Pontiff, and establish true Christian Churches?

What biblical evidence do we have that the Roman Catholic Church is possessed and moved by the Spirit of God.

You also express your personal belief in respect of the Pope being no Anti- Christ. However the Church of England and her founders held opposite views. Remember Cranmer, Latimer and Ridley. We should surely keep as close to the bible as these fathers in the faith and defend the little ones of Christ's fold against all error and preserve them as a chaste virgin unto Him (2 Cor. 11 verse 2)

Now my prayer to God is that Christian men of Aylesbury be united in Christ's cause and truth having love for the brethren and his dear children in the bonds of true Gospel unity and peace.

May the Grace of our Lord Jesus Christ be the cause and the communion of the Holy Spirit the means and life of His Church now and forever more?

Yours in Christian concern,

David Clarke.

In membership of Bierton Strict and Particular Baptist Church.

25 I GO FISHING FOR MEN

In May 1983 I was engaged to preach at the church in Bierton on Sunday 5th June 1983. I have always had that desire to catch men for Jesus Christ but how do you do it. I was now living in Aylesbury and a lot of my former friends were still in and around Aylesbury, having no hope and without God in the world.

I felt compelled to do some thing to get the message of the love of God in Jesus Christ, to them some how. Jesus had done for me and that I was preaching at Bierton Church I decided I should go and ask the Bucks Herald,a local news paper to give me some free advertising. I simply went to the Bucks Herald office and told them my story. I said I wanted to reach all my old friends to tell them what the Lord on, 5th of June that they were all welcome.

I was prepared to advertise but I know I was being cheeky in asking for it free. Little did I realize it but I was giving them their front-page news for the week. Before I knew it the photographer was out to see me and a reporter taking notes for a story. It all happened so quickly

The story appeared as follows on the front page of the Bucks Herald on Thursday, May 19th 1983.

Providentially this meeting was televised and can be viewed on Youtube

(Click here to view) **David Preaches at Bierton Chapel 5th June1983**

I felt the need to be very careful because in October 1982 I had already found some opposition from one part of the church and I was not out to cause trouble. They were against a certain good minister and visiting preacher because he had used the term Evangelical Repentance and that he read the Evangelical Times. I had defended this man in every way I knew how but for the sake of peace in the church decided not to asked this man to preach again. I was very sad and disturbed by this and I believed from that time Satan was provoked by my actions. And there was more to come. So for this reason I felt the need to be extra careful.

A News Paper Report

I was landed with a problem as I did not expect any of this to happen and I hadn't informed the church and so I felt the need to explain what had happened in case it offended any one. I felt relieved when no one was upset. I was landed with a problem as I did not expect any of this to happen and I hadn't informed the church and so I felt the need to explain what had happened in case it offended any one. I felt relieved when no one was upset.

The Bucks Herald

THURSDAY 19th May 1983 price 8d

Former thief says: Come and be helped

REFORMED drug-taker and thief David Clarke hopes he can pass on the secret which diverted him from a life of crime.

For David — now a Christian and Baptist preacher — hopes his belief in the Bible will help his former friends to make more of their lives.

SERVICE

And he is planning a special service at 5.45 on June 5 to try to reach the people who were once his partners in crime.

David (33) of Aylesbury Road, Bierton, was convicted of 24 crimes when he confessed to them after his conversion to Christianity on an LSD trip in 1971.

He claimed at his court hearing that Jesus spoke to him while he was under the influence of the drug, and has been determined to pass the message on ever since.

"It is now time I tried to spread the word to the people I used to know in Aylesbury when I was a teenager," he told us.

"There are still many of them left in the town, and they have gone through broken marriages, drug addiction and crime.

LECTURER

"I hope they will come to my service and see what Jesus has done for me," said David, who is now married with two children and lectures in electronics at Luton Technical College.

He returned to Aylesbury 2½ years ago to rebuild his life.

"My adolescence was spent taking all sorts of drugs and stealing. I am glad I saw the way out of that," added David.

The service will be held at the Strict Baptist Church, Bierton, and he has thrown open the invitation to all his "ex-drunkard", criminal and drug-taking friends in Aylesbury.

Come And Be Helped

Bierton Pulpit

The Bierton Meeting 5th June 1983

The following week I went fishing, looking in the pubs, and visiting people's homes looking for my former friends in crime, in order to bring them along to hear what Jesus had done for me and could do for them.

It wasn't long before the national news network were on to me and wanted the story which I believe appeared in one of the national news papers. I was disappointed in the write up because I felt it was trivializing the reality of what was going on. This is the official transcript:

Dear David

Here's what we put out on the national Telex service. Looking forward to seeing you at the service June 5th Yours Peter Game

From Peter Game, OX and Bucks NA

Catch: Service

Reformed crook David Clarke is hot on the trail of his mates in crime.

He's turned detective to trace thieves, drug pushers, burglars, bandits and drunks in a massive one man round-up aimed at changing their lives.

And it could result in the most bizarre meeting of shady characters a town has eve known.

David, 33 wants to pack them all into a tiny church at Bierton, bucks, and tell them how God saved him from spending a life behind bars.

And if the Local C.I.D. force at nearby Aylesbury, bucks wants to turn up and join in the hymn singing too they are welcome. David a married man with two children from Aylesbury Road, Bierton, is a lay preacher in the Baptist church.

He said, "God helped me and can help all my old buddies too".

David an Electronics lecturer at a Polytechnic explained:

" I 've already persuaded some old villainous pals to come along. I want to pack the church with criminals, but it's going to be a tough job".

The former thief and drug user left Borstal aged 18 and decided to lead a life of luxury based on crime.

"I was in a car ringing business, thieving vehicles and knocking them out again," he confessed.

" I've broken into an old peoples home to steal a colour telly, taken garage equipment, nicked from tills, walked of with speed boat engines, and taken drugs. I've even sold drugs and got involved in permissive sex.

"There were times when I used to keep an axe and a mallet in my car just in case. Now it has all changed.

His life took a drastic change when he "met Jesus Christ" during LSD trip and joined the Baptist Church.

And when detectives questioned him about an offence he did not commit he confessed to 24 he did carry out.

He Added " I've had a clean sheet for 13 years. I'm not going to preach the bible at the bad boys --- Just show them how God helped me and let them make up their minds".

Ends.

Memo to news desk: Service on June 5th. We believe this man is absolutely genuine in his actions.

Memo End.

Out Come Of The Meeting

The meeting went ahead as planned but not many people turned up. I heard that some did not come because they did not wish to be associated with each other. Pat Jones and Malcolm Kirkham were now enemies. Pat Jones had not long ago been around Malcolm's house to blast him with a shotgun. Malcolm had been in evolved in drug pushing and other things.

Mike West said he wasn't prepared to sit or be associated with drug pushers and criminal's etc..

I had spoken as faithfully as I could at that meeting of the Lord Jesus Christ and I remember saying from the pulpit how good God had been to me in blessing me with a good Job, a wife, a nice house, children being in church and many friends what more could a natural man want. I had comments made by several people that God had really blessed me providentially and I knew it.

On reflection it seems from this time I was battered from every way. First my church membership was lost, then my health, which affected my call to preach. Then my children were attacked, then my home was lost, and then my Job was lost. Then my faith in God was lost, which led to me giving up on my marriage.

My Troubles Appear To Begin After This Meeting

As I write this it reminds me of the story of Job who was truly blessed by God in his own soul and in material things, then Satan came seeking to destroy his faith in God. God gave Satan leave to do it but the end of Job best better than his beginning. Thanks be to God. I hope my story will reflect the same faithfulness of God to me.

Stephen Royce and family at Eaton Bray

Shortly after this time I met Stephen Royce and his family including his father and mother who were members of Watford Strict Baptist Church. Stephen had become a believer and was seeking to resolve difficulties that he had in receiving the wording of the added articles of the Gospel Standard.

He had been brought up at the Watford Strict Baptist Church, where Mr Hill was the pastor but he had moved to Luton Ebenezer and Mr Sayers's senior was the new pastor and his son Howard Sayers was a minister sent from the Watford church. At that time Howard made it clear he did not accept the added articles of the Gospel Standard that of course was no help to Stephen Royce or his father.

Stephen Added Articles

Stephen Royce was had become a Christian and believed he should be baptised but Mr Ramsbottom, the pastor of Luton, would not put forward his request to be baptised to the church as he in conscience could not subscribe in totality to these added articles.

This became a real problem to him and he wondered why he could not be baptised, as a believer and simply not join the Church meeting at Bethel chapel. As he could not in conscience agree with the wording of the Added Article because they appeared to deny scripture.

I fully understood his problem and felt for him so I put pen to paper (or type face) and sought to answer his questions, since I was a member of a Gospel Standard listed Church and sent minister from that Church.

My reply to Stephen Royce is published in,"The Bierton Crisis" and I believe was a scriptural answer and support to the non-offer of the gospel that we had declared to be the case in the Gospel Standard Articles.

The Holy Table

About this time, I took my children to church and I had my brother's daughter with me and she would have been about 5 years old. After the Sunday school before the morning meeting began I happened to place her cardigan on the table at the front of the chapel. This was the table used when conducting church affairs and for the communion. The pulpit was behind this were the preacher stood and preached. The table was where the hymns were announced and given out.

Mrs. Evered, in her lovely manor, came up to me and said that I was to take the cardigan off, "The Holy Table". I was shocked by this remark. What was this all about we now had a Holy Table? We were not Roman Catholic or High Anglicans. I was dismayed at such heresy and after the morning meeting I asked the church members to stay behind whilst I established what was going on. I began to realize I was unearthing more religious errors, which would have to be dealt with sooner than later.

I asked the few members of the church, in front of Mrs. Evered about the "Holy table". I said there was no such thing as a holy table in the New Testament this was religious error and just like the Roman Catholics and their superstitions. I said I would not stand by and let this error go unchecked. To my surprise and disappointment Miss G Ellis became angry and walked out saying she was feed up with it all. She said she would not want a pair of shoe put on the kitchen table and she walked out in anger. I thought to my self we are in two different worlds what was going on in the minds of the church and congregation at Bierton. I felt so taken up with zeal for the cause of God and truth I could have taken a large axe and cut the table up in front of every one. I decided to do it another way. I would use the "sword of the spirit".

Television Radio and Cassette Recorder

I was all too well aware of the issues regarding the television set as it was the general consensus of opinion it was wrong to own or view a television. This matter had arisen not only in our church but also anther churches that I had visited.

I had no problem with the television because I did not watch it and after all it could be switch off if one had one. I had been a television engineer working for Granada TV Rentals and had visited the Dicker, taking with me, in the company car, my Scots Presbyterian friend James. This was with the company advertising on the side of the vehicle, which had caused him embarrassment. I had also taken Mrs Evered, in that very vehicle, all the way to Brighten, to visit her relatives, including Mr Frank Gosden.

Also I had on many occasions taken our church members to the various anniversary meetings in my company car. All of these churches were Gospel Standard churches. So I was aware of the issues involved. I had discussed the matter with Mr Joseph Rutt, a minister from Bethel Church Luton, who had been very expressive of his opinions against the use and ownership, by church members, of a television set and had made his views known to all.

I am informed it is wrong for me to teach electronics

Mrs Evered had express it was wrong for me to teach the subject of electronics at Luton College because it helped students repair television sets.

It was therefore a matter I could not ignore but deal with in due season. I had discovered far more serious issues that needed to be treated first. I could well imagine the same kind of problems occurring over the Radio, Newspapers and the cassette recorder and future electronic means of communication.

Escorted out of St. Albans Abbey

In October 1983 I was informed that officials of St. Albans Abbey, a Church of England establishment, were for the first time in 400 years giving official recognition to the practice of the Roman Catholic Mass. This was probably as a direct result of the Papal visit to Britain in 1982.

They had invited a Roman Catholic Father Plourde to serve in the Anglican Church and he was to offer Mass on a regular basis at the St. Albans Abbey. This was in fact illegal and against the principles of the Act of Settlement.

No one seemed to care or could see what was happening I had studied the teaching of the Roman Catholic Church and found it in very serious error.

I felt constrained to support any kind of protest just to let people know what was going on throughout the world. The Mass had no place in the Christian faith.

I decided to take my two children Isaac John (5) and Esther Jane (4) with me to protest against this evil

I attended the meeting on a Saturday afternoon and before very long a Mr. Scott Person of the British Council of Protestant Churches stood up and made a formal protest. He was escorted out.

I waited a while and just before the meeting resumed I stood up and made my protest. I too was escorted out of the meeting with Isaac and Esther in my hands.

This event hit the headline news again in Aylesbury and also in the local news in Luton these articles appear as follows:

The Bucks Herald

19th October 1983

AN unholy uproar involving a Bierton man and others broke out at St. Albans Abbey on Saturday because of the involvement of a Roman Catholic priest in the service.

The protest by Mr David Clarke, of 187 Aylesbury Road, concerned Father Robert Plourde who, along with Methodist minister the Rev. Donald Lee, was being welcomed to the Abbey.

An initial protest was made by a representative from Maulden, in Bedfordshire, of the British Council of Protestant Christian Churches, who then left the Abbey.

Before the service resumed however Mr Clarke stood up and said he protested about a Catholic priest being appointed as an assistant in the Church of England.

Mr Clarke told the clergy and congregation that to invite what he described as

David Clarke

a Popish person to conduct Mass, was contrary to Christian principles and the Gospel of Christ.

The authorities of the Abbey were betraying the people into the hands of the Papal Anti-Christ, he stated. At this point he was escorted from the Abbey

accompanied by his four year-old son and three year-old daughter.

Mr Clarke, a 34-year-old lecturer of electronics at Luton College of Higher Education, is a member of the Baptist Church in Bierton, and himself preaches in various churches.

This was the first official service in the Church of England, as far as he knew, to give recognition to that way, he said.

A representative of the Abbey said the two part-time ecumenical chaplains had already been appointed and were being welcomed on Saturday at the interdenominational service.

Father Plourde would now be able to celebrate Mass in the Abbey for people who wanted to take it, she said, pointing out that all were welcome at the Abbey.

"There is a long tradition of welcoming all Christians, and of supporting Christian unity in the Abbey," she commented.

Teacher's protest in Abbey
The Bucks Herald front page

A Luton college lecturer was ejected from St. Albans Abbey after a stand up argument in the middle of a special service.

David Clarke was escorted from the building after protesting about involvement of a Roman Catholic priest in the proceedings.

This week 34- year old Mr Clarke, who lecturers in electronics at Luton College of Higher Education, Park Square, told why he challenged the welcoming of Father Robert Plourde to the service.

He said: To have a Roman Catholic priest appointed as an assistant in an Anglican Church is contrary to the Church of England articles of religion.

The service had been stopped by a protest from Rev. Scott Pearson, the Baptist minister of Maulden, representing the British Council of Protestant Christian Churches.

He left the Abbey, but before the ceremony could resume father- of- two Mr Clarke stood up to voice his opinions.

"I told the congregation the involvement of a Popish person was against Christian principles and offensive". He was escorted out of the Abbey with

178
his two children.

He said the welcoming of Father Plourde and Methodist minister the Rev Donald Lee on Saturday last week was part of a move to bring the churches together.

Mr Clarke of Aylesbury Road, Bierton Buckinghamshire, who sometimes preaches in the Luton Area, said he was saved from a life of crime and drug taking through Jesus Christ spoke to him when experiencing a bad LSD Trip.

I had some opposition and response via The Bucks Herald, our local paper and these are:

Thursday 20th October 1983

An Evil Wind Is Blowing

Sir, - It was a feeling of sick despair, all to often felt in these times, that I read in this weeks issue of your paper the account of David Clarke's conduct in St Albans Abbey.

In his position as a preacher at his local church he has maybe raised doubt in the minds of many and laid his own church open to criticism and most unfairly There is and evil wind blowing through the world and the despairing cries of victims caught in the midst of sectarian wars. Above their cries are heard louder voices declaiming "We do this for God" and each names God in different tongues.

Men and women of good faith striving for peace and brotherhood brought about the delicate and vulnerable progress towards unification of the various denominations slowly and arduously. Such a balance could be disturbed and for what purpose? Search the bible that you are so prominently featured holding, Mr. Clarke and there you find that Jesus preached love, compassion and tolerance. Not the condemning of hatred against those of us, of every faith and creed, who are still striving towards further enlightenment.

Christ's teachings are simple and clear cut. Are you certain you are following the true leader?

Mrs. Cecilia Brooks

30 York Place, Aylesbury.

NEWS/GAZETTE, October 20, 1983 Teachers Protest

Another upset person also wrote the following in the same paper:

Playing "Fantastic tricks"

Sir, - Like myself, many of your readers must have been filled with dismay to see your recent headlines **"Anti - Pope rumpus in Abbey".**

They must also have regretted that, when the two great Christian leaders, the Pope and the Archbishop of Canterbury, are striving to promote peace and understanding between religious denominations, well- meaning but fanatics should seek to destroy their endeavours.

Half the cold-blooded murders in Ireland wear the cloke of religion as else where in the world, whilst the Russians persecute Baptists and the Mujahedeen. And in Iran the unfortunate Baha'is - men, women and children - are martyred for their faith.

Do we want the days of the Tudors to come back and flames rekindled at Amersham or Oxford?

No- one should suppose that tolerance and indifference are one and the same.

The tolerance, in which I believe, means respect to others and for all God's creation- man and beast and plant.

It also means love for one's neighbour but, as Shakespeare wrote; Man proud man, dressed in a little brief authority, plays such fantastic tricks before high heaven as makes the angels weep".

K.M.D. Dunbar Firethorn
London Road Aston Clinton Buckinghamshire.

The Lord, through Malcolm Kirkham, encouraged me. I was move to write my reply to the newspaper and it appeared on the 27th October 1983, which was as follows:

Cannot Remain Silent

Sir, - I did not wish to provoke hatred, violence or anger when making my protest over a popish person now conducting the mass at the Anglican Church at St. Albans.

Can it not be seen my actions were of those of a loving and faithful Christian? All Christians believe, "faithful are the wounds of a friend ".

My protest was based on the fact that the Roman Catholic Mass has no place in the Christian Church since it is a blasphemy against the Lord Jesus Christ. (Article 31 Church of England).

The Roman Catholic Church proclaims a person cannot be saved unless he partakes of the sacrifice of the mass, nor experience the salvation of the Lord Jesus Christ.

My concern was for those newly seeking the Lord Jesus Christ and to indicate to them the devices of those who should know better.

I have a wife and family and twins on the way. I have a responsible lecturing post and teach people of all ages. I am experienced in danger and believe I should point out such dangers to the innocent.

I am currently teaching the gospel to a now reformed drug pusher, criminal and convict. Directing him and his wife unto the Lord Jesus Christ the saviour and not the Mass or any other device of men.

To Cecilia Brooks and K.M. Dunbar, who believe many were horrified

180

and dismayed, may I say I think not but be consoled with the words of a wise man (Acts 5.38) "Refrain from these fears and anxieties for if my actions be merely of myself it will come to naught: but if it be of God, ye cannot over throw it, lest happily, ye be found even to speak evil of the evil wind, that is said to be blowing, when in fact it is the Spirit of God.

As a preacher of Christ's love to men, I cannot remain silent but must oppose those kisses, though ever so sweet are deceitful.

My home is open to all that are genuinely seeking the truth as in the Lord Jesus Christ.

You may come to see the church at Bierton as well to hear the Word of God spoken.

DAVID CLARKE (Minister of the Gospel)

27/10/83

26 WADDESDON STRICT BAPTIST CHAPEL

In 1984 a Mr. Rose of Luton, a former trustee of the Waddesdon Hill Strict Baptist Chapel wrote to me whilst I was living at Bierton. Asking if we at Bierton Strict and Particular Baptist Church would wish to hold evangelistic meetings at the Waddesdon Strict Baptist Chapel during the time when Billy Graham was preaching in England and Mission England was going on. He suggested I wrote to the new Trustees who were now the Metropolitan Association of Strict Baptist Churches.

Our church at Bierton would not be interested in Billy Graham or want anything to do with Mission England because of their Arminian ways, so I wrote to the Trustees explaining what had happened and asked if few others and I could use the chapel during this period to preach the gospel. I explained this was Mr. Roses request and I was very willing to be involved. I explained we had a few Christian friends who would wish to be involved including the church at Eaton Bray.

The Waddesdon Hill chapel was a very quaint chapel out on its own along the village road in Waddesdon. It had closed down due to too few people attending. Each year since 1976 I had attended an anniversary service there conducted by a Mr. Collier, minister of Linslaid Strict Baptist church then Mr. Hill of the Luton Strict Baptist church.

Waddesdon Hill Gospel Standard Chapel

Waddesdon Hill Strict Baptist Chapel (G S)

Association of Metropolitan

I sent the following letter to the chairman of the trust.

Dear Mr. Knight   27/4/1984

With reference to our telephone conversation of Tuesday I write on behalf of a number of people with a request to hold public meetings for the purpose of preaching the Word of God and worship at the chapel situated at Waddesdon Hill.

This initial proposal is to hold three of four meetings during the summer months, say the 1st Saturday of each month, June, July, August and September, in the PM.

I am a Particular Baptist (and minister of the Gospel) in membership of Bierton Strict and Particular Baptist Church. Whilst our church does not wish to be responsible for such meetings they have no objection to my personal involvement and organization of any such meetings.

Enclosed is a subscriber list of names offering mutual help and support.

I understand you are to meet shortly and we would be grateful if permission could be granted to our request. If this is possible may we have a copy of the "Articles of Faith" and clauses in the trust deed with your reply?

Yours Sincerely,

David Clarke.

My request turned down

My request was turned down, as they wanted a properly formed church to take over the chapel such as the Limes Avenue Strict Baptist Church. I found this way of doing things very chilling and help formed my view of such organized associations. I would not commend them.

Try To Buy the Waddesdon Hill Chapel

Shortly after this after I had succeeded from the Bierton chapel and a few of us were meeting in our home at Bierton I was informed the Waddesdon Hill Chapel was up for sale. I thought perhaps this was a way forward and we could use the chapel to meet in and we may be in the position to form a church.

I wrote to the trustee's explaining my situation. I asked them to forward me a copy of the trust deed as I felt since I had attended the meetings held by the former trustee's it was quite probable that we would qualify to use the chapel if we fitted the characters of those set out in the trust deed.

I was invited to meet with the committee and put forward my case and during meeting one of the trustees said they wanted some one dynamic to go into Waddesdon village and make an impact. I thought this was not how I saw things. God was well able to do it his way. I replied it sounded as though he wanted the Lord Jesus to go there.

I am offered the chapel on unsatisfactory terms

I was offered the chapel on the basis that I form a church using their confession of faith, which was the 1966 Strict Baptist Confession. I said I could not do that because I believed them to be wrong but would be able to do so if they were, as the Gospel Standard Articles, without those added ones. My request and offer was turned down.

I offer to buy the chapel for 1 penny more than the highest bidder Not being prepared to let it go, I offered to buy the chapel and since they were going to sell it I would offer one penny more that the highest bidder. They were not prepared to do this. So I left it.

27 TRUTH CAUSES A DIVISION

Luke 2. 51

This section deals with those issues that I would not normally publish. However as a result of the very serious doctrinal errors and practice that I encountered I am fully persuaded that it is right to publish them as a warning for others. The following is an account of an issue that resulted in me withdrawing from the communion, over matters of conscience, due to the unresolved churches issues and departure from the truth and misconduct of the church.

The following sermon notes were made before and after I preached at the weeknight meeting, at the Bierton Strict and Particular Baptist Chapel, on Wednesday the 20th of April 1983. I believe that sermon was the instrument laid at the root of the error, which caused the division, and parting of the ways between the Bierton Church and I. This led to my secession on the 26th of June 1984.

Particular Redemption

I had clearly spoken on the subject of particular redemption and providentially one sermon was rerecorded and can be heard on YouTube:

A sermon preached a defence of Particular Redemption 1983 (Click here)

On Wednesday, the 20th of April, I preached a sermon, during our week evening meeting. The text being, this is a faithful saying and these things I will that thou affirm constantly. That they, which have believed in God, might be careful to maintain good works' (Titus 3 8).

In my attempt to apply the truth of this text, bearing in mind the current needs and position of our church at Bierton, I gave examples, by way of direct application.

I stated how we might be found to take heed to this exhortation if we restored a suitable children's hymn book which did not contain hymns expressing general redemption & universal redeeming love to all children. Some how a blue children's hymn-book, published by the Metropolitan Association of Strict Baptists Sunday schools, had been introduced to the Sunday school. I stated also it would be a good work to set our church in order even though some would not credit this to be a good work. That in this pursuit there may be a thing not acceptable to our natural carnal desires and us as individuals.

School Hymn Book

The National Association of Strict Baptist Sunday

The Children's Hymn Book

The examples given in order

We had no ruling authority and needed a pastor or minister for teaching and ruling well.

We should teach truth in our Sunday school and not error as was being taught by Mr King, such as "universal redeeming love" for all children. I asserted it was wrong to teach the children or led them to believe in general redemption and that a step to avoid this would be to restore a suitable hymn-book, which was in accordance with our own Confession of Faith..

Effects of this address

During this address I observed the countenance of Mr. King who shook his head from Side to side. This was at the point that I said it was heresy to teach the children Jesus died for them each one. He said, at another time, he knew not by what spirit I spoke that evening. Mr King was the only other male member of the church and had been sent by the church as a minister to preach. I do not know how long he had been a minister or when he was sent to preach but as such he was responsible for the things he taught.

A Church Meeting To Resolve The Issue

Mrs. Gurney after the meeting asked when we could have a church meeting to discuss these matters. Our quarterly meeting was due to be held that April so we booked the 27th day of April at 2:30 pm. At this meeting Mr. King red from the 23rd Psalm and was our appointed chairman. Mr King was a sent minister of our church and had been then one to propose that we become a Gospel Standard cause. He was a responsible adult and church member.

The chairman (Mr King) made introductory comments regarding his position as chairman and that by the next church meeting he would have fulfilled that office for one year and that he wished the church to seek a chairman to succeed him. This was because he could not conduct church affairs whilst there were disagreements amongst the members.

Chairman refuses to allow discussion causing Concern.

The chairman expressed his disapproval of the matter to be discussed since he said this matter could not be raised since, as it was contrary to the rule 15 of the Gospel Standard rule book of which we were governed. He stated Mr. D Clarke was out of order and must have the permission of the church to discuss this matter.

Mr. D Clarke expressed his view, that since it was a case of serious disorder and the Cause of truth would suffer prejudice if left for one month, rule 15 allowed for his action. Also that it would be wrong to leave the church for a whole month with such a charge being unanswered. (P.S. I believed, at the time, this delay was a tactic of Satan and so I then Devil was resisted, in the same way as Cromwell resisted and deposed the ruling king of England, who maintained "the divine right of a king to rule in unrighteousness".

Mr King Honourable Dismissal

to leave the church

Mr King asked for an honourable dismissal from membership. How ever I informed him, at the church meeting, he could not be given leave with honour unless he move to other church of the same faith and order, simply because he would not be subject to a lawful enquiry of the church as to the doctrines he was advancing. **See our Gospel Standard rules of conduct Rule 15.**

Chairman Comments Upon The Sermon

The chairman stated that I had made serious charges against the Bierton church and that he wished the ' chair ' to be respected and honoured by this ruling authority .

Chair opposed

After general matters had been discussed and church business had finished Mr. D. Clarke opposed the Chairman regarding the sermon preached explaining he wished the church to give their opinion as to their belief in respect of teaching the children and their unconverted Parents, at the Sunday school Good Friday meetings. This was because general redemption in opposition to particular redemption was being taught. I said my charge of them teaching heresy was justifiable for Mr. King had said himself, at the Good Friday service both last year and this year, Jesus had died for each one of the children. Also they were teaching the children to sing Jesus had died for them and he loves them all.

The matter was not resolved at that meeting so I gave the chair back to Mr King to conclude the meeting.

The Holy Table (No idolatry Here)

After the issue of the hymn book and my defence of particular redemption that matter regarding the Holy Table arose again. I also wrote to Mrs. Evered, in order to discuss and explore the matter further. This was because this matter was so serious it needed to be put right. Mrs Evered should have known better, after all it was here declared her intention to return the Bierton Church to true Christian practice and preserve the traditions that she had held from a girl now we were amongst Gospel Standard Baptists. She returned the letter to me unread. She informed me she knew the truth and nothing would change her mind. She inferred that I was young and did not know these things as she had been brought up with the truth.

This was blatant idolatry that could not be ignored. This whole matter and my attempts to resolve these serious issues are recorded in detail, along with all the correspondence to all concerned, in my publication, 'The Bierton Crisis', published in 1984".

I Preach A Moving Sermon in 1983

On the 26th October 1983 I had the responsibility to lead the prayer meeting on the Wednesday evening and speak from the scriptures as I felt lead. On this occasion four of the congregation got up and left, my sermon was obviously was a moving sermon.

Essence of the sermon: The Chapel not the House of God.

I explained I had been called by grace 14 years ago and had testified to them of the goodness of God to me. That was in saving me from a life of crime, drug taking etc.. I had learned about Jesus through reading the bible. I recalled the facts that I had come to the Bierton church because they too had knowledge of the truth of Jesus Christ, his dying for our sins. His justifying righteousness, and the Sovereignty of God in all his work towards us.

I said I believed God had called me to preach the Gospel of Jesus Christ and I had responsibilities to them all to make known what God had shown me.

I said the building was not the "House of God". There were no such things as holy tables etc.. and we must not reverence these things as was common amongst Roman Catholics.

At this point a member of the church shouted out. "Well is not this the house of God" pointing to the roof of the building. Then another rose to their feet saying this is just like a church meeting and walked out. Then two other persons, Mr. King and his wife and John Snuggs got up and left.

I was staggered and alarmed for I had not risen my voice, not spoke severely or in a hard way. Never the less the truth as revealed in Jesus Christ had provoked this reaction.

From that time Mr King withdrew from fellowship and no longer attended our meetings.

I then recalled a dream that I had, had previously and it had now come to pass.

I had previously spoken to Mr Collier about the problems that had arisen at Bierton regarding Mr King teaching general redemption and I had requested our church to invite him to help resolve those issues at our church. However Mr King did not wish him to be involved and the matter never was resolved. Mr Collier stated that we must change the hymn-book, as what we had was wrong.

Mr Collier Dies

It was a sad loss for us at Bierton in 1982 when Mr Collier died he had been a great help to me and the church at Bierton. Many people attended his funeral and Paul Watts his grand son and Dr Ian Paisley the minister of the

187

Free Presbyterian Church of Northern Ireland conducted this. Mr Collier had been a good friend and helper to the church at Bierton and he was surely to be missed.

Mr Crane of Lakenheath

Appointed Our Overseer

During this very difficult period Mr Crane responded to our request for help to resolve our difficulties and he did a very good job, and the best he could. However matters were never resolved during the time I remained in membership. We went to several church meetings in order to resolve issues that had arisen but unfortunately they were never resolved. Mean while other issues began to arise that needed to be dealt with.

Requested Help With Article 26

It was during my first year of preaching that I met Stephen Royce at the Eaton Bray Chapel at Eddlesborough. His parents were members of the Watford Strict and Particular Baptist Church and he was very keen to hear the things of God. At that time he and his wife was attending the Bethel Strict and Particular Baptist Chapel along with his wife and children. It soon became apparent he had believed and trusted in the Lord Jesus for salvation and I encourage him to join the church he was attending. Unfortunately for him he was presented with a problem because he found the wording of the Gospel Standard Added Articles in accurate, at best, and wished to come to terms with their meaning. He reason that because I was a sent minister from a Gospel Standard Church then I would be the ideal person to assist in resolving his dilemma. The particular article was number 26. He was informed that unless he could subscribe to them without hesitation or question then the minister of the Church would not put he forward as a candidate for church membership.

I really understood his difficulties, as I too had to deal with the same issues when our church at Bierton became a Gospel Standard listed Church. It is a very serious thing to adopt articles of religion that affect our conduct and practice in connection with other people. The way I dealt with the problem has been recorded in The Bierton Crisis under the chapter The Gospel Standard Article of Religion. My experience with the many and varied religious groups and opinions of the day served to ensure that I had an informed mind and conscience regarding Articles of Religion and practical conduct.

Mr Stephen Royce had a valid point and his questioning and concerns were valid. He deserved a good answer, so I did the best I could. See the Bierton Crisis for my answer.

I Am Asked To Help

It was because of Stephen's difficulty of just accepting these articles, without question he wrote to me and we discussed the whole matter. I in turn wrote my reply and suggestions as to how he could deal with the matter, I understood his problem completely and it was a real matter that needed to be resolved and not brushed away as though it did not matter. It did. My response and answer to Stephen is recorded in my book, The Bierton Crisis.

Stephen found this hindrance, preventing him form being baptised, a real Burden which had been placed upon his shoulders. In order to obey the Lord he requested just baptism rather than full church membership but this was refused without any scriptural reason why not. His response to a question that really was being asked by him was, what doth hinder me from being baptised.

What Doth Hinder Me Being Baptised

The answer he received was his inability to agree to something the he, in conscience, could not agreed with out adequate clarification, and a definitive clear statement of truth regarding the matter, prevented him from being baptised. I trusted that my answer to him was sufficient. You will have to ask him. In the end another minister baptised him and he was not required to become a member of a church.

Paul Rowland Singing of Psalms

One of our visiting ministers was Mr Paul Rowland who expressed his objection to the singing of hymns rather than the psalms. Mr Rowland also worked as a buyer for the Trinitarian Bible Society. I had no problem in the singing of psalms and was very interested in his objections, which were a matter of conscience. He also expressed his objections to the added articles of the Gospel Standard to which by now I was no stranger. As the secretary of the church I was responsible fro engaging our ministers. In order to accommodate Mr Rowland problems regarding the singing of psalms I agreed for him to provide us with psalm books and we sang psalms rather that songs from our Denham's Collection called the "Saint's Melodies".

It was interesting to talk to Paul as he also expressed his belief that the Presbyterian System was more scriptural and of course I had meet some Presbyterian's when visiting the Isle of Skye but believed them to be wrong on several issues.

Linslaid and Children's Hymns

Soon after Mr Collier died we joined their members on their Lords Day afternoon meetings. It was good to meet other believes and I had been invited to join them by Peter Janes. However I was surprised to realize that one of the ladies had chosen a children's hymn just like Bierton which taught general redemption and I began to realize things were not as it appeared and began to think was this replicated in other strict Baptist churches and was this just the tip of the ice burg ?

Meeting Richard Bolt

At this time I met an old acquaintance, a Christian man called Dr. John Verna who too had met Mr John Metcalfe. I had first met him when I first became a Christian, at the age of 20. He was a Doctor working at Stoke Mandeville Hospital working in particular with paraplegic patients. He used to help with the Hospital outreach meetings, which were held every month at the hospital. Several Christians from various churches had joined a group of Christian from the Assemblies of God Church in Aylesbury, to reach patients detained in Hospital. Each month patients were individually invited to the Saturday night gospel meeting held specifically for patients and staff in the Archery unit of the paraplegics department. They would be collected from the various wards in their beds and a different speaker, each month, would give a gospel address and we would pray for them.

Dr. John Verna and his wife helped and encouraged and worked with this group of Christians.

I talked with John about my position at Bierton Church and he seemed keen to help and support me. He introduced me to a dear friend of his a Mr. Richard Bolt from a place in Kent near Matfield. John Verna believed Richard Bolt to have an apostolic ministry.

He and Richard Bolt came to my home and we spent quite some time together and I was encouraged by them both to continue to seek God for direction. Richard Bolt was a very straightforward man, direct encouraging and thoughtful. A man of conviction And I believed had the fear of the Lord. I respected him for his honesty and sincerity. It was good to meet him.

I expressed my misgivings about my dealings in the Pentecostal Churches and my new position in the Strict and Particular Baptist church.

Both groups it had occurred to me went to extremes. One held to the belief in the gifts of the supernatural gifts and Baptism in the Holy Ghost (Spirit) and looked for and expected manifestations of spiritual gifts in believers including the working of miracles (Pentecostal). They were very subjective and looked inward to them selves for the evidence of God working in and through them. Whilst the other group (Strict Baptists) denied the operation of supernatural operation of spiritual gift such as speaking in tongues and gifts of healing etc.. but rather looked inwardly to the evidence of Gods dealing with them by how unworthy they might feel to receive any thing from God. That doubts of salvation were a good sign and an evidence of faith rather than presumption. Both group depended on God the Holy Ghost to work and save. I had concluded both groups could go to extremes.

Both Richard Bolt and John were convinced of the supernatural baptism in the Holy Ghost (spirit) and looked for and expected God to operate the nine gifts of the Spirit including the working of miracles according to Mark 16 verse 17. They believed in the fullness of New Testament Christianity and I was keen to learn and hear even though I was cautious and careful.

One thing I observed was that Richard had lost many of his teeth and I assumed this was because he had believed God for healing and looked to God for divine health. I thought to my self that if Christian were to expect and experience divine healing in this day and age then how come Richard had so few teeth. I did not ask him about his teeth, as I did not know him sufficiently to ask such a direct and personal question.

28 JOHN METCALFE TYLER'S GREEN CHAPEL

Whilst speaking to Dr. John Verna he informed me he and his wife had met with John Metcalf of Penn, near High Wycombe, Buckinghamshire and that some of the people there often had a stall on the Market Square in Aylesbury selling Christian literature and the bibles they sold were only the Authorized King James version.

I was interested and because I had recently picked up a small tract written by John Metcalf called "The Gospel of God", which was about the claims of the Papacy and John Paul the second. I wished to meet John Metcalf because I recalled our visitor to the Bierton Church James who had attended Mr Metcalf's ministry and I understood and agreed with his writings in the tract. This had been most helpful and encouraging to me.

John Verna and Richard Bolt left and I felt encouraged by our meeting and I decided to go and visit the Church at Penn so as to meet Mr. John Metcalfe.

One Sunday evening I decided to go and I took my daughter Esther, she must have been about 3 or 4 years old and we drove to Penn and found the old chapel called Tyler's Green Chapel, Bethlehem Meeting Hall. Old-fashioned metal railings enclosed it and the gate was locked with no way in to the front door. It felt strange because the people were inside and a meeting was being held. I thought to my self had this door been locked deliberately to give a psychological shock to late comers and the feeling of being locked out as would be the case of the 5 foolish virgins mentioned by Jesus in Matth 25 verse 2)[11].

It was damp outside and getting dark but I was determined to meet Mr. Metcalf so Esther and I waited outside, in the road, until the meeting had

11 I have since learned a Full Preterist view of Eschatology views this correctly.
See Our further publications The Parousia by James Stuart Russel for clarity.

finished. Eventually the meeting ended and the people filled out sedately and quietly. I took courage and walked up to the man I believed to be John Metcalfe. Not too tall, well dressed, with a cream or white raincoat and white or grey hair. He was very courteous and when I introduced my self and explained my intent. I asked him about the chapel gates being locked gates he smiled when I explained my thoughts about the 5 foolish virgins. He then explained they locked the gates to prevent vandalism during the meetings, as they had, had trouble in the past.

He informed his daughter and noted my persistence in waiting and that I had read his tract on John Paul the II, which seemed to encourage him. He then invited me back to his home for supper.

Esther and I were received graciously and we exchanged much conversation. Mr. Metcalfe's daughters made a fuss of Esther and gave her chocolate biscuits. I was invited to share my testimony of how I became a Christian and I deliberately decided to tell all that took place the night of my conversion holding nothing back.

(See full account of my conversion[12]). All was very quite and nothing was said that I remember. I explained my present situation at Bierton Strict Baptist Church and the issues I had encountered regarding Particular Redemption, Law and Gospel, Added articles and finally Holy Tables. I was asked about my work and family and I explained I was a Lecturer at Luton College and a minister of the gospel in membership of a Strict Baptist church.

I felt greatly encouraged and noticed how nicely the house was kept. All in a lovely garden, spacious and it was beautiful. It was old and charming just as a Royal house and John Metcalfe kept an Alsatian as a guard dog.

John Metcalfe was a charming person a man of conviction, decisive and uncompromising. He seemed determined to follow God. I liked him and admired these qualities. I felt I could learn many things from this man. He had dealings with the Rev Ian Paisley but opposed him for unknown reasons. He despised the title Dr. and Dr. John Gill for accepting such titles. Also he had known Dr. Martin Lloyd Jones and eminent Christian ministers but opposed many things.

After that evening I returned another time with my wife and we were invited to attend the meeting at Tyler's Green Chapel one Sunday morning when Mr. Metcalfe would be preaching. It was arranged that one of the members of the church would look after our four children whist we attended that morning meeting. This we did. This was a remarkable sermon and I had never heard such powerful preaching. I was greatly encouraged and I realized later to substance of his sermon was that contained in his publication

---

12   As told in this book Conversion from crime to Christ.

" Messiah". The sermon was eloquent, powerful and I believed very faithful to the word of God. I was greatly encouraged and admired the man and wanted to support his work.

After the meeting I was asked by Mr. Metcalfe how I had got on and he seemed to be looking for feedback. I had become unaccustomed to give any kind of feedback, which could give rise to puff the old man up (rightly or wrongly), so I found this situation awkward. I kept quiet even though I was moved with excitement and wanted to express how well I had got on with the message spoken. It was so encouraging that I wanted to tell all my friends in excitement come and here a man speak the things of God.

Paul Rowland And I Visit John Metcalf

It was shortly after this that Paul Rowland's, a minister in the Strict Baptist Church, who also worked for the Trinitarian Bible Society, came to preach at Bierton Church. He was a great advocate of the Free Scottish Presbyterian Church system and by conviction would only sing Psalms in Christian meetings. I spoke to Paul about John Metcalfe and invited him to meet him. Mr. Metcalfe seemed interested to meet Paul and I together, so we were invited across to his home at Penn one evening together.

The Shot Gun And Our Pockets Searched

Paul and I went one evening to John Metcalfe's home and we were received well and our coats taken to be hung up. We were invited to sit in a large lounge rather like a large study and library. It was beautiful decorated and very eloquent. John Metcalfe was dressed in a smart suit and tie.

John Metcalfe spoke about his work and recent publications the *Psalms, Spiritual Songs, and Hymns of the New Testament.*

The Beautifully produced song books

Paul Rowland got involved in talk regarding the Presbyterian Church and the Scottish Psalm Book. They soon spoke on doctrinal issues regarding the Law of Moses and legal Righteousness.

Christ Righteousness Imputed

John Metcalfe maintained that he opposed the views put forward by the Calvinistic Presbyterians who maintained the righteousness of Christ (that which he wrought out by obedience to The Law) was our justifying righteousness before God. He said he had, had a lot of opposition from the Scottish Churches because he maintained the righteousness of Christ is not mentioned once in the New Testament only the Righteousness of God. This righteousness being distinct from Law.

I was not full well aware at the time of the significance to this distinction and at first did not understand the issue. How ever the evening went well and was very stimulating and not without surprise. John Metcalfe posed us with a question as though it was a riddle asking was the fruit that Adam ate good or bad. It was as though he did not expect us to answer because he reminded us God had said his work was very good. I knew the answer straight away I did not need to think but thinking there must be some reason behind the question I awaited and Paul answered. This answer was not satisfactory to Mr. Metcalfe and the issue was discussed. I did not answer because shortly after this John Metcalfe reached behind a curtain and brought out a shotgun in a dramatic gesture and preceded to take out the cartridges. John Metcalfe was not amused when I laughed in amusement he said he was suspicious of our visit that the IRA had threatened him and had to be very careful. He also had just been informed that our pockets had been searched to check up on us and that tobacco had been found in one of the pockets. Mr. John Metcalfe later used this against the person in derogatory comments.

Our visit to Mr. Metcalfe was one not to be forgotten and was quite Remarkable.

This cause me to consider many things and I tried to understand and unfathomed the discussion regarding Justification. I had at that time been considering the view of eternal justification of Gods elect. I knew of the controversy of Antinomian and the legalists. I had shared with John Metcalfe a love of the writings of William Huntington and about Martin Luther's issue of Justification by faith.

It was the misunderstanding of the conversation that he had with Paul Rowland regarding Justification that made me consider the issues that I thought they raised and understood the truth to be. These were:

Justification

1 Gods act of Justification, when viewed from the point before the world existed, was from all eternity. In one sense the elect were justified in Christ from all eternity (in the mind of God). However the work and merits of a justifying righteousness was to be performed in time by none other than our

Lord Jesus Christ.

2 He was righteous by virtue of his person and spotless humanity. He did not become righteous by any works of the Law to Moses. He fulfilled the law and walked according to it.

The gentiles were never under the Law of Moses but rather by it excluded from the benefits that the Jews were promised to those who kept it. The Law never promised spiritual blessings only natural ones. All spiritual blessings, such as regeneration, adoption and the gift of faith, came only through the Lord Jesus Christ.

Also the Law of Moses was not, like the Presbyterian's Calvinist's say given to Adam as a rule to be kept and that eternal life promised to those who kept it. It was not.

I understood that in the Lord Jesus's righteousness sinners are clothed and accepted as righteous before God. This being the righteousness of God imputed to all that believe. This being the source and merits of a believer's justification.

3 In actual experience how ever, in time, the sentence of Justification takes place upon the person believing God, as Abraham believed God. It is received by faith and takes place in the conscience, when first we believe and receive the Lord Jesus Christ as our saviour. This is justification by faith. (Rom. 5 verse 1). From this springs the joy of salvation, which of course involves the senses of the soul. This experience is justification by faith.

Justification by Blood

It could only be brought about by blood and made effectual by blood. Jesus himself being made a vicarious sacrifice. That being by the death of Jesus in the cross. By His death our sins are removed and we be made clean from all our sins. (Rom 5 verse 9). Justification being the declaration by God that we, being clothed in the righteousness of Christ, we are counted righteous for Jesus sake.

This was not the issue

I learned later how after this was not the issue with Paul Roland and John Metcalfe.

The follow Saturday morning I had a telephone call from John Metcalfe, I did not realize it was him at first thinking it was Dr. John Verna and I addressed him as John. This did not go down well he said I was being too familiar and I must address him as Mr. Metcalfe. Needless to say I felt awkward and that this man was being unnecessarily rude. We got on to speak about the feedback he wanted and I said I had things to say but would rather wait until I saw him face to face rather than on the telephone. He became very impatient and demanded I say there and then on the telephone what I had to say. I felt threatened and awkward and was not at ease at all. So I decided I would say about the things I found awkward and unacceptable first explaining that the tract he had written was in fact in error.

His reply was, "look mate I have more theology than I would ever have in 1000 years. That my testimony of what Jesus had done for me was disgusting and that I was in the same danger as the Pharisees, which blasphemed the Holy Ghost during the ministry of Jesus. There the conversation ended.

During all this time my wife had been concerned about me becoming involved with the man as she had notice how much and effect he had on me.

That following week I was away on a week's study at Durham University as I was a student with the Open University. Here I wrote to Mr. John Metcalfe.

My response to John Metcalfe

Dear Mr. Metcalfe   26th July 1984

Further to our telephone conversation I have decided against meeting with you when I return from Durham for the following reasons:

You allow not the children of God to do as the apostle exhorts: " despise not prophesying. Prove all things; hold fast that which is good. Abstain from all appearance of evil" 1 Thes 5 verse 20 - 22.

My words to you on the telephone were that on the one hand I could rejoice with you thanking God for " here was a man I respected and trust in the things of God (for various reasons) whilst on the other hand I got cross with you and could take extreme dislike to you for what appeared to be a sinister way, This I took exception too.

Now you did not inquire as to what I meant but rather justified all your ways, methods and actions by stating your beliefs, saying that for the first time I had come under the preaching of the word of God in the unction of the Holy Ghost. That as the opponents of Christ questioned the spirit by which the Lord Jesus performed his mighty works, so too I come very close to their fearful condition.

You then stated your beliefs in respect of my own testimony; either you rejected what I said as true or was in doubt as to its reality and substance (correct me if I am wrong).

I am sorry if I offended you and your family when I gave my testimony, please forgive me. How ever I am not the only believer to speak of vile things. Deut 28 verses 53. Lam 2 verse 26 and Hos 1 verse 2 and many more. Do you impute guilt to these also as you do me? Never the less what I spoke was true and an actual account and not as you seem to imply an opportunity to speak of self. For that true account I offer no apology.

If you reject what I said as truth I protest I am no liar. And if you are in doubts as to the reality well I cannot add to or diminish what the Lord Jesus works or works not. You are entitled to your opinion but pray give me the same liberty to judge you, your preaching, writings and assertions.

I still do not understand your impatience with me questioning you regarding the statement in the tract, "The Gospel of God".

You say the issue at the Reformation was: Given the merits of Christ person, how are they imputed and his person imparted. Page 33. I said to you. I could understand the statement of " the merits of Christ's person being imputed but not his person imparted.

I gave you room to explain, owned an ignorance and awaited further light and even said I would reconsider the statement. Here however you said you knew more theology in your little finger than I ever would ever know in a 1000 years, given it were possible I should be granted such time; called me mate and kept me at a formal distance.

Well be that as it may I still await a theological precise statement, whether it be in realms of high and heavenly things or in terrestrial ones.

I say persons are communed with and not, with natures, imparted. Neither persons nor natures imputed. I would suggest your tract should read: Given the merits of Christ's person, how are these imputed and His nature imparted. I say I was not seeking to find faults; it stuck out like a sore thumb, just as my incorrect spelling may do.

Here again I beg your pardon and apologize for any seeming impertinence. I say to you this behaviour of yours displays no humility, of which you say is lacking in me. Also according to your judgment I am not low enough yet before God. You judge by appearances; so do I but are you right? Only God knows the agonies, the heart searching and tears shed since our conversation and that is no pretence.

On these points I have mentioned I beg your reply and answers. For how can two walk together if these differences divide? I certainly have no intention of being your enemy.

You said at one stage you wondered if I be teachable. Well I am allowing my feelings and reason to act in judgment over these issues. This I do as you set the example and encourage, or have I got this wrong as well?

I get excited for you, over the production of the Psalms and hymn-book and would like to have seen them in use. I hope my letter to you now will not cause that breach to prevent it.

I have read your tract 2 and have found both 1 and 2 very relevant, pertinent and well written. They search me. Particularly tract 2 and I find I have walked the path of your tract. May they be blessed of God for the furtherance of the Gospel and the purpose for which they were written?

I could comment on the tract 3 about Taylor Brethren but not unless you wish

Yours very Sincerely.
David Clarke.

Following this letter in hot pursuit I wrote the next letter this would have arrived the next day.
Dear Mr. Metcalfe,

I also think it wrong to speak of the merits of the person of Christ. The merits of Christ yes! But not the merits of his person. The reason for this is:

As the Son of God he is a divine person. By nature He is God. Essentially God by nature but personally the Son of the Father. To speak then of the merits of a divine person is abhorrent to the delicate and gracious soul for one cannot admit any imperfections in God nor demerit as to perfection's, councils, actions or purposes. God is by definition essentially righteous. Perfectly just and right in all and in everything. Whether this glory be revealed or veiled always was and ever shall be.

The scripture speaks of the Lord Jesus Christ being the express image of the Fathers person.

I admit a complexity; in that the Lord Jesus Christ is bi natural, that is to say he has two natures. Yet he is but one person, co.-equal with the Father and Holy Ghost. By nature eternally God taking unto into union with himself, at the incarnation, our humanity, that which he was not, becoming truly man. There is now then a union of divine and human natures (never to be dissolved) in the person of the Son of God, hence Christ Jesus the Lord is a glorious complex person.

We may speak of the merits of Christ Jesus for he is truly a human being, having a real soul created when made man; this man may accrue merit by virtue of living in this world being not only made under the Law of Moses but under every divine rule, him being subject unto his God and Father. The divine servant.

The expression then, "how can the merits of Christ's person be imputed?" I say is too loose and really the whole quotation should read: given the merits of the Lord Jesus Christ how are they imputed and His nature imparted? This being the question at the Reformation.

If you think I am being nit picking then what kind of 1000-year theological course do you advocate as being worthwhile.

I write this way because I trust it will be of help to you. You certainly have helped me in causing me to consider many things. I also add I stand to be corrected and ask you to do so.

I expect I have touched on your doctrine of justification and perhaps you have deliberately phrased your statement in the tract the way you have because they reflect your views of justification. Am I right?

Please excuse this hurried note but I must write, as I am able. Yours Sincerely

David Clarke

Durham. 25th July 1984.

My two letters were returned with no comments. I took it that, that was meant to express he rejected my observations or council, against himself.

29 I LEAVE THE BIERTON CHURCH

The events, which had taken place in our Bierton Church, had convinced me Satan's kingdom was being plundered. I had been instrumental in causing no small stir in the church. By October 1983 of that year the church was dysfunctional.

I had been engaged to preach and to conduct the communion service but felt unable to do so because in conscience it wrong for me to do so. This was because the communion represented the common fellowship we all had in Christ but our fellowship due to these severe difficulties divided our church. I believed until the issues were sorted out and the church was in order and of one mind in the Lord, it would be wrong for me to conduct the communion service.

Mrs. Evered, the person who had objected to the term's evangelical repentance, of course had pointed the finger at me. The incident regarding evangelical repentance was another serious issue, which I deal with in **"The Bierton Crisis"**. It was said I caused these difficulties since April 1983 as I had written to Mr. King, a member of our church, and a sent preacher from the church. Mr. King had been advancing views of general redemption, which I objected too and opposed him.

Our articles of Faith clearly stated a belief in particular redemption and also Mr king and Mrs Evered had been the ones to propose and second we join the Gospel Standard. So they had no excuse due to ignorance. I had attempted to correct these errors by speaking to Mr. King personally and finally ended up writing to him and also to Mrs Evered so as to make it quite clear what I was saying and found unacceptable. This letter was said by Mr. King to be, "Full of condemnation" and Mr. King had read parts of that letter to the church before he resigned. This letter is recorded in "The Bierton Crisis" and Mrs Evered had returned my letter that I had given her unread.

Not only this but the issue of Ladies wearing hats- I say head covering-had surfaced (not that I was against women wearing a head covering as the scripture taught this) but rather against this insistence of ensuring visiting unbelievers wearing them. Then there was the issue of "The Holy Table" all of which were heretical views and introduce by Mrs Evered, the church member who had insisted she knew best, and had known the truth since a girl.

I actually felt the old serpent there and I was about to stamp on the Old Serpent. Looking back I realize I had been contending not against flesh and blood but against those principalities and powers, which had kept many believers in bondage and chains.

I felt in the end it was me that was causing the trouble at the church and I should leave things alone. I now believe, on reflection that was a satanic suggestion. I had been standing for the truths of the Lord Jesus Christ but had met with all kinds of false religious spirits all of which, I was naming and opposing.

I Secede from the Bierton Church

From that meeting at the Bierton Church in April 27th 1983 until the 26th June 1984 when I seceded from the Bierton Strict and Particular Baptist Church.

I contended for the truth of the gospel of Christ our with our church members, in particular with Mr King and Mrs Evered, regarding these very serious errors in belief and practice.

The whole of the matter I wrote about and published my article to all our Trustees and all persons connected with the controversy. **This Publication was privately published in 1984 and circulated personally by me to all concerned and entitled "The Bierton Crisis" and as a second edition entitled "Let Christian Men Be Men". The text may be found at my Internet Archive https://archive.org/details/@davidolores Or a paperback may be purchased from Amazon.co.uk and Amazon.com.**

This ended in me seceding from the Bierton Strict and Particular Baptist Church on 26th June 1984. I did this because I saw no hope if people wished to remain in darkness. I could not act in faith by staying in a situation I believe I should withdraw from. According to our rule the church could have dishonourably dismissed me and my wife for the none attendance of the church communion, from membership but as no doubt advised by Mr Paul Crane our elected over seer, they had no real grounds. Neither my wife, Mr king, or me were dishonourably dismissed from membership of the church.

I inform all our trustees of my actions

I felt is my responsibility to inform our trustees of the whole matter and this record, and report, is contained in **"The Bierton Crisis".**

30 OUR MOVE TO SNAILBEACH

Lord's Hill Baptist Church

About that time I heard about a minister called Peter Hallihand who was a Baptist pastor of a church in Shropshire and he also was a representative of the Trinitarian Bible Society. He was preaching at a meeting in Dunstable and Mr Oldham of Leicester had also spoke well of him.

I went to hear him preach and shortly afterward we decided to visit him in Shropshire to outline our position. It was soon evident to me that if the church where Peter Hallihand was the pastor was in Bierton I would feel it right to be joining the Lordshill Church but we lived in Bierton and this Church was in Snailbeach, Shropshire. We both felt persuaded that we should move house and I should change my job if it was the Lord's will that we should join that church. I felt that if God was directing us this way, and I must make the moves and the way would be opened up to us.

The Chapel

Lordshill Chapel Snailbeach

We advertised the house for £97500 but dropped the price in to £92000 in order to sell. We were able to buy a three-bedroom bungalow for £37000 cash in Snailbeach, Shropshire. We moved in January 1986 and in order join the church. We were both very hopeful expectant and looked to God for support.

Our House

Our House In Snailbeach

I still worked at Luton and travelled there each Monday morning and returned to Snailbeach at the weekend. I stayed with Steven Royce and his family during the week and travelled home at weekends. I had hopes to obtain a lecturing job in one of the colleges in Shropshire.

Became depressed
Decided to move back to Luton
Graham Gardens
I recover from depression
Satellite TV
Paid To Leave

Second Bout Of Depression

It was shortly after this that my agony began and I really began to fell the effects of my depression. I never did get work in Shropshire and it never happened. I had attended three interviews, at three colleges, but failed to get any of the jobs - I wondered what God was doing. That year I missed out on my first promotion at work because they understood I was intending to move away. This knowledge all added to the aggravation I later began to feel.

During this time I experienced awful agonies of fear and doubts etc.. I began to believe I was like King Saul in the Old Testament, and the Lord had rejected me. I began to think that all my experience of God was of the flesh and not of God. I felt what I thought an Apostate would feel and that just added to my agony. I felt alone, isolated and very depressed. Depression set in and Steven Royce began to call me Mephibosheth, as he was a son of king Saul, who had gone to live at Lo-debar. (When I look back that was a very good description of my situation and position). I had never heard of the term manic depression, or bipolar mood swings, but on reflection and after being clinically diagnosed with manic depression I realised this experience was part and parcel of my mental condition at that time.

My wife also became very depressed and suffered all kinds of agonies. On a number of occasions she would ring me at work crying about the difficulties she faced. Isaac was being bullied severely and she couldn't cope. She felt hostility from some in the church and did not know how to manage. It all became too much.

I stayed at the Royce's for a period of 18 months during the week, whilst I worked at Luton College and travelled home to Shropshire at the weekend. I hated the journey and very often on the way back to work on a Monday morning I would have to stop and seek God for strength to continue. I was feeling so ill through depression. I began to feel that I had been cast away by God and was in the similar position as King Saul, in the Old Testament, having begun well but was later rejected by God. I felt as I thought an Apostate would feel, which in turn cast me down even further. I wanted to die.

Trade Union activity NATFHE

Luton College of HE

Whilst waiting to get a job in Shropshire in February 1985 I was asked to join the trade union Natfhe at Luton College (I had not joined as a matter of principle), which I had the opportunity to explain in these letters) and here is the letter asking me to join. The significance of this letter will become apparent when I write about my forced resignation under threat of dismissal at Luton College in 1988. I write about this later. It was the Trade Union NATFHE who acted in the interest of the Union in negotiating my terms of resignation. This forced resignation was the result of my first medically diagnosed hypo manic episode but at the time I felt it was simply due to my excessive work and the opposition that I experience at Luton College in seeking to develop a training centre for satellite television reception.

Dear Dave,

As a membership secretary for NATFHE I am writing to you to suggest that you might consider joining the union.

At present education is under attack as a part of the public sector of the economy, and although it is true that as lecturers we have a special interest in being opposed to reductions in educational provision, we can make also a case against these particular reductions in expenditure on more altruistic and objective grounds.

However, although NATFHE is involved in a great many ways in attempting to be a positive influence in education, I would be misleading you if I did not say that our trade union functions were fundamental to our existence.

For the immediate future, these trade union functions are going to include defending jobs, the conditions under which we teach, and as a spin-off the quality of the courses that we offer. (Not to be under-estimated).

In any attempt to increase student staff ratios this is always at risk, even if not a certainty, that working conditions can degenerate and become a breach of the agreements made between the Local Educational Authority, (our real employer remember, not the college) and NATFHE. We must be prepared to resist such moves where possible. Our policy must be to preserve the quality of the courses and the work that we do. Naive and simplistic assumptions that raising SSR's equals more efficiency need serious questioning. It smacks of "never mind the quality feel the width". The way in which efficiency is defined requires questioning.

If compulsory redundancy is proposed for any member of NATFHE our policy is to defend that member of the union. Of course, if a none - NATFHE member of staff is threatened with redundancy, and then we cannot be enthusiastic about defending that person on a personal basis (unless it has repercussions for our own members). Indeed if there is any suggestion that a NATFHE member is to be compulsory redundant we would have to insist that the LEA's human sacrifice would have to be drawn from the list of non-NATFHE lecturers. Any union has to take the position of "hands off our members" - it is its job to do this.

But not only do you have to think of self-preservation but also of your colleagues' positions. Will you be able to oppose a bad policy when directed against other people and act in what you might consider a fair, reasonable way, simply by standing alone? That I leave to you.

For some staff the way in which the Union works is not totally understood and we intend in the near future to issue explanatory notes to make this clear to members. We know that communication could be improved.

I hope that you will now seriously consider joining our ranks and push the proportion of membership above the existing Photo of 91.5 % of full-time staff.

Yours fraternally

My reply to NATHFE Union 5/2/85 and was as follows

Dear Roy,

Re: NATFHE

Thank you for your letter in respect of me joining NATFHE. I can see and understand your points of concern. However I am not a member of the union because of a matter of principle.

I fear God and am a Christian. If I were a member I would, as a matter of conviction, be obliged to contend against all actions, which were opposed to Christ and morality. This is not my calling as a lecturer.

My protection, in respect to my work, is by the hand of the living God. I know also if my colleagues were that concerned they too might seek divine protection, through Christ Jesus, as I do my self. It is He that watches over me and if according to his command I loose my job, then who am I to resist the living God.

If you like I could speak on this subject to all the members at national local and national level. I would also be prepared to debate or answer criticism of those that feel the need to do so.

Yours Sincerely,

David Clarke.

I was quite surprised to receive further correspondence on the same subject and it made interesting reading:

Dear David,

5/3/85

Thank you for extending the courtesy of a reply to my note to you.

I understand the position you take in your letter. Of course, in the end, it has to be a matter of personal conviction which will decide the matter of union membership and for you this is a stronger factor than for others, what I do not wish to do is of course create a clash of loyalties and principles for any one with genuine misgivings. In the end it will have to be your decision, so anything that I write here is done knowing that fact.

Not knowing the exact religious sect to which you belong I am at some disadvantage in the question, which I would pose to you. They might not seem to be addressing themselves to the points, which to you are the most crucial.

However, I gather that you accept the notion of predestination by saying that if you lose your job this would be "according to His command"

Please explain to me why the act of joining a union might not be counted as being determined by the living God, for how can one event be regarded differently from another in this way?

This might be particularly relevant if the job loss results from a central Government policy inspired by Monetarism, a creed that the market of capital should dominate the lives of people. Did not Jesus have something to say about the money changers in the temple? Is it a negation of God's work to be opposing the evil of the destruction educational opportunity for people? Why is it that a struggle against powers that wish to make worse the lives of people is seen in some way as not carrying out God's work whereas the actions of those damaging education is seen to be an act of God?

Although as a child I was christened as a Congregationalist, I became one who rejected the idea of God because fearing God did not make sense. To do some thing because I feared the consequences of not seemed to be abandoning one's human responsibility. Imagine the mass- murderers of the Nazi Regime claiming that they were carrying out Gods work. Of course this is an extreme case I put but it raises the point in an extreme way that personal judgements needs to be exercised in some cases and the act of exercising that judgement might be fulfilling God's intention. Surely there can be an active interpretation of predetermination as well as a passive one?

Anyway, if you resolve to maintain your position then it is your decision. At least I felt that your letter deserved some reply,

Yours Sincerely,

Roy Bride.

PS One member of staff has decided to pay equivalent to the annual subscription to the Teacher's Benevolent Fund, instead of joining.

My reply to the Secretary of NATFHE

I felt it right to reply to Roy and give further answers to his questions, as clearly he was not saved and had by his own admission turned away from God. I felt it an Ideal opportunity to speak of God's sovereignty and love in Jesus Christ. Here is my reply:

Dear Roy

Re: Our correspondence in respect of NATFHE

Thank you for your letter of the 5th February.

I am most intrigued by your response and am pleased you have given the consideration you have to my views, even though I think you may think me a little naive.

Without wishing to be too personal or cause offence directly may I take the liberty to answer some of your points? It may possibly be the means of enlightenment, to you in respect of divine predestination and man's responsibility.

Yes, I do believe, absolutely, in divine predestation as you put it; if by that you mean the end of all things is determined, therefore the means to that end are also determined. I would confess to believing the scripture, which states that God has determined all things, and all things come to pass according to His predetermined purpose. That our being made, or created, is for God's own glory and pleasure. Acts 2. Verse 23. And Rev. 4 verse 11.

That God has chosen some of the human race to obtain salvation by faith in Jesus Christ and left others to answer divine justice for their sins. Eph. 1 verse 4-5 and Jude 1 verse 4 and Rom. 9 verse 14-20.

In all this the glory of God is great, for we have a display of the everlasting love of God the Father, Son and Holy Ghost. A love, which is unchangeable and sovereign in its bestowment, God loving some and not all (contrary to popular belief) Rom. 9 verse 13-16. The reason for this love has nothing to do with what is found in the sinner, for this choice is without respect to actions done or capable of being done. In fact the choice was before the foundation of the world. Peter 1 verse 2 and Eph. 1 verse 4.

If it were based upon merit none could be saved, therefore it is a choice through grace alone not based upon works. Thus salvation is received by faith and not through or deeds of merit. Rom. 4 verse 16.

With respect to the chosen all things work together for their good. That industrial strife, famine, unemployment, sickness, death, in fact all evil work together for their eternal good. That these things are sent of God to us that we will learn not to rest in our selves but rather cause us to seek our all in him and depend entirely upon that which he has promised us in his own divine word. Rom. 8 verse 35.

In respect to our responsibilities: I agree with you we are responsible to do those things, which are right and sensible for our own preservation. If needs be we oppose evils and fight for those things, which are right and proper, not only for our selves but for the coming generation, but all in the bounds of "If possible live at peace with all men".

I do not however by this mean we should be stupid and allow all (as you rightly refer to the point of the Nazi oppression) to vanquish all that is opposed their Idealism. In fact any such system, whether it be communism, socialism, capitalism or any other 'ism should be resisted if it adopts those flaws common to corrupted human nature. I therefore say to you, since you appeal to scripture as a basis to oppose Monetarism and claim educational opportunity, that this is a work of God. Then use the whole of scripture to govern all your policies and by this means I might be inclined to help.

I would suggest the following and give this to you to consider:

1) Never engage in a fight unless it is a righteous cause. (God is on the side of the righteous)

2) That the battle be one you think you can win. (In which case God might be sought in prayer and divine aid is asked for).

3) Consider whether God has called you to fight the battle. (In which case there will be principles taught clearly in the scripture).

4) Consider whether the men you fight with are reliable and moved by the same principles and convictions (a divided army or kingdom is not likely to win any battle).

5) Fight with all your might for the righteous will hold on His way.

I am fully aware of the Nazi Regime and also the connection with the Roman Catholic Church. Also that the basis of the Third Reich was upon Jesuitical principles (See the secret History of the Jesuits, Edmund Paris) Not only so but Hitler and Mussolini were both sons of the Catholic Church and so the scripture is fulfilled in that the blood of prophets and of the saints and all the slain upon the earth was found in her (the Roman Catholic Church). Rev 17-18 verse 24.

My question to you is do you think your contention with monetarism is a holy war?

I believe a holy war is directed against any that oppose Christ and His Church - not one 'ism against Monetarism as you call it. I tell you if I believed this policy of Government were opposed to Christ in this matter of educational cuts then according to my five-point plan I would engage in the battle. That if I found none with me I would fight alone, just like David who fought Goliath, and like Samson who slew a 1000 men with the jaw bone of an ass. But I would not fight with or join hands with Apostates, atheists, unbelievers or heretics, for these would be in the way and could not wield the weapons of truth.

You suggest that it might it be according to the will and purpose of God to join the union to fulfil his purpose. To which I answer he would direct me to do so and I would know that calling in the same way I know my name is written in the Lamb's book of life that I am saved, my sins being forgiven me and I have divine protection. This knowledge I would derive from the scriptures of truth as I employ my reason to biblical principles and walk according to the faith, once delivered unto the saints.

Re. Your tentative inquiry to what sect of Christendom I belong - maybe you might review your knowledge of these sects and find a place for me, I would certainly be interested to see into which group I am pigeon holed.

Yours very Sincerely,
David Clarke

14 02 1985.

Recollection And Union Views Now

It is only now as I write this account, when I look back on these things, that I am beginning to learn some of the lessons I had believed in my head but not proved by actual experience of knowing God in the very depths of ones souls agony.

I now believe the NATHFE union are a valuable functioning body and I have no problem in supporting and being a member of such a union. This is because they have thrashed out with Management their rules of conduct, which, if employed, can result in very fair dealings with members. I think

Union services should be offered free to no- members. This I think would enlist more members.

Second Bout Of Depression

It was shortly after this that my agony began and I really began to fell the effects of my depression. I never did get work in Shropshire and it never happened. I had attended three interviews, at three colleges, but failed to get any of the jobs - I wondered what God was doing. That year I missed out on my first promotion at work because they understood I was intending to move away. This knowledge all added to the aggravation I later began to feel.

During this time I experienced awful agonies of fear and doubts etc.. I began to believe I was like King Saul in the Old Testament, and the Lord had rejected me. I began to think that all my experience of God was of the flesh and not of God. I felt what I thought an Apostate would feel and that just added to my agony. I felt alone, isolated and very depressed. Depression set in and Steven Royce began to call me Mephibosheth, as he was a son of king Saul, who had gone to live at Lo-debar. (When I look back that was a very good description of my situation and position). I had never heard of the term manic depression, or bipolar mood swings, but on reflection and after being clinically diagnosed with manic depression I realised this experience was part and parcel of my mental condition at that time.

My wife also became very depressed and suffered all kinds of agonies. On a number of occasions she would ring me at work crying about the difficulties she faced. Isaac was being bullied severely and she couldn't cope. She felt hostility from some in the church and did not know how to manage. It all became too much.

I stayed at the Royce's for a period of 18 months during the week, whilst I worked at Luton College and travelled home to Shropshire at the weekend. I hated the journey and very often on the way back to work on a Monday morning I would have to stop and seek God for strength to continue. I was feeling so ill through depression. I began to feel that I had been cast away by God and was in the similar position as King Saul, in the Old Testament, having begun well but was later rejected by God. I felt as I thought an Apostate would feel, which in turn cast me down even further. I wanted to die.

31 WE MOVE TO LUTON

During the time at Shropshire I tried to assess where had all my contending come too, and began to question many things. I was far from happy. And I felt forsaken by God.

It was then I decided to put family and myself first and move back to Luton where I had work. I felt in my soul I would answer to God for my decision as I felt I was going against what I believed He taught in the scripture that was to seek first the kingdom of God and His righteousness and then all these things will be added unto me. I thought we should put church membership first then family. From here I would try and sort out church after we were living together as a family. I had always believed we should put the things of God first and God will look after you.

I hated living like I was away from my home and family. When we were at Bierton I had always been able to read and pray each day, as the head of my family before they went to school but now we were fragmented. I hated it. I felt I should be with my family and not living like we were.

The prices of houses in the South were rising rapidly whilst those in Shropshire and in Snailbeach, where we lived were hardly moving at all. To give you some idea we had sold our house in Bierton for £92,000 in December 1995. This was a lovely 4 bedroom detached chalet bungalow with double gates and half moon drive way. We owned this house apart from a £24,000 mortgage.

We were able to purchase a three bedroom detached bungalow in Snailbeach for £37,000, which we purchased out right with no mortgage.

When we came to sell it and move back to Luton in 1988 it was sold for £41,000. This value had risen by £4000. At that time we bought Graham Gardens for £78,000 and had to raise £42,000 by way of mortgage. This was only a small 3 bedroom detached house however the awful thing to us was our old house in Bierton was up for sale for £199,000. These house prices had risen so much due to inflation we had to buy a house way down on valuation the list. Had we stayed at Bierton we would have owned a house worth nearly £200,000 or alternatively moved from Bierton to Luton we could have owned the Luton house with no mortgage. Instead we were in an inferior house worth only £78,000 but with a mortgage of £42,000.

Both my wife and I found this difficult to swallow and I felt robbed. This was to be a hurt to me for many years.

Whilst at Luton I began to recover but was still unhappy about the church situation.

I did not fell ready to re enter the Gospel Standard cultural set up due to the awful problems I had encountered whilst at Bierton. At the same time I was not free to get involved in churches which where not Calvinistic due to my experience in the Pentecostal Holiness Church. So we found our selves un-churched again. However I began to feel a lot better coming out of sever depression and I began to enjoy the simple things in life again and I could smile once more.

Discipline A Problem Teaching At Luton College

During all this time I still held on to my job and taught at Luton College. Discipline however was not my strong point. How to keep control of a class of 24 teenage students from various ethnic backgrounds was not an easy task. I adopted my own methods, one might say a manic method.

When I was training to be a teacher at the Wolverhampton Polytechnic one teacher, taking the subject of discipline in the classroom told us only of one method. This was my course in classroom management.

This lecturer had to teach a class of craft students and wanted to assert his authority before they got out of hand. Craft students are noted generally to be awkward to manage. He decided this would make sure he would have no problems with them later on in the course.

During the class when he was teaching technical drawing, he asked one of the students to go out to the building sight and bring to him a large plank of wood. When the student returned with the wood the lecturer took it from him and with one mighty karate chop, broke the wooden plank in two. He then proceeded to use the plank of wood as a ruler on the chalkboard just as though nothing had happened. He did not say a word to the students. The students stood back in amazement at this show of strength and took it as a warning. This was the lecturer method of saying to the class don't mess with me or you will get what this plank of wood got.

I found this story amusing and from this I was supposed to learn all about class management. With this limited knowledge I took it that you had to find your own method of discipline in the classroom so decided to have some fun.

One of the problems I initially found was enforcing the college rules. One rule was no eating of drinking food in the classrooms. How do you stop it? Sweet papers were evident, empty drink cans evident, so it went on whether they were allowed to or not. Even when they were told they still broke the rules.

I decided I would sort this problem my way. I thought if you couldn't beat them then join them. So I made it a rule that if I found them eating sweets or food in the class I would make them share them and help I would my self to their food. I proceeded to do so. It soon got around that I was taking their food. Whether this stopped the eating problem I do not know but on this one occasion the student got one over on me.

I saw at the back of the class two students messing about under the desk and their mouths were in operation. I stopped teaching and went to the back of the classroom and sure enough a lovely fat juicy Mars bar was in Chavda's hand. I had caught them red handed. I said come on you know the rules give it to me. Not without their protest I took it from him and looked forward to

211

a big bite. As I consumed this mouth of Mars bar the rest of the class burst in to laughter- they all knew- I didn't. I discovered pieces of white tablets mixed in with the chocolate. They had laced the Mars bar with laxative tablets and got their own back one me.

They were totally amused and from that time I had no real trouble.

On another occasion I had some trouble with Chavda again and could not stop him from causing a disturbance in the class. I must have ruffled his feathers as on this occasion he threatened to sort me out. He was and Asian about 17 years old and I must have been about 30 years old with out much experience in dealing with this type of situation. In my determination to sort this problem out I challenged him to do it in the boxing ring, thinking this would put as stop to it all. How ever the class took up this suggestion and he too went along with the idea- Yes- OK. How.

Oh dear I thought to my self-how am I going to get out of this one. I said they must go to the college Gym in the lunch hour and ask if we can use the boxing ring for half and hour. This sorted the problem out and we all got back to work. They must have been looking forward in anticipation to this fight out.

Sure enough off they went to the Gym during the break and shortly afterwards I got a telephone call from the women Gym lecturer asking me what was going on. She said they were not really allowed to do it. I seized on this and said good, please tell them that and that will get me off the hook.

They came back after break feeling let down as they were all looking forward to this boxing match. However there was no Chavda, nor was he there the next day. I was told that he had got wind of the fact that I was a welterweight boxing champion and was looking forward to sorting him out. This again landed me on my feet.

Muslims Want to Convert Me

During my time Luton College of Higher Education I taught classes with a lot of Muslims and other religions.

It was easy to speak to Muslim students about the things of God and they insisted they were right and God could not possibly have a son. From time to time I would visit their homes and meet their parents and they soon respected me.

I had gone through many trials and difficulties and believed I should speak to these Muslims about Jesus and what he came to do.

I could talk to them about the Omnipotent God, the Omnipresence of God and Omniscience of God and they began to think I would soon become a Muslim.

I was invited to there young persons meeting on a Friday evening so I took with me a Muslim missionary who had been looking for an opening to meet the Luton Muslim community. We had a reasonable time just talking and listening.

Word got around that I was interested in the Muslim religion and the student president of the Muslim community came to se me one lunch hour for a meeting.

I fact some of the students nick named me God and had rang in to the local radio station, Chiltern Radio in January 1988 to say they had named me God. See my reply.

There must have been about 10 or so keen Muslim students together with their president and I was speaking to them as best I could about the Lord Jesus.

I suggested I pray for them and with them. They said this has never happened before and that they pray different to Christians. They said they pray on the floor so I suggested we should do the same.

One of the students in his respect for me took of his jacket and placed it on the floor for me to kneel on and as I kneeled down they all kneeled down behind me as I lead them in prayer.

I prayed to the effect after thanks giving my God and Father would open the eyes to the truth to what I had spoken to them about.

Afterwards I was informed this had never happened before they had never prayed or had a Christian pray for them.

I did not see any results from that time but they held me with respect and were always curious to me.

I had met a Muslim missionary called Paul? At the time connected with Spicer Street Independent Church in St Albans and asked him to come with me to their Friday night religious instruction classes. This we did and spoke to them about the Lord Jesus Christ. I learned the address of greeting with the Muslim and it was A Salem Ali com (Hello) and the reply was walli com Salem (Good bye).

Entrepreneurial Enterprise

Coming out of Depression

I found it a great relief to be living near I worked. I had been living in a shared bedroom, at the Royce's home fare away from my family and in my car for over 18 months. I was good to be able to come home from work at lunchtime and return at leisure. I began to get well and be more involved in my work.

It was the year of the launch of the Astra Satellite and soon got involved in preparing training courses for satellite installation technicians.

At the same time we had difficulties with Isaac at school and eventually we had him accessed by an Educational Psychologist as he had Specific Learning Difficulties, which was called Dyslexia. The Bedfordshire County Council denied the word and would not accept Dyslexia as a reality. In the end we went to a leading Education Psychologist, Bev Hornsby in London to assess Isaac and this did the trick and got Isaac recognised as having learning difficulties. This was sufficient to get some him help at school.

I too had always had problems in reading, writing and spelling. I could understand concepts and problem solving was no problem to me but the ability communicate with the written word was virtually impossible for me. How I got though teacher training college I do not know. I often thought they must have been hard up for students at the time. I can how ever remember the Head of Technical Studies calling me to his office saying he was worried about my written work. He arranged for me to have remedial help. I went to one of two sessions but it I found it was not helpful at all. It was so boring and they had no Idea how to help me. It was only when I became a Christian that my desire to learn more and more about the things of God and what Jesus had done that I was compelled to learn to read and understand words. This leaning had helped me write essays to gain entrance into the Technical Teacher Training School at Wolverhampton. So in reality I taught my self and then I taught myself to type. With these skills came the revolution and a disgruntled wife.

The Apple Mac Computer

When I threw myself into my work at Luton College, after coming back from Shropshire, I purchase an Apple Mac computer. It was a Mac Plus with 1 Meg of RAM, multi tasking, (only 340 KB of Ram needed for WORD 4), 45 Mbytes of Hard disk and a dot matrix 24 pin printer. It knocked spots of any other computer available at the time. It was the best thing to me since the printing press in the 15 century. At Luton College we had installed PC's, which were slow inelegant beast's probably 8080 series (just before the 286) and only able to do single tasks. My Mac Plus became my friend and helper. My wife complained that I had spent the money we had set aside for her new kitchen, on my new Cyber (Pet). It was a wonderful helper to me so you might call it my cyber woman. No wonder my real wife complained.

This enabled me to write letters, memos, and technical notes and print them all straight away. I was able to communicate with the educational and business world. My ideas of developing a training school for Satellite Television was only able to work because of the use of the Apple Mac computer and printer. It freed me to communicate my ideas with the written word in a simple and uncomplicated way. I am sure I am dyslexic but I have never had a statement. We discovered later that my wife and Esther and

David were all diagnosed as Dyslexic and were given statements. Dyslexia is really regardless of what the authorities say s. David still receives help with his learning difficulties. He has exactly the same problem as I did.

My wife later received an educational award due to her Dyslexia when she started her degree course. She bought an Apple Mac PowerBook 170, which was beautiful and I would have loved it. This computer was portable and this enabled her to do all her written work, which other wise she would not be able to do. She graduated 3 years later with and upper Second in her Degree in Cultural Studies at Portsmouth University.

As you can see I am an Apple Mac fan and not a PC fanatic.

Entrepreneurial Venture Satellite Television

Soon how ever I had a run in with the management at Luton College. I had what I thought a good idea to make money for the college. At that time the Astra Satellite was about to be launched and Alan Sugar had announced he had intended manufacturing 3 Million satellite receivers that coming year all of which would have to be installed. I had been to a conference in London and met a satellite installation technician called Steve Holmes and I talked with him working with me at Luton College teaching about satellite systems. I wrote to the CAI (Confederation of Aerial Industries) suggesting the Educational Standards and Industrial technology come together in a joint venture to train satellite installation technicians and award a City and Guilds, or similar award from the start. At that time very few people had installed a satellite dish or receiver.

I spoke to my immediate boss, Derrick Curran but my idea did not register or he did not see that my idea was any good. I was not prepared to be put off so in the summer holiday of that year I asked to see the Director of our College a Dr Wood. I then explained my idea saying that our Centre for Applied Technology and Innovation (CATI) at Putteridgbury was in ideal venue to set up a training school to train technicians how to install satellite TV systems. I put it to the management that we together with the CAI, City & Guilds and the industry could earn money by charging reasonable fees for students. He thought it a good idea. I explained I was due to go to a meeting with the CAI in London in the next few days and he said he would direct my Head of School, Derrick Curran to go with me. I had recorded our meeting with my portable tape recorder so it was clear to me I had the backing of the Director of the College.

The meeting went well, Derrick was late but the CIA was sufficiently impressed with my idea of education and industry coming together to ensure quality and set standards. I invited them to come to Luton to discuss these things further. My head of school was sufficiently impressed to give me the go ahead and make all necessary arrangements.

I was able to contact many people in industry, inviting them to our meeting at Cati Luton. The purpose of the meeting was to show the technical facilities of the Engineering Faculty, to the CAI and other interested parties, so that a joint venture may be pursued with those concerned. Also to show the Cati conference rooms so that marketing and educational directors may consider using our centre for future operations.

Assuming a favourable outcome we shall form a working party of technical personnel to determine future course needs and make the appropriate arrangements to start training immediately.

The Satellite Television Venture

The Meeting on 7th September 1988
David centre by the Satellite dish

The following were in attendance at the meeting And many more.

CAI	Mr John Knight	CIA Executive
Sky Channel	Mike Aarons	Network Manager
City and Guilds	Mr Snell	Executive Representative
SAT TEL	Richard Stallworthy	Managing Director
Master Care	Jeff Belington	Commercial Director
Solara UK	John Breed,	Satellite Production Manager
Saturn Com	Andrew Demetrious	Managing Director
BSB	Bert Hurlock	Project Manager
	David Blackshaw	
	David Ayres	
	Keith Payne	

Granada TV	Roy Ward	Technical Services Manager
SES ASTRA	Pam Taylor	Manager
Open University	Prof. H Gower	Assistant Vice Chancellor
	John Martin	
Premier	Mike Tonnes	
	Ian Welders	
Amstrad	Alan Sugar	Managing Director
Grundig	Tom Carney	Managing Director
Racal	Bert Ferguson	Managing Director
Micro X	Chris Lack	Sales Director
Matthew Aerials	Steve Holmes	Director of Satellite Installations and LCHE Advisor
Mega sat		Managing Director
MSC Industrial	Mrs L Kelly	Administrator

Most of these people came to the meeting except Alan Sugar. I thought he might have arrived in his helicopter.

I even thought of inviting Arthur C Clarke but he would have had to travel from Sri Lanka.

I gave the address to this meeting, sharing the plan and ideas. I was introduced by our Vice Principle, (who himself was called Dr Clarke), as the Director of Satellite Communications - an impressive title, which suited me down to the ground.

The meeting went down well and things looked extremely good.

It was after this meeting that the problems began as a certain woman called Fiona Howorth took on the management of the training venture. She could not be depended upon as she changed her mind and ideas without any reference to me. She was the manager of a department within Luton College of Higher Education, - the Centre for Applied Technology and

Innovation called Cati. She generally cut across what I had arranged and I felt extremely frustrated with working or trying to work with her. I had thus far single-handed got the venture off the ground from nothing. I had got all the interested industries together and I was set to go. How ever this was not to be. The management wanted to take control, away from me.

A Problem

After several confrontations with Fiona Howorth and the management they decided to reduce my powers and make myself just responsible for the equipping of the workshop area and writing a textbook. I was told not to contact any out side organisations. They had decided to take over this venture as they planned to charge £100 per head per student. The CAI had indicated they might have 2000 persons wishing to be trained. I remembered how it was the women at the Bierton Strict and Particular Baptist Church, which had been the problem there, and here now, was another woman taking charge of my venture and I resented it.

I was angry at their decision because I knew they could not make things work, the way things were at College. They needed entrepreneurial skills and management to deal with industry. They did not have what it took to make it work. It was then that I wrote to the Director saying I had sacked Fiona Howorth and Derrick Curran and would sort things out my way. I had worked so hard to secure many thousands of pounds worth of sponsored equipment and had the support of the industry. It seemed a shame for me to stand by and see it fail, due to middle management incompetence.

I believed I had, at the time, the Directors backing for what I was doing and thought if he knew what was going on amongst the middle management he would not approve of them. I believed once he found out what was going on a few heads would role. I had the original audio recording of our first meeting when he gave me the permissions to do what I must to achieve our objectives, so I informed the management that I had this recording, which actually gave my commission to do what I was doing, and that I had the Directors approval.

My state of mind and manic activity

At this time I was feeling very happy and had many fluent ideas and was able to talk about them, virtually none stop. My senses were heightened and I appreciated colours, beauty and music. My libido was high and on one occasion, when rushing to London on the train, I was virtually stopped in my tracks to admire the beauty of a woman traveller.

A Take Over and I am Paid to Resign

The management at Luton College wondered what had happened to me and they no longer listened to me. They had decided they did not want me working for them and wanted to take over the work I had begun. The College management asked the NATFHE union to be involved but I was not a member so this was a difficulty for them because they did not want to deal with me directly. As a result I was suspended from work and the management asked the Chairman of the Union, Mr Tom May, to act for me and with them. He acted in the interest of the Union and he informed me it was in the interest of the union to do so. It was in the Colleges interest to pay me £6000 in lieu of notice, to leave my lecturing post. I did not really wish to leave but rather than risk being unfairly sacked I agreed to take the money and leave, provided I could have a good reference. I realised the Management could not handle the situation and it was in my best interest to leave. This was early 1988.

I was told by the Director to destroy the tape recording of our original meeting, which contained the proof that I had his approval for the venture that had I developed.

32 MANIC DEPRESSION OR BIPOLAR DISORDER

During this time, in fact the week I was suspended from work, I went to see my doctor and was signed off sick due to not being able to sleep and my hyper - activity when working on the satellite-training venture. It was then suggested that I had a bipolar mood disorder and was in a hypomanic state. A psychiatrist, at the Luton and Dunstable Hospital, later confirmed this diagnosis. My doctor prescribed some medication to bring me down from my high mood. This was Haloperidol, a typical antipsychotic drug, and also Priodel, with the active ingredient lithium. My mind had been filled with many ideas seeking to develop the training school for the satellite industry.

At the same time I realised that Michael, my brother, had very similar patterns of behaviour and I realised he too suffered from this kind of mood disorder except in his case he had no medical treatment. I recall speaking to his wife on the telephone. They just had separated and were going through a divorce. I related to her about my condition and that it was identical to Michael's and could be the reason for his current behaviour. I then realised he too was suffering from manic depression and this accounted for his mood swings in the past.

The effects of the medication that I had taken did not take place for a few weeks or so but when it did, it all happened on one day. I had been suspended from work due to my manic behaviour but I was not prepared to be put down, so I intended to continue my work from home. I had gained a lot of support from the satellite TV industry and secured over £30,000 worth of equipment, all for the training venture at Luton College. However being suspended from work left me high and dry, so to speak.

Having decided to go it alone, I advertised my own training program in the local newspaper and taught future satellite installers how to install satellite equipment from my home, at Graham Gardens, Luton. The man next door got a bit upset because I had 5 satellite dishes in the garden and he said it looked like a Radio Transmitting Station. We had a little write-up in the local newspaper about this training venture.

Third Bout of Depression

It was on one of these training days that this medication I had been taking took effect. I felt a wave of depression come over me, half way through the day, just like the first wave of depression I experience on the garage roof at Mount Street in 1975. I was teaching a group of students when it hit me. This depression was to last for a further 3 years. I became so bad I had to rely on further medication. I could hardly leave the house through the agony I was facing. I was struggling with the things of God and did not know how to handle the problems that I was beginning to face. I wondered why in the providence of God this had all happened and reasoned that I had given my self over to too much work, to the neglect of the things of God. I rejected the notion that I was suffering from manic depression as I thought it was simply due to excessive work and the opposition that I had experienced at Luton College.

Symptoms of Manic Depression

or a Bipolar mood disorder

What is often recognised and described as manic behaviour is seen when a person begins to have unusual ideas that seem brilliant and they are able to talk about them, expressing their thoughts with very rapid speech. They talk 10 to the dozen so to speak.

Accompanying this is the inability to sleep for any length of time. They wake early, with fluid ideas wishing to get on with the day. They find they have more strength than usual and are very active, hence the term used about children being hyperactive. They can go from one job or activity to another leaving neither finished. They will find no job too great and are prepared to take on enormous tasks.

When in the manic phase, or hypo state, a person can become very short tempered and impatient with others, as they wish others would keep up with them. At one time my wife sought to control me and she refused to stop ' having a go' at me. In response I held her up against the wall with my hands around her neck seeking to stop her from going on at me. I stopped when she slid down to the floor, as she could no longer breath.

Such people are impatient in conversation; often not allowing another to complete their sentences, as they wish to answer any objection or another persons idea before they have expressed it, as they think they know best. They believe themselves to be right and often argue their case till others either reject them or accept them.

There is an increase in libido, along with an increase in the body senses. Sight seams to be clearer, both natural and insight. The ability to appreciate art, music, poetry and spirituality, increases. There can be a desire to dance and sing and a delusion they are great singers and/or performers. It is as though the human senses touch, taste smell, hearing and sight are synchronized, enabling rapid communication between that person and the outside world that allows them to sympathise or react to historic events.

In short they feel on top of the world as if nothing could go wrong and they may well believe the world was made just for them.

In my case I experience all of these things along with the belief that I have a personal relationship with God, that Jesus Christ was my Saviour, and that all things, the good and the bad, would work together for my good.

However It is the low side that generally leads the suffer to seek help. In my previous lows I felt God had forsaken me and that I had become a castaway because of some negligence or sin in the past. Such fears and thoughts are unbearable and are really destructive. Once in that state there seems to be no way out, just as though one has been thrown down a pit hundreds of feet deep. There is no way out. I knew that William Cowper, of the 18C, the famous hymn writer who wrote hymns such as, "There is a fountain filled with blood" and "God moves in a mysterious way", suffered from melancholy which left him in total despair. I could fully enter into and feel the sense of his poetry and hymns. He suffered from manic depression.

I have since learned that many well known people suffer from Manic Depression.

List Of People With Bipolar Disorders:
Frank Bruno,
Russell Brand,
Kurt Cobain,
Ray Davies,
Stephen Fry
Paul Gascoigne,
Spike Milligan
Florence Nightingale,
Jean-Claude Van Damme,
Vincent Van Gogh,
Ruby Wax,
Catherine Zeta-Jones

All such experiences and more are to be related as my story unfolds and I hope they will be of help to any reader who has the same experiences or knows some one who may be suffering from manic depression.

I Work at Fareham College

At this time I applied for a job at Fareham College and was offered a place. I took up the position in September 1988 and I believed this was God's provision.

The Principal at that time was Mr John MacNab and the Vice Principal was Derek Feber, with Pam Robertson as the Bursar. I discovered later that Derek Feber was a Christian and helped with the Christian Union at the College.

It was a very fair interview and I believe the College selection process was very good in that it was truly an "Open Opportunities College". My record from Luton College was either acknowledged to be good or ignored or kept secret. Mike Pease, Head of Division, and Geoff Whitefield, Principal Lecturer, selected me for the post at Fareham College, on the strength of my own presentation.

A record was later made in my personal file of my former stay in Borstal, and conviction of possessing a firearm without a license at the age of 18 years.

I was very please to get the job but this meant another move and involved the difficulty in selling our house. I had to move into lodgings in Fareham. This was another Snailbeach situation, living in lodgings and travelling home at weekends. I missed being a father to my kids and living in my own home. This lasted for a further 18 months until we finally sold our house in Graham Gardens. During this time I was under a cloud of depression even though it was controlled through Lithium (Priodel). I was also, on reflection, experiencing the other symptoms, which accompany manic or bipolar depression.

Before I left to work at Fareham College, we were walking one day in the countryside on the Dunstable Down, and I saw for the first time in years, an erotic magazine that had been left by the wayside. My normal practice would be to turn away and not look at such a magazine but on this occasion I was tempted to look. The effect of these pictures were so great that I could not get them out of my mind and they followed me and were retained as erotic images for years to come. I did not resist this temptation and proved to be my downfall at a later date.

My wife had decided she would like to return to full time education and she took up the offer of a place on a degree course in Cultural Studies, at Portsmouth University. She had previously studied on an Access Course at

Barnfield College in Luton, when I was working at Fareham.

It took us 18 months to sell our house in Luton during which time we were living apart as a family yet again. I felt alone and still suffering from depression even with the medication.

We were eventually able to sell our house in Luton just before my wife began her first year on the degree course at Portsmouth University. We were able then to move into rented accommodation at 8 Queens Grove, Southsea and the children went to St. Jude's junior school, in old Portsmouth.

My Doubts About God

At this time I began to shut my ear to the Word of God and I allowed temptation to enter my thoughts. We been attending St. Judes Church in Southsea and I felt that I was as Steven Royce had called me, like Mephibosheth - crippled and living in Lo debar. Mephibosheth was a crippled and had been driven out from his rightful place in his father's kingdom (King Saul) and was living in a place called Lo-debar, a place of dry land and no pastures.

I began to entertain various sinful thoughts and then actions. I found greater arguments and reasons to explain away Gods dealings with me in the past. It could not be denied I had really believed in God and experienced many remarkably deliverances and provisions from God, but now the subtlety was in the form of such thoughts as these:

"How do I know that it is God working and not just the product of misguided interpretation of events? I.e.. Yes, you believed God worked for you and yes your life had been radically change by that belief or faith but surely all you believed could have been just not true - granted it would have effected your life just as it effects other peoples - but believing in something does not actually make it true. You have believed in something just like others and what you believed is not true". That was the argument and I began to accept it. (Reader - this is a lie from Satan, don't you believe it also)).

Reader, as you read this I want you to know that as Peter was astonished and all that were with him at the draught of fishes that they had caught when they fished at Jesus' command, I believe I have written this account at the command of Jesus, and we too will be astonished at the many fishes caught through this testimony of the loving kindness and faithfulness of God to me.

Although I did fall away from God I now recall what Jesus had said to me on the night of my salvation on the 16th January 1970. Jesus said, "David I will never leave you". And so it will become clear that He does restore and seek the lost and the prodigal sons.

Soon we were attending Titchfield church, but I still felt like the cripple in the New Testament lying beside the water pool at Bethesda. I wanted to be healed but had no one to put me in the pool. I took my family to church but it was more out of routine than any thing else and I was in a barren spiritual state.

I had needs but was turning from God at Titchfield church. Then I met my wife to be.

Moving to Fareham I Turn From God

Once we moved to Fareham I continued to listen to the arguments put forward by my wife when she was studying for her University Degree at Portsmouth University. This was a degree in Cultural Studies. She shared with me the current views from sociology, psychology and philosophy about the none - existence of God. The whole of such higher education worked from the presupposition, "God does not exist". This really was what they now called Post Modernism.

I heard about the philosophers such as Kant, Hegel, and Kierkegaard and learned about Existentialism. In essence I got the picture that were no absolutes at all. No God. No rights or wrongs. Nothing. Morality was changeable, and depending upon society. This suited me and helped me to turn my back on the Word of God. In this temptation I did not do as Job, a character in the Bible. I sinned and turned from God. This was my foolishness.

My Visit to Soho London

At this time I had occasion to visit London going to the Macintosh exhibition and on my way home I decided to re-visit Soho. I remembered my visit there when I was 13 or 14 years old. In one of the streets was a strip show being advertised with an entry fee of about £2.00. It was a con but I did not realise it at the time. I was dressed in a dark navy blue suit I paid my £2.00 and sat at a table awaiting for the show to begin. There was no one else there except a girly waitress who came to me and asked if I would like a drink. I agreed to a drink and it was presented to me on a tray with a bill. As I waited for the show to begin I looked at the bill and it was for £20. When I called the waitress to challenge the bill she said there would be no show until I paid the bill. I was not prepared to pay such a bill and sat there. I was than approached by another girl who said If I did not pay the bill I would not be allowed to leave and they would contact my wife and informed her where I was. This was not a threat to me so I simply sat there for 15 minutes or so, until finally I just got up and left. So you see it is very easy to get into hot water when dealing with shady business.

My Wife Questions The Reality Of God

My wife also began to question the reality of God and turn from the ways she once believed true. She entertained different thoughts and we both got involved in things, which were not of God.

I now believe that my sinful heart wanted to be free from God's rule so that I could be independent and do as I pleased. I think I must have thought, " If this is what is now believed by the highly educated and the philosophers of the day, then I am a perfect student of this new age so I will put it into practice" - and that is what I did. (I now deplore it - it is not education, but a lie). I took these views on board and began to argue the none - existence of God, being intent now to do my own things.

I argued since God does not exist there is no absolute right or wrong. All is relative. I in fact decided what was right or wrong for me. I actually became my own god.

I now believe God gave me up to my own sinful heart and left me to myself to practice sin. I did not know at that time what was in store for me. I was given over to indulge in sexual talk and activity outside marriage. I went off the rails and got into things I now feel ashamed to speak about. Those that knew me at that time will know all about it. I was wrong and out of order. Again, on reflection, I was displaying the many symptoms, which accompany a Bipolar mood disorder.

33 THE ROAD DIVIDES

Here I tell of my brother Michael's life and eventual imprisonment in the Philippines serving a 16 year sentence.

Michael Goes His Own Way

As mentioned already after the Bierton meeting, on the 5th June 1983, Michael did not really take what I had told the congregation very seriously. Never the less he continued his own life and began to prosper in business ignoring the things of God. His life had been unaffected. He becoming the Director of his own company **Tudor Charm Produces** and **Penny Wise**. But life's difficulties hit him, which led to him experiencing depression, divorce and the loose of all his money. It was this experience that led him to explore another adventure and start his life over again.

Paradise Movies

It was then [1991/2], Michael started his own company making movies, in Thailand, called "Paradise Movies" and he involved our Mum and Dad, who lived in Eastbourne, to sort all his finances out whilst he was away. He also took Jessica, his 10-year-old daughter, with him for the summer, which cause her mum great alarm when he did not bring her back to England. He said at the time that he wanted to get back at his ex - wife because of all the grief she had given him in the past.

In the end Michael's business in Thailand went wrong. His equipment was stolen and he ran out of money. We don't really know what he got into while in Thailand but Mum was so fed up with bailing him out with money and favours that she finally said she had enough of him as he was making her ill. We later got news of some of his activity through a News of The World Article, I learned later, from Michael, that this story was a complete fabrication.

Michael In Thailand

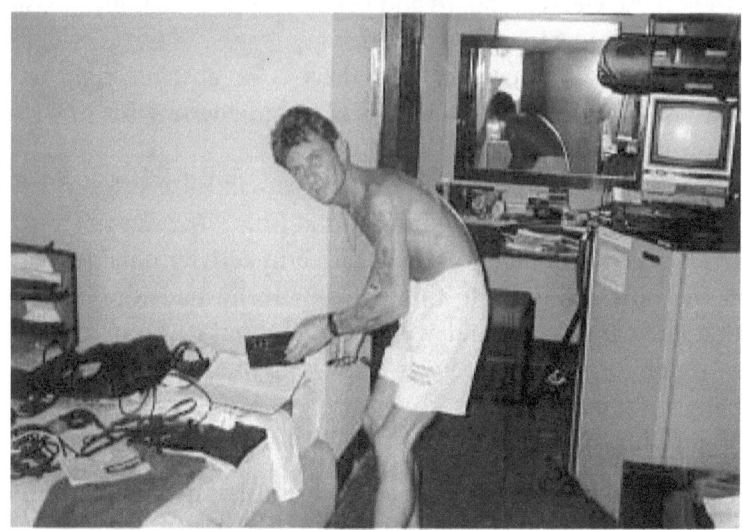

Michael and his Equipment

Paradise Movies

Paradise Express

News Of The World Article
January 19th, 1992
EXCLUSIVE by MARK CHRISTY

Michael The Pirate   **Michael The Policeman**

Sailors beware! A new nautical menace has appeared on the horizon - a con man Michael Clarke has set up a scam to keep himself supplied with booze and birds on a paradise beach.

He has ripped off scores of unsuspecting British yachting folk by offering them jobs in an epic sailing movie he claims is being made in Thailand.

Clarke's ad in Yachting Monthly magazine promises free return airfares and £40 a day for a five-day week. All he wants is a £55 insurance fee from applicants.

But there is No film and punters NEVER hear from him again.

Former Watford market trader Clarke reckons four square rigged sailing ships are going to be used in the movie 'Invasion of Thailand', set 200 years ago.

He calls himself Peter Timberlake and operates his con from the "Paradise Suite" in the Thai City of Patiya.

But his "Office Suite" is a seat in one of Patiya's hundreds of girlie bars. And his firm "Paradise Movies" Inc. Does not exist - though he does have a home movie video camera in a local pawnshop.

The slogan of "Paradise Movies" is "A cut above the rest". And when the News of the World found Clarke he was half-cut above the rest.

An investigator confronted him at Jan's Bar. "Yes I am Paradise Movies", he slurred. "But I've been up boozing all night and need to think before I speak to you."

Then he vanished and our man found him at The Jasmine, on Patiya's beach, - a bar offering girls for sex. He was working for £2 per night touting for customers.

Asked if he intended to return the cash he had defrauded, he replied, " I can't even afford the price of a beer".

Thai Police and Immigration officials are now looking into the fraud.

One British yachtsman who fell for the con is architect Fred Howell of Christchurch, Dorset.

He sent off his £55 after seeing Clarke's ad in November, and even rang Thailand to check.

Mr Howell, 55, said, "someone there said they would look for him in his office, so I assumed it was genuine" .

Yacht skipper Alan Stevens of East London, also wrote but smelt a rat.

"When I contacted Yachting Monthly they admitted they had lots of complaints about the advert", said Alan, 47.

No one from Yachting Monthly was available to comment.

Michael Writes Home Seeking Help

Needless to say Michael got himself into trouble and wrote home to our Mum and Dad for help. This is Michael's letter home that he sent shortly after this news article.

Punnee Bar Babbua Muang, Kanchanaburi Thailand 7100

Dear Mum and Dad,

10/06/92

How are you both? Keeping well I hope. It will be good weather in England so you will be able to enjoy your garden. It's been four months since your last letter, which you sent to Peunnee Bar in Kanchanaburi. That was the only letter I ever received from there. I did reply to that letter but everyone seems to be having problems with mail to and from England.

Last time I wrote I was working for a tracking company but after I set them up with two main agents they double-crossed me. Things here are getting from bad to worse. Six weeks ago I lost all my money £700. I was in my room on a raft house. A big storm came, which caused a lot of damage, a lot of my belongings went to the bottom of the lake 100 meters deep, together with my money and Passport. I reported it to the police and got a report to give to the Embassy in Bangkok. I wrote to the Embassy in Bangkok but so far no answer. In my letter I told them I had a photocopy of my passport and lost my money. I am in Thailand with no money and my visa is out of date about £400. I also told them I had no one in England to help me financially. The tourist police told me not to worry, as it was an accident, which should stop me from going to prison. Now I don't know what to do. At the moment I am living with a Thai family 80 Km east of Kanchanaburi at Sisawats Great Lake. They have several bamboo raft houses designed for tourists but they are in very bad repair so I am helping them to repair them so at least I get food and keep (but no wages). If we get tourists I will get some money but at the moment it is low season and the many political problems in Bangkok is not helping. If I don't hear from the Embassy soon I will have to try to go to Bangkok to see them.

I Have Been Stupid I Was Never Happy

I know that over the past few years I have been stupid. I have lost every penny, even my daughter, and my credibility. I am stuck in Thailand penny less. Even if I could get home where would live and what would I do? I am not well and I am not young and most of all I have no spirit to live. Even when I had money I wasn't happy. I know I had a reasonable job and a nice flat but I was so screwed up inside it was sending me crazy. Even when Jessica came to see me it was heart breaking for me when she went home. I know you both love Jessica very much and because of me you cannot see her, I wrote to her a couple of times but no answer.

Please Mum and Dad give me a few words of wisdom as I think that this depression could be the end of me. I thought of writing to Brandon Gibson in Australia but I don't know his address. May be he could help me with some money and I could work to pay him back.

All my TV and video equipment you sent I lost due to massive tax duty and also a crook that tricked me.

The weather here is hot every day. It seems the same, just like England's heat waves when you get them, but the water in the lake is clear and fresh and night air is refreshing. Every one I speak too says the tourist trade in Thailand is finished.

Marriage Break Up A Cause

Please write to me soon and let me know how every one is. Even a quick word to Jessica to say I love her would be good for me. Please when you write don't give me a lecture on how irresponsible I have been and on how much you have helped me. I know all this and am truly sorry. My marriage break-up I think was the cause of it but I don't know.

I expect my financial situation is very bad at home and Margaret and Chris think I am very bad. Please what can I do now?

Well today is another day and I have just heard from the British Embassy. They tell me that they have no financial resources to help me even though I lost my money and passport. They say I must have money sent from England to clear my over - stay, about £400 otherwise I will be in prison without a doubt. So now it's making me ill and this Thai family cannot help me much longer. I have written to a few people in Thailand to see if they can help me with a job but I don't hold much hope.

I have heard that in Bangkok I could possibly get a job teaching English but I would have to go to Bangkok to check it out. At least if I could get my visa in order and it would keep me straight with immigration and stop me going to prison. The Embassy pointed out any money should come through Thomas Cook Travel Agents and send it to their head office in Siloam Road, Bangkok and would only take 24 hours or so and on proof of I. D. I could draw it. But I would have to know when to go to Bangkok, which would mean a telegram here first to let me know from you. I know you think I have a damn cheek after all you have done for me over the years but I have no one else to turn to. I have written to David and Irene for help and advice.

A Fear Of A Thai Prison

I really am going crazy with the thought of going to a Thai Prison.

If you cannot help I will understand as I feel that you have done too much for me in the past and I should be old enough to take care of my self, but this is Thailand in the 3rd World.

I have just had a thought ----- for me to get to Australia. I need a return ticket out to get an entry visa and this I doubt if Brandon would do anyway but please try and locate his address for me.

Please send my letter on to David, as I do not know his new address.

Write soon and take care.

Your loving son Michael.

P.S. I have written to the Embassy again asking what will happen if I give myself up. I think they will hand me over to immigration to lock me up. Then the Embassy will inform you that I am in Prison but I don't know.

Mum And Dad Fed Up With Michael

Mum and dad were fed up with what they thought were Michael's irresponsible ways and they despaired of him. I think mum in the end sent him the money to get him out and back to England.

On a letter received from Michael Mum wrote "turning point" so I assume she felt Michael was changing his ways.

Turning Point

Mum writes turning point on the top of a letter dated 10th July 1992, sent by Michael from Sam's Place, Song Kwan Rd, Kanchanabari. Michael writes, "Last week I went to Bangkok to speak with the embassy but they told me no help can be given what so ever and the only way is to get some money from home to clear my visa overstay and an air ticket home. They said they would get their office in London to contact you. I have also written to Auntie Edith.

The straight facts are as follows: I have been on overstay since February 16th which is 100 B fine a day= £350 to date. And to clear it I must have the money to go to the immigration plus an air ticket home £300. If not I will go to prison and work off my fine for £2 per day. Then I have to pay for the air ticket and deportation costs, which doesn't get me anywhere. They will keep me in prison indefinitely until money comes. Every day I stay here is about another £2.40.

I am ill with worry. I do not have any thing left here or in England, only my family who have helped me time and time again. I have been so foolish over my life. I have no will power to go on living. I cannot face the future. I know I must find a way to get back to England. David said I could live with him for a while which could be good as I could not face living in Eastbourne. I would have to start where nobody knows me, as I can't handle being with people who know what's happened to me since I have been in Thailand.

Why did the Embassy tell you I was fit and well? How do they know how much I am suffering inside myself? At the moment I am living at the above address. My clothes I keep in a hold- all and I keep it in the toilet of a boat where I sleep on deck at night. I get food free but that's all.

Please, please help me, as I know the Embassy cannot. Please give me a ring with a word of encouragement. The best time is at 11 am your time. Just ask for Michael. PS. I have written to every one I know for help but no joy.

All my love Michael xxx.

Michael Returned To England

On Michael's return to the UK he came to live with me for a short period and it was then he began to work on his next project which was his idea of being a Travel Agent.

Michael and the Philippines

It was then he developed his ideas to form a travel business. He had met Freddie Laker earlier in his life and put together his business plan; "**Paradise Express**" and he informed me of what he intended to do in the Philippines, in February, 1995.

To keep this account short Michael got involved in arranging holidays for single men to take advantage of the easily available sex on offer by G.R.O's guest relations officers.

34 A DRAMATIC CHANGE IN MY LIFE

It was at this time, while Michael was in Thailand, that I now realised that I was searching for something that I hadn't got from within my marriage, even though I had a wife, four children, a nice house and a good job. I had come out of depression (a sever manic low) and was now beginning to climb higher.

My wife had begun her degree course and I felt she began to look down upon those who was not as educated as she was. Also I felt that she no longer respected me, as I was not an Art student graduate, just a mere low-level engineer. I had listened to the Post modernist arguments regarding morality and religion and became a perfect student as I began to deny the existence of God and to entertain the idea of an open marriage.

Meeting Silver Girl

For the sake of anonymity I have named my wife to be, "Silver Girl", due to the addiction I experienced through meeting her, or "Nurse Ratchet", depending on my mood as I write. Nurse Ratchet is a character in the film, "One Flew over a Cock Cuckoo's Nest", staring Jack Nicholson. Nurse Ratchet was a psychiatric nurse and it so happened I fell in love with a psychiatric nurse.

My Wife to Be

Silver Girl

The name "Silver Girl" is taken from the line of the song "Bridge over troubled Waters", by Simon and Garfunkel. In this song they make mention of Sliver Girl, which is of course the heroine needle that the addict depends upon.

One Sunday morning, in 1992, whilst my family and I were attending the Titchfield Evangelical Church, we met a lady in the car park, behind the doctors' surgery. She was blond and had four children with her. She was going to the same church that we were going to.

I soon discovered she was not the mother of all these children. She only

233

had two children and she was separated from her husband. My wife and I befriended her and we became good friends.

I had not long come out of depression and I notice my mood getting higher. I began to feel very happy. I began to be interested in my wife's studies at university and we began to do interesting things. Silver Girl became my wife's very close friend and at that time I was very happy and on reflection was rising out of depression into a manic high.

We met interesting people, Dr Geoff Parsons, a doctor in psychology and moderator of the local Macintosh user group in Southampton, who specialised in people's sexual problems. We met another Mac user, Richard Block, the former of B&Q; he was the original Block & Quail. My wife at that time had a crush on him but he was interested in health foods and alternative medicine. During this time I began to fall in love with Silver Girl.

Making Music

During this time my memories of former pop music came to the front and I recalled songs by the Everly Brothers and Billy Fury. I was so taken with these old songs that I ask one of my students, Jim Berry, who was a keyboard player in a local group and a former member of The Yarbirds, to compose a backing track to "Halfway to Paradise", by Billy Fury. This was before karaoke was well known and I took this track and played it at Silver Girl's party, singing the words, which were for her.

Falling in love

It wasn't long before I felt Silver Girl would full- fill my every dream. I knew this was wrong but with my newfound philosophy that I had learned from my wife's Cultural Studies at Portsmouth University I ignored my conscience and felt no one could say it was wrong. So because I wanted this relationship with Silver Girl, I denied the truth of God, in order to get what I wanted.

Michael Returns From Thailand

I was at this time, June 1993, that my brother Michael returned from Thailand and he did not look well at all, and on reflection he was suffering from depression but said nothing to me. He had nowhere to live, or money. So he came to live with me at our home in Fareham. He was quite content to live in our caravan, in our front garden and stayed with us until he was able to decide his way forward. He met Silver Girl and was aware of the developing relationship but said nothing. It was after this that he made the decision to return to our parent's home, in Eastbourne and it was there he earned money by buying and selling cars.

Highlands Road and the BMX Bike Frame

My mood was very high at this time and one day Isaac came home from school very upset because some lad up Highlands Road had tucked him up for £13.00. Apparently he had offered him a BMX bike frame for £13.00, as he wanted money that we later found out was to buy 1/8th ounce of Hash. Isaac gave him the money in exchange for the BMX frame but the lad would not give him the frame. I felt very angry and realized what I must do. I was dressed in an overall and said to Isaac come with me and we will find this person. I drove my motorbike with Isaac on the back and we toured the Highlands estate asking for the where about of this boy.

We were directed to a house where he lived and I marched up to the front door and knocked him up. When he opened the door Isaac confirmed it was him so I, without hesitation, marched into his house, not caring who else might be there and simply demanded "WHERE IS IT", meaning the frame or the money. The boy must have been about 16 years old and said he had neither. To which I replied, "Right go and get me something worth money", and he asked why and said is it for security", to which I replied, "Yes". He bought from upstairs a stereo system and a quick look found it poor quality so I said that is not good enough go and get a better one. When he returned with a better one I informed him he could collect the stereo when he paid back the £13.00. Then we drove off.

Isaac on his BMX Bike

Isaac flat Land

Motor Bike Burnt Out

The next day when I retuned from work I was informed that the next door neighbour's motor bike had been set light too and I then realized that this was done in retaliation for me taking the stereo system in payment for the £13.00 taken from Isaac. I was thankful that the bike next door was insured against such crime. That how ever wasn't the end of the matter as word had got around that they had hit the wrong bike and the next day my bike was taken and found burned out in the park, down the road to Appleton Road. I thought that's OK as I was insured too but I later discovered, to my disappointment, that I had to pay the first £150.00 on any insurance claim. I only paid £150.00 for the bike so I lost out and the Highland Road lads got one over on me. (I wonder who they are?)

Leaving My Wife and Children

Thinking totally of my self- I can't blame anyone else - and after my wife had discovered that I had a relationship with Silver Girl, I left her and moved out of my house, taking all the things I needed with me. I took our caravan and joined the Abshott Country Club, parking the caravan in their camping park. I was hoping all would be easy, that the dust would settle and things would turn out well. This was not to be the case because although I could see Silver Girl I felt so very guilty and this spoiled our times together as I tried to suppress my guilt.

My wife, with her newfound education and philosophy, had opened her mind to new ideas and she too had her own doubts about God. She had entertained the idea of another partner at one time and leaving me. However things had turned. I wanted to marry the girl I loved. But things were far from easy. I began to reason there was no God, no condemnation and so I could do as I pleased and I was going to get my woman at all costs.

"But the thing that David had done displeased the Lord". 11 Samuel 11 verses 27.

This is a quotation from the bible, which relates the story of David, the king, who committed adultery with Bathsheba and she became pregnant. The story tells how David arranged to have her husband killed, so he could marry her and cover up his sin. This happened - her husband was killed and David married Bathsheba but the baby died. They did however have another child who became the ancestor of Jesus Christ.

In my case things did fail. I had left my wife and got my girl but we were both very miserable and insecure with each other. Silver Girl realized she could not cope with the situation, as things stood. I became depressed and at the end of myself and had nowhere to turn for help. I was desperate alone in my caravan not being able to see a good future.

In this condition I knew I needed God but I did not believe in God. I knew I had wronged my wife, children and many others, in the process. I would have invented God, if I could, for I believed that only God could help us in our situation. It was impossible. I just needed to cry out for help, to someone or being, to deliver me from my utter despair.

A Prodigal Son

I knew that I could not pray to God (the God whom I remembered and knew from the scriptures) in my present state because of a truth, which had remained with me. It is written, God will not hear the prayer of the wicked. I knew that whilst I was not prepared to give up my sin, I could not pray since God would not hear my prayers – i.e. If I regarded that iniquity in my heart.

At that time when I was living in my caravan at Abshott Country Club, I remember reasoning how I might turn back to God in prayer. I shared my thoughts with Silver Girl and we both decided we had to give up our relationship because it was wrong and I ought to offer to go back to my wife.

At that time I met a friend, from the Lock Heath Free Church, and he made an appointment to see me, in order to talk through my dilemma and difficulties. He was a great help and support and encouraged me to seek God. Both he and his wife had been through divorce and difficulties and were able to appreciate all the heartache and pain that was associated with divorce and separation.

If it were not for the mercy of God I would have been totally lost and in an awful state of mind. I may have ended my life, as things were so bad. I had nowhere else to turn and I needed God more than ever before. I bless the Lord for He heard my cry.

It was then that the simple words of Jesus that helped me and washed my mind of the lies I had believed. Faith came to me by hearing the Word of God.

On reflection I now know God had called me back to Himself, as He was not going to let me go. As Jesus had once said to me he would never leave me. I left him but he came after me using life's difficulties to drive me home.

I spoke to my wife about the situation and informed her I would return to her if she wanted but thankfully she informed me she had found a partner and wanted to divorce me. This was in February 1993.

I Was Made To Walk The Plank

When I was told that my wife was going to divorce me I was thankful because I now felt I could return to be with Silver Girl without my conscience accusing me that I must return to my wife. I was shocked and taken back when I broke the good news to Silver Girl as I thought she too would be happy. This was not the case! She felt that I had only returned because my wife had rejected me, that I had wanted to return to her. Silver Girl maintained that this made her feel second best. I was speechless because it had been muted before that she could not feel secure with me as I had already left a wife and what would prevent me doing the same to her? She had reasoned that if I had the capacity to leave a wife and children, without a conscience than I would be a cold and callous individual.

35 NUMBER 2 HAYLING CLOSE

A Period Between Two Wives

In the early part of 1993 to 94 I decided I should find more suitable accommodation rather than live in the caravan throughout the winter. Silver Girl had her own house, living with her two children and we believed we should wait until we were married before we lived together. From this time our relationship was so unstable and insecure it was touch and go if we would ever make it together. It was awful for me as every time we argued Silver Girl would say she would move to Canada or France if ever she thought I did not want her or if we split up.

Anyway, I enquired about a room, which had become available in Hayling Close, in Fareham, It was here that I met Simon Noel and his cat "Baldric" who only had three legs. Simon also rented a room at number 2 and David Jennings was our landlord.

There was a rear garden that had overgrown with an ironing board in the middle and a tin foil food take away tray, formed into a do -it -yourself barbecue sitting on the board. I thought the garden was a mess, ideal how ever for a cat. This became my home for the next 3 years while I waited my release by divorce, which took place in August 1996.

It was here that I began to contend with my bipolar or manic mood swings. As the disputes, arguments and insecurities that I experience with Nurse Ratchet, plunged me now into those chasms of deep depression. However my creative mind, on a high, devised ideas to sustain the highs, to prevent my depressions. At one time during these depressed periods I had contemplated suicide, using my brothers shot gun, but I kept these things secret and told no one but a Samaritan Counsellor in Portsmouth. I fought the lows of depression by creating artificial highs, as will be seen by the things that I got up too during this period.

I Wanted More Room

After living in one room for a few weeks and sharing the downstairs lounge with Simon, I noticed the small bedroom was not in use and was filled with Simon's gear, so I asked the landlord if I could rent this room as well as the room I had. I wanted my kids to come and stay with me, from time to time. They were Isaac (14), Esther (13), Eleanor (11), and David (11), who all lived with their mother and they were students at Henry Cort School. I don't think Simon was please with this arrangement because that was Baldric's bedroom, and Simon also wanted it as a free office. Simon was a bit like his cat and was territorial as he placed one or two of his things everywhere, including the garage, just to say he lived there too.

Harrods of Abshott

I had far more time on my hands, than a married man would have had, and at that time I discovered "Harrod's of Abshott", the most salubrious shopping centre in Hampshire.

I soon learned there were other branches in Southampton, Gosport and Port Solent. There were many bargains to be found at Harrod's that I could not really refuse to buy. There were televisions, computers, washing machines, weighing machines, tools, equipment, furniture and clothing and they were generally all at rock bottom prices. "Harrod's" was in fact the local amenity tip – the dump. Now run by Shaun of Hopkins Recycling Company of Botley, Hampshire.

Shopping for other people

I often found my self-shopping with other people in mind, which meant that when I saw items of value that I did not really need I would buy the valuable article for someone I had in mind. I asked Simon if I could just put a few things in the garage and use it as a store. Not that it was Simon's garage but because he was the older, long-standing tenant, and he had taken over the garage for himself.

After a few weeks he began to moan about my televisions and other things being stored in the garage. I think he felt I was taking over the house. (Which I was).

The Television License

It was shortly after that we had a blazing row over his TV Licence and then he wanted my things out of the garage. His problem was that he had paid for a television license for his room, and not for the benefit of whole house. He did this because in the past the other tenants did not wish to club together and buy one license, for the whole house, so he had bought his own and informed the licensing authority that the other tenants needed to buy their own as he was not prepared to pay for others to watch TV at his expense. This was Simon's way to ensure that no one else at the house could benefit from the license he had bought.

Now Simon had not told me about this history however things began to fall into place because a week previously he had slipped a note under my bedroom door, which was from the TV licensing authority wanting me to

239
buy a license.

You see I never watched the TV but he did. He was unemployed and watched his TV all alone in his own room but had been caught watching it without a licence and was required to renew his license and possibly face a fine

His drift was this; if I were to contribute half the money to renew his license then I could watch the TV set in the lounge because his licence would cover that as well. This sounded very reasonable at first but I felt there was something more to the scheme than Simon had let on, so I said no. This niggled Simon.

What niggled Simon was the fact that I repaired TV's and videos in the lounge, and I had also started storing them in the garage. Simon did not like it because he began to think the Licensing Authority did not trouble the house to inspect for licenses simply because he had paid for one already. In effect he thought I was benefiting from him having a licence - I should pay.

He had the garage and because I refused to buy a TV licence he was not very cooperative with me and did not want me storing TV's and other things, in the (his?)

I Had Moved In And Simon Knew It

I had moved in and he knew it and he felt if I had a TV or repaired them in the house then I would have to buy a licence. So Simon did have a point. However as far as I was concerned I only collected TV's from the dump and repaired them with other people in mind. I did not need a TV even though most people did. I suppose I felt that the TV license was a good earner. For me and my argument went like this; I repaired televisions for other people to watch and so they would have to buy their own license and of course the government would be helped financial by my service. So really I felt I should be exempt from a licence. This was my drift and I still think there is some mileage in my argument.

Simon was not happy and I am sure he thought I was most unreasonable but he never thought to discuss it with me he just went off "Half cocked." One evening it happened - as I repaired a TV set in the lounge that evening he became very angry. He came at me in a frenzy and threatening to hit me with a chair, as he smashed it across the table. He was a well-built man and about 6 feet tall and he could have flattened, me if he had hit me, but I stood my ground and he scurried off back to his room.

I Take Over The House at Hayling Close

It was soon after this that Simon left because he had, had enough of me and he took the other tenants with him, leaving the house empty. It was now that the landlord offered me the whole house for £400 per month and gave me permission to rent out the other rooms. This was unfortunate for the neighbours, who did not share my interests. I took over the house and my habits continued. Shopping at Harrod's continued. The more people I knew the more items I found to buy and so I soon filled the garage with wonderful items of value.

I Take in lodgers

My first tenant was a Mr Alan McCarthy, a window cleaner who had come from Manchester, although he had lived in Fareham for some time. I said he could have a room for £40 per week. I hadn't realised, but he had been living in a motor vehicle ambulance in a garage, somewhere near Segensworth throughout that winter, and had severe problems due to possible drug abuse and his broken marriage. I discovered he was a baptised member of the Mormon Church but was not actually practising. I think he appreciated the fact that I took him, in without references. He had a few pounds, but that was all.

For Alan things were not easy and I am sure he felt a bit like Jonah (a character from the Bible) as things started to go wrong for him the moment he moved in with me. In straightening out his room he attempted to nail down the floorboards only to find he put a nail through the central heating water pipe that Sunday evening and water was running everywhere. Alan felt he was to blame and found it difficult to cope with. Nevertheless I soon fixed this, to his relief.

My next tenant was Sean Land (some say Private Land). He was a friend of Alan and had been living in his Ford Fiesta during the winter nights too. I think Sean also had problems with drug misuse, a broken relationship and was not able to see his daughter. Sean had a more personal problem- his music and his feet. His music was too loud and his feet smelt.

It was their music, which caused the neighbours to complain to the council. We were served with noise monitoring forms and threatened with confiscation of equipment if the noise level was not kept down. It was difficult to convince these lads of the amount of noise they were making.

The next inmate was Mark, another acquaintance of Alan and Sean. Occasionally Mark's girlfriends stayed the night.

Joe Neve was the next to take up residence; he loved cars and was in an out of trouble with the police all the time.

It was from Joe that I obtained my lovely Fiesta, a 1.4 cc engine, in nice condition, for £40. This car took the place of my car (TAN 707Y), which I bought, from a Motor Vehicle lecturer at Fareham College.

My Best Car

David's Fiesta

One of the best cars I had (Cheers Joe)

A Run in with the Police

The problem with older cars is that they tend to go wrong but a Fiesta can be easily fixed. One evening, coming back from Gosport my exhaust pipe was blowing and I got pulled over by the police on a routine spot check. I was given a "Producer", which is a note to get the car fixed within 7 days. On my way home however, I had to pick up my daughter, Esther, from the Locks Heath Free Church, and in the dark I realised my indicators had stopped working when I was nearing the church. I noticed another police car coming in the other direction towards me and I felt anxious and thought "oh dear" as my indicators were not working and I would now be pulled over again. So I quickly pulled into the church car park. I then left the car unlocked and tried to enter the church only to find the doors locked. I then felt certain the police were about to come back to the car and check it out. I had lots of things in side, which looked like I was moving house but to a policeman it would look like I had robbed a house. Not wanting to face another interrogation from the police I decided I would just leave the car and come back to it later. So I went around the back of the church, walked up the road and rang up Esther to find out where she was, but first I had to climb a fence, a wooden spiked fence. As I straddled the wooden spiky fence, I slipped and felt the spike go up into my groin. I was stuck, in pain, straddle across a fence, almost hanging by my testicles. This was because I did not want another rectification certificate for my indicator lamps or a fine.

I managed to get down from the fence and hobble up the road. My inside legs felt wet and warm. It was not too painful so I hobbled to the phone and found out where Esther was.

After this I decided I had, had enough. I thought to myself - what I am doing here hobbling about in pain waiting for the police to leave me alone. I told myself that I would return the car, confront the police, and just go home, as it was only the winkers that had stopped working. I was hoping that the police had gone by now.

As I walked back down Hunts Pond Road the police car had parked along side my Fiesta. I marched up to them and asked directly could I help them, as they were busy checking the car over. I had left the doors unlocked and they were now checking to see if I owned the car. They could see all the stuff in side and it must have looked as though I had robbed a house. They asked me who I was and did the car belong to me and what was I doing. I then explained to them I had come to collect my daughter but the youth group had closed earlier and she had been picked up. By this time a returned radio call to the police radio confirmed I was the owner of the car (Thankfully I had it registered in my name and it was taxed and I had an insurance certificate). They then left me and I drove home. The winkers were not even mentioned.

All I did was retire to bed as I was not well and did not see the damage that I had done by being spiked with the wooden stake. I slept in my clothes and called for help the next morning. When my wife -to- be came, who was a nurse, she said I must go to hospital as I was damaged. The stake had pierced my left testicle sack and blood was everywhere, all down my trouser legs and it was difficult to see the extent of the damage.

After going to QA Hospital I was examined and it was felt I would have to go to St Mary's Hospital for surgery, as it was a severe wound. It was there that two male Indian doctors dealt with me. "This won't hurt," said one of them and I saw like a huge syringe needle in the other man's hand. They opened my legs (I felt very embarrassed and humiliated when they asked how it happened) they thought that I was a burglar running from the police.

I Was Sewn Up And Eventually Released

It was a very near close shave and I felt God had a sense of humour and I must learn a lesson. I wonder if you could tell me the lesson. E-mail me with your thoughts. The torn jeans were hung up in my lounge for a along time as a token to remember.

My House Becomes Full

The next inmate was Rob White, a friend of Sean, who had nowhere to live, so he had Baldric's bedroom. Rob had a small Jack Russell, called Sally, and shortly after that Rob's girl friend Carla Walsh needed short-term accommodation. Carla was only 16 years old and I was informed her mother had kicked her out. She moved in as well - I had tried to get alternative accommodation with a girl called Angie - which is another story. Needless

243
to say Carla and Sally ended up at number 2 Hayling Close.

Our Household

Sam Jones& Bruno, Carla, Sally, Rob and Joe Neve

By this time Alan had met a girl called Samantha Jones from Manchester and she bravely moved to Fareham to be with Alan. Sam had a son called John and a small Jack Russell, called Bruno and they were looking for a home of their own. They all ended up at number 2 Hayling Close. Sam's son John spoke with an accent just as I had done when I moved at 5 years old from Oldham to Watford. He would always ask me technical questions about how to repair things and Sam soon realised he had become my apprentice.

Sam and Alan

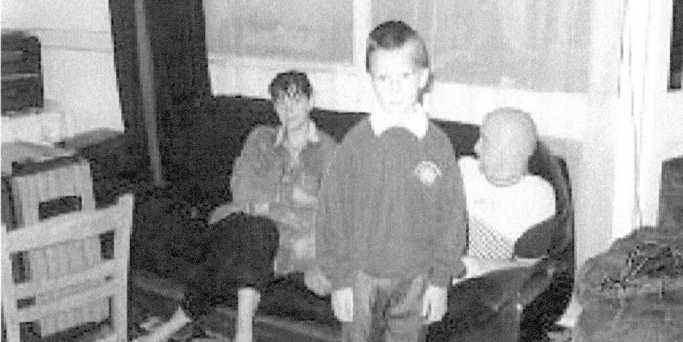

John My Apprentice

Joe's friend Kinder soon wanted somewhere to live as he had just come out of prison so the lounge had to be his room. The lounge had been my room and so I had to move out.

If you have tried to live in a house with 10 or 11 people and two small Jack Russell's - it is quite taxing. Sometimes Sean and his friends would stay the night so the house was quite full. It was Rob and Carla that cause a bit of a stress as they always left their washing up undone. They always denied it so I ended up by installing a "No bodies washing up sink" , which I had managed to scavenge from Harrod's.

How To Deal With No bodies Washing Up

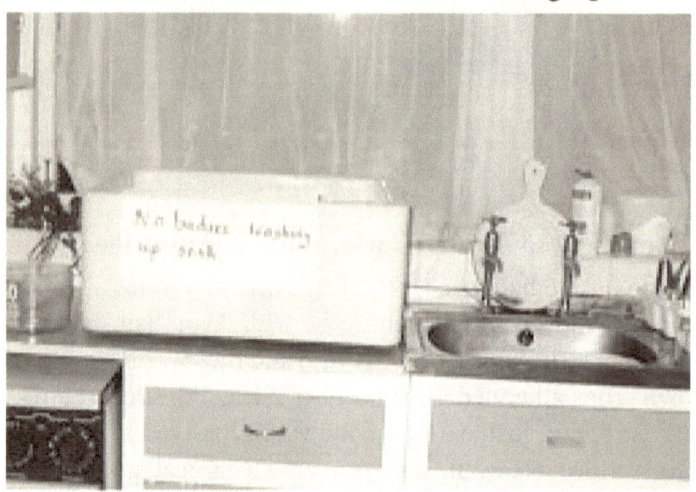

No bodies "Washing Up Sink"

The House Court

About this time my go-kart, which had been given me by a farmer who attended in Wantage Strict Baptist Chapel many years ago, was stolen from outside my wife's- to- be house in Stubbington.

After making a few enquiries I found out who had taken it so I decided rather than get these youngsters (16 year olds) into trouble with the police I would give them a chance. I spoke to one of the culprit's mothers (he is P.R. of Stubbington) and told her what I intended to do and she was most obliging and appreciated me not involving the police. I knew where the kart was and went to the house and sure enough the lad was there. I simply said I had come to collect the kart. He was unable to say a word as there it was in the back garden, so I got him to help me put it in the Fiesta. I told him that I wanted to see him and his friend at 8.00 p.m. the next day as I was taking them to my house for a hearing.

Alan Macarthy

Alan the House Court Judge

At 8 p.m. the next night, I collected these two lads (their names are withheld) and I had assembled in the lounge at number 2 Hayling Close a lounge villain, ex-convicts, friends and renowned characters from Fareham. Rob White's brother was there, who has just been released from prison. These made up the court. Alan McCarthy was the judge.

The two 16 year olds stood (in there peer group they would have been considered cool and hard) as quiet as mice. I think they were asked whether they pleaded guilty or very guilty. After listening to me, then to David White, and a few others they were warned of the dangers of stealing goods etc.. We did not want them ending up like some of us. They were fined £25 (the cost of a powder coat re-spray) and given time to pay. The money was paid on time. We heard no more about these lads. I hoped they learned their lesson. If you know them get them to e- mail me as they are on my list. nbpttc@ yahoo.co.uk

I Move Into A Tent In The Back Garden

My lodgers were generally people who really needed help. Their friends began to want to live with us and gradually the house was full. Of course the neighbours found this household too much to cope with and some believed that we had become a religious sect.

I decided after this time to move out in the garden to make room for Kinder, Joe's friend. So I built a spacious tent in the garden out of scaffold poles and an awning from Harrod's. It was a lovely (tent) room. I had a wardrobe, drawers, and table hi.fi. system etc.. Some said I was like Lawrence of Arabian living in the comfort of a lovely tent in the summer. I enjoyed my stay that summer but then the winter came.

The Garden Where I Lived

David's Tent   Inside David's Tent

At that time one of my mature students from Fareham College offered me a room in his house, in Locks Heath. I stayed here until November 1996, when I had planned to marry Silver Girl and then we could live together. This was to avoid Fareham Borough Council charging us with over- crowding a domestic residence.

Lads At Number 2 Hayling Close

The Tent Comes Down   **Sean and His Friends**

All these lads are on "Dave's List"

Do I Need A Good Woman Or A Minder?

On reflection, as I look over this period of my life, I realise that I was not safe living on my own but rather needed a good woman behind me but some would say I needed a minder. I'm of the opinion that if Silver Girl been a real help to me, the neighbours would have been spared an awful lot of trouble. She would have been sensitive enough to help with the situations that arose and ensured that I considered the neighbours.

It is for this reason I now blame Silver Girl for all the troubles that the neighbour's had at Hayling Close J. If had we been living together in a proper relationship she would have ensured the neighbours were not troubled by the things I got up to. Instead she was living away from me, as a single parent, doing a full time job. I now maintain that had she been the homemaker I wanted and not the stereotypical women chauvinist, claiming equal rights with men, then the neighbours would have had a reasonable time through her help. So I really feel that Hayling Close had Silver Girl to blame for all their troubles, to this day. That is my story and I am sticking to it (tongue in cheek).

Crime Prevention Programs

Whilst Michael was suffering in prison in the Philippines I was at home reassessing my own life in light of my returning Christian convictions and responsibilities towards my children. I was concerned about Isaac's future and wanted to keep him from becoming a criminal. It is on reflection that I am now able to define certain social activities as CPP's because these were identified as the best way to meet people and steer them away from crime. This meant joining recreation groups or inviting them to join you in any creative activity. I believe these programs are necessary to prevent crime. Also to bring fulfilment to those involved because generally people who are creative need to be actively engaged in good social activity, otherwise they are prone to be involved in crime, in one way or another. One such CPP is that of the BMX social network, which Isaac my son got involved in when he was 13 or 14 years old. And to do this he needed a BMX bike.

Portsmouth Skate Park

This was the place were many BMX'ers road their bikes and met many of their friends. And it was there that I first meet Dennis Wingham who did a back flip on his old battered BMX. I was very impressed. It was here that Isaac got hooked into what I call a CPP (Crime Prevention Program) as it kept him busy and out of trouble. It provided a social network for friendship and good activity, which is better, them crime. There are sensible and famous people at the Skate Park such as Ephraim Catlow, Isaac Clarke, Denis Wingham, Jim Stevens, Rodney Burnham, Jamie Knipe, Colin Hunt, Martin Hunt, Ronnie Johnson (Remo) DJ Jon Pratt, John Hopkins, Richards Wells, Stephen Drain (Drainer) Anthony Pill (Pill) and many more.

248

Dirt Riding in Skelly Woods Fareham

Isaac and Luke Fuller at Skelly Woods

Any way Isaac got involved in BMX riding and made many friends and at that time they got into " dirt" riding and him and his BMX'ers made Skelly Woods into a great BMX dirt track. The Council eventually kicked them out which was a real shame.

Hasting and Backyard

Another yearly event for BMX'ers was an event held near Hastings where BMX'er from all over the country, including riders from America would come and ride. It was a real good event and most people camped overnight on common ground. I took Isaac, Esther and their friends in my Transit van and that was were we slept. These CPP's, such as Portsmouth Skate Park and Backyard events involve those participating in good recreational activities thus keeping them busy, out of trouble and good creative competitive fun.

On Top of my Van

Isaac Luke and friends at Backyard event in Hastings

Isaac Clarke King of Southsea 2011

The evidence that confirms my believes is that Isaac got linked into BMX and skate board riding from an early age and this year won the 2011 King of Southsea Award. He has never been to prison and managed to avoid becoming a criminal. Unlike me who became a convicted criminal at the age of 17 years old.

The Award

Isaac's King of Southsea Trophy

Other Criminal Prevention programs

Realizing the value of such program's I began to get involved in all sorts of social activities, which involved Music, Drama, Art, Public Relations. This was the time of my separation from my second marriage, which I will be speaking about later. It kept me busy and occupied and also opened up social networks which enabled me to meet other and share the gospel with them on their terms. There are such a programs such as Faith and Foot Ball, involving Pompy players such as Darren Moore, Linvoy Primus and Mick Mellows. I am sure there are others programs but such programs are needed in our day to prevent the kind of riots that we have recently witnessed in our country.

Being In The World Yet Not Of The World

Through my experience and getting involved with these activities I have just mentioned I realized there was not virtue in isolating oneself from the world like some religious people believed we should do. There are many religious groups like this and have such mentality such as the Brethren, Strict Baptists, Jehovah's Witnesses and so on. I also believed we should be leaders of men rather than followers and it was good to be in touch with critical issues of our time rather than be "several steps behind". Those that are several steps behind seek to provide answers to questions that people are no longer asking. I believed it was right to be both relevant and different as if we fail to be relevant, we cannot be heard. Also if we fail to be different, we have nothing to say. In the meaning of John 17:14-15 14'I have given them your word, and the world has hated them because they are not of the world, just as I am not of the world. [15]I do not ask that you take them out of the world, but that you keep them from the evil one.

BMX stunt at Portsmouth Harbour (1995)

During this time my son Isaac rode his BMX with the riders from Portsmouth and I went from time to time to meet the lads at Portsmouth Skate Park. On this occasion these lads were having some fun riding and old BMX bike, up a ramp and over harbour wall, and into the sea. One Sunday afternoon Esther and her friend Emma Jean was there and I had with me my daughter Elly and Jim Gold and we arrived in my Fiesta. It looked great fun riding into the sea on this bike so I decided to have ago. I had never done it before and wanted to pull off a back flip, so I asked some of the lads how to do it. I followed their instructions to the "T" and sure enough up, up and over; I managed to pull off my first back flip on a BMX into the sea. The crowed was great they cheered me on. My daughters were getting concerned and begged me not to do it again s it looked dangerous but I wasn't deterred.

Back flip over the Fiesta

To make it more fun I drove my Fiesta side ways on, at the harbour edge, and got the lads to put the ramp up against it. I was going to do a back flip, jumping the Fiesta into the harbour. Thankfully Dennis Wingham took the lead, with his crash hat on, and pulled of a great back flip over the Fiesta in the sea. My turn next, I had no crash hat, and my girls were begging me not to do it but I peddle as hard as I could, up the ramp, up into the air, pulled back and sure enough a back flip landing in the sea. The crowd gave a great cheer and coming out of the water, on camera was asked how old I was and had to think for a moment. I was 45 years old. The cried He's the King.

Here is the video link to The Harbour Jump

Harbour Jumping Video

Jim Stevens Rodney Burnham Keith Cowern Jamie Knipe Colin Hunt Martin Hunt Isaac Clarke, Dennis Wingham, Ronnie Johnston (Remo) DJ Jon Pratt, John Hopkins, Richard Wells, Stephen Drain (Drainer), Anthony Pill (Pill) and loads of the rest of the old Southsea skate park locals... Were all there.

A Fresh Look at Christian Marriage

At this time I began to take a fresh look at Christian marriage and studied what the Bible had to say. When sharing my findings with Silver Girl she agreed and we wanted a Christian marriage. I thought that much of societies troubles of the day were due to the influence of television and programs which portrayed the modern views of the world, many of which I believed were wrong. In particular I blamed the inequalities between men and women and the over reaction in society to redress these problems. I felt that those women who were claiming equal rights with men were contributing to all the evils in the world. My conclusions and my understanding of what a Christian marriage is all about are recorded under the chapter heading in this book, '**A Fresh Look At Chrisitan Marriage**'[13]. I accepted every tenet

---

13   Please see the subject in my book Mary, Mary Quite Contrary listed as

252

and sought to live this way with Silver Girl.

I began to learn, through the many arguments I had with Silver Girl, and those problems that I had with women in the past, that the problems were due to them having lost sight of their created roles as helpers. They had become dictators. In every case that I had met I noticed such women loose their beauty and become the proverbial nag, or nagger. At one time such women would have been ducked in the ducking stool (I.e. a trial by water) as being a witch i.e. one that control a man by subtlety. Maybe that was my manic reaction to my trouble with women.

It took me a long time and much pain to realise that women are far more sensitive to situations than men and that women are best to judge such issues, which cause others to be upset. Men just do not think. They certainly do not think like women. Hence my new proposed book "Electronics made easy", which is a humorous book making use of those differences between men and women, by describing the operations of complicated electronic circuits in a new light. I tried this out whilst teaching students about the operation of a tuned circuit whilst at Fareham College, the inductor having the characteristics of a man whilst the capacitor has the characteristics of woman. My students loved my illustrations. We made a video of one lecture and I am sure John Cleese would find it most amusing.

Seeking to help Alan and Sam

On one occasion Silver Girl and I went to help Alan and Sam as Alan had gone out for the evening with his friends to a night club, leaving Sam on her own and she was concerned that Alan might be returning to his former bad habits. We both went to see Sam and I suggested it would be good for us to pray together for her and with her as I had hoped that they might find God's help. In conversation I said to Silver Girl, when referring to Alan who had gone off to the nightclub, "There go I but for the grace of God". In other words if I did not have Christian values, I might be just like Alan, wanting to go out to a nightclub, with his mates, when I could have been at home with my family and not seeking the life of single man, without responsibilities.

This really caused Silver Girl to react, she fell really insecure, and wanted to talk about the matter immediately rather than give Sam the support we had come to give. I was aware that this was just the beginning of another row and wanted to talk to talk about it later, not in front of Sam. So I refused to talk about it there and then. The atmosphere at number 2 went so tense that Sam left and went to her room, and of course we were of no help or comfort to her. Eventually Silver Girl got up and left, walking or getting a taxi back to her home. She felt I was saying that I wanted to go out just like Alan and

further publications.

that it was only the fact that I believed in God that prevented this. She feared that if ever I turned away from God then would be off leaving her. This of course is nonsense. Every Christian will admit the human heart is capable of many wrong things and that God is the one who keeps them from falling. I am not sure if this matter was ever resolved or if Silver Girl understood what I was saying or meant.

36 MICHAEL AND THE PHILIPPINES

"Paradise Express" 1995

Michael during this time had new ideas and sought to develop his ideas to form a travel business. He had met Freddy Laker earlier in his life and put together his business plan; "Paradise Express" and he informed me of what he intended to do in the Philippines in February, 1995. He had been to Angeles City, in the Philippines, and identified many nightclubs, hotels and travel attractions and agreed to work with those businesses already functioning in the sex industry. Michael intended to sell package tours aimed at single men, to take advantage of those attractions already functioning. I felt it was wrong. I had already spoken to him, at our mum and dad's home, after I had seen his advertising for his "Paradise Express". He was advertising holidays, in the English National newspapers, for persons to enjoy the sexual attractions, which was offered in Angeles City, in the Philippines.

The Brochure

Front & rear cover of "Paradise Express"

He maintained it was all right that they loved that sort of thing and every one was into it. He maintained that it was perfectly above board and legitimate. However I was not happy about it and asked him how would he like some man to use his daughter Jessica as a sexual attraction and be one of the girls he was advertising. He said he wouldn't but out there they are different – and maintained they loved it

Michael is Arrested in the Philippines

It was a very shocking and sad to hear the news in June 1995 on the television, that Tuesday lunchtime, at Fareham College. It was announced that an English sex tour operator had been arrested and remanded in custody in the Philippines, to await a trial.

At that time I had no real idea what the actual charges were against him but realised it was to do with his travel business, involving all the existing exotic night-life and sex attractions in Angeles City. I had no idea that the allegation was to do with child prostitution.

The ITN news at 10, that evening, showed a video clip of Michael apparently directing an enquirer to a child prostitute. The pictures were very convincing and I felt very sad and groaned in side, I was shocked because I had no reason to ever think Michael would be involved with child prostitution. He had always been straightforwardly blatant with what he had done in the past and so I had no reason to believe he was involved now in the said sad and awful crime until now.

Michael had written to the Eastbourne Herald asking Anne Marie Shields to contact mum and dad as he could get not through to them. He wrote, "I'm fine but the thought of being on possible Death Row is getting to me. My attorney is great so far we a winning. An armed escort has transferred me from the military jail and I am now at the Headquarters N.B.I. Olongopo City".

No doubt Mum and dad were not responding the way Michael wanted this was probable due to the last time he got in trouble in Bangkok, Thailand. Mum had to do so much for him and deal with all his affairs. Mum had become ill and couldn't deal with the demands he kept placing on them for financial help and dealing with his affairs in England.

Our Mother Dies

It was the 29th February 1996, that my mother died, leaving my father a widower and the stated cause of death being pulmonary embolism, deep vein thrombosis of the leg and Coronary artery thrombosis and atherosclerosis. I was of the opinion that the awful news of Michaels arrest in June 1995 and imprisonment in the Philippines, was contributory to her death as I felt she really died of a broken heart.

No Sympathy for my Brother

I too had little sympathy for Michael because Mum had bailed him out of Prison (for not paying he visa) in Thailand and no sooner had come home he was off and gone to the Philippines and was in trouble again. His travel business was immoral (from my point of view) as it was trading on the promiscuous nature of persons not bound by Christian values. It was encouraging fornication and I was opposed to him and this activity and I had told him so, before he went to the Philippines. Just like I warned Ken Knight about his bogus insurance scam.

I learned later that Michael had protested his innocence from the beginning and maintained that a certain Fr. Shay Cullen, an Irish Priest, was behind the set up and apparently it was he who directed the ITV news video crew to entrap him on Baloy Beach.

The full NBI report of this incident was brought to me by Suny Wilson, the English man who was sentenced to death, on 16th September 1996, after he was acquitted, on the 19th December 1999, when he returned to the UK. This report clears Michael of the said charges but seriously indicts Fr. Shay Cullen. I never saw this report until January 2000 some 5 years after the event. This information is all recorded in my publication Trojan Warriors.

Michael was set up (entrapment)

Michael had been found guilty of "Promoting child prostitution", in the Philippines in October 1996 and sentenced to a term 14 to 16 years. To be served in New Bilibid Prison. Muntinlupa City, Philippines. Had always protested his innocence. His sentence was announced on national ITV news and it was the previous ITN news clips, which were used as evidence to convict him in the Philippine court. It was awful it made him out to be selling children for sex. The exact nature of the offences was not clear from the News item.

I had written to Michael several times and I found it difficult really believe he had been selling or promoting child prostitution, as the ITN TV camera portrayed. He had written to me and I have the whole story written in his own hand, as to how he was "set up" by Martin Cottingham, Adam Holloway and Fr. Shah Cullen.

Michael maintains the TV camera was cut and spliced to make out he was doing some thing he was not. He also describes what actually took place between Malcolm Cottingham and his friend Adam Holloway, as they pretended to be holiday seekers with Paradise Express.

Michael was very bitter against Shay Cullen and this showed in his letter to me, he really believes him to be the real culprit of these evil actions. He outlined his life style as a man having a luxury life style and in a lovely mansion with bodyguards etc.. And soliciting funds from abroad, using headline-catching news to attract further funds from abroad. These things he wrote in his letters.

37 MY DIVORCE AUGUST 1996

As far as I was concerned my former marriage ended at the time my wife decided to divorce me and I accepted this because of what I had done. However it took a long time to complete the legal process and finalize the divorce, which took place on the 26th August 1996.

Would I Ever Marry Silver Girl ?

I was working through my beliefs in respect to what the bible said about wronging, divorce, remarriage and I knew from my knowledge of God that my sins would have to be dealt for me in order for me to receive benefit and help from God. I knew from the bible that this provision had already been made the Son of God, Jesus Christ, dying for sins, the sins the world. It was in this provision that I trusted and believed in God. I could have no relationship with God whilst I was still in my sins and they had to be forgiven. I believed God for the forgiveness of sins and the gift of righteousness. I had done what I thought I needed in to put things right with my wife and family. Silver Girl and I had promised each other to have a Christian marriage. We went through many struggles and conflicts of conscience and sometimes I feared the worst would come upon us. I endured many painful feelings and many struggles in conscience being accused in conscience of many things and felt I had wronged my children, as they too had gone through all kinds of hurt. All of which I regret having put them through it all. I wanted to be at peace with and all those that I had involved.

Silver Girl experienced much insecurity as she felt I would be returning to my wife at any moment. She began to reason we had both used her in order to repair our marriage and that I would return to my wife and then she would now suffer loss. It was this insecurity that made her fell the need to separate from me in order to avoid getting hurt. This of course bread insecurity in me, as I could not bare the thought of her leaving me.

Having re-looked at marriage and what the bible has to say about it I came to believe that my marriage to Silver Girl took place the moment we had exchanged or promises to each other, which had taken place in September, 1996. I say this because there are no instructions, or examples in the bible, as to how a marriage actually takes place. So I concluded this must be culturally defined and not dictated by God. I also learned that a legal marriage can be and may well be a very real help to couples feeling insecure. I now think that marriage, as is commonly known in our culture, is a reasonable practice. I wanted to be legally married to my partner as soon as I was legally divorced in August 1996, but this was delayed. However this was not to be and would come later.

The Place of our Marriage

Rebekah's Field is the place where Silver Girl and I exchanged our promises of marriage. A time and place, which was far more romantic than the Registry Office, and as far as I was concerned was the time and place of our marriage. It was in September 1996 and was beside the horse trough in Rebekah's Field, Stubbington.

I was so delighted about the event that I wrote a song about the situation and this is called "Rebekah's Field". This song was sung at Oliver's Bar, in Gosport, when our band entered a Beat the Band competition on 5th May in 2000 as I will relate later on. Video links below:

Here is the Video Rebekah's Field at Home

Rebekah's Field Oliver's Bar Gosport

The Horse Trough in Rebekah's Field

As I look back on this event I believe I must have been on a manic high as I also sung my other song, "Can your Remember", at the same event.

A Wedding reception at Asda

I began to feel much happier at the prospect of us living together as man and wife and we both wanted a simple and legal ceremony, at the Fareham Registry Office. How ever upon reflection I realize my mood was rising and I was high as we were preparing for a simple wedding and I took Silver Girl's off the cuff comment about having wedding reception in Asda quite literally and arranged it with the management at Asda, in Fareham. I simply asked if we could have our wedding reception in their store and the management were very obliging. Once the local news got hold of our plans they were very interested in the story and before we knew it local and national newspapers published the story. This was all too much for Silver Girl and she pulled out of the wedding. However this didn't stop the story going to the press. Here is the story:

FAREHAM / Pressure too much for bride-to-be (THE NEWS, Friday, November 22, 1996)

Asda reception couple put their wedding on ice

By TANYA JOHNSON

A Fareham couple due to celebrate their marriage with a reception in a supermarket have postponed their wedding.

David Clarke and Silver Girl were due to tie the knot at Fareham Register Office this afternoon.

The ceremony was to be followed with a reception in the self-service cafeteria at Asda in Fareham

More then 20 guests were expected for a £2.50 -a-head meal of roast chicken, lasagne and hot pot.

Yesterday Dave 47, contacted The News to say that is was not going ahead. "I regret to say the pressure has been too much", he said. "Silver Girl has called off the wedding."

It is too much for her to cope with. I am very upset.

Dave an engineering lecturer at Fareham College did not elaborate on his girlfriend's reason for cancelling the wedding.

Silver Girl who is expecting the couple's first child is a psychiatric nurse.

Both were getting married for the second time. Dave, of Hayling Close Fareham has four children from his first marriage, and his new wife lives in Stubbington and has two children.

Yesterday Dave said: "We want a nice wedding but without frills, which cost a lot of money. "But we hope the wedding will go ahead at a later date.

Continuing in their unconventional style he added: " I don't think my wife will be disappointed if I don't give her a wedding ring but I'm not sure how she will react to the ball and chain that I have made.

Just some Fun

Dave's Ball and Chain

He said he has not ruled out the possibility of a honeymoon in a tent he lives in this summer in the garden of his home.

Asda Wedding

Silver Girl

38 MY MARRIAGE AND 11 HAYLING CLOSE

With my future so uncertain I decided to buy a house of my own and had hoped it would become our marital home, if ever we finally go it together. This proved to be a good move, as I needed a retreat whenever Nurse Ratchet and I had a disagreement. Never the less I tried ever so hard to work on our relationship.

The Fareham Registry Office

We had always planned to get legally married as soon as I was free. However until that time I felt it a good thing to buy a house so that we could start our married life in a new home. I was able to complete the purchase of number 11 Hayling Close in January 1997 and move in straight away. By this time we had arranged our legal marriage at the Registry Office, which took place on 21st February 1997, with a reception at the Oast and Squire. On this occasion I had to rearrange my teaching schedule that Friday afternoon for many of my students attended and after this we had our honeymoon in Bournemouth.

I know I was definitely on a manic high on that day as I took with me, in my chauffeur driven car, a manikin dummy dressed, in Silver Girl's cloths, this was just in case Silver Girl did not turn up so I would then marry the dummy instead. I must have been on a high , I am sure I was. After our honeymoon were returned to my wife's home in Stubbington and entered the next phase of our life together.

I Build An Extra Room Above The Garage

We never did move into our house at 11 Hayling Close but rather made our family home in the house belonging to my wife. We then lived together for the first time along with Silver Girls children.

I decided to build a workshop in the garage and an extra room in the roof space of the garage, which we called The Den. It had a purpose built stair way, leading from the garage, up to the room and a small door leading through the wall into the boys bedroom, with a lock and key for private access. I then fitted a velox window giving plenty of light to the room. It was great and my wife's son and his friends loved it, as they often had sleep overs there.

I also made the garage my workshop were I could repair the items I had bought from Harrod's. It was a good workshop.

My Father Dies

After my mothers death in 1996 my father lived alone, in their home at Eastbourne, until 3rd March 1997, when he died of the same problem as our mum, Pulmonary embolism and Deep vein thrombosis of the leg. My brother Michael and I along with my sister were left money in their will and I was then able to write and inform Michael, who was in New Bilibid Prison of this. Although it was very sad for us all it was a real help to Michael, as he could not go about clearing his name and getting released from prison, in the Philippines. It is money that it needed, particularly if you are a foreigner and in jail.

An Insecure Marriage

During this time I had been subjected to divorce from my first wife, which involved a long legal battle regarding money. This was unusual because we had been divorced in August 1996 and my father had died in May 1997. For some reason the financial settlement had not take place at the time of our divorce and subsequently settled in court, after my fathers death. Prior to this I had the news of my brothers 16-year prison sentence in the Philippines in October 1996. And it seamed as though one bad thing followed another. I also saw the devastating effects of my marriage break up upon my children, which I could not share with Silver Girl, as this would only serve to increase her insecurity. I could see their needs and knew that I had been responsible for the hurt that I had plunged them into. I felt totally insecure and felt Silver Girl would leave me or tell me to go. The Insecurity that we both felt was great and marriage do not bring the security I needed and thought it would. It was a real problem and without speaking about things too personal I had to seek God, more, and more, and more, as life went on. I needed help from God because I was not managing or coping well at all with my daily life. The stress that I found myself experiencing was unbearable and I eventually sought personnel counselling from "Off the Record", at Fareham College.

Financial Settlement And Divorce Won't Help

During this time we spoke to Nurse Ratchet's solicitor because she was anxious about my former wife's financial legal claim on her assets. She was distressed saying she did not want her getting her hands on her mothers money; money that had been left her, when she was married to her previous husband, by her mother. That money was used to increase the value of their home and she wanted her children to benefit and not my former wife. We were led to believe she might have some valid claim because we were now married and joint incomes were taken into account in financial settlements. She said she would do anything to stop her getting her hands on her mother's money.

Taking Silver Girl's words and meaning literally, I asked the solicitor a hypothetical question saying, "How would we stand if we were divorced"? To which I was informed of the impractical nature and legality of such a plan. This how ever was the cause of our next series of arguments and Nurse Ratchet reported this incident to one of the elders of our church saying that I had proposed a divorce, leaving her devastated. Of course this was nonsense and there was no way that I could reassure her otherwise. She maintained I was proposing a divorce, causing her to feel so insecure with me.

I Was A Murderer

At one time she awoke in the early hours of the morning with the notion that I was a murderer and had killed a prostitute at Port Solent. She had concluded this because she had noticed, a few weeks earlier, that my attention had been drawn to the headline news on the TV, about the murder of a prostitute at Port Solent. She concluded that the reason why I took notice of this news item was because I was the murderer. It was crazy, I could not reason with her, even after explaining that the reason why it took notice of the news was because the incident had taken place so near our home. It was shocking. As a result of this crazy dream she wanted a divorce and went to see the minister of the church at the Locks Heath to discuss divorce.

The Spare Rib

Another incident took place involving my comment about the delectability of a spare rib. This argument was number 365. One evening I was eating out with Silver Girl and her brother and his girl friend at "Chiquito's" in Port Solent. During the meal I simple expressed my pleasure and how tasty the spare rib was, stating that I felt it was intoxicating. This phrase "Intoxicating" generated a chilled silent mood in Nurse Ratchet, which was felt by all and a dark cold cloud descend upon us all at the meal. Not a word was spoken, for the rest of the meal, and Nurse Ratchet's brother asked, "was there a private issue going on between us?"

I was not told about the reason of this chilled silence until later on that evening. It was then I learned that Nurse Ratchet had believed, understood and stated, that I was rubbing something in to make her feel bad. I had no idea what she was talking about, however it turned out that I had used this word, "intoxicating", a few months earlier during a conversation with a friend of hers. On that occasion I was asked to express how I felt about an experience I had with another woman some years ago. I simply said that it was, "intoxicating". Nothing more was said.

Nurse Ratchet however picked up on this word and stated that at the meal table in Chiquito's I was taunting her by saying the spare rib was intoxicating. She insisted I was deliberately saying this word to upset her and make her feel bad. This of course was nonsense but there was no way that I could convince her otherwise. Such a thing would not have entered my mind to do.

Rebekah Is Born

My wife gave birth to our lovely little girl on the 8 June 1997, at Queen Mary's Hospital in Portsmouth. She had very dark hair and blue eyes when she was born. And as she grew up I got her to help me. Even to repair items that I had bought from Harrod's.

264

Working In My Workshop

Rebekah and her daddy helping him

My workshop was set up to repair the many items I bought from Harrod's and by this time Harrod's had moved from Abshott to Segensworth. It was there that many of my students did there shopping. In fact one of my students, Lenny Butler, actually worked at Harrod's and he was a very intelligent student. We laughed at some of his ideas about repairing electrical goods; for example instead of replacing a fuse, in a piece of electrical goods, with the correct size and rating, he would insert a nail or wrap silver paper around the broken one and more often that not it would work. That was Lenny for you.

Rebekah and Her Dad

Helping Repair a Strimmer

I use to involve Rebekah in all I did around the house

Our First Holiday Away In France

This was a disaster as far as I was concerned. Rebekah was a few months old, Nurse Ratchet's had friends in France and we were able to stay there. We took her son and his friend in a Mitsubishi Space Wagon that I had renovated. I don't know what the trouble was but Nurse Ratchet went into none of her cold chilled none communicative moods and I notice she pick holes in all that I did.

Insecurity

How ever the insecurity we both found our new marriage was real problem that we both felt and without speaking about things personal I had to seek God more and more as life went on. I needed the help of God because I was not managing or coping very well at all. The problems involved the relationship between the children of our former marriages and my new wife, the proverbial stepmother. After we had been arguing for several days and as a result expressed my beliefs about the relationship between men and women. I shared my concluding observations with Nurse Ratchet saying I now believed that any relationship between a man and woman could not work in harmony, without the help of God.

My Belief Sends Silver Girl Around The Bend

This observation of concluding belief of mine sent my wife around the bend, and she was very upset with me. She wanted to know what would I do if I ever turned away from God again and we were having difficulties- would I remain married to her? She had totally missed the point as to what I meant.

I had come to the conclusion that we both needed to apply Christian principles in our marriage, to resolve the many personal difficulties that we were facing, and the many personal arguments we were involved in, so we could survive. In other words the scripture outlined general rule and guidelines on how to relate to each other a way that enabled the Lion to lay down with the lamb, so to speak, and the lamb not get devoured by the lion. Hence taking heed to the word of God was having God in ones life. I felt we both needed such help. Unfortunately she just could not see my argument and she felt threatened by it. I could not assure her otherwise.

I believed that if we had both been resolved to seek the Lord and be directed by His word in every thing then we would be blessed with a God honouring marriage, in other words a harmonious loving, happy family life. Any thing less than this would be a failure and second best.

I questioned Nurse Ratchet as to why she was upset but she would not explain this to me. She later wrote to me but lost the reply and so she wrote again to explain her upset. Her reply is entitled "Marriage" and included in this article.

No Way Forward Without The Help Of God

I had stated to Nurse Ratchet that the bible contained instructions as to how we should love each other and go about resolving difficulties i.e. 1 Cor. 13 verses 1-13. I stated that all of these God given, inclinations and abilities, to live at piece one with another, are given to those seeking God. That we should pray to the Lord to grant us supplies of these special abilities. That we are called upon to exercise these gifts in our times of difficulty this is the help of God without, which there will be no harmony.

I maintained, "God has spoken to us". I maintained that unless we take heed to these directives and exercise these graces such as patience, long suffering, forgiveness in our marriage, then the relationship is doomed to failure. In our case we need God's help and we should not to ignore it.

Nurse Ratchet objected to this (she being a trained adult mental health nurse) by saying there were many none Christian marriages that have good relationships without God. So I was wrong! Again she missed the point.

I went on to explain that I believed that many people exercise love; patience etc.. With one another because they have learned that is the best way forward. It is in fact the way, which God approves of and directs. They have learned it from their past experience, traditional up bringing, or what ever, but in the end they are only doing those things that God has so freely spoken about in the scripture. That is why their marriages work. You might say a pound spent in Manchester and a pound spent in London was equally valid and it did not matter if was spent by an atheist, Muslim or Christian. The pound spent was good currency because it was the currency of the realm.

I stated since God has made man in his own image he may use the natural gifts of love, patience, forgiveness and long suffering, as these work, and so their that is why they have successful marriages without realizing they have been helped by God.

I was saying that we needed the help of God in our relationship and marriage in order to survive. Just like these people. They may be unbelievers and deny the existence of God but they posses and display those natural gifts of wisdom, which God had given them. That was what we needed. I believed however the we needed to learn directly for the bible and exercise the directives given to us plainly in His Word because to that day our marriage was not working. I believed we were doomed to failure because we hadn't learn these natural laws. I felt this was the same with every thing connected to the Christian religion. This is the same with every thing. In Churches who seek to go contrary to the Word of God and promote thing opposed to the plain teaching of Scripture they are doomed to failure. Just like appointing women elders or homosexual bishops.

I also mean that the moment the marriage relationship ceases to reflect the image of Christ loving His Church and the Churches submission to Christ it is a failure and not functioning as the designed purpose of God. When this happens, as was happening to us we both suffer loss. Distress of mind and soul and feel all the in-securities that it exposes one too.

What I have said before about me not leaving is true. I will never leave you. If you kick me out and insist I go; then that is different. But I would not leave because I have promised you and I keep my word; that is the image of God in me.

What may happen to others depends upon their own view and way of acting. I have promised never to leave you on any grounds, misery, despair or any reason. What more can you require?

I would not leave you and go off with another women, because of what we have together if our marriage fails. This is because I believe a failing marriage can be restored if we follow Christ

I would like to know that this is your vowed intent too i.e. Not to leave or divorce me because of your promise or covenant of marriage.

David Clarke   2nd December 1997.

Do not let the sun go down on your wrath- in other words sort out the problem with the other person before you sleep that night.

Love one another-consider the other person before you say or do anything.

Husbands love your wives as Christ loved the church.

Wives reverence your husbands.

Children obey your parents in the Lord.

Etc..

39 OUR FIRST SEPARATION

This took place early 1998 and was due to unresolved problems that were all due to "the baggage" we both had carried from our former marriages.

We had, had the problem of me being a murderer, the spare rib, the hypothetical divorce and my first girl friend when I was 16. The problems were generally relating to the children of our previous marriage, past relationships or our misunderstandings, fears, miss trust. My fears were those of being deserted by Silver Girl.

Our arguments generally produced a knee jerk reaction resulting in Nurse Ratchet insisting I leave her, or me walking out in total frustration. It wasn't long before I was compelled to leave by Nurse Ratchet and I returned to live at number 11 Hayling Close.

At that time in April 1998, Nurse Ratchet wrote a letter to me stating certain things that were hurtful, unnecessary and derogatory comments about my eldest son Isaac. Isaac, unfortunately for him, discovered this letter, in my kitchen at Hayling Close and read these things about him. He felt very angry with Nurse Ratchet and he decided he did not wish to see her again. He then informed his brother David. They both believed she was the cause of all their mothers hurt and the family breakdown and their pain. They always maintained that Nurse Ratchet had never express sorrow or given an apology to them, or their mother, for the hurt she had been responsible for. This was the source of the animosity between all my children and Nurse Ratchet and as a result it was not helpful and only led to more resentfulness between my wife and children, in particular David.

Off the Record Counselling

Due to my utter despair feeling down and unable to cope with the situation I was in, I sought the help of the Hampshire, "Off the Record", counselling service, offered at my college. This lasted for a whole two years of regular, once a week sessions. I learned that I had became the victim in our relationship and I was unable to express how I felt about a problem. I was able to say what I thought about a situation but not how I felt.

I learned also that I was not responsible for another persons feelings either. So I began to practice saying how I felt about uneasy situations, rather then say what I thought. This meant if I expressed how I felt about something no body could argue or deny my feelings. If however I said what I thought about something, then my thoughts could be argued about.

So in an argument and some one were to retort to me some thing like this, " You are an evil bastard and you make me feel sick," It would not help if I were to respond like this," I think you are nasty piece of work" and you deserve what's coming to you. This would not be a helpful way of response and would prolong an argument.

Had I said, "I fell hurt and angry when you call me an evil bastard and I hear what you say about feeling sick", However lets talk about the problem and see why you are angry" then may be you will feel better and we could try and resolve the matter.

I then began to realised I was not responsible for feelings and she needed to take responsibility for how she felt. I could not make her feel anything. For instance if she were to say to me, "You make me feel sick" then she was really saying she felt sick which may have been as a result of some thing I said, did or inferred, How she felt was her problem and she was to take responsibility for her feelings, not me. I was not to blame for how she felt. It may be that what I said or what I did resulted in her feeling certain things, in which case the matter could be looked at and any bad feelings could be examined and alleviated or redressed. But I was not responsible for her feelings; she should take responsibility for them her self.

I learned about the trinity of roles in our harmful marriage relationship. The Persecutor, the Victim and the Rescuer. The outstanding emotion in the Persecutor was anger and was Nurse Ratchet. The outstanding emotion in the Victim was hurt, rejection and loss. I felt I was the Victim in our relationship. In the role of Rescuer the outstanding emotion was sympathy and love. And so it could be seen in my life that because of my experience of rejection and hurt I took on the role of Rescue, seeking to help the homeless and disadvantaged and finally got into trouble at Fareham college when I stepped in to ensure one of my students passed their practical exams, after he had made a simple mistake. I will tell you later.

It was at this time I felt the name Nurse Ratchet was more appropriate to call my wife because of the way she needed to control me, our marriage and my children.

We tried to resolve our problems but all to no avail. Nurse Ratchet appeared to experience so much insecurity that it leads her to believe unusual things about me.

Argument 368 Kneeing In The Testicles

This is just one series of incidents that I numbered argument 368. I had actually lost count of the number we actually had but it seemed we had one for each day of the year. This was argument 368 the third one in the second year of our marriage. In this dispute Nurse Ratchet was furious with me and kneed me in the testicles and refused to go to church with me, that evening. She wanted to discuss something that she was upsetting her, just as we were about to leave for the church. I had arranged to take to church that evening Isaac my son, Luke Fuller, Isaac's friend, Joe Neve, a drug dealer and addict, and Eleanor my daughter as this was an evangelical meeting. She wanted me to cancel what I was doing and insisted that I stay with her and sort out the problem she had.

This argument was brewing. She was not prepared to wait. I wanted to wait till a later time and if possible have a friend present to discuss the matter, in a safe environment. I had good reason to avoid this type of argument because of what I had experienced before. On a previous occasion Silver Girl and I were with out, with our new daughter, on a trip to Salisbury. Nurse Ratchet was upset over something that I had either said or had done. She insisted that I had never got over a relationship with a girl friend some 30 years ago (my first girlfriend, Susan Alwright, from Aylesbury). On this occasion she got out of the car extremely upset carrying our daughter in her arms and proceeded to walk home. Of course that was unsafe for her and our daughter.

So I had reason to fear such talk would lead to inappropriate action on Nurse Ratchet part. I also felt responsible for my children's welfare and important to take my children and their friends to hear the Gospel of our Lord Jesus Christ. I had the opportunity that I rarely had and they were prepared to come to the church that night. I had been helped at the church and to tell all my family of what the Lord had done for me. Nurse Ratchet felt otherwise and rather than be dictated too by my wife I refused to obey her voice and do what I believed was the right thing to do.

On this occasion she kneed me in the testicles and wanted me to leave Stubbington, and live elsewhere, and me to leave our home in otherwise she would find somewhere else to live and take Rebekah and her children with her.

This also lead to Nurse Ratchet's daughter ordering me out of the house and because I ignored her she left instead of me and told her in-laws to be that she had been kicked out.

All such arguments were very unpleasant and hurtful occasions. All of them brought on by an argument of similar nature and complexity as the one I felt was being prepared for me at that moment. It was Nurse Ratchet's determination and insistence that we talk about the issue right without considering me that I felt was an abuse. I felt abused. It was my intention to steer away from such disastrous discussions unless we had some Christian help at hand so we could avoid further hurt and needless pain.

Just Say I Love You

Try a different way 1997 – 98

The argument we were having often involved my children from my first marriage. On one particular evening an argument was looming and at the prayer meeting that night, at the Warsash church, I requested prayer and support. It was suggested to me I try another way. Rather than respond and argue over matters simply say " I love you" and to repeat it every time she wanted to argue. I was to say no more. I took this on board and agreed to give it a try. I returned home and as the contention began in the bedroom. I simply said, "I love you" and repeated this without saying any more. My wife was convinced I had gone mad and wanted me to say more. She then called her daughter in from her bedroom to witness my response. I simply repeated, "I love you".

If I Were You I Would Hit Him

My wife was furious and her daughter said to her mum, "If I were you I would hit him", I began to have real fear that a more serious argument might occur and then some form of violence would take place and I wanted to leave the house until she had calmed down. So as she left the room I quickly took my clothes and slipped out of the bedroom, into the little room, that I had made above the garage and locked the door behind me. I heard a commotion at the other side of the door, between my wife and her daughter, as they were wondering where I had gone. So I just lay down on the floor and kept very quiet. I just wanted to be left alone. I was hoping things would calm down and the heat would go away but my wife did not give up. Eventually she made a search for me by going into the garage and climbed up the staircase that I had made in the garage, to the roof space where I was. She found me lying down with my eyes shut, as though I was sound asleep. She opened the door to the inside of the house and called her daughter to say she had found me and pointed out that I looked unconscious.

I Dare Not Open My Eyes

I felt I did not wish to show I was awake in case she was more furious with me so I kept quiet. My wife felt by body and I was cold so she switched on an electric fire and place it near my legs to warm me up but it was so hot I began to burn. How ever but had to keep still and feel the pain. I still kept quiet. I then heard my wife' s daughter say how selfish I was, thinking I had attempted suicide, and was not thinking of my daughter. I then heard Nurse Ratchet call my former wife on the phone asking had I done any thing like this before. She then called the doctor, it was late at night and things were getting worse for me. I dare not wake as trouble was now really brewing for me. I just lay there until the doctor came. When he arrived I simply open my eyes and said I was fine and that we had, had an argument and I just needed to be left alone. The doctor was fine and left the room and he informed my wife to just leave me alone and that I would be fine.

Suicidal Thoughts

Soon after this time I informed the members of our prayer group that I had experienced suicidal thoughts, all relating to the troubles in our marriage and the fear of my wife leaving me. It was at that time one of the Elders prayed with and for me after, which then I began to get better, "The black dogs of depression", left me for a while.

I had learned to respect medical opinion and it was now my opinion to maintain my stability by continuing with my medication, which is the prescribe treatment for manic depression or bipolar moods swings. It was a bit like Oliver Cromwell's advise to his army, when they were going into battle he said, " Trust in God and keep your powder dry". And so with me call upon the Lord and keep on with the lithium. The ups and downs of our new relationship brought with it the highs and lows of emotion. Van Gough once said that emotions were the captains of our lives. I was certainly driven by powerful emotions at this time. I was responsible, during all this time to have my blood levels checked and to take my medication. This I did as regular as clockwork and kept in touch with Dr Walmsely, even when I was signed off as needing care. This was because I was aware of my reality and fear of depression.

Nurse Ratchet Is Jealous Of My Song

After this meeting I felt the desire to compose a song in praise to God, for the help I had received, and I wrote the following entitled, "Spirit of the Lord Come down" and was able to sing it at the Warsash church. This desire was an expression thanks for the support I had received from God during my recent awful times. However when Nurse Ratchet heard my song she expressed she was jealous, as it was not about her. I found this response incredible and it portrayed to me she had deep-seated insecurities. Realising this was the case and wishing to assure her she had no need to be jealous, I re-wrote the words for her benefit. This new song was called, "Can your remember". Unfortunately I was never able to sing this version of the song as we separated in November 1998, but that did not stop my plan to sing this love song to her the next year. Not only did I re write the song but also I practised it many times and sung at various venues after we separated. Finally I decided it should be recorded and be release as a single.

Joining the Warsash Church

At this time sometime in October 1998, a few weeks before our second and final separation, we had attending the Warsash Church for some time and Nurse Ratchet, without notice, began to attend the church in Titchfield, on her own, without informing me of the reason, so continued to attend the Warsash church. It was then that I was asked, by one of the elders, to become a church member. This however was one of the last things on my mind, so I said I would consider it.

40 OUR SECOND AND FINAL SEPARATION

The resentment, between Nurse Ratchet and my children, led to our second and final separation. This took place on the 4th November 1998 when I left and retreated to 11 Hayling Close, dreading the future, as I felt so low in my mood.

Nurse Ratchet had repeatedly stated she wanted me to leave and if I wouldn't go she would get her ex husband to come and remove my things. I finally realized I would have to go and so I made all the necessary preparations, regarding finance and securing my personal things. I left the morning of that day, as I knew once I had gone I would have no cooperation from Nurse Ratchet to resolve anything.

On a previous occasion I had given Nurse Ratchet £4,000, this soon after my fathers death but she said she did not want it but would look after it for me until I needed it. So I opened an ISA account in her name and deposited the money. It was during the weeks before I left on the 4th November, that I realised I would have difficulties getting the money from her, never the less I had asked her for the money. She refused and would not give it to me. And still continually told me to leave. So I wrote to the ISA bank, in her name, informing them of our change of address i.e. To 11 Hayling Close and the following week I wrote to the company to close the account asking for the £4000 signing the letter in her name. I was thankful it was successful and I receive the cheque for £4000 plus interest. Never the less it was this action of mine that sent her around the bend with anger and was the reason for her saying I was a hypocrite.

It was with great sadness that I learned, to my dismay, that Nurse Ratchet had purposely been very difficult and awkward with me, those weeks before hand, in order to drive me out and away from our home. I learned this after reading her secret diary written in October 98. The entry reads,

"The more horrible you are to someone the more Dave is drawn to them-- he always sides with the ones being got at. So I'll be even more horrible and he may go to his darlings. His loyalty to me is disgusting."

I realise this now that this accounted for her unacceptable behaviour towards my children and my subsequent desire to protect them from it was but a natural instinct and a Christian principle that I followed.

She continued to write, "I'm sick of hearing their names. I wish he'd just live with them at wonderful number 11".

On Thursday 15th October, 1998 she wrote, "I'm am full of rage and feel sick and in knots. I hate all of them" --They have evil in them--they needed to be away from others.

Nurse Ratchet, the psychiatric nurse, had made up her mind about my children as can be seen by what she wrote and referred to them as the "KLU CLARKE CLAN."

I knew there was a problem and had previously suggested we get help from the Family Mediation Service, because I knew things between us all we so caustic. Unfortunately Nurse Ratchet felt differently. She was offended that I should suggest such a thing to her as she was a trained Adult mental health nurse and so did not need any help in mediation. On the 26/10/98, her diary entry wrote, "I want to kill him."

It was the following week that Nurse Ratchet stated to me that Eleanor and Esther were no longer Rebekah's sisters but another girl Gillian was, who baby-sat for her. At the same said she wanted Rebekah to have another father.

My Children

The Clu Clarke Clan

I discovered these things written in Nurse Ratchet's secret diary when I returned to our home, the week after I left, whilst she was at work.

I left and took all my things on the 4th November 1998.

Nurse Ratchet's problem with me joining the church at Warsash

During the weeks leading to my escape the thought of joining the church at Warsash was one of the last things on my mind. Things at home were so difficult I could scarcely think of any other thing wishing to solve the problems in the marriage. However I wanted to be more involved in the church and I felt so rejected by Nurse Ratchet, it felt as though God was saying. " If your wife rejects you, I will receive you". With this feeling and reason I agreed to join the church and felt wanted.

Nurse Ratchet was later informed, by one of the elders, after we had separated in November, saying that I was about to become a member of the church. I learned she felt angry about it. She did not like it and was very upset for some unknown reason. She did not feel I should be allowed to join the church on the grounds of all the allegations she had written about to the Family Mediation Service. See letter dated 8/12/98. She wanted an explanation from the elders how they could admit me to be a member. She felt I was a hypocrite and that I joining the church felt like I had another woman. Nurse Ratchet told one of the elders of the church how she felt about me joining the church in front of his daughter Gillian, who later related this to my youngest son David. In response to this he felt very angry with Nurse Ratchet and he informed me that she had been saying bad things about me and that I had another woman. He felt that these evil things were the cause of her son being upset and awkward with him.

When David informed me what Nurse Ratchet had been saying about me I decided I would have to ask Nurse Ratchet and her son about it the next time I saw her. When I spoke to the Nurse about it I discovered this was not true and that all she had said was that it felt like I had another woman when she learned I was to join the church.

Nurse Ratchet then demanded David make her and her son an apology, face to face, and she wanted me not to see him again until he apologize to her and her son for repeating these things. I saw David and told him I wanted him to apologies to Nurse Ratchet he said he could not face the agony of seeing Nurse Ratchet face to face and agreed to send a letter of apology

Nurse Ratchet Upset With The Church

The nurse was angry at the church for considering making me a member as she felt I was not worthy. She wanted to ask the Elders all about it, however she said she could not face going to see them. I received a letter from the Nurse stating that she did not want me to join the church and that if I did she would take it that I did not want reconciliation. She said it showed to her that I wanted a permanent separation. I felt so frustrated as this was not true and I felt this was black mail that I was not prepared to give in to this form of control. At that time I asked the Nurse for my unpublished book, written about my time at the Bierton Strict and Particular Baptist church but She refused to give it back to me and I felt very much alone. I later published this book in 2003 and it is called the, "The Bierton Crisis".

The Elders felt she was wrong and it would do no good to speak to her.

I Decide To Join The Church

Having decided not to give into this blackmail I wrote the following letter to Nurse Ratchet on 10/12/98

Dear SG

I have spoken at the meeting tonight explaining your request to speak to the elders at the church and who ever, about their decision to accept me as a member of the church.

I explained how you felt very upset and angry since I had done awful things to you (what ever they were). I mentioned in particular your forged name explaining of course I knew you were angry about and that I had said other things to you, which may of hurt you in our arguments. I also informed them that I had apologized to you and asked you if I could put any matter right.

I explained you felt me joining the church was like me having another woman that they were not helping us get back together but doing the opposite.

I explained to them what Elder RB had said and his advise to you about Warsash and also what your minister had said about Warsash church, stating they were wrong etc. That both RB and the minister were in agreement with you, I should not be allowed to join the church because of what I had done.

I did the best I could but they felt you were wrong. They said you were welcome at Warsash Church any time and they love you. Will said you had been invited to be a member but you did not respond. He said he had often asked you to see him to help with the kids and me but you would not.

John and Sue C were there and Sue seemed to understand you and I am sure she would help if you went to see her.

I had hoped they would have offered to sit with you at a meeting with who ever you wanted to be there, in order to answer your questions, but they did not feel it would help at all. They assured me you are very welcome at Warsash church and that Brian had been in contact with you.

I explained how you said if I join you will take it I want separation. They encouraged me to continue seeking the lord and honour Him. All of which I said I would be doing anyway. Since writing to you about the Derek situation I now realize Abraham would have never offered up Isaac as a sacrifice if he had allowed his wife to stop him from obeying God. We do not know if Abraham told Sarah about his intention to offer up Isaac in sacrifice but we do know in other things she obeyed Abraham and was a help to him and not an obstacle. You know I believe God and He has given you to me. It is right and fitting for me to obey God and you me.

I have to admit I now find your warning threat hurtful and I take it very seriously. That is warning about me joining the Warsash Church. I have explained to you that my wishing to join the church did not mean I wanted separation from you at all but I simple wanted to follow Jesus, in every way I could. I have never wanted separation from you; it has been you all along wishing separation - not me.

In fact it would be my hearts desire we both be members at Warsash. So why not think about it. Why have you left Warsash anyway? I will step aside for a while if you want to go.

I now realize if you are telling me you will still take it I want a separation if I join the Warsash Church, in spite of me telling you otherwise, then you are threatening me. I take it you will forsake me if I join the Warsash Church.

I take it you are threatening me for being a Christian. I believe my Jesus whom I depend on will never forsake me and has spoken to me from His word about this very situation and this is what he says:

Matthew 19 verse 29. Every one that hath forsaken houses, or brethren or sisters or father or mother or wife or children or lands for my name's sake shall receive an hundred fold and shall inherit everlasting life.

I love you more than you have ever felt or known and I believe you were given me by God as my hearts desire. I am sorry for all the wrong and hurt

I have caused you please forgive me.

You now tell me you will want permanent separation if I follow Jesus in the way he wants me to go. I want to follow Jesus. You have told me I stand to loose you if I follow Him.

You have already said I cannot take Rebekah if I join the Church on Sunday, even though I really want you and her with me. I am sorry this is your attitude and intention but I now know what I must do.

If the Lord will I will be joining the Church at Warsash on Sunday 13th December 1998. I assume you will stick to your word but please ring me and say I can take her. I will talk with your minister friend, R B, D.C. and V F, any one if you think I need help or if you want me too. I am free Friday and Saturday.

I love you, please do not forsake me. We have a lot to look forward too in the Lord.

Love David.

I Decide Against Joining The Church

After careful consideration I decide not to join the church thinking this would help so I explained my situation to B T and his wife and B and I and they said they would speak with us both and help. I wrote the following to Silver Girl.

Dear Silver Girl,   20/12/98

I realize you may not be aware but I did not joint the church at Warsash last Sunday. I was hoping my decision not to join would help our reconciliation as you expressed you were not happy about it. I also took the liberty to ask B and I and B T and his wife to help us by talking through things with us. They all said they would be pleased to help.

I have a Christmas present for Rebekah and would really like it to be to her from us both - how do you feel about that? Is there any way I could see you for a short while during Christmas as I miss you so very much (If you haven't given up on us).

Yours in love

David.

Summery

I would encourage my readers, who are considering marriage, and wish to know what the bible says about men and women relationships, to read and understand my article on Christian marriage.

Women Elders and the Church at Warsash

My times and difficulties in dealing with my wife was enough to put me on guard against the rise of women taking prominent places and positions of authority in our present age. Can you imagine how I felt when the following episode took place at the Warsash Church?

It was the beginning of the New Year; January of 1999, after some of the elders and members of the church had left to form a new group meeting, at the Hilton Hotel in Farlington. It was then announced that the elders of Warsash Church were asking for nominations to elect further elders and that these positions were open for women to apply. This took me by surprise. I understood the church was wishing to follow the New Testament pattern of church order and practice. After all they since called themselves the "Jesus is Lord" church and from my understanding this was going against His principles.

I recalled that they had asked me to join the church recently because they wanted to increase the membership and make a stand in the United Reformed denomination against two issue causing dispute at that time. The two issues were the appointing of homosexuals to leadership and the appointment of women elders.

When I raised my concern with the elders I was met with opposition and despite my documented evidence, pointing out scriptural reasons, showing their error I was finally told to remain silent whilst I continued going to the church. This was my cue to leave the church as conscience dictated a better path to take. It was then I wrote about this matter in my book entitled, **"Mary, Mary Quite Contrary"**, which is my response and opinion regarding the matter of women being elected to the position of elders in a church. The essence of the matter from a Christian point of view is this:

1   Since the fall of Adam God curses them both along with the serpent and the ground. Adam would suffer hardship, that thorns and thistles would grow, and so earn he would have to earn living by the sweat of his brow until the day he dies. To the woman he said that she would be in great pain in childbirth and her natural desire would be to rule her husband but he must rule over her.

2   In Christian marriage the man is the head of his wife, in the way that Christ is the head of his church. As the church is to be subject to Christ so the woman is to be subject to her husband.

3   This order has to do with the fall of Adam and Eve in the Garden of Eden and since God placed this curse on His creation after the fall, then that order remains to this day.

4   We should follow the order, set by Christ, for all relationships between men, wife, children etc. And not think we know better.

This order of relationships still continues to this present day, as demonstrated by the fact that the curse, placed by God on his creation, still remains. Therefore so should the order between men, women, children, church and elders remain in the church?

As a result and after discovering similar problems relating to women taking on leadership roles in a church in the Philippines I wrote an account of my run in with the elders at Jesus is Lord Church at warsash in my book **Mary, Mary Quite Contrary,** or Alternatively, " Does The Lord Jesus Want Women To Rule As Elders In His Church? I then left the Church and began meeting with a new group of Christians called The Christian Gospel Church that met in the Hilton Hotel in Farlington.

Letter From My Brother

My brother Michael had written to me in 1998 asking me to help him and I could tell from his first letter he was in a very bad way. He told me of another Englishman, Suny Wilson, who had been "set up" for a crime he did not do and was sentenced to death in 1996. Michael use to visit him on Death Row and spend time together. The Philippine Supreme Court acquitted Suny Wilson, on the 19th December 1999 through the help of Alan C. Atkins and Errol Wilkinson and he had given Michael a small paperback entitled "Mere Christianity" by CS Lewis on his release. Michael read this book and was later convinced that Jesus was the Christ the Son of the living God.

Michael's Letter Indicating A True Change Of Mind And Heart

Dear David,   7th May 1999

With regards to me writing my life story etc., for you to include in your book! Please David forgive me but I am so screwed up, I just could not handle it right now. It takes me all my strength to just write this letter to you...

I am so very pleased that you are concerned for me and that you include me in your prayers and your fellow Christians. I do believe in God and Jesus Christ but even though I pray and ask him to please forgive me, for all my sins, and to help me to be a better person and to take over the rest of my life on earth and to lead me into heaven - I do not want to go to hell because I know that what I am suffering now is nothing to the perpetual hell which would await me after physical death on earth. My faith is not strong enough and I am so very, very, confused. Even if I get out of here what am I going to do with the rest of my life. I am looking very old, skinny, withdrawn. I have not smiled in almost 4 years. Where am I going to live? How can I earn a living in my condition?

Oh, David I am so very afraid of the future and it hurts me so much to even think about it. I have become old before my time and all I can see is loneliness in some dingy rented room and no chance of ever finding some one (a lady) to love and share things with. Oh, David what am I going to do?

The only thing that stops me thinking about suicide is that hell will be waiting for me and the torment there will be a million times worse. Will I ever smile again? Will I ever love again? Will any one love me again? Is it possible to be happy again? I do not have any reason to live and that is so very frightening. Oh, David I know you have your problems that may be greater than mine and to be honest I do not know how you cope. How do you manage to keep working and keep your home going, the loss of you wife must be absolutely unbearable? May be you can suggest how I tackle my problems of the future, for me there simply is no light at the end of the tunnel.

When I leave here I don't even have a pair of shoes. I will have to start all over again but the question is how do I start all over again? I simply have no will to live and I just could not cope with living on my own as I know I would not be able to fend for my self. To think of buying a property is really out of the question. What do I do? What do I do?

Another reason why I cannot think of writing my life story is because I am truly ashamed of many of the things I have done and I don't really want to broadcast my evil past for every one to read. I have confessed to the Lord and I just hope He will forgive me.

You asked me how I felt about you becoming a Christian 30 years ago. Well I was quite proud of you but felt you were a little over the top but I never mocked you in any way. My heart broke with Karen Mead and the collapse of Tudor Charm and my divorce I will expand on that some other time so please David not at the moment, you may have to wait until I am released.

At the moment I am taking each day at a time and I keep praying that I will be acquitted of this horrible conviction, which I hope will give me added strength to face the future. I am sorry my letter is so depressing, all I can do is pray to out the Lord for strength and guidance.

Once again David thank you again for not forsaking me and I am sure you will be always there to give me support.

Please give all my love to the Children

41 HOW MY LIFE WAS EFFECTED

Whilst going through all these difficulties and emotional trials I am sure, as I look back, that I subconsciously created manic highs in order to avoid depression. This is my theory. Any way I did my utmost to be good at my job and also find another outlet to express my emotions.

In my endeavours to do my best for all my students I got my self into trouble at Fareham College, towards the end of the summer term. At that time of the year we held a practical examination, for the Electronic Servicing 224 course and I along with an external assessor, from Portsmouth College, was responsible to conduct the practical tests for the RTEEB Examining Board and to mark their work and ensure there was no cheating. It was a recognised national standard test.

On this occasion one of my better students, who had paid for his own course fees, made a simple error in the test he was conducting. I noticed his mistake and realised that this could result in a failure. So I altered his script to read correctly. Unfortunately the external examiner noticed the change and alerted the senior management of the College. I justified this action, to myself, because I was the best person and only person to judge if this student was capable to do such practical work. He had proved himself to me over the two years I had taught him and I knew him to be good. He just simply made a mistake. Fortunately the student was unaffected as he has sufficient marks to pass regardless of my alteration but the matter was brought to a disciplinary hearing and I could have been dismissed. In mitigation I had several personal testimonials, from former students, speaking on my behalf regarding my previous good conduct and beneficial help they had all received, which resulted in me getting written warning for one year. One former student was Mike Fisher from Gosport and Michael Evans from Petersfield.

John Sawyers funeral

At that time John Sawyer, one of my students died. He was a diabetic and lived alone at 6 Ranson Close, Titchfield.

The police rang me one morning asking if I knew John Sawyer. I explained I was his course tutor at Fareham College and he was one of my student doing a City and Guilds course in Electronics Servicing.

The policeman explained John was found dead in his home at Titchfield and he had no relatives to contact and my telephone number was the only contact they found in John's house.

I had known John, as a student at College, for about two years and had visited him at his home. He had shared with me about his life and his struggles with Fareham Borough Council about his workshop that they stopped him building.

He was quite a well-liked character amongst the staff at Fareham College. He loves his wife, who had died a few years previously, and so he returned to college doing mechanical engineering and electronics as a hobby. He was a mechanic and engineer having all kinds of good electronic and mechanical equipment.

Since John had no relatives we decided at college to make arrangements for his own departure. It was muted at first we hire a proper vicar to conduct the funeral. It was then I stepped in and said I would be pleased to conduct his funeral.

Several students and staff came to his funeral including Geoff Whitefield our Head of School and our Health and safety officer Marilyn Dufour.

Our technicians and staff were his coffin bearers whilst I spoke a few relevant words about John and his life. I related that Jesus at the tomb of Lazarus wept. It was a natural thing to feel and express grief. I said had John been a believer he would have gone to be with Christ but he had made no profession of faith, as far as any one knew. So I couldn't say any more.

It was a sorrowful occasion but John had a respectful funeral and he left us with good memories of him self.

It was commented after the funeral that his coffin was so heavy they suggested John had taken with him his tool kit.

It was also said I made a better preacher than a lecturer; little did they know that, that was my real calling.

It can be said that I cater for all my students' needs although I have not yet been a mid wife. Nor have I conducted a marriage.

Steven Murray

During this time in May 1999, I had a mother call to my home, asking if I would provide accommodation for her step-son Steven Murray, who was 20 years old. He looked very much like my own son Isaac. I was reluctant to take him in as he was without work at that time and the only means of paying any form of rent was to apply for Housing Benefit. He assured me that he would find work very quickly so I gave him a chance and took him in.

I also felt I could help him and shared with him my past life and my Christian beliefs. I knew nothing of his past background although I sensed it had been difficult. I encouraged him to come to church with me and gave him s draft copy of my book Converted on LSD Trip.

I encouraged him to attend Fareham College and enrolled him on an electronics course, as he was very knowledgeable. I also encourage him to repair items that we had bought from Harrod's and re-sell them to earn pocket money and he was very successful.

I took Steve to church with me and he showed a keen interest in Christianity and got involve with the church, helping out with the PA system. He soon expressed faith and need of God and was baptised in the Sea at Lee-on-the-Solent.

I was delighted as this was what I expected from any one who believed the gospel of Jesus Christ. This was just as it happened to me over 30 years

283
ago.

The News Thursday, June 24, 1999

LEE-ON-THE-SOLENT / Former drug user and thief tells of his new Christian outlook

Baptism At Sea Marks Start Of My New Life

By Lorna Vicars

A reformed Fareham drug user and thief was baptised in the sea to mark the start of a new life. For years Steve Murray, 21, took drugs, stole cars and burgled houses- but when he became a Christian his life changed. Steve of Hayling Close took the plunge, at the slipway at the Lee-on-the Solent Sailing Club. About 30 friends and relatives watched as an elder, from the Church Steve attends, carried out the baptism. Steve left school six years ago at 15 and became qualified in painting and decorating and carpentry. He spent the next four years when he was not working smoking cannabis and taking ecstasy and amphetamine drugs. He said, "I was getting into trouble with the police – thieving cars and motorbikes". "When I was not working I was rebelling. I did not know why I carried on doing it. I felt comfortable doing it in a way.

Steve Murray

Steve Murray baptised in the sea

By Rev Peter Jacobs of the Christian Gospel Church

I used to hang about with people who wanted bits fro their houses and it started of with me shop-lifting and petty things. Then people needed cars, and I went on doing it myself because I wanted the stuff.

"I wanted to change but I felt there was no way out".

Steve remembered the first time he prayed two years ago when he was told his then girlfriend Tyrone Finlayson might die giving birth to their daughter Rhiannon.

He said, "I was surprised to find myself praying and they both made it through".

"It has gone from there".

Steve became a Christian and has been going to the Christian Gospel Church, which meets in the Hilton National Portsmouth hotel, in Farlington.

He chose to be baptised in the sea following the example of John the Baptist in the bible.

After months of being unemployed Steve is now working as a Bar Steward at the Forte Post House Hotel in Titchfield.

He said," It is not like my life has stopped. I still go out and drink and have a good laugh – I just go to church every Sunday".

"It is like an emptiness has been filled and it gives me something to aim for and I have got someone there. I pray and hope every thing to be all right.

"I see a happy future".

The very next week he got a job as a barman at the Post House Forte, Segensworth and shortly after that he was able to see his own daughter for the first time in months. I gave him my wedding suit as a baptism gift as he needed a suit of cloths.

I took no notice of those people who began to give me evil reports of his past behaviour believing he was a new man in Christ. Unfortunately I became concerned at his continued heavy drinking and gambling and also his miss treatment of girls. I prayed for him and so did our church. I had another young lodger and they both generated a lot of loud noise from their music and the neighbours complained. Later my daughter's bicycle was stolen and I had to sort things out so I gave my other lodger, called Dan, notice to leave. He soon complained to me that I had given Steve special treatment over him and he felt this was because he had been baptised.

It was soon after this, whilst Steve was helping at the church one Sunday morning, that the collection money (£400) was taken, and shortly after this my motorbike, that I had just purchased, was stolen. It was a 250 cc Honda Super Dream. It was returned however with damaged front forks, a broken lock and missing wing mirrors. It was strange that Steve had asked to ride it the day before and assured me he had a full drivers license to drive it. Steve, Dan and Steve's friend, denied any knowledge of the bikes disappearance and it return.

The Bad Boys

Steve Murray and Dan Bullimoore

They say they did not take my Motorbike

I then got a call from Steve's boss, at the Post House, to say he had not been to work and he now no longer had a job. It was after Steve told me he was going back on housing benefit, as he was not working sufficient hours, that I gave him notice to leave because he was now lying to me.

I received a call on the 27th July 1999, from the Cheque-cashing bureau in Fareham, regarding a cheque, apparently issued to Steve Murray, which was not honoured, for £220, so I was advised to go to the police. When reporting this to the police it turned out that Dan also had drawn £100 from my account along with a further Nationwide withdrawal of £380.

Even after this when Steve and Dan had gone I had things stolen from my house. What really got me upset was when my Fender Strata 1983, American Stratocaster, was stolen form my house along with my 8 track digital recorder. The police recovered the Guitar from Steve Murray. When I reported the story to the local News it was reported in the Paper. The only real problem resulting from this was the fact that the senior man at our church had a go at me and was not very happy. He seemed very concerned about the name of the church but showed no concern for the fact that Steve Murray had robbed me and taken advantage of me seeking to help him. I felt that since the scripture mentioned the good and bad events such as the bad conduct of Judas, then I felt it quite OK for the world to know Steve Murray's

286
conduct.

42 MICHAEL'S CALL FOR HELP

One Year On And A Change Takes Place

Just after one year I noticed a remarkable change in Michael's outlook and his state of mind. It was all for the better. I gradually felt able to read and digest the National Bureau of Investigation Report (NBI), which clearly clears Michael of charges made against him. This record goes on to a recommendation that Fr. Shay Cullen, Michael's Complainant, be deported on the grounds of him being and undesirable alien in the Philippines. (See report appendix 01)

Michael had written to me in 1998 asking me to help him and I could tell from his first letter he was in a very bad way. He told me of another Englishman, Suny Wilson, who had been "set up" for a crime he did not do and was sentenced to death in 1996. Michael use to visit him on Death Row and spend time together. The Philippine Supreme Court acquitted Suny Wilson, on the 19th December 1999 through the help of Alan C. Atkins and Errol Wilkinson and he had given Michael a small paperback entitled **"Mere Christianity"** by C.S. Lewis, on his release. Michael read this book and was later convinced that Jesus was the Christ the Son of the living God. Suny Wilson's Story is told in **"Sentenced To Death"** by Alan Atkins and Earl Wilkinson. It is also available as a Youtube Video:

Sentenced To Death Suny Wilson (click to view)

Here is Michaels letter:

Dear David,   July 3rd 2000

Just a few lines wishing every thing are OK With you and you are being to sort out how you will be able to see your daughter on mutual terms.

There is no movement with regards to my case with the Board of Pardon and Parole because as of today my prison records have not been sent from the prison document section to the Board. Every thing moves so slowly it really drives me crazy.

I am still reading a lot of Christian books. The one I am reading now is "Joy Unspeakable" by Dr. Martin Lloyd Jones. It is all about the Holy Spirit and I believe that baptism of the Holy Spirit is some thing distinct and does not always, as some people think happen automatically at conversion. The Holy Spirit is within every believer at conversion YES but the baptism can come at any time when Jesus Christ chooses to out pour it upon us. And if us Christian's are not aware of this and do not seek this ultimate experience

I believe they are quenching the Holy Spirit, by not praying for it, and not just for them selves but for the whole Christian Church. "Revival". Etc. Your are always in my prayers Michael.

News Of Michael's Conversion

Michael wrote to me again to me in 2000 with news of his conversion to Christianity and of him being baptised, in a 45 gallon oil drum in New Bilibid Prison, by Lucas Dangatan, a former inmate, who was now a Religious Volunteer (RVO) working in New Bilibid Prison and Pastor of the New Bilibid Prison Theological Institute (NBPTI) in the prison. I finally believed Michael was telling the truth about his conviction. That he too had been "set up" for a crime he did not commit. This was clear to me after reading the National Bureau of Investigation (NBI) report, written by the Bureau in 1995. See Appendix "Trojan Warriors" to read the report. This report was brought to me by Suny Wilson, who himself had been wrongly convicted on a charge of rape. He called me on the telephone, on the 25th December 1999, soon after he returned to England, to introduce himself and he then came to see me with news of Michael and to give me the NBI report.

I Write Our Story

It was as a result of my recovery to faith in the Lord Jesus Christ and the run in with the Elders of the Warsash Church I felt able and compelled to write my story of conversion from crime to Christ, which resulted in my second book, "Converted on LSD Trip".

As I was putting the final touches to the first edition of Converted on LSD Trip, I felt compelled to include Michael's story (this is a STOP PRESS story) and must be told by Michael himself but in his letters to me when, I asked him to write his side of the story to compliment, "Converted on LSD Trip" he wrote in May 1999, "with regards to me writing my life story etc. For you to include in your book! Please David forgive me but I am so screwed up I just could not handle it right now it takes all my strength just to write this letter to you".

Cast Your Net The Other Side Of The Ship

I had a strong conviction that our story could be of great help to others and although I had tried to tell it in England a scriptural verse pressed hard on my mind it was, And he said unto them, **"Cast the net on the right side of the ship"**, **"And they were astonished, and all that were with him, at the draught of fishes which they had taken"**. Luke 5 verse 9.

The sense I gathered was that for years I had toiled to fish for men in my home country to win them for Christ and now I was to cast the net on the other side of the world rather than the ship to catch men for Christ. I shared this idea with the Church one Sunday and announced my intention to go and help Michael in the Philippines.

I had concluded that God in his wisdom had allowed all these things to happen to me and Michael, both the good and evil, to bring me to the point of testifying to the truth, of the goodness and mercy of God. It is my pleasure to do so. It is now as natural for me to glorify God as it is for a bird to sing.

May 12th 1999.

Our Church Writes To Him

Celebrated his conversion and we sent him a new leather bound bible and a couple of tapes and some friend wrote to him. He said also he was very pleased my fellow Christians were praying for him and were concerned about him. He expressed he was so very low and did believe in God and had asked forgiveness for all his sins and trusted in him. He wonders could any one ever love him and would he ever smile again or could he ever be happy again. Another reason why he could not think to write his story was because he said "I am truly ashamed of many things I have done and really did not wish to broadcast my evil past to every one at that time". He had confessed to the Lord and just hoped he would be forgiven.

Good News

In July 2000 Michael wrote he was reading Christian books and at that present time was reading, "Joy Unspeakable" by Dr Martin Lloyd -Jones. I was very encouraged and soon realised he had become a Christian when he expressed his wish to work in full time Christian ministry.

It became very apparent to me and to others that God had demonstrated His goodness to another undeserving sinner. Michael John Clarke. This was indeed good news to say the least. Armed with this good news and my intentions, I told my story to the religious correspondent at The News Portsmouth, Lizzy Millar.

THE NEWS Saturday August 12th 2000

ON THE left is Dave Clarke - college lecturer and committed Christian. On the right is his brother Michael - currently languishing in a prison cell in the Philippines.

Gordon Smith Contacts

And as a result of the me publishing my story, Converted on LSD Trip, the Bucks Herald News paper published and article in the Aylsebury Paper and as a result of my book Gordon Smith and an old friend of mine contacted me, from Dorset, where he was living. We there and then, on the telephone, agree to go on our mission to the Philippines to bring assistance to Michael and celibate his conversion to Christianity. It was decided we would visit for

3 weeks, as this was the longest time we could visit without a visa.

Portsmouth News Item

Dave spends much of his spare time trying to help young people turn away from a life of crime. Now he is on his most important mission yet - trying to save his brother's soul.

Dave converted to Christianity almost 30 years ago, after sharing a life of crime with his brother in their youth. But his brother Michael went further off the rails and is now in a jail in the Philippines.

Dave, 52, of Hayling Close said, regular letters from his brother showed he was sick of his lifelong criminal past, and was thinking of becoming a Christian. He said: 'Michael wrote to me saying he was despairing and suicidal and asked me about my faith. 'I've been praying hard for him and believe he has now come to know the Lord as his personal saviour. I think he is listening to what I write.

Both brothers were notorious criminals in Buckinghamshire where they lived in the 1960's. They were jailed for malicious wounding, which involved shooting a woman in the face with an air weapon at Margate.

Dave said: "When I came out I knew everything there was to know about crime. It was a good school".

"I was determined to have the best of everything and went about it with determination. "I was riding on my brother's reputation. I thought he was cool, but others may not have done so. I set up a garage business for stolen cars.'

The New Article

HOPE: The Clarkes were gangsters in their youth – now one is a Christian while the other is locked up in a Filipino jail

I pray I can save my criminal brother

by Lizzy Millar and Darren Beck
The News

ON THE left is Dave Clarke – college lecture and committed Christian.

On the right is his brother Michael – currently languishing in a prison cell in the Philippines.

Dave spends much of his spare time trying to help young people turn away from a life of crime.

Now he is on his most important mission yet – trying to save his brother's soul.

Dave converted to Christianity almost 30 years ago after sharing a life of crime with his brother in their youth. But his brother Michael went further off the rails and is now in a jail in the Philippines.

Dave, 22, of Hayling Close, said regular letters from his brother showed he was sick of his lifelong criminal past and was thinking of becoming a Christian.

He said: Michael wrote to me saying his was despairing and suicidal and asked me about my faith.

I've been praying hard for him and believe he has now come to know the Lord as his personal saviour. I think he is listening to what I write.

Both brothers were notorious criminals in Buckinghamshire where they lived in the

1960s. They were jailed for malicious wounding after shooting a woman in the face with an air weapon at Margate.

Dave said: When I came out I knew everything there was to know about crime. If I was a good school.

I was determined to have the best of everything and went about it with determination.

I was riding on my brother's reputation as a lout. I set up a garage business for stolen cars.

Dave went to borstal for 12 months while his brother, who denied the charge, went to Maidstone prison for two years.

Father-of-five Dave went straight after converting to Christianity in 1970. He moved to Fareham where he

began teaching electronics at the town's college and became involved with the Christian Gospel Church.

His brother went on the run after being given home leave from prison but was recaptured and served his full sentence.

Michael is now four years into a 16-year jail sentence in prison in the Philippines for promoting sex tourism.

Dave Clarke, left, and his brother Michael – they grew up to share a life of crime

Dave Clarke, left, now prays for his brother Michael

Islands' seedy sex business

MICHAEL Clarke discovered the Philippines and its cheap sex in 1996 when he set himself up as a tour operator.

He placed an advertisement under the name Paradise Express in Exchange and Mart and produced crude brochures describing a 12-night holiday as the dirty dozen and with photos of bikini-clad woman as well as giving details on how to find a Filipino wife.

Clarke, who is divorced with a daughter, had been arrested for agreeing that under-age prostitutes should be procured after he had been captured on a hidden camera. He is appealing against conviction.

Dave said he hoped his

A picture from one of the brochures

brother would now tell God and give up crime.

He added: I regret all the hurt and pain I caused but I realise I had to go through what I have because what I talk to tried to keep them out of trouble I have credibility.

The News Saturday, August 12, 2000

Dave went to Borstal for 12 months while his brother, who denied the charge, went to Maidstone prison for two years.

Father-of-five Dave went straight after converting to Christianity in 1970. He moved to Fareham where he began teaching electronics at the town's college, and became involved with the Christian Gospel Church.

His brother went on the run after being given home leave from prison but was recaptured and served his full sentence.

Michael is now four years into a 16-year jail sentence in prison in the Philippines for promoting child sex tourism. This crime he has always denied.

MICHAEL Clarke discovered the Philippines and its cheap sex business in 1995 when he set himself up as a tour operator.

He placed an advertisement under the name of Paradise Express in Exchange and Mart and produced crude brochure describing a 12-night holiday as the dirty dozen and with Photos of bikini clad woman as well as giving details on how to find a Filipino wife.

Michael Clarke, who is divorced with a daughter, had been arrested: for agreeing that under age prostitutes could be procured, after he had been captured on a hidden camera. He is appealing against the conviction as an

Irish priest set him up.

Dave said he hoped his brother would now find God and give up crime.

He added " I regret the hurt and pain I caused, but I realize I had to go through what I have because when I talk to kids to keep them out of trouble I have credibility.

Lizzy Millar The News

12th August 2001.

Our local news reporter Liz Millar of The News wrote to Michael, via e mail and asked the following questions " as follows:

Liz also wrote these questions for Michael in 28th Aug 2000

Questions for Michael Clarke

1) How do you plan to get out of prison?

Answer - Conditional Pardon by way of voluntary deportation

2) How can we be sure you've changed your ways?

Answer - It is my Lord Jesus Christ that has convicted me of all my Sins, but regards to the crime I was convicted for, which I will always maintain my innocence as Fr. Shay invented this crime.

Cullen who is an Irish Priest and he himself has been charged with Rape and a warrant is now out for his arrest with NO BAIL granted. The Victim is a 7-year-old girl.

Several foreigners have become a victim of Fr. Cullen and The Modus Operandi of him is now under investigation by the Secretary of Justice whom hopefully in the long run will vindicate me completely from this present conviction.

The fact that I am now a true Christian and my FAITH will safe guard me from the temptations of the Devil. It is the same FAITH that assures me of eternal life. AMEN.

I Encourage Michael To Be Baptised

I wrote to Michael in order to encouraged him and said he must now be baptised (Dipped) and I gave him the words as he had expressed into what name or on who's authority should he be baptised? I said In the name of Jesus (his authority) and get immersed water, in the name of Father, Son and Holy Ghost (Spirit). I said he must get one of the inmates who was a Christian to dip him or one of the Christian works that he knew.

These he did and on the 16th September Michael was baptised, as a Christian, in a make shift 45-gallon oil drum.

Michael is baptised 16th September 2000. Philippines

To: "'David Clarke'" <david@dclarke49.fsnet.co.uk>

Baptism in New Bilibid Prison

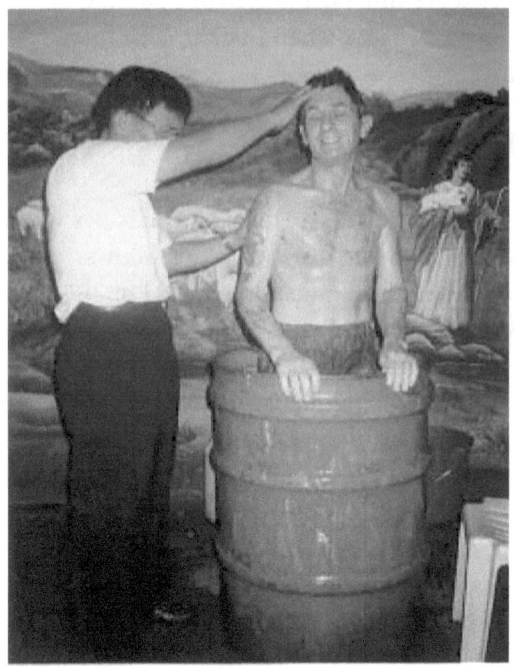

Michael Baptised in New Bilibid Prison

Subject: My visit today to Michael

Date: Tue, 19 Sep 2000 16:37:09 +0800

He sends you this reply.

I was baptised "by immersion" on Sept. 16th 2000 a photo, the photo is now being developed.

Your suggested words were used even before I received your views. YES please put on the web sites the NBI report. But do not give any details whatsoever as to my past criminal record this is personal so just say in general terms that over the years he did many things that were wrong including breaking the criminal law. This also concerns any newspaper stories about me. NO DETAILS only general.

Regards to Liz Miller's question asking, "what does he expect the new story will do to help him".

ANSWER

To expose the truth about the fabricated case against me brought about by Fr. Shay Cullen. But I believe that God will use this situation to expose the works of Satan and in doing so I have surrendered myself to the Lord and have devoted the rest of my life to saving other lost souls.

I have forgiven Fr. Shay Cullen for his evil acts and hope he too confesses his sins to the lord as well as publicity otherwise I know that he is not a Christian and the Lord will punish him in his own way.

Ps Michael was first imprisoned June 7th 1995 - date of sentence Oct 11th 1996 to date 5 years 4 months in Prison

The Baptism Group in the Prison

Michael's Baptism Group

(Pastor Lucas- bottom centre)

I was over the moon with delight and I wrote and told him this was the way forward and we will go on together with Gods help and strength get him clear or acquittal and out of prison.

My Redundancy at Fareham College

It was in March 2001 that I was given 6 months notice my compulsory redundancy. I had taught electronics at Fareham College since September 1988, however student numbers had declined over the years and the college had decided to no longer offer the courses I had taught. I felt very insecure and was not sure about the future on all fronts. With this bad news and sense of despair I tried to speak to my estranged wife. I was concerned about our future and I had the need to talk about our finances but she state that she wanted nothing to do with my house, my money, or anything and wanted nothing do with my brother, as she stated he was a paedophile.

I felt so alone and realised I had to look after my own interests and my brother. I knew if I had no income she would not get any money from me for maintenance for my daughter and have to rely on other sources. And so since she wanted nothing to do with my concerned I felt there was no reason for me to stay in the U.K when I could be in the Philippines, giving assistance to my brother who needed me.

This was the moving cause and reason of our first mission to the Philippines and enabled me to make the decision to go. My wife would have to see to her life on her own.

Fareham College Principals Response To My Book

"Converted on LSD Trip"

The story of "Converted on LSD Trip" was an embarrassment to some people, including the Principal of Fareham College who was my employer. The Principal being Malcolm Charnley. I just could not understand this no one seamed to realize what was happening and it was clear the book was judged by it's cover. The Principal wrote:

"I do not wish to be associated personally or professionally with a book entitled "Converted on LSD Trip" with it's over reference to drug taking". October 2001.

This was presumably because the book had been published whilst I was working at Fareham College. In my true story I mention my work at the College and my turn away from God and so was probably an embarrassment to the College. It was remarked by some that my story might have been just too much for the College to cope with and that my imminent redundancy from the college was the result. The strange thing was that whilst all this was taking place the College was under considerable pressure from the Health and Safety Executive who were examining it for not dealing correctly with problems of asbestos on its premises.

The College was later fined (February 2002) on four counts, a sum of over £23,000, for exposing staff and students to asbestos dust. This however was after I finished work at the college, in August 2001. My redundancy fro Fareham College made it possible for me to complete our Mission to the Philippines.

Portsmouth Consultant Psychiatrist Approves My Book

The irony was that at the same time Dr. Philip Fleming, the consultant psychiatrist of the Kingsway House, the centre for Substance Misuse Service, Portsmouth had written a forward to the second edition.

Dear David,

I attach a brief review of your book as requested. As you will see I found your experiences of great interest and I am sure your book will be of help to many.

295

Philip Fleming

PORTSMOUTH
HealthCare
TRUST

"Converted on LSD Trip"

This book, the personal testament of David Clarke, in an autobiographical style. It charts his life, which became one of criminality and drug taking though an experience in 1970 of finding God whilst under the influence of LSD. Cynics may say that this was just an effect of drugs, but it is clear that the experience changed his life. Later when in court facing charges he admitted to many other crimes and was fortunate in receiving three years conditional discharge and not a prison sentence.

Since then David has combined his work as a lecturer in electronics with his mission of spreading the word of God. This is a scrupulously honest book recording both the difficulties he has faced as well as the successes in his life since 1970. A continuing worry is the fat of his brother, currently serving a long prison sentence in a Philippine jail who himself has recently found God.

"This is an inspiring story of a life that has been turned from crime to a positive account and may be of help to others who find them selves direction-less and involved in crime and drug misuse".

Philip

Dr. Philip M. Fleming. MA. BA, Bch. FRCPsych. DPM.

Consultant Psychiatrist with special responsibility for drugs and alcohol services. Kingsway House is the base for these services in Portsmouth. May 2001

Knowing these things I felt that middle class morality or the morality of this world stank and not all men have faith to see beyond and outward show of righteousness. Some went so far as to say "I must withdraw the book from circulation". They believed it would do harm and not good.

43 OUR FIRST MISSION TO THE PHILIPPINES 2001

The Decision To Go

The decision to go and help my brother Michael was made in May 2001. Gordon and I went on our first mission to the Philippines taking with me 8 copies of my book, Converted On LSD Trip, to be given to The President of the Philippines herself, Gloria Macapagal Arroyo, The Director of New

Bilibid Prison, Richardo Macala, The Director of New Bilibid Theological Institute Lucas P. Dangatan, and The Undersecretary of Justice Jose Calida. The City Mayor Olongapo City.

The full itinerary and record of the mission is told in our book Trojan Warriors. We had a very successful mission in August 2001 through to October 2001. Gordon and I not only preached the gospel to many inmates in New Bilibid Prison but also in **Angeles City Jail, Barretto District Jail** and various churches in different parts of the Philippines.

Our Visit To Angeles City Jail (Click to view)

Trojan Warriors

Michael had worked hard with many inmates of New Bilibid Prison since his conversion . These men too had been converted from crime and worked together to help each other.

In August 2001, at one particular meeting within New Bilibid Prison, Michael and I had an idea (vision), which came to us simultaneously. We believed it would help and assist those inmates who had been converted, from crime to Christ, to write their testimonies and so we requested 100 men to write an account of their conversions. We promised to return the next year with their life stories printed in a book that we named there and then, **"Trojan Warriors"**.

It was purposed that each man upon their release would be able to take a copy of their book, with the accounts of the 100 men's conversions from Crime to Christ, as their own tool for evangelism. So upon their release they could go back to their own cities, towns of villages and tell of all what the lord had done for them and others.

It was this proposal that we worked together with Lucas Dangatan the whole of the next year to gather the hand written testimonies and put them together in our book, **Trojan Warriors**, that we were able to publish in September 2002.

Further proposals

We developed our ideas of helping inmates by the proposition of forming a Teacher Training College within the prison. This was to assist and help the work that was already ongoing amongst prisoners. Our idea was well received and **William C. Poloc** was one of the first inmates to be released and go home to his own city to preach the gospel in **Baguio City Jail.**

It was with this idea Gordon and I went to see the Undersecretary of Justice, **Jose Calida,** with proposal to allow men from our training college be released from the, **"Big House"** to go and teach the gospel within the Medium and Minimum compound prisons. Our proposal was met with great encouragement and it was suggested that due to the problems of security it was envisaged them prisoners from the Medium and Minimum Compound could be transferred to the Maximum Compound to partake in our teaching programs. We also spoke to Director of the Bureau of Corrections, **Ricardo Macala**, about our proposals and he agreed that with the support of the President herself this could be achieved.

The Same Gospel Truths

Michael and I had both experience the salvation of God and deliverance from sin and a life of crime by the saving knowledge of Jesus Christ. We knew the gospel was the power of God unto salvation to all who believe and felt constrained to teach these things to all we could and to help others to do the same.

In conference we had independently come to understand and believed the doctrines of grace which are referred to as Calvinism and we knew very few of those professing Christianity were in the dark and in fact some opposed these truths. This did not stop us working along side those who differed from us as we knew the truths of God are spiritual and a man needs to be taught by God these things in His own time. Jesus knew all truth and those he came to save were in the dark but that did not stop him coming along side and helping where he could.

End Of The Mission

Before leaving home for the UK one of or critics wrote a very complimentary account of our work which is listed below and I must say I felt good after such compliments. As the writer says we were just ordinary men doing what we felt we were called by God to do.

News Reports Of Our Mission

PRESS RELEASE

Reporter Alan Atkins. 11th September 2001

TROJAN HORSE MISSION TO THE PHILIPPINES

4th August- 10th September 2001

Preaching to prisoners including those on "Death Row", New Bilibid Prison, and Philippines. By Alan Atkins.

When first learning of the intended visit by self-styled evangelists and former Lecturer, David Clarke, from Fareham, Hampshire, and Gordon Smith from Merely, Nr. Bournemouth, England, to the Philippines, a number of resident foreigners were angry and dismayed. This was not for the fact that the pair wanted to share their experiences of conversion to Christianity that was their business. Rather, it was the deeper motive of purportedly attempting to assist in the early release of David Clark's brother, Michael Clarke, from the hell-hole that is called New Bilibid Prison, where he had been sentenced to serve 16 years. The angry resident foreigners, all of whom are involved in fighting to obtain justice for many foreigners falsely convicted in a country where the justice system is decidedly faulty to say the least, believed the visit would be detrimental to their own efforts.

Initially, the pair was to be accompanied by Albert Wilson, the Dover resident who had obtained acquittal and release from a death sentence just eighteen months previously. It was believed that certain local vigilante organizations, which had been screaming after his acquittal, would have drawn adverse publicity, which would have hampered the efforts of the locals.

German, Harry Joost, and Britain, Alan Atkins, had dispatched angry missives to David Clarke stating that they both could not see just what good the mission would achieve. Both believed that it would set the cases of incarcerated foreigner's back, as living here for many years, they fully understood the Philippine psyche. Vocal criticism by foreigners would lead to the Filipino authorities digging in their heels, just to show whose country it really was.

David Clarke, in particular, had a genuine reason to visit. There is little doubt that his brother, Michael Clark, convicted of running tours for paedophiles, was cleverly encouraged to make a silly, facetious remark while being secretly filmed by a British television company needing sensationalism. The case was gleefully seized upon by the self-styled "paedophile - busting priest", Father Shay Cullen. Cullen, who has a huge property overlooking Subic Bay, obtains millions from donations to support his children's home, which, incidentally, only contains between 26 and 36 children at any one time. Michael Clarke is only one of the high profile convictions he has obtained against alleged foreign paedophiles. Each conviction is accompanied by fanfare overseas, mainly in Germany and Italy, and results in a massive inflow of cash.

David Clarke, learning some of this, had every right to visit the Philippines and assist his brother. Michael Clarke now claimed to have also been "re-born" being baptised in an oil drum in the prison yard. David Clarke, before arriving, did make one concession to local fears.

Discussions dissuaded Albert Wilson from visiting with him, so one problem was out of the way. David Clarke and Gordon Smith duly arrived and met with their Philippine hosts and coordinators, to begin a massive program of preaching not just in Bilibid prison, including to prisoners on Death Row, but also in various areas within reach of Manila, including the cities that used to host the huge U.S. bases, **Angeles City and Olongapo City.**

In these places, they not only preached in various non-conformist churches, but inside the jails. To the amazement of their local critics, they achieved an amazing success, especially in the prisons. **Literally hundred of prisoners** expressed that they wanted to learn more about the Gospel and themselves "be saved".

The religious will say this is a miracle. To the cynical, analysis tends to induce just how big a failure the Catholic Church has been in the Philippines. In the Philippines, well over 80 percent claim to be Catholic.

Indeed, most will have been baptised in a Catholic Church. Yet as over 54 percent drop out of school in primary, and even those who go to Mass will only listen to the homily, most of them know very little about Christianity. The fact that two very ordinary men, not wearing the "magic" vestments of priesthood, relate in simple terms, stories and the meaning of what is in the Bible, must have a huge impact. For the first time in their lives, they understand what being a Christian really means.

What makes it even better is that David Clarke readily confesses to them that 30 years previous, he was an incarcerated criminal, and that he discovered Jesus on an LSD trip. These men could, and did, relate to him. He was one of them, once. David's book, **"Converted on LSD Trip"** has just been published, which tells the whole story.

Critics Silenced

The critics have been silenced and instead applaud. Both David Clarke and Gordon Smith carried out their mission with dignity and respect for the Philippine people, and in fact, had proved to be a credit to the British people. Positive results have been achieved. They have suggested a scheme where prisoners can enter the ministry and preach in other prisons. This is under consideration. If their scheme is adopted and prevents recidivism, then their mission will indeed have been worthwhile.

Alan Atkins   11th September 2001
(Correspondent from Manila)
Trans World Radio

On my return from this first mission I was asked to relay an account of the mission work we was doing and again providentially this too was recorded Here it is on Youtube Sky Digital 888

A Joint Effort, We Worked Together

We worked the next year very closely with Michael, Lucas Dangatan, a former inmate and now Religious Volunteer, to write the book. It was published in September 2002 and in fact in the end 66 men submitted their testimonies which were all published. The book, by chance, was written with 365 pages, one page for every day of the year and 66 testimonies for every chapter of the bible.

In this book we outlined our proposals for a Teacher Training College that was to be run by prison inmates to help in the process of rehabilitation and reformation.

A copy of the book was given to each of the inmates on our return visit in October 2002. The Articles of Religion of our **Trojan Horse mission** were clearly stated and they were a transcript of the Bierton Strict and Particular Baptist Articles of Religion of which I remained a member by default.

William C. Poloc Sent to Baguio

William C. Poloc was our first Trojan Warrior to be released and his testimony is number 62 in our book, **Trojan Warriors.**

He was due for release in August 2002 and Michael and I commissioned him to return to his own City in Baguio and preach in the City Jail and Benguet Provincial Jail. He did very successfully.

We Fund William Poloc

We funded him with a monthly of Php 6600 per month, plus expenses and he did a very good job. He was commissioned to write a field manual for others to read as to how to take the gospel into the prisons of the Philippines. William did a very good job and went to Baguio City Jail and Benguet Provincial Jail and taught the gospel to may inmate and the ministry of Trojan Horse was recognized as a good work able to help in the rehabilitation of prisoners.

Again the doctrinal basis of William's work were Calvinistic or monergism as he calls it. These are in fact articles of religion of the Bierton Strict and Particular Baptist, 1831.

This meant we were all Calvinists holding to the truths of predestination, the sovereignty of God in terms of creation, providence and salvation.

William O. Poloc was released from New Bilibid Prison in August 2002, after serving 14 years. He was the first of what we hoped would be many inmates to be released. Trojan Horse planned to support financially many such men to do the self same work that we had commission William O. Poloc to do. This was the reason for the development of the Teacher Training College.

You can read Williams Poloc's testimony, which is number 62 in our book **Trojan Warriors.**

William O. Poloc Or First Trojan Warrior (Click to View)

William Poloc Our first Trojan Warrior

In August 2002

William Poloc was released, after serving 18 years in New Bilibid Prison. He was the first of what we hoped would be many inmates to be released, with the support and financial aid of our New Bilibid Teacher Training College.

Williams Poloc's (Extract from Trojan Warriors) Testimony number 62 in our book Trojan Warriors

Inmate William C. Poloc

Name: William O. Poloc
Age: 47 years old 3rd January 1954
Status: Married 3 children
Prison No: 140226-P
Dormitory: 13-A
Crime: Robbery with Homicide
Sentence: Life Imprisonment
Served: 13 yr. 6 months
Detained: Since 1988
Family: Address: 207 C. Michael St., Lower Engr's Hill, Baguio City, Philippines 2600

Dear Guys,

Greetings in the sweetest name of our Lord and Saviour Jesus Christ.

Hey guys! If you ain't be doing right now or maybe something's gonna be fussing you over, just put on your stuff, get rid of those hanky-pankies from your mind and do allow me to drive you into a footing you can be able to size up...."Who you are, what you are, and where you are".

Guys just do me a little favour by going over these few lines. You know I really mean business. I don't want making any "tse-tse buret-tse" (exaggerated stories) with you neither I go roaming around the bush because I know in some degrees you're indeed a spoiled brat like me before. Well. If my A, B, C, would hit you directly below the belt, that's gonna be a sure sign that I made an impact... No pain, No gain. Right!

On August 22nd 1989, I was sentenced by the court to suffer the penalty of life imprisonment for committing a crime of robbery with homicide. Qualified as and insular prisoner, I was then immediately transferred from Baguio City Jail to the National Bilibid Prison. Maximum Security Compound, Muntinlupa City. The place is a couple of hundreds kilometers away from my home. The legendary hell inhabited by hardened criminals coming from different places of the country. Killings, stabbings and rumbles are common activities and a daily experience caused between gangs before.

My early years in prison were indeed a mess. I could hardly adjust myself with the unusual and unpleasant environment. The climate was too hot for a country boy like me. I felt sick dealing with different people around. People who know no other things but to invent tes-tse buret-tse just to deceive others. Sometimes I became morally inclined when my family comes to visit. After all, I am back again to my abnormal situation. Life in prison for the past eight years was a bitter experience in my life. Until one day that was in June 1995 I happened to attend a fellowship of born again Christians. I just don't know what prompted me to get assembled with these enthusiastic people. It was my only first time to join worshiping God demonstrated by dancing and clapping of hands. I really felt irritated and thought to myself that these people had gone all insane. I just wanted to step out of that rumpus place but there was some thing from within that's gonna be pulling me to stay over. Eventually I tried to relax myself and with curiosity, observe the next event that would take place after the singing. Mean while a man rose from his seat, positioned himself at the pulpit, and confidently delivered his message. I could not understand why at that very moment my attention was focused on the preacher's message. It was a message of hope, a hope for sinners like you and me. A hope that isn't temporary a lasting one authenticated by the blood of Jesus Christ. I was deeply moved and had been responsive by the preacher's message. It was very interesting and encouraging, however, intimidating. In my perception, I sensed that the preacher was emphatically hurling the message to me. But how did he come to know my spiritual needs? Besides it was only the first time we met each other. Nevertheless, whatever the intent of the preacher in delivering his message, I don't care. I don't care if it hurts me, being a sinner. I am drawn by his message and like it. I wanted to grasp everything he's trying to say. Finally, the conclusion of the preacher ended in a simple statement of challenge, which says. "Brothers, true hope can only be experienced through faith in Christ".

As I lay on my bed in my little room that very night, the message flashed back in my mind. I tried to recapture and meditate everything he said and found out my self that I am one of the worst sinners living against the will of God. And as a result, I deserve the menacing punishment of hell. The glowing presence of the preacher's massage that morning became real into my mind. I was convinced that through faith in Christ was the only way to elude the consequences of being a sinner.

It was on the evening of June 1995, that I decided to accept Christ in my little room. Dragged by my will and emotion, I cried to God for the forgiveness of my sins. I asked God to give me a new life. The following day I felt like being a new man, I perceived that there was joy, peace and hope stimulating over my whole being. After a couple of months I committed myself to a church and was baptised. I really felt God was working in my life and wanted to equip me with his word. So I enrolled then in a Theological Institute and by the grace of God I was able finish a 4-year course, a Bachelor in Theology. At the same time I endeavored to be active in every spiritual activity by preaching God's word to other churches here in prison, evangelism, and sharing God's word to my co- inmates.

Lots of them were surprised to see the changes that miraculously transpired in my life. And this led some of them to come and accept the Lord as their personal Saviour.

People over here call me a doctor. I remember a certain Englishman by the name Michael Clarke. Every time he had a problem he used to consult me asking for a prescription. Of course I have got to give the best spiritual medicines that will heal him. In fact that is the reason why they call me the doctor.

From now on, Muntinlupa the former grave of the living dead became the centre of evangelism for Christ. Missionaries and Evangelists from different places thronged the place to preach the Word of God. Consequently lots of my co- inmates arose from their graves (spiritually speaking) they've come to accept Christ as their Lord and personal Saviour.

Guy's! Have you considered the questions? Who are you? What you are? Where you are? . The Bible says that we are all sinners, therefore, each and every one of us deserves death (torments in hell) but because of God's loving-kindness he gave us the antidote in the person of Our Lord Jesus Christ to save us from the impending wrath of God.

Guy's it is time for you to think it over. You're in danger; you're in need of a Saviour. Salvation is now! The Bible says that ... do not boast about tomorrow, we do not know that day may bring forth. (Prov. 27.1)

If any one cares to write to me it would be my pleasure to respond. C/o

304
my family home address. September 9th 2001.

Gordon Smith saying good-bye to Dr. William Poloc.

Gordon had just prayed to the Lord that one day he would bless him with a new leg because he is due for release in August 2002 and wants to be a Trojan Warrior Outreach Officer, in the jails in his mountain Province in Baguio City.

Can any one help?

Our Second mission to the Philippines

By October 2002, we had 66 testimonies, of some of the most notorious criminals who had testified to their conversion from crime to Christ. Twenty-two of these men were on **Death Row**, and I had the privilege of putting together this book with their stories written for all to see.

William Poloc and Gordon Smith

A Bionic Leg would be a Blessing.

Our book was published and printed and we shipped over 100 copies for each inmate that had submitted their testimony, and we went on our second mission to continue the work we had begun.

William Poloc had returned to Baguio City and commenced a work in the City Jail and Benguet District jail and during my visit I had the privilege of baptizing 22 prisoners in Baguio City Jail and 8 souls in Benguet District Jail.

Trojan Horse International

During the next year Michael, along with Lucas Dangatan, a religious volunteer (RVO) and pastor of the New Bilibid Prison Theological Institute within the prison, worked together to collect and verify these testimonies. I worked here in England and wrote our book, "Trojan Warriors" in which the vision we all shared is recorded and at that time was to be realised.

44 Our Second Mission To The Philippines

Our second mission had taken one year to prepare and we took a team of 5 from England. Gordon Smith, Alastair Sutherland, Andy Macdonnell, Catherine Farr and Dr Richard Kent. On this mission we distributed our book to each prisoner that had written their testimony. Twenty Two of these were prisoners on **Death Row** and after our main meeting with the inmate we visited **William C. Poloc, in Baguio City,** or first Trojan Warrior to be released and go back to his own home to preach the gospel. This mission was thwart with difficulties and opposition.

Baguio City And Benguet Provincial Jails

We visited both Baguio City and Benguet Provincial Jail, in December 2002. William had worked continually in Baguio City and Benguet Provincial Jail and as a result of his successful work I had the privilege of baptizing 22 inmates in Baguio City Jail in December and further 8 souls in Benguet Provincial Jail, all of whom had become believers through the ministry of our sent man William O. Poloc. You may see the Youtube video relating to this mission

Our Second Visit To Baguio City (Click To View)

Twenty Two Inmates Baptised In Baguio City Jail (Click to View)

William is committed and he continues to this day as an independent minister.

William Poloc our sent man at Benguet Provincial Jail

William Poloc Talking To The Warden

Benguet Provincial Jail

William Benguet Provincial Jail

Michael and I Meet Together

In January 2003 Michael and met within the prison and summarized our plans and desires for the future as can be listened and viewed in the following Video on Youtube.

1 Trojan Warriors: The Beginnings

2 Trojan Warriors: The Vision

3 Trojan Warriors: Our Doctrinal Basis

These videos outline the beginning of our plans, the common vision and goal and our doctrinal basis for acting for which we learned later some men were opposed to us teaching these things.

45 A REVOLT IN NEW BILIBID PRISON

Eat what is set before you asking no questions

Very early after we arrived on our second mission I was privilege to stay late in the prisoner and attend a function organized by a VIP inmate in the prison. It was a Saturday night and in Maximum Compound. This was a Privilege that was not opened to all RVO's.

There were many in attendance including inmate Commanders. Mayors and V.I.P's from Malacanang Palace. It was an exclusive Saturday night gathering of significant men in New Bilibid Prison.

This was not a religious group but men of the world. We were given food and drink and were accompanied by a **God Marshall Rescuer** as a bodyguard. (These men are specially appointed prison inmates- there are about 240 of them and they dress in black and are allowed to carry a wooden baton to show their sign of authority). These were not allowed in to the meeting but Michael and I were invited guests.

307

The next day it was reported that Michael and I were drinking wine (The Filipino "Born Again" Christians believed this to be a moral evil and was wrong) not only that but we were mixing with sinners.

This report spread quickly like wild fire throughout the prison. The fact was it was not wine but probably gin, which may have been made by the inmates. I learned later that it is in fact alcohol which was banned in the Prison. I have also since learned that inmates manufacture there own alcohol, in order not to be daunted by rules they do not respect. This drink is called **Tuba**. It seemed to me that these men did what they wanted an in fact actually run the prison.

Challenged

I was approached the next day by a lady RVO pastor called **"Cita"** who asked had I been drinking wine in the prison the night before. She seemed amazed that any one could do such a thing. I felt grieved in my spirit and realised that the spirit of those under law bewitched these people setting a bad example to unbelievers. They felt they should not touch or taste certain things like wine or taste certain things. I.e. These were of the opinion that righteousness was a matter of do's and don'ts rather than that of imputation of Christ's Righteousness. They did not seem to realize that it was not what the ear or drank that made a person unclean but rather the evil thoughts and gossip that came from within them defiled them.

They had fallen from grace or had never been freed from natural religion and they sought to bind others to their religious views.

Recollections of the Strict Baptists

Note. (I recalled my experience as a Strict and Particular Baptist minister in England in 1983) they were far stricter over many other issues than drinking wine.

One example was the Television. It was considered wrong to own a television set and watch such programmes as this was a means of defiling the mind and conscience and that we must keep our selves unspotted from the world. In their communities you were not allowed to own a television, because to watch such programs, brought the World into your home. So to them it was also a bad example to young believers who we desired to walking up rightly and not be conformed to this worlds standards.

To own or watch a television would be could be considered to be on par with a sinner, prostitute or atheist. They argued that if you use your liberty to watch the Television Set (even though you had a switch to switch it off) you could easily see things you should not be watching and be responsible to allowing your children and other weak believers to sin and stumble. So in order not to be **a stumbling block**, it was the Elders principle that no member of the Strict Baptist Church could have a Television set. If they did have one they would be put out of the Church Communion.

I recalled that these people allowed smoking and drinking wine but not the television Set.

It was as a result of this wrong censorship of someone else's conscience and liberty that I decided to publish my third book that is entitled "Touch not Taste not" or **The Bierton Crisis 1984**, in which I describe in detail my succession from the **Strict and Particular Baptist Church** situated in Bierton, Buckinghamshire England U.K. This I wrote in 1984 and had a limited circulation.

I now recall that it was exactly fourteen years to the day, after my call by grace, and conversion to Christ, on the 16th January 1970, that I withdrew from this Church as a matter of principle and conscience, which was the first and only church I had joined. This took place on 16th January 1984.

I seceded from the Bierton Strict and Particular Baptist Church because they had turned away from living and depending upon the grace of Christ to another Gospel. A so-called gospel of keeping Law, traditions and customs of men. It was in fact the Law of Moses that they taught was a rule of life for the Believer and not the rule of Christ him self, which the Bible called the **"Perfect Law of Liberty"**. They maintained they kept the Law of Moses, including the Sabbath and did not watch the Television, or use an audio tape recorder to record sermons. All of this enabled them to keep them unspotted from the world, or so they thought. I was very concerned over all these issues and I was ashamed to be amongst them who should know better.

The whole of these issues I contended fought with for a long time period of time. This is the substance of **"The Bierton Crisis 1984"**[14]. I now realise why I was directed to write about it. I believe the publication of this book in the Philippines will help many and further the cause of Christ and His Gospel. It will be used to help many in the Philippines and elsewhere.

Rejection By Sonlight Ministry

On November 23rd, 2002 , I went to New Bilibid (Medium Security Compound) Prison and Pastor Obispo Gani met me on the way and I informed him that I had the permissions from the Department Of Justice (D.O.J) to make the video of the inmates receiving their free bibles that were being given them by Gideon's International.

There were with him members of a group called **"Sonlight Ministry"** who were from the Maximum Security Compound and Pst. Obispo Gani was one of them. Gani was one of our Trojan Warriors and was our acting

---

14 Please see Our further publications at the end of this book

secretary and legal advisor, as he worked for the Department of Justice. They informed him they did not want to be associated with me.

I was surprised at this as the lady spokesman was the one we had asked **if she could** distribute our book **"Trojan Warriors"** to all our Warrior's at the Maximum Security Prison during the main event.

This group now did not wish to associate with me and decided not to allow me to go with them to give the bibles to inmates.

I was informed they were having a go at Gani for working with us. The reason apparently was that it had been reported that **I was a wine drinker and that we worked and mixed with notorious sinners in New Bilibid Prison,** and so I was not a true Christian like other more righteous people.

Gani said to me he was the Lord's free man and works where ever the Lord directed him (a good answer I thought) and so I soon realised how that Satan seeks to work in men to stop the good work of God being done. Gani suggested the problem was jealousy.

They said they were suspicious of our motives for making the video and were critical of our book Trojan Warriors.

They were in fact very dishonourable and I decided to bring the matter to the attention of their senior Pastor Dr. Tuico, who at that time was in America. He was one of the host pastors who had invited me to preach in New Bilibid Prison last year. I had met him and his wife and I was looking forward to see him on his return from the United States.

A Big Problem

Gani later shared with me in words which he describes as "a big problem", he said **"we have a big problem"**. He had received a text message from Dr. William O. Poloc who had been texted by an inmate at New Bilibid Prison reporting that Michael and I had gone to building 13 one evening recently and were drinking Tuba. That we were drunk and singing songs with two Bakla's (lady boys) late at night. That our conduct was known and our conduct was known to all the guards and all the inmates and was wrong.

I was told that the reason why members of Sunlight Ministries did not want me to video them giving away bibles was because I drank wine. They also were suspicious of us thinking we might put the video to misuse.

My answer to Gani was, " **I had no problem with drinking wine**". I accepted he and others might have. That I am not a drunkard and no one has ever seen me drunk. I confirmed that I did drink wine with sinners and others.

I also reminded Gani that I use to sell drugs, deal in sex and drank to excess before I was converted from crime and my sins to Christ on 16th January 1970. That my conversion was from sin, death and hell, in fact from crime to Christ.

I too stated to Gani that no one has come to me personally about this so called drinking or alleged misbehaviour except others who has acted on hear say. The gossip that had carried these stories were just the same as that spoken against the lord Jesus Christ in his day.

I accepted there was a concern for me as they felt that it was a bad example to prison inmates and not a Christian testimony. How ever that was their problem. Jesus drank wine and mixed with sinners and at night, so why think we should behave differently.

They said they did not want me to be rejected by the people who maintain drinking wine was a sin. They suggested I might be causing a **weaker brother to stumble**. One RVO went so far as to ask one of our team members (Trojan Horse International) not to smoke or drink at her home as it reflected on her, not because of it was unpleasant to her (she drank wine in private) but rather it was a bad testimony to unbelieving people.

My Question Is Who Is The Weaker Brother ?

My initial response was to ask whom have I caused to stumble as I certainly was not aware of any one who had turned into a drunkard through me drinking wine with sinners any where. To the contrary I have spoken and encourage men to turn from strong drink to Christ.

I have no problem with what I have since learned with what they call "**Tuba**", except (My tongue in cheek reply) that I would encourage The Director of the Prison **Col. Ricardo Macala** to set up a manufacturing plant to produced bottled Tuba and legalize it. The prisoners could mass produce it and it could then be marketed abroad. I suggested that it could be as popular as Scots **Whiskey.** I may in fact be writing to suggest this to him and if he thinks it is a good idea he could write to the D.O.J. for such permissions.

Gossip Begins

Pst Obispoe Gani was then forced to leave Sonlight Ministries by Dr Oliver Tuico and due to his concerns about me drinking wine and mixing with sinners he withdrew from the Trojan Horse and joined Rev. Lucas P. Dangatan and the elders at NBPTI and the NBPCC group. It was then that the rumours began. It was reported that the Trojan Horse had 40 American sponsors and that we had received 4,000,000,00 dollars in donations.

In December 2002 I learned also that Lucas had not registered our ministry with the securities Exchange Commission in the Philippines. He had been given the money to do so months ago. So due to the trouble we were experiencing I asked Lucus to return the money that we had given him , which was in his bank account and was 1.1 Million Pesos.

Four days later we receive the petition from his men to get us out of the prison. He had instructed his men to write this petition to get us out of the prison.

It was also reported that Shay Cullen Michael's enemy had alerted the Catholic Church against our **book Trojan Warriors** and the Philippine Government had banned it.

It was also reported that I was a dishonourable visitor to the Philippines. That I had left my wife and daughter in England and was selling our family home because I had a girl friend in the Philippines.

They tried to ban us from the prison by denying our existence and they said we were not part of them.

It seemed that these men felt we were getting sponsored money but they were getting nothing. This was completely untrue as we had no money given to us from any one and Michael and I funded the whole mission from our private funds.

It so happened that the mount of money that was available for the mission was £40,000.00 and only Lucus was aware of the amount of money we had.

These men did not like our Calvinism and the fact we had spoken against women elders as they were being supported by women RVO's and they did not want to upset them. It was these RVO's who did not smoke, drink or mix with sinners late at night.

I call it Arminian righteousness and I call them the don't doers.

Gani had also spoken to a lady who had offered to renew my visa. She was given the money to do this but she did not do it. When Gani heard of this he suggested they contact the Bureau of Immigration and Detention and have me deported on the grounds of visa overstay. They were really against us and wanted us out of the prison.

None of them had seen the vision we were working too in seeking to bring help tom many of them and in assisting them in their declared intent to preach the gospel of Jesus Christ to men.

As a result of these evil reports word was sent back to England, from within NBPT/NBPCC, to my church, Gordon, Alastair and wife. These reports were believed and acted upon and no one asked me about any of these things except I got word that my sanity had been questioned by Gordon.

As a result of these evil reports emanating from the NBPCC, back to England, my Church withdrew moral support to me personally and Trojan Horse International Ministries.

46 FIRST PETITION AGAINST TROJAN HORSE

312

Get The Trojan Horse Out Of Here

Difficulties had arisen in the prison.

Michael and I had mistakenly believed these men in the prison would have the same desire as us to teach the gospel to all who they could. Michael and I had both experienced the power of God in delivering us from our criminal sinful past. We thought it would be a straight forward task to train and teach these men who had no religious traditions the gospel and how to share the true with others. We were mistaken.

This was because there were many religious volunteers who had gone into the prison before us and gathered groups of men together teaching their version of the gospel. I also realized what attracted most men was the amount of help in terms of food of goods that these religious volunteers gave them. Remember these men had no source of income and their food ration was 1 Kg of rice a day. There problem was that if they did not tow the line and follow the directive of their RVO they would not get their allowance. And if the RVO took exception to another group who they did not approve of then the prisoner would be discouraged from having any thing to do with that other group and if they did they would not benefit from that RVO's supply of goods. And if a particular RVO took exception to another person of group and disagreed with them then a word in the inmate ear would be sufficient to turn a nominal believer against them. I was personal informed by one lady RVO that one inmate had deceived her and gone so far as marry her in order to get support.

This happened in our case. There were many women RVO's who were called Pastors and they opposed the truth of predestination they were what I call the don't doers. They taught it was wrong to smoke, drink or sing secular songs. At the same time but they gossiped told lies about people behind their backs all which was really wrong.

This is what happen with us. I asked these elders, as part of their studies, to write an essay on the role of women in the church. Word came back to me that they would not do so as they did not wish to upset the lady RVO's who called them selves elders or pastors. Remember the scripture did not allow women to teach or usurp authority over a man in the church. These elders at NBPTI refused to write the essay as they did not want to upset there women RVO's. They also wanted me to stop teaching about God choosing men to salvation because their RVO's had taught them that they had free will

The Don't Doers.

The essence of the problem was that they had fallen into the trap of thinking and teaching they could please God by their don't do deeds. Do not smoke, do not drink wine, do not mix with sinners late at night, do not sing secular songs and so on.

A Denial of Imputed Righteousness

They seemed to be ignorant of the fact that the gospel taught that the righteous life of the lord Jesus Christ was imputed (reckoned to the account) of the believer and it was in that righteousness they stood perfect before God. They did not have to produce a righteousness in order to be accepted by God. This righteousness was a free gift, not earned and given to all who had been chosen to salvation. These believed if they denied themselves the thing they were forbidding they pleased God and it showed others they were good Christians. This was nonsense.

The bible says that the testimony they should have is a display of the love they have for others not gossip and back biting and speaking evil of others who were not like them.

On the 6th December 2003 I received notification of a petition regarding our Trojan Horse Mission. These men and elders had written to Rev. Lucas Dangatan about an incident that they were concerned about and had also sent a copy to the prison authorities.

Elders Responsible

Pst. Edwin B Tubiera	Pst Jose M. Franco	Pst. Ricardo C. Benitez
Pst Ricardo C. Bangcado	Pst. Salcedo A. Bagking	Pst. Hector R. Maqueda
Pst Tomas A Buchanilum	Pst. Anthony C. Dolin	Pst. Mel F. Nicolas
Pst. Cielito R Gan	Pst Basilo B Malarbob	Bro Domingo Lucag
Bro. Fatai Albi	Bro Pablo R Bebayle	Bro Enriquque A Yabanez
Bro. Efren C Roxas	Br. Arnel R Espina	Bro. Fausto V Manigding
Bro Domingo Alacids	Bro. Rufo Llenarisaz	Pst Adonis L Balad

Copy Furnished To: Supt. Office 1-OIC Office 1- File

Rev. Lucas P. Dangatan, Jr Pastor, Anthony Dolin. Assistant Pastor, Edwin D. Tubiera, Jose M. Franco, Richardo C. Benitez,   Adonis   L. Balad, Saledo A. Bagking, Hector R Maqueda, Jose C. Bangcado

and **Elders:**

Effren C. Roxas, Arnel R. Espina, Domingo R Lucag.

The Essence Of The Complaint Was This

On the 15th December 2002, in the afternoon Michael and I met with the elders to hear the complaint, as they had convened a meeting to decide the future of **The Trojan Horse office** as it had been brought to their attention that Michael's attitude and behaviour, to some of them, had been unacceptable. He was irritable and awkward and ill mannered, which was contrary to certain rules.

Also it had been noted that Michael had been seen drinking Tuba and smoking in the prison and in our Trojan Horse Office. That a certain **Richard Gatwood** had been seen late at night in the office and Michael and he had a drinking spree with us. That when I left the office I was smelling of Tuba. This was their complaint and to them a bad thing. None of this had been checked out to see the truth of the matter.

Trojan Horse Office

Michael have built the Trojan Horse Office during our mission to the prison, on derelict land next to the bible institute study room, with the full permission of the owner Rev. Lucas P. Dangatan. It was used for all our mission work and housed all our equipment such as our video camera, television, printer and laptop computer. Michael also had permission to sleep there as a care taker and we use this for our ministry work.

It was later revealed that they were unhappy about Michael using the office as a dormitory they called it a Cabool and now it was not an office but Michael's room. They did not like this because no one else was allowed in our office it wasn't like an office they wanted i.e. That they could use it at anytime at all. It was stated that no one was allowed to use the schoolroom as his or her Cabool or as their own room so they **wanted rid of the Trojan Horse Office**.

They stated they did not know what we were doing in the office and they did not believe Michael. It was stated Michael was a liar.

The summery was that drinking Tuba and smoking was wrong and against the rules of their institution and they were concerned about Michael bringing disrepute upon them. They argued and said that Tuba drinking was not allowed in the prison and if caught it would lead to prison discipline. Any behaviour, which broke the prison rules would leave their Bible Institute open to questionable behaviour, which they did not want.

I Summarized My Response As Follows

I felt at first, on their first presentation of the problem, that there misgivings could be resolved but I was mistaken.

The issue about Richard Gatwood was a straight forward one as they had been miss informed by a gossip monger who slept in their school room and was their water carrier. Had they asked us about the matter I would have told them all about what happened but they never did.

Richard Gatwood was an inmate from London doing a 40 year sentence and had come to see me wanting help and I sought help him in what ever way I could. He had brought the Tuba and had a drink with Michael. I didn't like Tuba . When the guards came to fetch Richard Gatwood to take him back to his dormitory he tipped the tuba down the drain as it was against the prison rules. That was where the smell came from. Drinking Tuba was not immoral but distorting the truth and spreading gossip was.

I too had been disappointed with Michael's attitude and behaviour and had spoken to him about this during the second week of our Mission. The Team had also witness my opposition to him but they did not approve of me arguing with him over these issues in front of them, or others. That as a result I had sacked Michael from his position as Executive Director to his great disappointment and so I had dealt with the problem.

I was also unaware of the rules of their institution and prison rules. I was disappointed in Michael for not informing me or deliberately breaking the rules. That I had asked Pastor Andy to direct me to two good men who would spend time with me to share with me the values and ways of their culture- nothing had happened. I wanted to know about customs, which were different to the West and may affect the Bible Institute.

They Broke Prison Rules

I was aware that Tuba was not allowed in the prison and I knew of many rules that some of them did not keep such as possessing cellular phones and drinking whiskey or Gin secretly. Some drank Tuba. I stated that I had no problem in conscience over drinking Tuba or wine with sinners and I informed them that I was not a drunkard.

I stated that I did not smoke but could do so if I wanted too. I chose not to do so. My belief being that **the Kingdom of God is not about eating and drinking** but righteousness and joy in the Holy Ghost. That what one drank or eat did not make a man unclean but rather that the evil thoughts that came from the heart and spoken words that came out of his mouth defiled a man.

I stated that That I as a guest was very happy to keep the rules of the house this was the least I could do but stated I believed them to be wrong to expect me to stop drinking with sinners such as Bucla's (Girl Men) outside the prisoners in homes or bars or night clubs as I sought to preach the gospel to men in the entire world. I stated Jesus drank wine with sinners and so did I. That I was prepared to follow Christ.

It was stated that they expected Michael to stop smoking and drinking and sleeping in the office.

I knew also other people slept in the adjacent school room office so I asked for time to talk with Michael about this as he had been called away.

My Reply To The Elders Meeting

I wrote the following

To: The elders Christian Church NBP   19th December 2002

Further to my meeting on Sunday may I say that I now fully understand your position in seeking to secure the integrity of your institution. Michael and I fully support your endeavours. I was unaware of the problem that you had in Michael sleeping in out Trojan Horse Office. I understood that he was sleeping there as a matter of security, looking after all our equipment. I did not realize you had a policy that no one was allowed to sleep in and have a personal room at the NBP Institute..

In light of this problem and my knowledge of Michael, I have suggested to him that he seek alternative accommodation in the New Year. This will prevent further problems with NBPCC through any inappropriate behaviour on his part. Mean while he will abide by the rules of your Institution.

The Use Of Trojan Horse Office

It is proposed that the Trojan Horse Office be in continuous use by officers of Trojan Horse. That it be set apart for Trojan Horse International use. In practice this means myself and Pastor Lucas P. Dangatan would share the office within its function continuing even after Michael's release.

That this office be used for Trojan Horse business, which will include:

Video productions, Counselling, Interviewing, Administration Business, Meetings, Teaching, Etc..

I would like to continue the developments, which we have already set in motion. I believe this will greatly increase the good work, which Rev. Lucas Dangatan has been responsible for in teaching the gospel and Training Teachers.

I would also like to add that I have offered my services to teach on a voluntary basis Theology and develop links at University levels in the United Kingdom and abroad.

Trust this meets with your approval and acceptance and we apologies for any undue harm.

David Clarke

Copy furnished to:

Andy Dolin

Lucas Dangatan

Michael Clarke

47 SECOND PETITION AGAINST TROJAN HORSE

My Response Ignored

I felt my response to these inmate pastors was very reasonable and workable but it was just ignored. No one spoke to me or mentioned my

317

response the them and instead a second petition was raise against us two weeks later, as can be seen below.

by NBPCC **directed by Lucas P Dangatan**

Dear Rev. Clarke

30th December 2002

We the undersigned Pastors-Teacher/Trainers are inmate-students from the different Churches inside this Compound, are withdrawing our unconditional support from the **"Trojan Horse Book"** for the following reasons to wit:

That we were not consulted and informed of the true objectives plans and purpose of the so-called **"Trojan Horse Ministries".**

That **NBP Christian Church/NBP Theological Institute,** where the trainers and teachers belong, does not, in any way, directly or indirectly, connected with the Trojan Horse Ministries;

That the NBP Teachers Trainers school is none-existent and fictitious;

That **we were duped** into believing that the **Trojan Horse Warrior Book** would be solely compiled purely of our testimonies; but it appeared that there were some **irrelevant topics/materials** inserted/annexed therein;

That there is no truth to the allegation that the Trojan Horse Ministries is supporting the NBP Christian Church financially, spiritually or any other means;

That we came to know that the Trojan Horse Ministries is not registered with the Securities and Exchange Commission and even in England;

That the **self-imposed leaders** (brothers David & Michael Clarke) are persistently showing conduct un becoming of real Christian ministers.

That David Clarke could not fully perform his function as a minister because he has presently marital problems; and

That our membership with Trojan Horse Ministries is considered null and void ab initio.

Let copies of the document be furnished to proper authorities for their information.

List Of Inmates In Opposition

	Name		Group
1			
2	Anthony Dolin		NBPCC
3	Antinio Dolin		AGCMA
4	Antonio Satiquila		SMECC
5	Arnel Espina		NBPCC
6	Arnrdi Macalfe		AGMCC
7			
8	Art Pangillinan		SonLight
9	Basilio Malarbob		NBPCC
10	Blessie Valasco		AMCG
12	Bonifilo Martinez		SMECC
13	Celso Daluz		AGCC
14	Danny De La Cruz		AGCC
15	Danny Moreno		SMECC

16	Edwin Tubiera		NBPCC
17	Domingo Emroy		PWBM
18	Domingo Lucag		NBPCC
19	Eddie Sernadilla		AGCMI
20	Edison Quillantang		SMECC
21	Ernesto Ibias		AGCMI
22	Fernando Gujar		OMI
23	Garry Cave		NBPCC
24	Hector Maueda		NBPCC
25	Jeremy NestorDolosa		NBPCC
26	Jose Bangcada		NPCC
27	Jose Franco		NPBCC
28	Leonito Baquiran		IFMFM
29	Manuel Gaño Jr.		NBPCC
30	Manuel Atadero		FJW
31	Marcial Llanto Jr.		CBFC/NBPCC
32	Marion Lazaga		NBPCC
33	Moise Maspil		NBPCC
34	Nilo Ardon		NBPCC
35	Norberto Del Mundo		IFM FM BOC
36	Gogie Candelario		SMECC
37	Rolando Pagdayawan		SMECC
38	Romeo Ibay		BNPCC
39	Romeo Orio		SMECC
40	Rommel Deang		AGCMI
41	Rudy Hugo		SMECC
42	Ruro Lleñarizas		PWBM
43	Sales Adic		SMECC
44	Sergio Jorolan		NBPCC
45	Tiddoro Laot		SMECC
46	Winnie Gacoyo		SMI
47	Jammie Jacobs		
48	Domingo Alacidis		NBPCC
59	Ricardo Benitez		
60	Aronis Balad		NBPCC
61	Mel Nicolas		NBPCC
62	Romeo Dianos		IFMFM
63	Ronald Labrador		IFMFM
64	Mario Biniahan		NBPCC
65	Salvador Baging		NBPCC
67	Cielito Gan		HNPCC
68	Ferninand Emocing		HNPCC
69	Efren Roxas		NBPCC

Copy Furnished To: Supt. Office 1-OIC Office 1- File

The Men Who Opposed Our Work

Lucus P. Dangatan   Anthony C. Dolan Jr.   Edwin D. Tubiera

Jose M. Franco   Hector R Maruaeda Jose C. Bangeda

Salido A. Banking Salido A. Banking Domingo R. Luag

The principles upon which these men worked were not derived from the scripture but rather natural man's religion, the same morality of the Sadducee's and Pharisees who condemned Jesus.

I call it **Arminian Righteousness** or the **Does and Don't religion.**

These men condemn smoking, drinking and singing secular songs and yet they will condemn a man with hearing him speak for himself, **back bit spread gossip and lie,** all of which he gospel of Christ condemns.

Leviticus 19, 18 You shall not take vengeance, nor bear any grudge against the children of your people, but you shall **love your neighbour as yourself:** I am the Lord.

These men give the gospel of Christ a bad name and they are said by some to be **Clingy Christians,** as they give Christianity a bad name. The principle being it is not that which goes into the mouth defile a man; but that which cometh out of the mouth, this defiles a man.

This people draw nigh unto me with their mouth, and honourer me with their lips; but their heart is far from me.

How I responded To This Petition

My first instinct was to ignore these matters as it seemed that it was a deliberate attempt to discredit and deny the work we had and were doing. All these accusations were based on gossip lies and untruths. They were now denying all the work that had been done by myself Lucas Dangatan and

320

others. **At least they acknowledged were not funding their institution and had any part of it.**

Who Funded Trojan Horse

The reality was we had funded the whole of the Trojan Horse Mission, Lucas and William Poloc's ministry. That Lucas Dangatan had handled over 1.5 Million Peso's of Trojan Horse International money that was used in visiting the many prisons and cities that we had gone too. It seemed these inmates and so called elders had no knowledge of these things **or were wilfully ignorant of them.** They were in fact denying the work that had been done

I was thankful that William O. Poloc was a living testimony to the truth and could confirm the work we had all done. We had fulfilled our promise of returning to the Philippines with the book **Trojan Warriors,** to give to each one of them that had written their testimony. They could use their book to tell of the great work that God was doing in the 66 men's lives that had testified to being converted from crime to Christ.

Our Evidence We Were A Ministry

The following outline of the Trojan Horse ministry was submitted at the request of the **Christian Mission Association** as part of the application for my full time Missionary and Visa Application.

Outline of Trojan Horse International (TULIP) Phils. Incorporated ministry

August 2001 to April 2003

Work commenced in August 2001 and:

1. Helped the New Bilibid Prisons Theological Institute with ministry, finance and encouragement.

2. Throughout the year from September 2001 to October 2002.

3. We assisted Rev. Lucas P. Dangatan and the teachers at the New Bilibid Teacher Training College with finance and continued support.

4. October 2002 to November 2003 we assisted 6 Philippine Pastors on Mission work in Angeles, Olongapo, Benguet Provincial, and Baguio City Jails.

5. Gave gifts of books printed in England and the Philippines to inmates and VIP's.

6. Supported local pastor of churches in Muntinlupa City and district.

7. Established an Incorporation that was S.E.C. Registered as a none profit charitable organisation with Filipino members in March 2003.

8. Opened Local Bank Account with the Philippine National Bank.

9. We opened a Trade account with Globe Mobile Phone Philippines.

10. Formed affiliations with the National Director of the Values

Formation Foundation Internationals Inc. (VFFII).

11. I was appointed a chaplain. Secured sponsorship from Apple Mac Computer Centre to assist Inmate Pastors in New Bilibid Prison in terms of 7 computers worth Php. 300.000.00.

12. Monetary Gifts and monies invested for the work of the ministry to date. All supplied by Trojan Horse International (TULIP) Phils. Incorporated.

	Date	Amount Php	To Whom Purpose
1	August 2001	270,000,00	The Reformed Presbyterian Church of the Philippines to support and help the ministry of Director Joseph Kim.
2	August 2001	234,000.00 108,000.00	Laptop Video Camera
3	August 2001	3000.00	Electric Meter NBTI Elders
4	September	85,000.00	Pastor Castillo for a Lap top for his ministry
5	October 2001	14,400.00	Rev Lucas Dangatan for assistance and Pastoral work
6	January 2002	54,000.00	Lucas Dangatan Ministry work
7	October 2002	400,000.00	Pastor Lucas Mission work in Angeles City, Baguio City, Benguet Provincial Jail.
8	October 2002	225,000.00	Books as gifts for education of inmates.
9	August 2002	60,000.00	William Poloc of Baguio City to January 2003 for ministry work in Baguio and Benguet jails and expenses
10	November 2002	11,000.00 28,000.00 14,500.00 12,000.00 50,000.00	Further laptop Second hand. CD Burner Fire-wire Drive Laser Printer Video Camera and Tapes
11	February 2002	20,000.00	Apple Mac Computer to Ronaldo Lopez
12	February 2002	20,000.00	2X Apple Computer

13	August 2001	84,000.00	Travel Expenses to local ministers and assistance
14	August 2001	315,000.00	Books for Inmates and VIP's Converted on LSD
15	July 2001	90,000.00	Transit Van
16	April 2001	144,000.00 36,000.00	16 Track Digital Recorder Drum Kit
17	April 2002		
18	August 2002		
19	September 2001	54,000.00	Computer 189/5400 to be brought from England
20	September 2001	108,000.00	Laptop G3
21	April 2003	9,9000.00	Refrigerator
22	April 2003	63,000.00	Living costs and assistance to pastors

Total Amount spent on ministry alone = Php. 2,562,800.00
Future Planned work

1. A second mission to Baguio City Jail in May 2003 with Philippines Pastors.

2. A mission to the Colonial Jail (Iwahig Palawan) with Philippines Pastors

3. A mission to the Kingdom in August 2003 with two Philippine Pastor to solicit funds for future work in the Philippines

4. Purchase property for office and residence for workers and inmates accommodation. Livelihood projects such as agricultural and appropriate needs that will assists the families. Export of Philippines products. Half way home and mission offices for outreach workers in their own City or town.

5. Promote Tourism to the Philippines from Europe for Christian minded people.

6. Promote work exchange programs for Government and private business.

7. The bring the Transit van, computers and equipment to the Philippines for mission work.

Prepared by:

David Clarke

Director of Trojan Horse International (TULIP) Phils. Incorporated

I did not need to defend myself from their misguided false statements misinformation and accusations. They had the responsibility to ascertain the truth about false accusations and not me. It was apparent they believed by denying the existence of The Trojan Horse they would benefit some how. I recalled that when Jesus went accused he did not defend himself against false accusations and was lead like a dumb sheep to his slaughter with out any protest.

Scripture Directive Ignored

The allegations made by these men were fabricated but mixed with some truth. The incident with Richard Gatwood was never looked into and so they never learned the truth about what happened

What they wrote was a fabrication and wrong. It was slander. None could be substantiated by facts, as many points were just not true. In spite of my writing letters and reply's to all the petitioners the scripture directives, as to how to deal with such issues, were just ignored. As can be read in my book, **Before The Cock Crows, ISBN 9780953947331.**

All Trojan Warriors Had Withdrawn Support

In January, I learned from an e-mail, sent to me by my pastor from England, that all trojan warriors had withdrawn their support from our Ministry. This was the first I learned of this.

At the same time Gordon and Alastair announced their withdrawal from Trojan Horse, giving no reason for their withdrawal. This information was not true as not all Trojan warriors had with drawn as many were still with us including **Alfredo R. Nardo ,**the Mayor of Death Row and other men on Death Row and William O. Poloc from Baguio.

I learned that lies and evil reports had been sent back to England about our ministry via certain people. Also rumours about my failed marriage had spread through out the prison. Gordon an Alastair failed to inform me of these developments and my Church did not ask me about any of the alleged difficulties that had happened during the mission.

My Pastor instructed me that I must subject my self to the eldership of Lucas and the NBPCC elders during my stay in the Philippines.

It was evident that he was completely ignorant of our work and the ministry we were involved in and accepted and acted on he evil reports sent to him from various sources. These sources were Pst. Obispo Gani, Gordon and Alastair. Lucas also was in communication with my wife and those in England.

As a result I was informed that my church had with drawn their support and refused to give me a letter of confirmation to say that I had been a good Church member. I had requested this letter to support my application for a missionary visa in the Philippines. So can you imagine how I felt when I was let down. This letter was required by the Christian Missionary Association who had offered to help secure my full time missionary status visa in order for me to continue the work in the Philippines at minimum cost.

Silence Spoke loudly

I asked Lucas P. Dangatan to write and inform my Pastor the truth and reality of events as this was his responsibility as he was in constant communication with him and Gordon.

I Was Given Just Silent Treatment

The NBP Theological Institute was not a biblically constituted Church and not registered with SEC and so it was unreasonable and against the scripture for me to be subject to un authorised authority.

The members of NBPCC were all convicted criminals and it was unlawful for them to register any association with SEC until a period of six years had elapsed after their release from prison. All of these men were still in prison except Lucas and Pst Obispo Isagani. My pastor in England was just unaware of these things and so I felt forsaken.

I Was An Outcast

I was an evangelist and an Ambassador for Christ under authority to him, but **an outcast to these religious men**. As far as authority goes in connection with our Trojan Horse International ministry Lucas and the mission team were under my authority. This was because The Teacher Training College venture and Trojan Horse International were working together. I was the Director and Lucas the President. It was an organisation in reality and not fiction as these NBPCC elders were now saying. Gordon and Alastair had no authority and were no longer in Church membership in any church as the Lion of the tribe of Judah had ceased to exist before we left to the Philippines.

I had no recourse to speak to their co equal colleagues or elders in England. Pst. Obipo Isagani had trouble with his Pastor Tuico with who I was in correspondence and had left his ministry at Sonlight Ministries to Join Lucas in the NBPCC elders, in December 2002. Dr Tuico was not happy with Pst Obispo Isoganie's conduct.

Conclusion
Men Pleaser's Cannot Please God

It was my conclusion that men pleaser's always think about what other people think of them.

Men Pleaser's are like silly sheep they follow the crowd and not the Lord. They need a crowd to feel secure, this is because they have no confidence in the Lord to stand for truth and righteousness. They have the reward by the applause of men when they act to please the crowd.

My exhortation to such who know they are like this and have been men pleaser's, is to seek God to give you a sense of His Awe and Might and His Holiness. Once you have seen the Lord, in His Glory, the **Fear of the Lord** will drive the **fear of man** away, like chaff, that the wind drives away, when the wheat is sifted.

My letter to Lucas P. Dangatan

January 20th 2003

Dear Lucas,

Re: Teacher Training College New Bilibid Prison

Further to the elders petition, and my request to you asking for your response and to send a letter to my church, along with an explanation to the elders of NBPCC. I am not sure as yet what your response is for you have not informed me. Gani has withdrawn, so has Gordon and Alastair.

William has informed me **he is with me in the Trojan Horse Mission to Baguio and La Trinidad**. I await the call to go and help baptise them. Are you going to come ?

I have with me all the written communications between us regarding the proposals and the development of The Teacher Training College, which you was in charge of from the beginning to this present day. These Elders have denied it's existence.

You sent me the details, photographs and status of the Teacher and Trainer and these have been published in Trojan Warriors

I have the details of the equipment we were considering purchasing, which includes a photocopier, to the tune of 65,000.00 Pesos.

It was you who wrote suggesting the change from a school to concept into a college, to which I agreed. And worked with you in it's promotion.

Further to this I in responded and took this on board. I took it very seriously and spent much time and effort representing our College at the highest possible levels, in the Philippines and to officials in Britain and the British Government.

Gordon and Alistair will confirm this if you ask them.

These representations were not fictitious, but based upon the proposals and ideas and realities that you informed me off and I accepted and promoted. Your we appointed as Our President by me.

You appointed Fernando Perez and others and I backed you in all you did. It was you who wrote to the office of the President and we received the reply regarding the opening of the **Trojan Horse Office in Laguna**. All of this was publicly known is known and was shared knowledge between myself, Gordon and Alistair and also Michael and many others.

William Poloc was the first inmate (Trojan Warrior) to graduate and be sent into the mission field according to our objectives as clearly stated and outlined in our publication, **Trojan Warriors.**

It would seem that either you did no inform your men at NBPTI, or the elders composing NBPCC, or some thing else has happened.

Do Not Call A Liar A Liar

Dr Hini says if I call a person a liar it is the highest insult so I will avoid using this term at the moment. Some one is not being honest some where. Some thing has happened. Please sort it out.

You are the one responsible to solve these evils as you are the President and Senior Pastor at NBPTI. **I actually feel you have a revolt on your hands** and the Elders have actually taken over from you.

Am I right? If so I can help you. Just call me as I am quite willing to take them all on. I have asked you to respond to me, in a Christian manor please do it for your sake. I am not on trial you are. You know what to do and I have asked you to do it.

Either way the Lord will honour his sent servants. It may be they are killed on duty. I am not ashamed to own my Lord and be counted with those who resist the Devil and stand for the truth and righteousness.

I wonder has Shay Cullen spoken to you or C.G.M. Regarding our book Trojan Warriors ? I have been informed that Pst Obispo Gani has informed you that the book has been rejected by the Catholic Church. If so you must tell me. Do not be taken in by such evil. I have been inform this may be the case.

I would like you to do as I ask. Please write to my Church and sort the problem out with NBPCC before I do.

Evil in New Bilibid Prison

I have witnessed great evil in New Bilibid Prison and I would value an explanation. I have seen a public live demonstration of a live chicken being ripped apart by its legs. This was by a Cebu dancer, before 1000's of inmates and visitors at New Bilibid Prison, on the Basket Ball Pitch. It seemed like this man was offering a sacrifice. He then bit into its side with his teeth. The poor chicken was alive and the man pulled out its intestines with his teeth, for the entire crowd to see. The Congress man was there, including the God Marshals. They all, or most looked in pleasure and gave applause. It did not seem to bother them.

What are you going to do about that ?

The chicken's intestines were pulled out of it's inside by the man's teeth. Intestines hung from the man's mouth and it's blood ran from his lips out of his mouth.

Fire-eaters and dancers in native costumes danced around the Catholic statue of St Nino. Giving praises to some thing or some one. What was that all about. I was shocked. This was idolatry.

This was awful. I witnessed one dear lady shocked and was horror stuck. When I went to comfort her. She reacted by vomiting when she saw it.

Why oh! Why!

Don't your men Petition about that ?

Why not revolt against such evil.

Are you children and not men and are gut less ? Where are the men of God, in New Bilibid NBPCC?

Why! Oh why? And who has bewitched you all!

You are taken up with issues of wine and smoking. You seek to take the speck of dust from out of a man's eye, yet you gulp down camels - your men gulp down 10 camels at once.

You Hypocrites

You let these things go and say nothing. You sing your songs and back bite and seek to defend your selves. You let such evils go on unchecked.

Why no protest from NBPCC Elders ?

I will be doing something about it. I have arranged to see Commander of the Cebu men to find out about this practice. Will you accompany me and assist me to make a representation on behalf of Christ? These men do this in the name of Christianity!!!!

I say unto you all, I am ashamed of you all. I say this in the name of my dear lord Jesus Christ and exhort you all to repentance.

Yes my view of Christianity is different to your Elders view. I love Christ. Who do they love?

Remember also I asked you to accompany me to preach the gospel to the tribal terrorist who beheaded the missionary last year. You said you would come with me when were on the way to Baguio to preach in Baguio City Jail. I hope you will keep your promise or shall I ask William to come.

Are you coming on the Baptism to La Trinidad at Benguet District Jail?

Yours in the name of our Lord Jesus Christ

Love David

Ambassador for Christ (Away from home, in a strange land).

Praise His name.

Baptisms in Baguio and Benguet

In January 2003 just after this revolt we went to Baguio and baptised 22 inmates in Baguio City Jail and 9 inmates in Benguet Provincial Jail, all the result of the work of William O. Poloc, or first sent man as a Trojan Warrior.

48 THE WORK PLANTED IN BAGUIO CONTINUES

William C. Poloc's Work In Baguio City

Thankfully our work in the Philippines was not in vain and we can report that our man William O. Poloc was our sent minister of **Trojan Horse International**. This I believe is confirmation, or the first indication that many such men will follow. I was called by the lord and sent by the Bierton Church and now my brother Michael had been called and we had now sent William O. Poloc on his mission that as we will show has been very fruitful. I believe this to be a vindication, by the lord, that I stood for the right things when at the Bierton Church in my contention for the cause of God and truth and also with those, in the Philippines, that turned from the way of grace, to follow the traditions of men.

I tell the truth in my defence and confirmation of the gospel of the Lord Jesus Christ. I believe we are living proof of the truth that all things work together for good to them that love God and are the called according to his purposes. Rom. 8 verse 28. That the things that have happened to me have turned out rather for the furtherance and confirmation of the gospel.

News from the Philippines

Re: News Up date confirming the ministry

Wednesday, 28 March, 2012 1:32 From: "William Poloc sr" <williampolocsr@yahoo.com> To: "David Clarke" nbpttc@yahoo.co.uk

To God be the glory!

We are all doing great anyway and my family as well. Regards to everyone. God bless!!

In Christ.

Dear David,

God's work here in the Northern Philippines bloomed most especially here in the city of Baguio.

The Baguio Christ- Centred Church also multiplied with the following daughter churches and other ministries.

We have:

2   The Pilot- Christ - Centred Church,

3   The Kamog Christ - Centred Church

4   The Christ - Centred Church Theological School (TULIP).

5   The Christ- Centred Radio Ministry, The Christ- Centred Jail Ministries etc..). We'll, we are truly blessed by these works He has entrusted to us.

Pastor's Day

Christ - Centred Ministries Philippines
Registration of Trojan Horse International

Due to the opposition that we experience from within New Bilibid Prison I felt it the right thing to do to register our ministry with the Securities Exchange Commission my self with the help of a Filipino Particular Baptist Pastor.

The Registration of Trojan Horse International

It was on the 16th January 2003 that I met a Particular Baptist pastor Ronaldo l. Lopez, at the Internet office in Muntinlupa City and we shared our experiences. He Stepped in and assisted me in many ways and for which I am very thankful to this day.

I noted the day, as this was exactly 23 years to the day of my conversion from crime to Christ. With Ronaldo's assistance I registered our Trojan Horse international (TULIP) Phils. Incorporation with the Securities Exchange in SEC Building, EDSA, Greenhill's, Mandaluyong City.

Our Security Exchange Registration Certificate

Trojan Horse International (TULIP) Phils. Incorporated Registration Certificate

(The necessary proof of our existence in the Philippines).

Our Registration Certificate (Click to view our Articles of Incorporation)

Missionary Visa For the Philippines

The first thing I needed to do was to secure a full time visa permit to continue my stay in the Philippines and mission work to the Jails. In order to secure the necessary details I wrote to the Police in Fareham in the UK, Mr Ramsbottom, the pastor of Luton Bethel Gospel Standard Church, Mr Janes, one of our Trustees at the Bierton Church, Mr Crane our Church overseer from Lakenheath Strict Baptist Church and also Mr Peter Jacob an elder of the Portsmouth Gospel Church. This was in order to secure confirmation of my affidavit stating who I was and my credentials. I had present evidence to the Philippine Authorities of my legitimate credentials.

Sadly but thankfully I received some help from the UK. Mr Ramsbottom replied to my request and so did and also Mr Janes but the sad thing was Mr Janes, one of our trustees of the Bierton Church, did not tell of the closure of our Bierton Chapel. Also Mr Peter Jacob due to the bad reports, which were spread in the UK about our work in the Philippines, refused to help in any way and would not confirm that I had attended their meetings and had been in good standing. I felt so alone and let down. I recalled at that time that it was this man, along with one of his elders and a so called lady Reverend that who opposed the first publication of my book **Converted on LSD Trip**.

I am sure the Apostle Paul felt forsaken, as I did when he wrote, For Demas hath forsaken me, having loved this present world. 2 Tim 4 verses 10.

Help from the Chief Chaplain

The appointed Chief Chaplain for the Philippine Prison Ministries Rev. Monico Carany assisted me and with his direction and assistance of the **Christian Missionary Services** at Pasay City, I had to undergo medical and psychological examinations including X-rays, HIV tests and intelligence tests, and as a result I was cleared and accepted and had a Psychological Report. I was thankful for this as I had herd from the UK my mental health had been called into question.

Medical And Psychological Examination. Date 2nd April 2003.

Interpretation Of findings

The subject possesses an average intellectual functioning and is able to express his thoughts and views. Has been noted to be responsive and open to social contacts. Observed to be work orientated and has a very positive outlook in life.

Emotionally, the subject manifests slight insecurities and loss. Evasive tendencies are relatively minimal.   Remarks:

Recommended.

My application was accepted and my admission status from a temporary visit under Section 9 (a) to Quota Immigrant Visa under Section 13 of the Philippines Immigration Act of 1940, as amended in my favour and granted to Rev. David Clarke a British National on the 10th April 2003.

It cost us in excess of Php 100,000.00 (£1000 GBP) to gather together and pay for all the required tests, examinations and documentation. The result was that I could permanently work, according to our Articles of Incorporation throughout the Philippines, as a missionary and return to the UK for two months of the year before having to return. It was some comfort to learn the results of this examination as I had heard that my sanity had been called into question and it had been rumoured that I was ill.

I had Incensed Religious Carnal Men

The truth of the matter was I had incensed the religious carnal mind, in certain religious men, who were then moved by another set of principle other than that the gospel of our Lord Jesus Christ. I was thankful for the scripture record that told me this was a normal reaction from ungodly men. Then answered the Jews, and said unto him, Say we not well that thou art a Samaritan, and hast a devil? Jesus answered, I have not a devil; but I honour my Father, and ye do dishonour me. John 8 48-49.

Working Within New Bilibid Prison

It became necessary to begin our work again within New Bilibid Prison and so to this end we appointed Gonzales Arnel Perpiton Bautust as our Religious Volunteer (RVO) and he worked with twelve inmate within the prison.

Religious Volunteer Appointments

My Status was established as an Extraordinary Religious volunteer which brought with is certain privileges to work with in the prison

We Buy Land Within The Prison

We were able to purchase a small lot of land within the prison and Arnel worked with the prisoners and built a function room to conduct meetings. (Not that this was possible as all property belongs to BUCOR, but inmates can claim ownership by continued use of land for what ever purpose).

 Funding Of The Mission

I don't' wish to really talk about money as the Lord provided funds for his work in His own way. How ever because evil men and people who pry into other peoples business, and also to silence the gainsayers, for the record both Michael and I provided all the funds from our personal resources. And between September 2000 and May 2005 we provided all the funds for the mission work, to the tune of £50,000.00. English pounds and on Michael's death he left £10,000.00 to his daughter.

We received no funds from anywhere else except a gift from the Christian Gospel Church, of £400 in July 2001. Our Trojan Horse funds supplied all the return airfares for all our 4-team members, all their accommodation expenses and travel arrangements for the 2002. The Trojan Horse mission was paid for by Michael and I. We had no funds from anywhere else and we did not seek sponsorship. The accounts for our Trojan Horse are available upon request.

Our RVO Arnel   **David Clarke RV**

My RVO Identification for New Bilibid Prison

49 MY RETURN TO THE UK
The Closure of the Bierton Chapel

I returned to the my UK, in July 2003 and I spoke to Mr Crane, our Bierton church overseer as he informed me that the Bierton chapel had been closed for worship, on the 22nd December 2002. I recalled noting that this was at exactly the same time that I was continuing my ministry, preaching and teaching the Gospel in Baguio City, where 30 souls had confessed their faith in the lord Jesus, and that being through the work of William Poloc, who was our sent man. As a result I baptised 30 souls who had been added to the Church, so confirming the ministry of William C. Poloc. I had baptised them in my capacity as a sent minister from the Bierton Strict and Particular Baptist Church.

Mr Crane suggested that I return to Bierton and reopen the chapel and he informed me that the Association of Grace Baptist Churches LTD (South East), 7 Arlington Way, London EC1R 1XA, had taken on the responsibility of the churches property. They had taken the Bierton Church Trust Deed from the lawful Trustees, Mr Janes, Mr Martin, Mr King and Mr Baumber who had expressed they were too old to bare the responsibility of looking after the chapel.

It transpired that our Bierton Trust Deed had been lodged with one of our senior church members solicitors, which is a fact that is important when registering property with the Land Registry for the first time. They had recovered the Bierton Trust deed from the Solicitor of our church member when she died.

When I approached the Association of Grace Baptist Churches LTD to use our chapel for the ministry work they refused permission. This was because they wanted to sell the chapel and profit from the sale. They had hastily gone on with demolition work, contrary to the terms of trust, seeking to sell the Chapel, at a profit once they had acquired planning permission. Where as I had already negotiated and planned that summer to bring two Filipino Particular Baptist ministers to the UK to visit various churches and our chapel would have been the ideal solution for some of our meetings. The Association of Grace Baptists Churches LTD were not concerned or interested in carrying out the wishes and desires of the original church founders and church members of the day. To their shame.

They first of all denied that we were a Gospel Standard Church and my standing as a member of the Church. When I sent them a copy of my book, "The Bierton Crisis 1984" and letters of confirmation from Mr. Ramsbottom along with Mr. Cranes confirmation that Mr Crane had suggested and supported my request to re open the chapel, they tried to say I was no longer a member. This was despite my bringing to their attention the fact of our strict rules, in relation to cessation of membership ensured that I by default remained a member of the church along with Irene Mary Holloway and Mr A king. The truth was that I along with Irene Mary Clarke (now Holloway) were still church members as our membership continued. The Church never terminated our membership and Mr Crane confirmed this in writing and I had presented this information to the Association of Grace Baptists Churches LTD with my application to use our chapel.

When I stated that they were not the lawful trustees, as the Church had not elected them to that position, I was ignored. I asked them to confirm that the copy of the Trust Deed that I held was one and the same as the one they had recovered from our deceased church member, they refused my request. This was because the trust deed states who were the legitimate Trustees, how they are to be elected and the responsibility of church members.

Trustees were to be elected by the church and to be men who believed and supported the doctrines stated in the indenture. The reality was that the Bierton Church was a Gospel Standard Cause and had no association with Grace Baptist churches. The church would never have elected this Association to be its trustees because their beliefs were those of the London 1869 Baptist Confession, and not those of our Church, which was the Bierton Church and Gospel Standard.

50 MICHAEL'S DEATH AND BURIAL

Michael sadly died in New Bilibid Prison before our vision of bring help and release to many had materialized, on the 27th May 2005 and was buried in **Olongapo City** cemetery by Harry Joost, from Baloy Beach and we held a memorial service of celebration regarding his life, death and conversion, from crime to Christ at our Bierton Baptist Chapel.

Michael Exhorting Men On Death Row

Michael preaching on Death Row in New Bilibid Prison

I had always considered Michael as a member of our church at Bierton when he was baptised according to my instructions, in the Philippines. I had received him and others too as a Christian and was considered to be a member of the body of Christ. And so in my continued role as the Director of Trojan Horse International (TULIP) Phils. Incorporated I conducted a memorial and thanks giving service for Michael at our Bierton Chapel Cemetery. Friends were invited, including Dave Courtney and Malcolm Kirkham. For their own reasons they did not attend the memorial meeting Malcolm Kirkham did attend an audience with Dave Courtney at the Britannia pub that evening. A meeting that I had arranged for us that evening.

In the above picture we see Michael speaking to men on Death Row giving them words of encouragement and consolation as their hope was to be in the lord not man.

Further Good

Malcolm Kirkham as I have already written about and my friend in early years has read my book and listed to my story and he too at the end of his life has confirmed that he too turned around from his life of crime as a direct result of my influence. It is my hope too the Dave Courtney does the same.

Our memorial service at our Bierton April 2005

Michael's Tomb Stone Bierton Chapel Cemetery

Bierton Chapel Cemetery

Several men from New Bilibid prison have been released and gone home to their own cities to preach the gospel. They are former drug dealers, killers and real criminals. William C. Poloc is just the first fruits of the harvest. You may read their testimonies in our book **Trojan Warriors**.

Michael In His Coffin

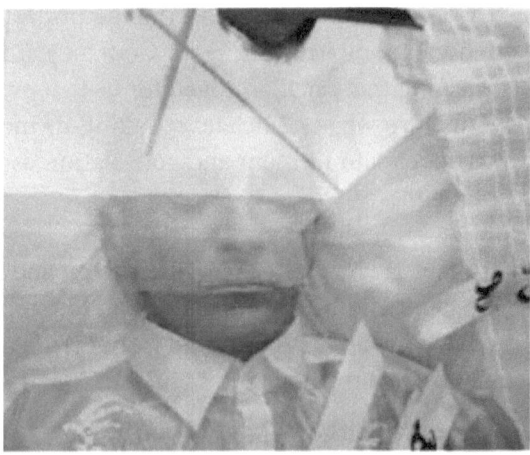

Michael Tomb Stone Or Plaque Of Remembrance

He Being Dead Yet Speaketh

51 TESTIMONY 41 MICHAEL JOHN CLARKE
(Extract from Trojan Warriors)

14th August 2001

Dear Reader,

As you may have gathered, I am the older brother of David Clarke, the team leader of the Trojan horse Mission and it is my privilege and honour to use this opportunity to tell you that the Bible is FACT and not fiction, and Jesus Christ is ALIVE.

In this testimony I will only highlight certain parts of my life, as David has already covered some of it in his book Converted on LSD Trip.

In addition to this, I invite you to access our www.biertonparticularbaptist.co.uk which shows quite clearly how God allows evil, (which in my case was the fabricated criminal case brought against me) in order to show that he is the Almighty God. Everything that happens is the bringing to pass of His

Divine plan, which was conceived in Eternity.

Prior to my first visit to the Philippines in February 1995, my concept of Christianity was that I only believed that there was a God, and that was enough. I considered myself to be 'normal' and in control of my own destiny – how wrong I was!

As a tourist I first stayed in Angeles and Olongopo Cities. I was amazed at the abundance of 'Girlie Bars' and night-life. It was crystal clear that sex was on the menu at a very low price.

On my return to England I formed my very own 'Paradise Express' travel business, the aim of which was to offer low cost holidays to my fellow countrymen. I thought I was on to a winner, because there are no such things as 'Girlie Bars' in England.

To cut the story short, within a few months my business was up and running and I returned to the Philippines to welcome my first influx of customers.

On June 5th 1995 I was arrested for promoting child prostitution, and later sentenced to 14 to 16 years' imprisonment. I have, and always will, protest my innocence. There were no child victims or child complainants; my reference to girls was only a general reference to girls as in 'Spice Girls', the pop group. I was not promoting children; I want to establish that in your mind.

After this, as you can imagine, I was very bitter and full of hate. Why, why, why have I been wrongly convicted, I would ask myself. I just could not understand why God would allow such a thing. Suicide was constantly on my mind.

A foreign Christian Missionary worker who encouraged me to seek the Lord for the answer to this big question then gave me a bible.

For the next few years I read the bible, and attended numerous so-called Christian gatherings, all of which seemed to differ in their interpretation of the Scriptures, which left me more confused. One day my friend Suny Wilson was acquitted from Death Row, and on his release gave me a book 'Mere Christianity' by CS Lewis. After reading it my eyes were opened to the truth. Everything began to make sense and I was drawn unknowingly to 'Jesus is the Christ' fellowship. Rev. Joseph Kim was the head pastor. He could see that I was thirsty and over a period of several months loaned me a vast array of books, which he assured me, would illuminate my mind further regarding this great mystery of mankind's creation.

I soon realized that for the last four years the Lord had been pulling me to him. He broke my yoke of bondage – I was saved from the power of Satan and given eternal Life. God revealed to me that he had to let me taste a little bit of hell in order to save my soul. God's Grace saved me alone. He gave me faith and the ability to repent from my former life.

After I was reborn, the Holy Spirit became very active in my life, and taught me to forgive the people responsible for my wrongful conviction. The power of Christ led me by force to a makeshift baptism in a 45-gallon ex-oil drum, in order to proclaim to the world that I was indeed one of God's chosen people. With me were 24 other believers who were baptised unto death and new life in Christ.

I have now devoted my life to the Lord and urge everyone to read, study, and meditate on some Words of scripture: The Book of John, chapter 3. Humble yourselves and ask God to come into your lives.

If anyone feels the need to write to me, please do not hesitate, as that would be a sure sign that God is drawing you near to Him. Please use my address in England for correspondence. I pray to the Lord that he may bless everyone who reads this book and I ask the Holy Spirit to guide him or her to the Book of Revelation 12.11

Signed by: Michael J Clarke, Ambassador of Christ.

Duly witnessed by: Pastor Andy C. Dolin, Associate pastor, NBP Christian Church.

Message to the World (August 11th 2001)

From Michael J. Clarke

It is my pleasure and to the GLORY OF GOD to proclaim that by God's Grace I have been saved from the power of sin and hell. Through FAITH and BELIEF that JESUS IS THE CHRIST I have now been granted ETERNAL LIFE.

This same message of Salvation is available to everyone and who ever truly believe will be saved. The Bible is FACT not fiction and I implore everyone to read, study and meditate on John 3 and ask the Lord to have mercy on your soul.

It is my prayer that my plea will also touch the hearts of all the bar owners and operators in Angeles City who knew me in 1995 when I was operating my Paradise Express travel business. Even though they know that I was charged and convicted for a crime that was totally fabricated, it doesn't alter the fact that the life I was then living was saturated in sin. My master was the devil, of which I was totally ignorant. It is my duty to tell you that you are all being totally deceived and living in a false paradise. Take heed of my words of truth and change your life's direction, with JESUS at the helm. I am not telling you to abandon your business! Just change the menu, kick out sin and promote tourism of a different nature in this beautiful country and your rewards will surpass your wildest dreams.

I have now completely forgiven my complainant and pray for his soul. I realize that God allowed him to be used by Satan in order to bring about my salvation.

At 10 am on August 12th I will be giving my testimony live on the Internet, God willing, here in Bilibid Prison. My brother David is the team leader of the 'Trojan Horse Mission' whose aim is 'Setting captives free'.

For further information

Or e-mail David:

May God Bless you all, signed Michael John Clarke.

BELIEVE IT OR NOT

By Michael Clarke

A MESSAGE TO ALL MY BROTHERS IN CHRIST

We are at war and as Christians we become members of 'God's Army'. We are all involved in this warfare whether we like it or not, and whether we are aware of it or not. Heaven's war is now on EARTH and it's no joke!

The Bible clearly tells us that the 'origin' of this war began in the cosmic realm, before the creation of man, in an 'Angelic' rebellion against the 'Lordship of God'.

How could such a rebellion happen in the presence of our God Almighty? The Scriptures help us with this (Deut 29-29) 'The secret things belong to the Lord our God, but those things are revealed which belong to us and to our children forever.'

This war will not end until the final judgment of evil supernaturalism. Until this final judgment, Satan, together with 1/3 of God's former angels that he managed to persuade to join him, will continue and become positively worse. - 'The number of fallen angels is unknown'

Assured of victory

Although the Scriptures clearly show that God will have the final victory in this war, the battle will continue with Satan's army doing its utmost to try and stop mankind being re-united to its rightful Father, God Almighty.

Be prepared

Once we accept this reality we need to condition ourselves, so to speak, and put on our 'Spiritual Glasses' of Warfare. If we underestimate this warning we will, without a shadow of a doubt, become casualties of war. The Bible itself is a training manual for all God's Army. However, to make us more efficient, God has inspired many Christian writers, who have had first hand experience of life in the mission-field, to highlight the importance of this training, together with the dangers that await the unprepared. God's message on this topic is readily available in Christian bookstores and public libraries. Good instruction on this subject awaits all that are prepared to join a Bible study class.

Knowing the enemy (2 Cor. 2-11)

'Lest Satan should take advantage of us, for we are not ignorant of his devices'

Unfortunately many Christians have a false sense of security! They tend to focus all their attention on Jesus and ignore the abundance of scriptural warnings. When this happens the adversary is delighted and his 'soldier demons' will attack (1Pet 5-8) ' Be of sober spirit, be on the alert. Your adversary the Devil prowls around like a roaring lion, seeking someone to devour.'

Warning

Scripture clearly shows that it is possible for true Christians to be devoured by the Devil because the warning was given directly to them, but this does not mean that we shall loose our salvation because that is impossible. We shall suffer calamity for not abiding in God's armour. To confirm this read 1Tim 3-6 and 2 Tim 2-26. Also Paul warns us of this reality in 2Cor 11-3.

The War

This is best described as a 'sin war' in three dimensions:

Sin is personal, it comes from within. It is our fallen nature, which is always inclined towards evil. The classic description of this inner warfare of our flesh against the indwelling Holy Spirit is found in Gal. 5 16-21.

Sin is social, it comes from without. This is the problem of the world with all its temptations. The classic description of social sin is found in 1 John 2 15-17.

Sin is supernatural; it comes from above, directly from Satan and his demons, principalities and his powers. Eph. 6.12

The third dimension is the most difficult to understand and to handle. It is also the most frightening:

DEMONS. What are demons? God has not chosen to reveal the origin of demons, but it appears that they are not in the same class as the fallen angels, but are somehow directly associated with Satan's rebellion and are members of his Army. Having said this we can conclude that demons are individuals with supernatural evil powers.

My main concern is to draw your attention to the reality of these powers. To underestimate this fact is fatal, just as to overestimate the problem could also make things difficult for Christians. Satan can and will take advantage of both these situations. However if we reject these powers, we must come up with another reason for the Son of God having come into this world.

Having said that we can be sure of ample protection, not only from the direct indwelling of the Holy Spirit, but also the ever present protection of God's own Angels and their powers, which, according to Scripture is twice that of Satan.

Demons are best described as evil spirits assigned to individuals on a personal level, whose main purpose is to influence the individual's mind and to control their will. This is what the Scriptures mean by 'demon possessed' this does not mean possession, as this implies total ownership. Satan and his demons don't own anything apart from their own evil. They are usurpers. God owns everything. However God holds all persons responsible for their own actions, and it must be understood that there are different levels of demonetization, ranging from mild to very extreme.

Can Christians be demonized?

Most believers would hold the negative view based on the assumption that the Holy Spirit will not or cannot dwell in the same body as demons. There is not a single verse of Scripture, which states that true believers cannot under any circumstances be demonized. On the contrary, Scripture is full of warnings of such a possibility.

The presence of the Holy Spirit does not, of itself, prevent demonetization, just as it does not, in itself, prevent the Christian from sinning. The Holy Spirit is not afraid of demons, and will enter the body of a believer even if they are there. All believers prior to conversion have become demonized to some degree, and, the amount of sin and the amount of power it had over them will determine the amount of power needed to completely free them from this bondage of sin. In a lot of cases it is a matter of the person still dwelling on their past, which is used by the demons to torment them.

Church history

A study of the writings of the early church fathers reveals that they understood that the Christians could be demonized. Because of this they created a 'Lay order's exorcists who took new believers through deliverance after their conversion to Christ and before their public Baptism.

Worldwide contemporary experience is now unanimous in the view that some true Christians under unusual conditions of sin can be demonized. It is also possible for a believer to have picked up a demon or demons after conversion, through their own sin and/or the serious sin of others committed against them. It could also be caused by heredity, parental rejection, and contact with demonized persons, curses and even rock music. These are just some of the ways that the demons gain entry either before or after conversion to the body or the mind and hide deeply within the person's structure. It is through lack of discernment and ignorance that Christians render themselves so vulnerable to demon attack. Example: Let us assume that our body is a house, and in that house there is a basement, which we shall call our inner structure. In this basement there is 'garbage' which in our case is our emotional and/or spiritual 'garbage'. Demons are like rats – they feed on 'garbage' in some cases this garbage has been there for years and will take a lot of time and effort to remove. If it is not removed the demons will continue to feed. Likewise if the rats are removed and the garbage remains, they will surely return, with others, and continue to feed.

The Answer: In most cases a person can handle this problem themselves. The new life of every born again believer is in constant battle with the old self, and in this battle the Holy Spirit which is inside them is constantly bringing to the surface all this deep- rooted garbage, which is brought before the Lord by way of repentance. This is 'sin garbage'

True Repentance: If you only repent ' about' or 'over' this 'sin garbage' it will remain like food for the demons to feed on! You must repent from your sins, which will leave them dead. This is very important; otherwise it will have no effect. Your repentance must be a <u>sincere pledge</u> …you must clean the basement.

Final words: Please heed my warning! This war is Real. If you feel that you want to know more about this warfare I highly recommend the following books:

Christian Warfare by Dr Martin Lloyd Jones, Defeating Dark Angels by Charles H. Kraft, The Devil's Disciples by Jeff Godwin (a must for parents).

The rest of Michael's story is told in our joint book Trojan Warriors and the book, **The Rise And Fall Of Brother Bobby.**

ISBN 9780953947331 by Jeff DuBuisson

52 ESSENCE OF MY LEARNING

I am able to conclude from my own learning and experience that there are certain truths taught in the bible which are fundamental to effect a change of life in a person.

The first of these things are:

1 To accept the reliability of the bible
2 To accept the truth that bible tells of the origins of man the purpose for our existence.
3 That we are accountability to God
4 To accept the bible that tells of judgment for the way we live and act toward each other selves.
5 To believe that God does forgives sins
6 To accept what the bible says as to who the lord Jesus Christ is.

7   To receive the truth that Christ died to pay the debt
    of man's sins

8   To believe that if we believe the truth and turn from
    our wrong ways then all our sins, past present and
    future are forgive.

9   To accept that every one who believes the gospel
    (good news) are the children of God. It does not matter what your
    past has been.

10 To accept that a person who receives Jesus Christ becomes a new
man   and all his past wrong is wiped out and a new life begins.

11 Understand the doctrines of grace.

There are many more things but sufficient to know that all of these things are expressed in theological terms and may be further examined by considering the follow subject matters that I treat in my other books, **Bierton Strict and Particular Baptists, The Fall Desperation and Recovery, Trojan Warriors** and **Mission To the Philippines.**

The main issues are:

1   The Sovereignty of God
2   The Doctrines of Grace
3   The Infallibility of Scripture and the relative
    Accuracy of the Authorised Version of the bible.
4   The Deity of the Lord Jesus Christ
5   The new birth
6   Predestination
7   Articles of Religion
8   Drinking wine, Mixing with sinners,
    Worldliness, Sabbath Days
9   Eschatology
10 Head coverings
11 Hymn Singing
12 Singing secular songs
13 Baptism or baptisms
14 Women elders

All of which need to be address by those who are teaching the Christian Religion.

My Return to The UK

Due to the very remarkable opposition and learning experience we had in the Philippines I realised the way forward is to educate people in the same way that Michael and I had done. This would give them a grounding in truth and religion and help them in their own way of reformation and rehabilitation.

It is our belief and vision that a similar work and help in the process of reformation and rehabilitation can be accomplished in our prisons in the UK.

Positive Responses From British Prisons

A draft copy of **Converted on LSD** was sent to over 30 prison chaplains in the UK, Including **HMP Belmarsh, Manchester, Risely, Lindsholme, Parkhurst, Erlstoke, Feltham and Hull** and as a result almost 500 copies was requested for prison inmates. As a result a special edition has been produced called **Borstal Boys** that addresses some of the criticisms that were received about the draft edition sent to prison chaplains. Two hundred and fifty copies are being sent to inmate in 40 prisons before December 25th 2013.

This punk rock opera, **Borstal Boy**, has been designed to be performed in British prisons and other public venues.

It is believed that the gospel is the power of God unto salvation to those who believe and God has not chosen many wise or noble men but rather the weak, despised the castaways, even prisoners and criminals, to work reformation in their lives. It is believed this unique way will get the story of reformation to people who would not otherwise hear it.

53 NO REST FOR THE SOLE OF MY FEET

Gen 8 verse 9.

But the dove found no rest for the sole of her foot, and she returned unto him into the ark, for the waters were on the face of the whole earth: then he put forth his hand, and took her, and pulled her in unto him into the ark.

Serious Errors Held

By A Strict Baptist Minister

On my return to the UK I sought fellowship with like- minded believers, only to find more serious errors and practices were found amongst those who should have known better. A minister and Pastor of a Strict Baptist church in the south of England told me that I would not be accepted into membership by any Gospel Standard Church. This was because I had questioned his views on the Law of Moses .

And so in my case on my return to the UK unlike the dove of Noah I was not received back into the ark of church membership.

This was because I had stated to him that if he held the position he then he would have a problem with the Sabbath. I sought to be of assistance to him, as he would certainly find his belief in the Law of Moses a stumbling block to himself and also to others, if he taught those things. I wanted him to be honest with him self.

He informed me, in agitated tones, that my views would exclude me from membership of any Gospel Standard cause. I knew from my continued membership of the Bierton Gospel Standard Church that this issue was no isolated problem. And also I was the sole remaining member of our Bierton Church. I had returned to the UK, from mission work, and our chapel had been taken unlawfully and immorally, by the Association of Grace Baptist Churches LTD, and later sold. So what was I to do? And now I was told I would not be welcomed in any Gospel Standard Church. My response was one of dismay and hurt. So I decided I must write to this man as he was in serious error believing I could help him. His reply was far from satisfactory and less then gracious without any attempt to enlighten me to his un-scriptural position.

Here is this man's reply:
The Ignorant reply from the Unnamed Minister
2nd December 2003

Dear David,
It is not my custom to answer letters of this nature.

However, I have been persuaded by many friends to make this brief reply. I am thankful to be the recipient of your letter and not the writer.

David, the views that you hold on the Law and the Lord's Day are wholly wrong and derogatory to the person and work of Christ. I can assure you that neither the church at B, nor the church at HE (of which I am a trustee), nor P, SS or hold your errors, and would never receive into church membership those that hold such notions. Furthermore, there is not one church on the Gospel Standard list that holds your views or would receive into church membership any that believed such none scriptural notions.

I have learned the hard way, David, never to enter into endless questions of this nature and soul destroying controversy that brings nothing but pain to the brethren and disturbs the peace of the churches, "But when ye sin so against the brethren, and wound their weak conscience, ye sin against Christ" (1 Corinthians 8:12). "But avoid foolish questions, and genealogies, and contentions, and striving about the law; for they are unprofitable and

347

vain (Titus 3:9).

May God grant you light from his Word to turn from your errors? Please respect my wish not to publish my letter in any of your books. Yours sincerely:

Un-named Minister.

How To Deal With Such Correspondence

This letter was in fact a reply to my letter that I sent to him in connection with the issue we were talking about. I had written to this minister seeking to help him as he had problems with the Sabbath. He had stated to me that I imagined strange things in connection with the gospel and so I wrote in order to establish a starting point to seek to resolve this difference of opinion and his problem. In fact his reply revealed gross errors on his part and demonstrated the need to defend the gospel truth.

Letter Minister of Strict Baptist Church

This is the letter that I sent to this minister which resulted in his rejection of the me and the truth that I maintained and advanced.

Date: 18th November 2003-12-10

Dear Un- named Minister (By request)

I too hate controversy. So please let us not be contentious.

The truth is given to us as light in order to shine in a dark place and I would not be faithful to its cause if I remained silent over an issue, which the scripture speaks so plainly about. I believe the distinction between Law and Gospel is a real distinction, which the scripture clearly speaks about. An argument, which rests upon a fact that one has held a view for 30 years and has contended over it, carries no weight when it opposes the plain teaching of scripture. A child who has no learning, in the school of the wise, but who believes the straight foreword words of scripture, is wiser than the men of this world who have read and studied all the works of many theologians.

This only would I learn of you received ye the Spirit by the works of the Law or the hearing of Faith. The contrasting statement in this instant is between works done to or according to Law or the hearing of faith, which is without reference to works done to Law. The Law in question is the Law, which came by Moses, and which was 430 years after the Gospel had been declared to Abraham. The Law here is the 10 commandments, which was delivered at Mount Sinai. I am not imagining this (as you have suggested) but quoting the plain teaching of Gods word.

Satan hates the truth and his ploy is to ridicule those who teach the truth. He will use underhanded methods to pick at the child of God by saying such things by saying ah! "That is your own imagination, you are wrong". This is because he hates the truth and does not wish the child of God to be free from the condemnation of the Law. But the child of God will be safe if he sticks close to the word of the Lord and he will not be confounded. The Law came by Moses but grace and truth by Jesus Christ. The Law came by Moses. Not Adam, Noah or Abraham. Those who say otherwise contradict the word of God. The epistle to the Galatians is very clear about this. All arguments to the contrary are wrong and it does not matter who argues them. I am not being contentious by stating what the Scriptures say, as this is the Word of God, without comment or alteration or explanation. The plain word states the Law, and by which I understand to mean the 10 Commandments, came by Moses but grace and truth by Jesus Christ.

This is without controversy and must not be gain said. Those who seek to change the plain meaning of these words are the ones causing contention and being controversial. They wrest the Word of God. The scripture does not say the Law came by Adam, or Noah, or Abraham, but by Moses.

The contention between the child of God and child of the bondwomen is foretold by the allegory of the two sons of Abraham Ishmael and Isaac. There was a contention then, so it is now. There will always be a contention between the spiritual man and the natural man. The Apostle makes the point that the one who contends for the Law as a rule of life is the natural man, or son born to the bondwoman, whilst the spiritual man is the heir of promise and the true son.

It is always the son of the bondwomen who will persecute the freeborn Son who is the seed of promise. This will always be the case. I am then going to ask you not to persecute me because I speak the truth, as stated here in this part of God's Word. There have been many books and many sermons spoken upon this subject and great minds have wrested with these issues. I maintain that it does not matter if the whole of the Christian world, and its writers or preachers were to opposed to the truth here spoken off, it will not alter the truth that the Law came by Moses but grace and truth by Jesus Christ.

The Law in all its glory came by Moses, to a people who had been chosen to be separate from all other people. It came to the Jew and not the Gentile. This Law, which came by Moses, excluded the gentiles from the covenants of promise. It did not include them.

Unless this can be agreed upon this straightforward statement of truth then we can go no further. There is no point in seeking to go further because if one seeks to alter truth in order to make scripture t our system of doctrine and religious thinking then we will be deceived and not be those who rightly divide the word of truth.

I am open to discuss these issues with you, or with any one, but will not contend with you. It does hurt when you say it is my imagination when I recite the scripture. I know that I have a tender conscience and I would not wish to harm a child of God and if you are lead by the same Spirit you too would be grieved you if you know you hurt a child of God. I would never mean to hurt you, in any way so please do not get offended if I express that you are wrong on an issue of doctrine, that you mentioned and came up in discussion.

I am open to correction but this must be from the Word of God and according to it. I am very clear in my understanding of many scriptures and I am also aware that I am not clear on others. When I speak that thing that I know why do you find it strange that I can be so certain.

The problem that you have A----, with your view of Law, will be that is that of the Sabbath Day. The Sabbath according to Moses is the seventh day of the week (Saturday) not the first Day of the week. And this cannot be altered or changed. You have the problem of wresting the scripture if you try and alter the scripture to make it t your view of Law and Gospel. I believe I can help you in this matter, by sharing with you the scriptures, but you will need to be patient with me and not get wounded with me or upset if you disagree with me. I would also ask you not to get personal with me by saying I have an imagination, which is wrong. I felt your spirit was wrong towards me in your retort at that point. Please forgive me if I came over to you like that, in such a manor.

Yours Sincerely
In the name of our Lord Jesus Christ.
David Clarke. 18th November 2003

Conclusion to the Response
Of the ignorant reply of the un-named minister.

This method of response by this un-named minister to my genuine letter to is ungracious, un-scriptural and very hurtful. This is not the answer of God but that of a carnal religious man whose rule of life is the Law of Moses.

He advances no scripture truth to confirm his view regarding the subject of Law and gospel. It is as though his ears were Psalm 58 verse 5. His ears were stopped like a deaf adder and though I speak ever so scripturally, logically and with moral persuasion he would not listen. Therefore how can he respond to the truth? Then just as the adder he seeks bite. I was thankful for the promise in scripture that says, they shall take up serpents; and if they drink any deadly thing, it shall not hurt them; they shall lay hands on the sick, and they shall recover. Mark 16 verse 18.

This conduct and the way of response to me in my pilgrimage was that wrought by the Mother of Harlots. This being demonstrated by his persecution that began when he wrote stating that I would not be accepted into membership of any church, holding the scriptural views of the gospel of our Lord Jesus Christ.

No wonder he did not wish for me to publish what he wrote. He is a bully and wishes to give me a bashing metaphorically , behind closed door, and then seek to bind me to silence and then walk out of the room, pretending nothing had happened. Not so, as I am set for a defence and conformation of the gospel, and will not remain silent.

It is for this reason there is a need to teach the next generation of men the glorious truths of gospel of the Lord Jesus Christ. It is of paramount importance. This is the reason for the project that is now called the Bierton Particular Baptist College.

My Response To The Unnamed Minister

I did not respond immediately to this letter but have left the matter for almost 10 years. The time however to has come to deal with these errors and other like errors.

Here is my response to that letter:

My Observations And Responses

To: Minister of the Gospel Strict Baptist Church Date: 18th November 2003

This letter suggests that such people who have views of the Lords Day and Sabbath day, as I do and teach, are wrong. To say he is like a weak brother like other are weaker brethren, and they have a tender conscience, is a subtle ploy of Satan. That such views are hurtful to them and because they have a tender conscience towards the Lord and the their weakness must be considered by others is wrong. They cannot hear the truth. I believe this to be false. It is a deceit and the answer of Satan.

In this matter there is no problem, as no Christian would wish to offend the weak believers conscience, in the thing that he allows himself to do, and so cause a weak brother to stumble. I put it to the reader that this man's righteousness, the Un-named Minister is one of the flesh and so carnal and therefore not from Heaven. This man is seeking to bind the free to the bondage of Law, Sin and Death. The trial by re will reveal this in due course.

Let the Lord Jesus be the one to judge.

The reality is that such who assert their views on others as this man does, and insist we follow them are the ones who cause division. They say others must follow them and their way. This man is an elder and one who is the strong as Peter was, and the Jews who through bewitchment joined those who wanted to circumcise all believers. These were dogs. In fact dumb dogs. A dog without a bark is of no use to warn of approaching danger.

They caused the dispute by saying unless these converts be circumcised and keep the Law of Moses they cannot be saved.

And as such we are instructed to mark them that cause divisions and offences contrary to the doctrine, which ye have learned; and avoid them. Rom. 16 verse 17. Paul and Barnabas had no small dissension and disputation with them. Act 15 verses 1.

Also When Peter came to Antioch, Gal. 2 11, Paul withstood Peter to the face because he was to be blamed. Paul and Barnabas had strong contention with him and rebuked him openly. This was because Peter had been carried away with the Jews dissimulation. So too, in this issue, the un-named Minister is wrong along with those who too dissimulate; as he caused the division as can be seen in his letter.

David is excluded from the privileges of a gospel church because he follows the Lord Jesus. And so the scriptures are fulfilled they that live godly shall suffer persecution.

To cap it all he thinks it right to beat me up metaphorically, behind closed doors, and then bind me to silence so as not to inform other of what he has done and said.

Set for a defence and Confirmation of the Gospel. I fell the time has come to earnestly contend for the faith once delivered to the saints. Grace be with you all in the name of our Lord Jesus Christ.

I Maintain The Scripture Teaches

The new man of grace is a new creation and he has a new nature whose motions are those of a good man. He also is possessed of his old nature that always seeks to dominate the new. Those who experience the new birth are those who were chosen by the Father, in Christ before the foundation of the world. They have been regenerated and are free to respond to the Gospel by believing in the Lord Jesus Christ.

Their right standing before God is based upon Gods act of Justification, where by the righteousness of the God man Jesus Christ is imputed to them, and in that righteousness they are declared just.

They are given the grace of faith to believe all the truth of God, and by faith have peace with God when they look too, and depend upon, the

352

finished work of Christ, in his death. Who by it made full atonement for their sins?

The sentence of justification is passed upon the conscience of the believer as they rest in Christ and look to him for all their salvation. The Lord Jesus is their true Sabbath rest.

Therefore if any man be in Christ, he is a new creature: old things are passed away; behold, all things are become new. And all things are of God, who hath reconciled us to himself by Jesus Christ, and hath given to us the ministry of reconciliation; To wit, that God was in Christ, reconciling the world unto himself, not imputing their trespasses unto them; and hath committed unto us the word of reconciliation. 2 Cor. 5 verses 17

Now then we are ambassadors for Christ, as though God did beseech you by us: we pray you in Christ's stead, be ye reconciled to God. For he hath made him to be sin for us, who knew no sin; that we might be made the righteousness of God in him. 2 Cor 5 verses 20.

54 BIERTON PARTICULAR BAPTIST COLLEGE

Bierton Strict and Particular Baptists continues

I continue the ministry that I was commissioned too by our church, in 1982 and despite the fact that religious men have taken away our chapel. It has been decided to operate in a different way. All communication with the Bierton Strict and Particular Baptist's may now be directed to our office address 11 Hayling Close, Fareham, Hampshire, PO14 3AE.

This ministry continues in the form of the Bierton Particular Baptist College, which is an Open Internet Cloud facility. It is set up to teach and educate students wishing to educate themselves in Doctrinal and Practical divinity or theology.

Initially this will be in the form of an Access Course to Higher Education, To also teach men to preach the gospel of Christ, which will include historical and sociological studies. It is planned that our course of study will be underwritten by the Open University or a similar qualifying educational body. This will give graduating students educational status to continue their studies any where in the world.

The doctrinal basis for this college is the Articles of Religion of the Bierton Strict and Particular Baptist Society (Church), founded in 1831.

As the former Secretary of the church I still hold a copy of the original indenture relating to the founding of the Bierton Church and the minutes of our meetings, which can be read on our web site. This indenture specifies how the church is to elect its own trustees. The trust is a 1000-year trust, which commenced in 1832.

Our trustees failed in their responsibilities to the trust and our Bierton

Church Chapel, and property, have been disposed of and religious men have taken the inheritance, yet the work of preaching Christ to men goes on. I write and inform my readers all about this in my book, "The Bierton Strict and Particular Baptists, My Testimony and Confession." Alternatively: Set for the Defence and Confirmation of the Gospel.

Oliver Cromwell

Oliver Cromwell soon learned he had to train the men of England in the art of warfare to achieve his objectives. Likewise the Israelites needed help in their day of trouble. Remember the scripture:

Now there was no smith found throughout all the land of Israel: for the Philistines said, lest the Hebrew make them swords or spears:

So it came to pass in the day of battle, that there was neither sword nor spear found in the hand of any of the people that were with Saul and Jonathan:

I Sam 13 19.

Education Is The Way Forward

Since the Philistines have taken our Bierton Chapel this cannot stop the work of God. The Bierton Particular Baptist College is like the Open University, were students might partake in a disciplined course of study by distant learning. Leading to a degree of knowledge in Doctrinal and Practical Divinity. The basic foundation will be based upon the First London Baptist Confession of faith, 1646, 2nd Edition, and all associated learning will be treated. Including history, the social influences of the 17-century. Oliver Cromwell's cause in England and Europe. The study will include the works of men like John Bunyan, Dr, John Gill, Dr John Owen, Joseph Philpot, William Huntington to name just a few.

Our Bierton Church articles of religion were written in 1831, which was before the Gospel Standard magazine was first published. However we aligned ourselves to the Gospel Standard Cause, in January 1981.

Those who know their history will be aware of all those conflicts and contentions that have arisen, so our philosophy is to start from the First London Baptist Confession, 1646, which is fairly comprehensive, and learn by examining these tenets and principles of truth by means of academic study and not indoctrination.

In our studied we will be treating the subject of the value and reliability of the Authorized Version of the bible, in order to ensure faithful reference to the Word of God.

A Note To Prospective Teachers

We welcome those who are being taught by the Lord to offer their services. We are sorry we cannot pay you. If you feel directed to offer your help we would welcome your application. Please send us an e-mail to that effect.

A Note To Prospective Students

We welcome those who feel they would benefit from a course of study. We know from experience the value of education for it is the truth that sets men free. Please send us an email with your request to enrol and enquiries regarding the curriculum.

Remaining Member Bierton Church

I, David Clarke am the only remaining active member of Bierton Particular Baptists Bierton. I am a sent minister of the Church and the full proof of my ministry are those 30 souls that I baptised in Baguio City Jail and Benguet Provincial Jail, in December 2002. This ministry activity being carried out by our sent man William C. Poloc whose testimony is published in our book, *"Trojan Warriors"*. This ministry being under my Directorship.

Before the Cock Crows

During my work in the Philippines, from October 2002 and July 2003, I was able to register our ministry with the Securities Exchange Commission, calling it **Trojan horse International (TULIP) Phils. Incorporated** and we were accepted as a bona fid ministry, which allowed us to work in all the prisons in the Philippines.

During our mission I kept a diary and wrote about the work we were doing. This is to be published in our next book, which tells of the good and bad events that we encountered. Sadly Michael died in New Bilibid Prison in May 2005, before our vision to bring help to many in the Philippines was realised.

Should I Obey God or Man?

In 2018 I gave a copy of my book,   The Bierton Crisis, to the Pastor of Hedge End Strict Baptist church asking if after reading my story if he would consider an application for church membership but to this day I have had no reply. As I mentioned earlier I had been told by another Strict Baptists pastor from a church in Bournemouth that I would not be accepted as a member in any Gospel Standard church due to my views on the Sabbath.[15]

I realize that I had considerable opposition and not every one was behind our work but I was not easily moved off course that was because by the fear of the Lord and not man, I chose rather to obey God and not be directed by the wisdom of men that are without faith towards God. I call my readers to look at the results of our mission recorded in this and our other publication to judge, as it is my opinion that Christ has been honoured and God has

---

15 Please see our publication The Doctrines of The Sabbath 1662 listed under further publications.

been glorified. And even though I had made enemies (I don't understand why), I took encouragement from the commendation that I received from Prince Charles in 2002. This was because on my return to the UK in 2002, I sought to work among young people in our area, to steer them away from crime and drug use. In this work a made a documentary video highlighting the problem of drug use among young people in Stubbington. The video was sent to the schools, police and Prince Charles and it is his response that encouraged me to continue the work we had begun not only in the Philippines but also now in the UK.

Our forth book **"Before The Cock Crows"**, tells the story of our second mission and relates the success, opposition and final registration of Trojan Horse International (TULIP) Phil's. Incorporated, with the Securities Exchange Commission, a bona fid Christian organisation in the Philippines.

Website Address for the College:

http://www.BiertonParticularBaptists.co.uk

E mail: nbpttc@yahoo.co.uk

11 Hayling Close Fareham

Hampshire

PO14 3AE

United Kingdom

FURTHER PUBLICATIONS

All or these publications are available as hard copies books from Amazon. co.uk. And have been reprinted by Bierton Particular Baptists.   Or PDF copies available on request nbpttc@yahoo.co.uk

Amazon.com,   Amazon.co.uk,   Amazon.de
Amazon.fr,Amazon.es,   Amazon.it,   Amazon.co.jp
Amazon.ca,   Amazon.com.au.

<u>LET CHRISTIAN MEN BE MEN</u>

This was originally published as 'The Bierton Crisis' and is the personal story of David Clarke a member of the Bierton Strict and Particular Baptist church. He was also the church secretary and minister sent by the church to preach the gospel in 1982.

The Bierton Church was formed in 1832 and was a Gospel Standard cause who's rules of membership are such that only the church can terminate ones membership.

This tells of a crisis that took place in the church in 1984, which led to some members withdrawing support. David, the author, was one of the members who withdrew but the church did not terminate his membership as they wished him return.

This story tells in detail about those errors in doctrine and practices that had crept into the Bierton church and of the lengths taken to put matters right. David maintained and taught Particular Redemption and that the gospel was the rule of life for the believer and not the law of Moses as some church members maintained.

This story tells of the closure of the Bierton chapel when David was on mission work in the Philippines in December 2002 and when the remaining church members died. It tells how David was encouraged by the church overseer to return to Bierton and re-open the chapel.

On David's return to the UK he learned a newly unelected set of trustees had take over the responsibility for the chapel and were seeking to sell it. The story tells how he was refused permission to re open or use the chapel and they sold it as a domestic dwelling, in 2006.

These trustees held doctrinal views that opposed the Bierton church and they denied David's continued membership of the church in order to lay claim too and sell the chapel, using the money from the sale of the chapel for their own purposes.

David hopes that his testimony will promote the gospel of the Lord Jesus Christ, as set out in the doctrines of grace, especially Particular Redemption and the rule of life for the believer being the gospel of Christ, the royal law of liberty, and not the law of Moses as some reformed Calvinists teach, will be realized by the reader.

His desire is that any who are called to preach the gospel should examine their own standing and ensure that they can derive from scripture the doctrines and practices they teach and advance and that they can derived the truths they teach from scripture alone and not from the traditions of men or their opinions however well they may be thought of.

List Price: $11.99
5.25" x 8" (13.335 x 20.32 cm)
Black & White on White paper
256 pages
ISBN-13: 978-1508465959
ISBN-10: 1508465959
BISAC: Religion / Christian Theology / Apologetics

A System of Practical Truths
Authored by Dr John Gill DD, Created by David Clarke CertEd
List Price: $8.99
8.5" x 11" (21.59 x 27.94 cm)
Black & White on White paper
176 pages
ISBN-13: 978-1543085945
ISBN-10: 1543085946
BISAC: Religion / Christian Theology / Systematic

THIS IS BOOK 1 Treating The Subjects:
Of God, His Works, Names, Nature, Perfections And Persons. And Contains:
Chapters
1 Of The Being Of God
2 Of The Holy Scriptures
3 Of The Names Of God
4 Of The Nature Of God
5 Of The Attributes Of God In General, And Of His
Immutability In Particular.

A Translation of The Quran

By David Clarke

This Publication treats the subject of the Quran and the reason for presenting this is due to a rise in Islamic terrorism which has caused great concern to many in the West. So with the current massive influx of Muslim's migrating from the various parts of the world into Europe, Great Britain and the USA, it seems reasonable to discover the roots of Islam in order to deal with the problems that have occurred. Our Politicians seem clueless on how to deal with this enemy and when they are questioned they appear to know relatively little about Muhammad and his teaching. One of our greatest Prime-ministers in Britain William Gladstone declared the Quran an "Accursed book" and once held a copy of Muhammad's Quran up in Parliament, declaring: "So long as there is this book there will be no peace in the world". Winston Churchill was one of the greatest leaders of the 20th Century, who served as Prime Minister of the United Kingdom during World War II and again from 1951 to 1955. As an officer of the British Army in 1897 and 1898, he fought against a Pashtun tribe in the north west frontier of British India and also at the Battle of Omdurman in Sudan. In both of those conflicts, he had eye-opening encounters with Muslims. These incidents allowed his keen powers of observation and always-fluid pen to weigh in on the subject of Islamic society. While these words were written when he was only 25-years-old (in 1899), they serve as a prophetic warning to Western civilisation today. "How dreadful are the curses which Mohammedanism (Islam) lays on its votaries! Besides the fanatical frenzy, which is as dangerous in a man as hydrophobia in a dog, there is this fearful fatalistic apathy." Churchill apparently witnessed the same phenomenon in several places he visited. "The effects are apparent in many countries: improvident habits, slovenly systems of agriculture, sluggish methods of commerce and insecurity of property exist wherever the followers of the Prophet rule or live." He saw the temporal and the eternal tainted by their belief system. "A degraded sensualism deprives this life of its grace and refinement, the next of its dignity and sanctity," he wrote. The second-class status of women also grated at the young officer. "The fact that in Mohammedan law every woman must belong to some man as his absolute property, either as a child, a wife, or a concubine, must delay the final extinction of slavery until the faith of Islam has ceased to be a great power among men," he noted. "Individual Muslims may show splendid qualities, but the influence of the religion paralyses the social development of those who follow it. No stronger retrograde force exists in the world." Well before the birth of modern Israel, its terror tactics and drive for world domination were felt. "Far from being moribund, Mohammedanism is a militant and proselytising faith. It has already spread throughout Central Africa, raising fearless warriors at every step, and were it not that Christianity is sheltered in the strong arms of science, the science against which it (Islam) has vainly struggled, the civilisation of modern Europe might fall, as fell the civilisation of ancient Rome." With the influx of Muslim people from the various parts of the continent along with their culture all of which is shaped by the teachings of Muhammad in the Quran. Some objections and Observations are as follows: Islam means submission Islam does not mean peace Multiculturalism is a failure. Islam denies the natural rights of women An Objection Halal Meat An Objection To Shari-ah Law Objects to Female Genital Mutilation (FGM) An objection to Jihad which seeks over throw Western culture through education, Social activity, political activation and Law. For this reason, this publication is made available for education purposes. With this prayer that God may grant us all wisdom as to how we may respond to the rise and threat of Islam.

MARY, MARY
QUITE CONTRARY
THIRD   EDITION
Does The Lord Jesus Want
Women Elders To Rule As
Elders In His Church ?

David Clarke

By David Clarke

When treating the subject of women elders in the church we are not dealing with the affairs of a secular society and so it has nothing to do with women's rights, equality of sex or race in the world. This matter only relates to men and women in a Christian church. It is about the rules of the house of God, which is the church of the living God and rules for those who are members of the body of Christ and members of an heavenly county. The Suffragettes Emmeline Pankhurst 1858 -1928) was a Suffragette and worked very hard to bring equal rights for women to vote as men. In the year of her death all women over 21 gained the right to vote. The Suffragette movement brought about many changes for the better in a secular society but not so for women seeking to follow Christian principles. One of her famous quotes was, "Trust in God She shall provide". Terms which do not reflect Christian beliefs. We know God will provide and He is not a she. In the USA and the UK, women's political rights were brought into general political consciousness by the suffragettes and since then there have been legal rights granted to the Lesbian, gay, bisexual and transgender groups, same sex marriages, along with the development of the feminist movement and the appointment of persons from the LBGT community to responsible positions in the Church of England. All of this has caused conflict in the Christian community due to differences beliefs of right and wrong. This book seeks to show what the bible has to say about the role of women in the church and family. Since these rules are taught by the Apostles of Christ they are the word of God to us and we should obey. The secular world may differ and turn from the narrow path taught in scripture but we should follow the word of God, this is our wisdom.

TROJAN WARRIORS

Setting Captives Free Paperback – 16 Feb. 2015 Trojan Warriors is a true story of two brothers, Michael and David Clarke, who are brought up in Aylesbury, Buckinghamshire, England. They became criminals in the 60's and were sent to prison for malicious wounding and carrying a fire arm without a license, in 1967. They both turned from their lives of crimes in remarkable ways but some 25 years apart, and then they worked together helping other prison inmates, on their own roads of reformation. David the younger brother became a Christian, after a bad experience on LSD, in 1970, and then went on to educate himself and then on to Higher Education. He became a baptist minister and taught electronics for over 20 years, in colleges of Higher and Further Education. Michael however remained untouched and continued his flamboyant life style ending up serving a 16 year prison sentence, in the Philippines, in 1996, where he died of tuberculosis in 2005. When David heard the news of his brothers arrest on an ITN television news bulletin he felt compelled to wrote their story. And then when he heard of his own brothers conversion from crime to Christ, after serving 5 year of his sentence, he published their story in his book, "Converted on LS Trip", and directed a mission of help to the Philippines to assist his brother. This book tells the story of this mission. They then worked together with many former notorious criminals, who were inmates in New Bilibid Prison, who too had become Christians and turned their lives around. This help was to train them to become preachers of the gospel of Jesus Christ . This book contains

364

the 66 testimonies of some of these men who convicted former criminals, incarcerated in New Bilibid Prison. They are the, "Trojan Warriors", who had turned their lives around and from crime to Christ. Twenty two of these testimonies are men who are on Death Row scheduled to be executed by lethal injection. Revelation 12 verse 11: And they overcame him by the blood of the lamb and the word of their testimony and they loved not their lives unto the death.

THE PAROUSIA

James Stuart Russell

Foreword By Ed Stevens

The word "Parousia" (par-oo-see-ah) is not a household word, but students of endtime prophecy know it is a reference to the Second Coming of Christ. It comes from two Greek words ("para" beside, and "ousia" state of being) and literally means "to be beside" (present with someone). It came to be a more specific reference to important people coming for an extended (but not long-term) visit to one of their subject territories (a "visitation"). It can refer either to the initial arrival or the afterward presence. It is used in the New Testament almost exclusively of Christ's Second Coming.

Russell examines every significant New Testament text about Christ's return, to see when it would occur and what it would be like. Since he believed the Second Coming occurred in the first century at the destruction of Jerusalem in AD 70, his view is labeled "Preterist."

The word "Preterist" is another prophetic term with which many are unfamiliar. According to Webster's Unabridged Dictionary, a Preterist is "a theologian who believes the prophecies of the Apocalypse have already been fulfilled." A Preterist is the opposite of a Futurist. Futurists teach that the three major endtime events (parousia, resurrection, judgment) are still future in fulfillment, whereas Preterists teach these events have already been fulfilled. Some may wonder what difference it makes?

Everything crucial to Christianity is at risk. The Deity of Christ, the integrity of the apostles and prophets, and the inspiration of the New Testament is at stake. How so?

Jesus and the NT writers repeatedly make time- restricted predictions about His return and the other endtime events. They do not merely suggest that Christ's Parousia might occur in their lifetime, they unequivocally affirm it.

Liberals, skeptics, and Jewish/Islamic critics use those "time statements" to discredit Jesus and the New Testament. Inspired men cannot make mistakes. Since Jesus and the NT writers predicted Christ's return to occur in their lifetime, and it supposedly didn't happen, they assume Jesus and the NT writers were mistaken.

Indeed, if we cannot trust their prophetic utterances, we cannot trust anything else they say. Christianity is totally discredited if those predictions failed to materialize exactly as they prophesied.

You might wonder what these "time texts" are? Matthew 16:27-28 is a good example. This book deals with every one of them. They were not mistaken when they predicted Christ's return in their lifetime. It really occurred, at AD 70.

Theologians who study endtime prophecy consider Russell's book a classic defense of the Preterist view. It is this book, more than any other during the past 125 years, which has moved so many toward Preterism.

Many in the Reformed faith (e.g., R. C. Sproul, Sr., David Chilton, Gary DeMar, Ken Gentry, Gary North, Jim Jordan, et al) credit Russell's book as having a significant impact on their eschatological views. R. C. Sproul, Sr. says he looks favorably at Preterism because it is the only view of prophecy which effectively counters the liberal-skeptic-critic attack. He has written much to recommend Russell's book and encourage the spread of Preterism, even though he does not go as far as Russell does. In his Foreword to the 1999 Baker Books reprint of The Parousia (pp. ix-x), Sproul says:

Russell's work is valuable chiefly for his analysis of the time-frame references of New Testament prophecy and his understanding of the main reference to the parousia. ...Russell's book has forced me to take the events surrounding the destruction of Jerusalem far more seriously than before, to open my eyes to the radical significance of this event in redemptive history. It vindicates the apostolic hope and prediction of our Lord's close-at hand coming in judgment.... I can never read the New Testament again the same way I read it before reading The Parousia.

Until this book appeared in 1878, Preterism had little systemization. This book began that process, and remains one of the most consistent and comprehensive explanations of Preterism available. The Preterist view flourished in Germany and Britain. But America, still recovering from civil war, took little notice. In global terms, its impact is still marginal, but it has seen significant growth in the past ten years, and the Internet is one of the big factors stimulating that. What the Gutenberg printing press did for the Protestant reformation, the Internet did for the Preterist reformation.

The Internet is the perfect place to publish helpful material like this. One of the first books to be posted on Preterist websites was Russell's Parousia. Even though the electronic version has had many readers in the short five years it has been available, it has not diminished demand for printed copies. This book is destined to remain a Preterist classic.

Russell did a remarkable job of interpretation compared to previous centuries. He pointed the way in a number of areas that we are only just now beginning to develop further. He devoted over 170 pages to the book of Revelation. One of his best statements is there. He uses the "time" statements in the first three verses of Revelation to show how crucial the date of writing is to the interpretation of the book:

It may truly be said that the key has all the while hung by the door, plainly visible to every one who had eyes to see; yet men have tried to pick the lock, or force the door, or climb up some other way, rather than avail themselves of so simple and ready a way of admission as to use the key made and provided for them. (Parousia, p. 367)

Russell leaves no excuses for Futurism. His survey of all the "Parousia" (second coming) references is a tour de force in Preterist exegesis. This book was the first wave of what has become a whole storm of books defending the AD 70 fulfillment of endtime prophecy.

Futurists and Partial Preterists for too long have hidden behind the excuse of wanting explicit "time indicators" before assigning a text to AD 70. Russell and modern Preterists have exhaustively shown that all NT endtime texts have first century "audience relevance" written all over them, which functions as an implicit time indicator. The New Testament was not written to us originally. We are reading someone else's mail. The primary task of a Bible interpreter is to discover what the original author intended to communicate to his original audience, not just to ask what it "could" mean to us today.

THREE DIFFICULT TEXTS SIMPLIFIED

There are three scriptures which most partial preterists think are yet to be fulfilled: Acts 1:11, 1 Cor. 15:20-57, and 1 Thess. 4:13-18. Russell shows that an AD 70 fulfillment is the most consistent interpretation of these texts. However, he does not deal very much with Acts 1:11. As a result, many Futurists and Partial Preterists have used this text to teach another major return of Christ still in the future. Modern Preterists have now shown that these three texts contain implicit time indicators and contextual clues which connect them inseparably to the Parousia and final consummation in AD 70. For a fuller explanation of these three texts from a Preterist perspective, see the three books written by this author (Stevens Response To Gentry, Questions 5 About The Afterlife, and Expectations Demand A Rapture).

https://www.preteristarchive.com/Hyper/2002_   stevens_rapture.html

In those books, we deal especially with the typological imagery of Christ's ascension into the cloud- filled heavenly Holy of Holies to present His own blood to make final atonement, and His "second appearance" back out of the heavenly temple to announce atonement to His anxiously waiting saints. The Acts 1:11 reference to the return of Christ is easy to apply to AD 70 when we realize it is speaking of the reverse of the visible ascent of Christ in Theophany form. His descent would follow the same Theophany pattern as His ascent, meaning that it would be visible like His departure. He ascended visibly with clouds and angels in the presence of a few disciples, and the two angels (Acts 1:10-11) promised that He would descend visibly "in like manner" in that same Theophany pattern to only those disciples whom He wished to see it. Both the going away and the return were "cloud comings" (Theophanies) accompanied by angels. He left the same way He would return (in clouds with the angels) to appear to his anxiously waiting disciples ("How long, O Lord?" and "O, our Lord, come!"). They expected His return before all of that generation died. Some of them were promised to remain alive until His return, and that they would literally "see" it before they all died (Matt. 16:27-28 and John 21:22f).

Even some partial preterists (e.g. Kenneth Gentry in his book, Before Jerusalem Fell) have agreed that Rev. 1:7 (which mentions a "cloud coming" or Theophany which "every eye would see") was fulfilled in AD 70. Since most expositors connect Rev. 1:7 with Acts 1:11, it seems reasonable to assign both Rev. 1:7 and Acts 1:11 to the visible Theophany that was seen by the Jewish people just before the war in AD 66. Notice what R. C. Sproul, Sr. said about the angelic appearances in the sky in AD 66 and its connection to Rev. 1:7 – "...theop Old Testament prophets, when speaking of a real historical visitation of God in judgment upon cities and nations, used exactly this kind of language in a metaphorical way to describe that coming of divine judgment.... As some 19th century scholars...Jonathan Edwards...B. B. Warfield and others have suggested, what Jesus is talking about here on the Mount of Olives [Matt. 24:3] ...is the end of the Jewish age. And that the coming that he's talking about, and that he's warning these contemporaries about over and over again... that was coming on that generation...was the judgment of God that was coming on Jerusalem and the temple in the year 70 AD.... Was Jesus visible? Did "every eye see him" [Rev. 1:7] and all of that? No. Although, one of the weirdest passages you ever read in ancient history is the paragraph that is found in Josephus [Wars, Bk 6, Ch 5, Sect. 3]. I quote it in my book [The Last Days According to Jesus, p. 124]... After talking about some remarkable, astonishing celestial events that some people had reported, he said, "Besides these a few days after that feast, on the one-and-twentieth day of the month Artemisius ...before the setting of the sun, chariots and troops of soldiers in their armor were seen running about among the clouds...." ...The overwhelming testimony of the contemporaries (and he was there as an eyewitness) was that people did see something in the clouds. And what is it they saw? They saw chariots. Is that the first time the chariot throne of God is seen in the clouds over Palestine? What took Elijah to heaven? What were the whirling merkabahs [chariots] Ezekiel beheld? Was not the basic symbol in the Old Testament of the movable judgment throne of God, his chariots of fire? And here we have the testimony of many, many people saying they saw these chariots running about the clouds right before the end of Jerusalem. ...It lends credence to the further application of Jesus' predictions of what would come in this judgment of the nation of Israel and of the city of Jerusalem..." [R. C. Sproul, Sr. "Last Days Madness" speech, 1999 Ligonier Ministries National Conference in Orlando. Bracketed material inserted by the author of this Foreword.]

Eusebius (Ecclesiastical History, Bk 3, Ch 8, Section 5) quotes this same material from Josephus, and Tacitus (Histories, Book 5, "About The Jews") alludes to the same events. Sproul's comments stimulate several thoughts. If Rev. 1:7 was fulfilled by the appearance of angels and chariots in the sky at AD 66, and if Acts 1:11 is speaking of the same judgment coming (or cloud coming, Theophany) of Christ, then what text teaches a still future visible coming of Christ? If the angelic armies literally seen in the clouds at AD 66 were the fulfillment of "every eye shall see Him" (Rev. 1:7) as Sproul has allowed as a possibility, then it was also the fulfillment of Acts 1:11! In Matt 16:27-28, which R. C. Sproul, Sr. affirms is AD 70, it states that some of those disciples would not taste death until they saw Christ return. It therefore seems logical that the visible coming of Christ at AD 66-70 which is mentioned in Matt. 16:27-28 must be the same coming dealt with in both

Rev. 1:7 and Acts 1:11.

The commander of the angelic hosts (Christ) was present with His angelic armies on that occasion (AD 66), just like Rev. 19:11-21 pictures for us. This was the visible return of Christ with His angels to judge His enemies and reward His saints, as both Rev. 1:7 and Acts 1:11 had predicted. Matt. 24:29-31 and Luke 21:25-28 also indicated there would be visible "signs" accompanying the return of Christ with His angels to raise the dead out of Hades, perform the judgment, and reward His faithful saints. This fulfills the "in like manner" terms of the Acts 1:11 text. Both Rev. 1:7 and Acts 1:11 fit the Matt. 16:27-28 "visibility" pattern.

It is also clear from the similarities between 1 Cor. 15 and 1 Thess. 4 that these two "parousia" texts are speaking of the same AD 70 return of Christ. Since both texts state that the resurrection will occur in connection with the "parousia" (1 Cor. 15:23; 1 Thess. 4:15-17), and since the NT does not distinguish between two different parousias separated by thousands of years, and since this parousia is said to occur in the lifetime of some who would "live and remain" until it occurred (1 Cor. 15:51; 1 Thess. 4:15), then it is clear that these two texts were fulfilled in AD 70. This forces some adjustment in our concepts about the nature of fulfillment once we get the time of fulfillment straightened out. All three of these difficult second coming texts have been explained from a consistent AD 70 fulfillment. This leaves partial preterists nowhere to hide. We can thank Russell for pointing the way toward this approach to these three texts.

A LITERAL RAPTURE

Another area in which Russell greatly served the interests of future generations was the rapture. Four other scholars within a generation of Russell also taught the idea of a literal rapture in AD 70 (Milton S. Terry, E. Hampden-Cook, Richard Weymouth, and William S. Urmy). There are minor differences in the way each of these men described it, but all agreed there was a removal of some true Christians in connection with the return of Christ in AD 70. Modern advocates of a literal AD 70 rapture (such as Garrett Brown, Walt Hibbard, Arthur Melanson, Ian Harding, Ed Stevens, and others) go further to assert that all true Christians (and nothing but true Christians) alive at the time of the destruction of Jerusalem were "snatched away" to be with Christ in the spiritual realm. Russell suggested that only some Christians were caught up – a "partial rapture" with the sleepers or unwatchful Christians left on earth. But it seems from Jesus' sharp criticism of that group in Matthew 25 (and in the book of Revelation) that the sleepers or unwatchful were not true Christians. The tribulation and apostasy eliminated the insincere. By the time of the rapture the only watchful, awake, and "worthy ones" were the true Christians. There would have been few (if any) pretenders and "mere professing Christians." So in either view, the group of saints actually raptured is basically the same, whether we see it as only the watchful Christians, or as true Christians only.

The arguments we all use to establish the necessity of a literal rapture in AD 70 are exactly the same. The strongest arguments are the Biblical "expectation statements." Scripture alone is our standard, not scripture plus history, tradition or anything else. The only authoritative material that we can use to make any final decisions about what did or did not occur in AD 70 is the Bible. If it says the Parousia was going to occur in AD 70, that should be enough. We shouldn't have to be convinced by history or any external arguments. If the text of scripture says something is going to occur within a certain time frame, then we are bound to believe it, regardless of whether we can find external historical or traditional support for it, and regardless of whether our credulity is stretched to the breaking point. The same thing happened in the field of archaeology in regard to the Hittites and Darius the Mede. The Bible was the only evidence we had for the existence of these people for a long time, yet that did not make advocates of sola scriptura doubt the veracity of the Bible. So for sincere believers, the question boils down to this: What did the NT writers believe, teach, and expect to see, hear, and experience at the Parousia? Did they expect to experience the Parousia in any conscious way? Did they expect to "know" it had occurred afterwards? Or did they expect it to happen totally in the invisible realm without being consciously aware of it in any way? It is these Biblical "expectation statements" that also need to be examined, not just the "time statements."

We Preterists have pressed Futurists with the "time statements," and rightly so, because they are "sola scriptura" arguments. They are Biblical statements that need to be dealt with. So are the "expectation statements." What the "time statements" do for Preterism in general, the "expectation statements" do for the rapture view in particular. The time statements nail down the "time" of the parousia and its related events, while the expectation statements reveal the content and "nature" of those events in the experience of the Church.

Just because the Parousia may not have been validated historically in the way some might have preferred, it never stopped us from seeing it as a fulfilled "fact." The "time statements" forced us to believe that it must have occurred, regardless of a lack of historical confirmation. Even if we are unable to find external historical proof for a literal rapture in AD 70, it does not invalidate the Bible's affirmation of it. Our concern is simply, "What does

371

Scripture actually teach?"

Rapture advocates have been accused of teaching a rapture based only on external historical "arguments from silence." Not so! Scripture is the driving force. The expectation statements are Biblical arguments, just like the time statements. The time statements help establish the time of fulfillment, while the expectation statements help determine the nature of fulfillment. As you study the following list of Biblical passages, find the answers to these two questions: (1) What does Jesus say is actually going to be seen and experienced by His saints at the Parousia? (2) What do the NT writers and pre-70 Christians indicate that they were expecting to actually see and experience at the Parousia? (Matt. 16:27-28; 19:28; 24:31; John 14:2-3; 1 Cor. 15:51-54; 2 Cor. 5:1-4; Phil. 3:20-21; 1 Thess. 4:15-17; 2 Thess. 1:6-10; 2:1; and 1 Jn. 3:2). These texts show clearly what the first century Church expected to experience at the Parousia.

Paul said that when Christ would come to cast His enemies "away from His presence" and gather His saints (2 Thess. 1:6–2:1), that the saints would "marvel at Him" in His presence and in the presence of all who have believed, and Christ would be glorified by their collective presence with Him "on that day." That doesn't sound like a very silent occasion to me. Did they fail to "recognize the time of His visitation" and remain silent (as if it had not occurred). They should have been celebrating and proclaiming the fulfillment of His Parousia (if they were still around). There is a strange silence here, at the very time when we would have expected anything but silence, when they said they would be marveling at Christ in His presence. Their silence does not match their expectations, unless they were doing those things in the heavenly realm (no longer on the earthly scene).

If all living Christians remained on earth after AD 70, why didn't some of those who saw these incredible events in AD 70 say something about it? Why the silence, if they were still around? Russell and the other four scholars mentioned above proposed the literal rapture to explain that silence. Silence is not a significant argument all by itself. But as Sherlock Holmes would agree in the case of the dog that didn't bark when a supposed outsider broke in, sometimes silence is significant, especially when the circumstances would force us to expect otherwise. Expectations demand our attention even in the case of silence, if the Bible clearly teaches us to expect something other than silence. And it does.

For more indepth studies of the rapture at the parousia in AD 66-70, see this author's book entitled, Expectations Demand A Rapture, and the excellent series of articles written by Ian Harding.

THE MILLENNIUM

Russell was uncomfortable with any view of the Millennium which ended at AD 70 (p. 514). He considered such a short duration of the millennium (40 years or less) to be "so violent and unnatural that we cannot hesitate to reject it" (p. 514). He suggested the millennium only began at AD 70 with a limited "first" resurrection and judgment (of the righteous only), and is still ongoing in history and moving toward a yet future final resurrection and judgment of the rest of the dead (the wicked only – p. 518). It seemed to him that the Millennium was "introduced parenthetically" as an exception to the AD 70 time limits of the rest of the book (p. 514).

He noted that some people (such as myself) consider the idea of a Millennium after AD 70 as challenging the imminent time indicators throughout the book of Revelation. We would prefer a 40-year millennium (AD 30-70) which stays within those time limits.

Russell places a flashback to AD 70 at the end of the Millennium (Rev. 20:10), so that the white throne judgment in Rev. 20:11ff takes place in AD 70. Preterists who take the 40-year approach cannot disallow his flashback, since we insert one at the beginning of the millennium.

Russell's millennium interpretation deserves careful consideration. He acknowledged his understanding of it might not be perfect, and held out the hope that succeeding generations "will soon correct what is proved to be erroneous, and confirm what is shown to be right." (p. 535)

In conclusion, I have to repeat how impressed I am with Russell's exegetical work here. Many thousands of Bible students all over the world have been, and will continue to be, blessed by this book. We send this reprint forth with strong encouragement to seriously and objectively consider everything he has to say, and to "search the Scriptures daily to see whether these things are so." (Acts 17:11)

Edward E. Stevens
Bradford, Pennsylvania July, 2003

DIFFICULTIES ASSOCIATED WITH ARTICLES OF RELIGION
Among Particular Baptists

Articles of Religion are important when dealing with matters of the Christian Religion, however problems occur when churches fail to recognize there is a growth in grace and knowledge of the Lord Jesus Christ in any believer. When a person first believes in the Lord Jesus Christ they cannot possibly have a comprehensive knowledge of a churches constitution or its articles of religion, before solemnly subscribing to them. The author David Clarke has introduced the Doctrines of Grace to Bierton Particular Baptists Pakistan, situated in Rahim Yar Khan, Pakistan and bearing in mind his own experience with articles of religion he has compiled Bierton Particular Baptists Pakistan articles of religion from the first Bierton Particular Baptists of 1831,of which he is the sole surviving member, the First London Baptist Confession, 2nd edition 1646, and those of Dr John Gill, in order to avoid some of the difficulties encounter by Particular Baptist during the later part of the 19 century and since. This booklet highlights the problem and suggests the Bierton Particular Baptists Pakistan is as step in the right direction.

Isaiah 52:8 Thy watchmen shall lift up the voice; with the voice together shall they sing: for they shall see eye to eye, when the LORD shall bring again Zion.

BISAC: Religion / Christianity / Baptist

Contents

Introduction

Articles of Religion Important

Authors Testimony

Bierton Particular Baptist Church

374

THE DOCTRINE OF THE SABBATH 1622

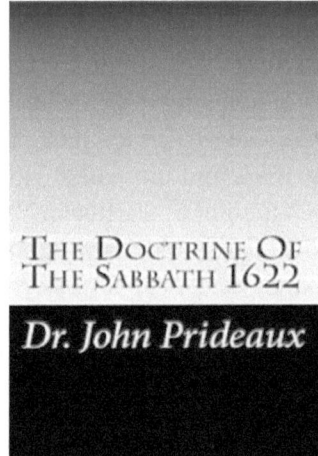

by John Prideaux (Author)

Of all the controverts which have exercised the Church of Christ, there is none more ancient than that of the Sabbath: So ancient that it took beginning even in the infancy of the Church, and grew up with it. For as we read in the Acts There rose up certain of the sect of the Pharisees, which believed, saying,

375

that it was needful to circumcise the people, and to command them to keep the law of Moses; whereof the Sabbath was apart: Which in the general, as the apostles labours to suppress in their first General Council, held in Jerusalem: So did S. Paul, upon occasion of whose ministry this controversy first began, endeavor what he could against the particular, shapely reproving those which hallowed yet the Jewish Sabbath and observed days, and months, and times, as if he had bestowed his labor in vain upon them. But more particularly in his epistle to the Colossians, Let no man judge you in respect of a holy day or of the new moon, or of the Sabbath days, which were a shadow of things to come but the body is of Christ. Both which expressions of Paul are in this following discourse produced to this very purpose. Yet notwithstanding all this care both generally of the Apostles and more especially of Paul to suppress this error; it grew up still and had its patrons and abettors.

This reproduction of, 'The doctrine of the Sabbath', by Dr. John Prideaux has been presented for those who have been troubled by the insistence of those religious people who insist that the first day of the week is the Sabbath day and to be kept holy, as dictated by the law of Moses. It is not. We include also Dr. John Gill on the subject of the circumstances of public worship as to place and time. It is the view of this publisher that the time and place of Christian worship it is a matter for the Christian community to decide and is not legislated in the scriptures.

BEFORE THE COCK CROWS PART 1, 2 AND 3

The Daily Diary Of Trojan Horse International: Volume 1

BEFORE THE COCK
CROWS (PART 1)
Setting Captives Free
David Clarke

David Clarke the Director of Trojan Horse International CM encountered remarkable opposition from various quarters in New Bilibid Prison, Muntinlupa City Philippines between October 2002 and July 2003.

Most of those who opposed the mission were men from among Asia's most notorious criminals in the National Penitentiary, which is situated on the Reservation at Muntinlupa City, 1770, Philippines. If one were to judge the success of the mission by that amount of opposition that it experienced, then the mission was a remarkable success. Newton stated that to every force there is an equal but opposite one to oppose it and like Newton, David suggests that to every proactive work there is and equal but opposite reaction and so if this reaction were to be the measure of success, then the mission was remarkably successful. It also serves to demonstrate that God always triumphs. That God saves, not by might, but by His Spirit. That God puts to fight thousands of his enemies and empowers the one's and two's, that trust in Him in order to show that Salvation is truly of the Lord. This prison comprises of three Compounds and penal farms housing over 23,550 inmates, which are all under the control of the Department of Justice (DOJ) and the Bureau of Corrections. (BUCOR). The Chaplaincy, headed by Msgr. Helley Barrido, is responsible for all religious groups and voluntary work done within the Prison. "Death Row" is in the Maximum Security Compound where over 1200 men are housed and they are all under the sentence of death. Some are doubly confirmed and due to be put to death by lethal injection. Trojan Horse International C.M. was established in the early part of 2001 and composed of a team of two from England, David Clarke and Gordon John Smith. The mission was set up as a Christian ministry, seeking to bring assistance to Michael John Clarke, David's older brother, and many inmates at the Prison. This was where Michael had been incarcerated, for a crime he did not commit, and was serving a prison sentence of 16 years. He had been baptized as a Christian. In an old 45-gallon US Oil drum, on the 16th September 2000 in the Maximum Compound. Michael, like his brother David, had been converted from crime to Christ whilst suffering the bitter effects of this form of injustice in the Philippines. How ever Michaels conversion was some thirty years after David who had been brought up in Aylesbury, Buckinghamshire and had been converted from crime to Christ, at the age of 20 years old, on the 16th January 1970.

By John Gill

The Gospel According to Matthew was the first written gospel and published sometime between (AD 31-38). It was written before Mark's (AD 38-44) and Luke's Gospel (AD-61).

Matthew was a Jew and one of the 12 Apostles of the Lord Jesus Christ and named Levi. He was a tax collector for the Romans. There are two strong traditions that Matthew made a personal copy of his gospel and gave it to Barnabas, a companion of the Apostle Paul.

Matthew tells of the birth and lineage of Jesus. The life death, resurrection of the Lord Jesus Christ and the final words of Jesus before his ascension into heaven.

This publication is presented knowing that Matthew penned his gospel that contains all those things the Lord Jesus wanted him to publish.

Matthew records the Olivet prophesy of Jesus concerning those fearful things that were to come to pass within the period of that generation and after his ascension.

It is the intention of the publisher that this will assist in making the gospel known to all people and is published in two parts PART 1 chapter 1 to 16.

And PART 2 chapter 17 to 28.

This book introduces a view of Bible prophecy which many have found extremely helpful in their Bible study. It explains the end time riddles which have always bothered students of Bible prophecy. It is a *consistent view* which makes the book of Revelation much easier to understand. It establishes when the New Testament canon of scripture was completed, demolishes the liberal attack on the inspiration of the New Testament, and is more *conservative* on most other issues than traditional views. And there is *no compromise* of any essential Biblical doctrine of the Christian faith.

The key to understand any passage of scripture has always been a good grasp of the historical setting in which it was originally written {*audience relevance*). Two thousand yeas from now our history, culture, politics and language will have changed dramatically. Imagine someone then having to learn the ancient language of "American English" to read our USA newspapers! If they saw one of our political cartoons with a donkey and elephant, what would they think? How would they go about understanding it? Not only would they have to study the language, but also our culture, history, politics and economics. The same applies to Bible study. If we are really going to understand what all the "donkeys and elephants" (beasts, harlots, dragons, etc.) Symbolize in the book of Revelation, we will have to seriously and carefully study the language, history, culture and politics of the First Century. Of course, the truths essential for salvation are couched in simple language that everyone can grasp. But there are numerous scriptures in the Bible which are "hard to understand" (cf. 2 Pet 3:16), and Bible prophecy is one of those things which must be approached with much more focus on the original historical art cultural context (audience relevance)

One of the main purposes of this book is to provide a closer look at the historical framework behind the New Testament. Many hove found it helpful to lay aside (at least temporarily) the legion of speculative opinions about the book of Revelation, and look at a more historical alternative, which is that *the book of Revelation was written to the first century church and had primary relevance to them.* It warned of events that were about to happen in their lifetime, and prepared them for the tribulation and other events associated with the End of the Jewish Age.

Atheists, skeptics, Jew, Muslims, and liberal critics of the bible use the supposed failure of those end times events to occur in the First Century to undermine the integrity of Christs and the inspired NT writings.

Non-Christian Jews laugh at this supposed non-occurrence, and use it as evidence that Jesus is not the Messiah. Their forefathers in the flesh rejected Jesus in His first coming because He did not fulfill the Old Testament prophecies in the materialistic and nationalistic way that they were expecting, even though Jesus told them that His Kingdom was not of this world, and that it would be within them instead. Yet it seems that many futurists today are expecting that same kind of materialistic and nationalistic kingdom to arrive at a future return of Christ Are they making the same mistake about the Second Coming that the Jews made about His first coming? Jesus repeatedly said His Kingdom is "not of this world" and that it would "not come with observation." It is a spiritual entity, and it has arrived We live in it. Both futurist Christians and non-Christian Jews need to realize this.

Christians are finally beginning to seek alternatives to the fatally flawed *futurist* interpretation. This book introduces the Preterist view.

"Preterist" simply means past in fulfillment It means that Christ has already fulfilled His promise to return and consummate redemption in Himself and His ongoing spiritual kingdom (the church). We should be like the noble-minded Bereans and "search the scriptures daily to see whether these things are true" You might want to have your Bible open alongside as you read.

Edward E. Stevens
INTERNATIONAL PRETERIST ASSOCIATION
https://www.preterist.org/
Bradford, Pennsylvania
April 17,2010

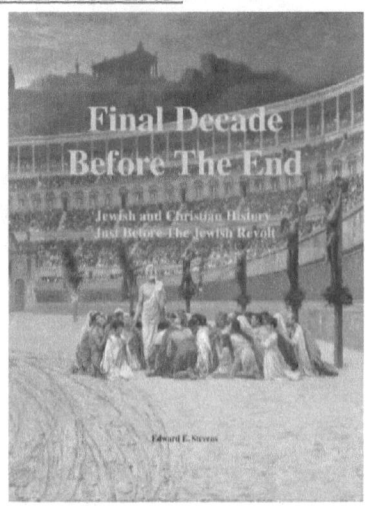

Introduction

Ever since the booklet, **What Happened In AD 70?** was published in 1980, there have been constant requests for more detailed information about the Destruction of Jerusalem and the Jewish, Roman, and Christian history associated with it. Over the years since then I have studied Josephus, Yosippon, Hegesippus, Tacitus, Suetonius, Eusebius, the Talmud, Midrash, Zohar, Pseudepigrapha, Church Fathers, Apocrypha, Dead Sea Scrolls and other Jewish/Christian writings, trying to determine exactly what happened, when it happened, and the effect it had upon the Church.

Then in 2002, after I began to promote J. S. Russell's view of a literal rapture, the demand for historical documentation of the fulfillment of all eschatological events dramatically increased. That forced me to dig much deeper. So in 2007 I put together a 21-page chronology of first century events. Two years later in 2009, we published a more substantial 73-page manuscript entitled, First Century Events in Chronological Order. That helped fill the void, but it did not go far enough. It only increased the appetite for a more detailed and documented historical reconstruction of first century events.

The book of Acts does not give a lot of details about the other Roman and Jewish events that were happening while Paul was on his various missionary journeys. For those events, we have to go to the other contemporary Jewish and Roman historians such as Josephus and Tacitus. The closer we get to AD 70, the more important all of those Jewish and Roman events become. They form an important backdrop behind the Christian events, and show how all the predictions made by Jesus were literally fulfilled. Every High Priest and

Zealot leader that we encounter from AD 52 onwards are directly connected with the events of the Last Days. Things are heating up, not only for the Christians, but also for the Jews and the Romans.

Paul on his missionary journeys was clearly following a plan which was providentially arranged for him by Christ: (1) to plant new churches among all nations and not just Jews, (2) appoint elders and deacons in every church (Acts 14:23; 1 Cor. 4:17), (3) write inspired epistles to guide them, (4) instruct his fellow workers to "teach these things to faithful men who would be able to teach others also" (2 Tim. 2:2), and (5) establish the Gentiles in the Church and make them one united body with the Jews (Eph 4). Everywhere Paul went, he followed this pattern. We see this clearly as we study the historical narrative in Acts and Paul's other epistles that were written during this time. These are essential patterns that the apostles evidently bound upon both Gentile and Jewish Christians, and which were intended to be the pattern for all future generations of the eternal Church (Eph 3:21; 2Tim 2:2).

We begin our study by looking at the most likely dates for Matthew (AD 31-38) and Mark (AD 38- 44), and then proceed to the first three epistles of Paul (Galatians, 1 & 2 Thessalonians), which were written on his second missionary journey (AD 51-53). Including these five books in our study allows us to date all twenty-seven books of our New Testament, and show how the NT canon was formed and completed before the outbreak of the Jewish War in AD 66. The study of New Testament canonization in itself is a good reason for reading this work, without even looking at the historical fulfillment of all of the endtime prophecies that we document here.

After looking at the dates for those first five books, we then move on into the third missionary journey of Apostle Paul which began in AD 54. It was during this final dozen years (from AD 54 until AD 66) when the birth pangs and signs of the end started increasing in both intensity and frequency, along with a quickening pace of NT books being written. We show how 19 of our 27 NT books (70 percent) were written during those last five years just before the Neronic persecution (AD 60-64). The Great Commission was finished, and the rest of the endtime events predicted in the Olivet Discourse were fulfilled during that time of "tribulation" upon the church and the "days of vengeance" upon the unbelieving Jews (Luke 21:22).

Edward E. Stevens
INTERNATIONAL PRETERIST ASSOCIATION
https://www.preterist.org/
Bradford, Pennsylvania
April 17,2010

www.ingramcontent.com/pod-product-compliance
Lightning Source LLC
Chambersburg PA
CBHW020918140626
46545CB00015B/100